Mainstream of the Modern World Series

EDITED BY JOHN GUNTHER

THE SPANISH CENTURIES

Books by Alan Lloyd

THE SPANISH CENTURIES

THE MAKING OF THE KING: 1066
(U.K. TITLE: THE YEAR OF THE CONQUEROR)

THE DRUMS OF KUMASI

The Mainstream of

DOUBLEDAY & COMPANY, INC.

the Modern World

THE SPANISH
CENTURIES

by Alan Lloyd

Garden City, New York, 1968

Library of Congress Catalog Card Number 68–11807
Copyright © 1968 by Alan Lloyd
All Rights Reserved
Printed in the United States of America
First Edition

FOR MY WIFE, DAPHNE
Whose Patience Is Beyond Reward

1436674

CONTENTS

Author's Note

If the hours spent reading this story prove in any part as enjoyable
and informative as the years spent writing it, my gratitude will be
increased toward the innumerable scholars, past and present, without whose expertise such a book would, of course, be impossible.
My hope is indeed to have produced an agreeable pastime for the
many leisure readers who are fascinated by Spain and her background, particularly those desiring some simple orientation in the
complex drama of Spanish history. Should a few be stimulated
to pursue the subject further, then perhaps the shortcomings of
my endeavors will to some extent be offset. To this end, a list of
titles relating to various phases and aspects of Spanish history is
included, most of which will, in turn, suggest further reading.

Vivid, la vida sigue,
los muertos mueren y las sombras pasan;
lleva quien deja y vive el que ha vivido.
Yunques, sonad; enmueced, campanas!

Live, for life continues,
the dead die and the ghosts pass;
he stays who leaves and he who lived lives on.
Anvils, ring! Church bells, be silent!

—ANTONIO MACHADO

Part 1

A TIME FOR DEDICATION

"One king, one law, one faith"
Isabella the Catholic

Chapter 1

COME FOLLOW THE SILVER CROSS

The old road from Córdoba to Granada winds south across the plain of Andalusia to the River Genil, a tributary of the Guadalquivir, then twists east, upstream, toward the snow-capped Sierra Nevada. The way through the Genil Valley, still guarded by a crumbled Moorish castle, is flanked by sloping olive groves and tawny, involuted mountains. Beyond the range to one's right, lie the Mediterranean and the not far distant coast of Morocco. Beyond the hills to the left, the Guadalquivir flows sedately and timelessly back to Córdoba, continuing west to Seville and the wild marshes of the Marismas before emptying into the Atlantic. It is a road basking in the near-African warmth of Spain's southernmost region. Mules and oxen labor unhurriedly in small fields bordered with hedges of cactus and cistus, where flitting goldfinches echo the reds and yellows of the wild flowers. In the valleys, dark-skinned children hunt lizards and chameleons while their elders cultivate the orchards, the *huertas* and *vegas*. Here, almonds, figs, jujubes and pomegranates ripen in a climate verging, by northern standards, on continuous summer. In some places, rice and cotton are growing. Where the route runs beside water, pink and white flamingo can be seen wading amid prickly pears and oleanders. Then, as the path winds higher, cork oaks, sweet chestnuts, and carob fill the slopes. The sun scorches the uplands. Ibex range on the mountains, while flocks of sheep and goats graze the lofty and arid pastures. This countryside of Andalusia has changed little in five centuries, since the last days of Moorish domination. Here and there, as in the Córdoba Mosque and the Alhambra at Granada, stand reminders of a brilliant Arab civilization. Andalusian culture retains many Oriental traces: persistent habits of language, costume, music, and dance. In contrast to the reserved and dignified Castilians to their north, the people hereabouts are salty and vivacious, with something of a passionate Eastern temperament. Indeed, though not altogether typical, the inhabitants of one part, the highland Alpujarras Valley, are still half Moorish, descendants of men who fought alongside the emirs in the final clash between the cross and the crescent in Spain.

It was from the heights above this road, in the clear sunshine of early June 1486, that the dust of an approaching squadron could first be seen by the Muslim hillsmen. As the convoy, bound from Córdoba, jogged nearer, a multiplicity of pennants, banners and richly clad principals marked it as an escort of major importance. The knights, a peacock train of high fashion and glittering arms, were the cream of Christian chivalry in the south. Their horses, many caparisoned after the style of the riders in vividly colored silks and cloths, were choice Andalusians and Arabs. The focal point of the column was a woman. On closer observation, it could be noted that she wore a black hat with a brim to shade delicate blue-green eyes, a scarlet mantle, and a velvet skirt with underskirts of brocade. Medium in build and alluringly proportioned, she had the fair skin and auburn hair much admired by the Spanish. Her features were mild, and when she smiled a somewhat cherubic face became pretty. In other company, she might have passed for a young matron of nobility on a country picnic. Her appetite, however, was more ambitious. Queen Isabella of Castile, first lady of Leon, of Aragon, Sicily, Galicia, Majorca, Gibraltar, Rousillon, Sardinia and Biscay, to name but a few of the prerogatives listed in her title, was bent on adding yet one more jewel to her diadem.

For all her responsibilities, not to mention the discomforts of the road, her composure was unruffled. "Con blandura"—with graciousness—was Isabella's constant maxim. Graciously she had welcomed the military escort sent by her husband, Ferdinand, to guard her on the journey. Graciously, she had distributed alms and consolation to the injured left by the army of invasion. Graciously, in

precise and elegant Castilian, she chatted to those about her as
they now pursued the line of communication. According to a
contemporary historiographer, her conversation, though not un-
leavened with gaiety, tended to be earnest. Vulgarity she discouraged, while her sense of Christian propriety sometimes weighed
heavily on the lusty instincts of the ranks. Graciously, but firmly,
she had forbidden the time-honored services of camp prostitutes
to her awed, if frustrated, warriors. During halts, she ate daintily,
sparingly. It was her habit to take little or no wine. She conveyed
in everything an air of gentlewomanly decorum. As the sovereign's
escort wound resplendently through the sierras, perhaps no more
than a single clue hinted at the sinew beneath the royal velvet. Isabella rode with the gritty aplomb of a trooper.

In fact, at thirty-five she had spent much of her adult life in the
saddle. The start of her queenly career had been marred by a mis-
carriage while riding to raise recruits to counter early opposition;
her last child, one of twins, had been stillborn after an ill-advised
journey to a council of war. The queen's labor pains had actually
begun at the council table. Of her four surviving children, none
had escaped a rude measure of jolting at various stages of embry-
onic development. In twelve dynamic years of authority, Isabella
had traveled tirelessly, not only among her own dominions but in
those of her husband, suppressing disorders, settling disputes, creating new laws and unities. Her reforming zeal had not always
been popular. She had chivied the complacent, chased the impious,
and appropriated the powers of great families and baronial institutions to further the aims of herself and her husband. She had
not been above taking a drawn sword to Ferdinand's soldiers when
she found them retreating. But her most potent weapon was fem-
ininity, and the writers of her time left no doubt that she used it
with inspired virtuosity. For them, Isabella the obsessive and calculating hustler was overshadowed by the vision of pious gentility,
an image with much appeal to the gallantry of the Spaniard. In
an age infused with mysticism and romance, it was especially mag-
netic. The queen's secretary and chronicler, Pulgar, though not entirely uncritical of the woman, told how her mere presence at the
battlefront put fresh heart in tired men—"it seemed as if all the
hardships of campaigning, all the downcast spirits and confusion,
were overcome and vanished."

Isabella's arrival at the camp on the Granada road was managed with customary refinement. Perched on a rail saddle gilded with silver, her mount itself covered in crimson velvet, the queen fingered gold-embroidered reins and beamed beautifully upon everyone at the reception. One body of troops, accompanied by some of the most ostentatious grandees in the army, had advanced several miles to meet her. Others were drawn up nearer their lines in battle order, each unit dipping its banner as she passed. Yet others ran forward to catch sight of the queen and her personal suite of almost fifty riders. "The welcome," wrote a local observer, "gave Her Highness much pleasure." Ferdinand waited patiently on a chestnut charger. Slightly younger than Isabella, swarthy with full lips and jowls, and bright, amused eyes, he watched the progress of his wife with advised admiration. Though he was a person of worldier tastes—his resourcefulness as a general and politician was matched at times by a weakness for gaming and the boudoir—he knew better than to disparage her precious talents. He was nothing if not a shrewd judge of usefulness. It was the criterion on which most of his friendships were based. Behind Ferdinand's impassive countenance lay a Machiavellian mind, a calculating machine as skeptical and materialistic in its plottings as Isabella's was earnest and metaphysical. Not that he was lacking in affection for his spouse. Nor Isabella for her manly Ferdinand. Perhaps her intensity found its complement in his calculating nature. At all events, the partnership had proved a remarkable success, their combined personalities exerting a cogent influence on Spanish politics. In the few hectic years of their marriage they had raised the tone of the monarchy from a cacophony of dissonance and corruption to a paean of crusading ardor. As champions of Christianity against the wide-ranging specter of Islam, Spain's Catholic sovereigns had soared from individual nonentity to become, already, the talk of Europe.

It was a continent still echoing the warning of an anxious pope. In constant peril, it seemed, from the Muslim hordes of Africa, ravaged by barbaresque corsairs and hammered by the Turks, the whole underside of Christendom was beset by the infidel. With Mahomet II at Otranto, threatening Rome itself, the incumbent pontiff, Sixtus IV, had issued a passionate call to his widespread and frequently quarrelsome flock. "Let those who are at a distance from the enemy not regard themselves as safe," he beseeched. "They, too, will bow the neck beneath the yoke, be mowed down by the scimitar, unless they come forward to meet the enemy— an enemy who has sworn the extinction of Christianity. A truce to sophistries! It is the moment not to talk but to fight!" The sentiment, coinciding with the Spanish initiative, had drawn to the sovereigns' camp not only the lofty magnates of Catholic Spain and their followers, but a host of adventurers, both priestly and secular, from many other regions of Christendom. Perched in the surrounding hills, the Moorish scouts could report an incredible pageant of hostile arms: a force as sublime to the eye, in its feathers and finery, as it must have seemed ill-fitted to the rough task ahead. The historic rivalry of Spain's top nobility, bent at last to a common cause, was expressed in a vaunting array of opulence. Each warlord vied with his neighbor in the splendor of his costume, the chic of his pages and lackeys, the burnish of his knights and retainers, the extravagance of his emblems, the din of his trumpets, the very shine on the salt pots in his baggage. The Duke of Infantado, for instance, had mounted five hundred men of his household for the crusade. Many were magnificently armed and dressed. Fifty of his horses were caparisoned in gold-embroidered cloth, while others were housed in brocade. Even his pack mules wore silken halters and harness embellished with precious metals. Such men might visualize dying in glory, but they had no intentions of living in austerity. Their campaign tents were pavilions of colored silks boasting fluttering pennons and done out with costly hangings. Their camp tables shimmered with candelabra and services of finely wrought gold and silver.

This grandiose style was emulated by many of the foreign volunteers. From France came a particularly swashbuckling contingent, complete with fancy surcoats and plumes in their hats. Germany, Switzerland, and Italy provided a number of high-stepping individuals. But perhaps the most pretentious of all, to a degree touching parody, was an English adventurer, Sir Edward Woodville, who appears to have borrowed the designation of his elder brother, Lord Scales, to impress the solemn and title-conscious Spanish aristocrats. Woodville's following, a band of tough professional brawlers from the hardy shires of England, was scarcely the last word in social graces. Hearty feeders and drinkers in the Anglo-Saxon tradition, they made few concessions to the relatively sober Spaniards, and their quarter of camp was notorious for its revelry and sudden tumult.

Woodville spared no effort to make up for their lack of finesse. On the arrival of the queen, he staged a late and dramatically exotic appearance. "The Count of England arrived with great pomp in a strange manner," it appears, "coming after all the others in full armor on a white horse covered with blue silk which reached the ground and was trimmed with a white band of a hand's width starred with gold and lined with purple Ceuta cloth. Over his armor he sported a French doublet of black matt brocade and a white French hat with plumes, while, on the left arm, he carried a small round shield with gold bands, and a helmet of such a strikingly new style as to be the object of general admiration. Followed on decorated horses by five brocaded and silk-clad pages, and a number of his lieutenants in gorgeous apparel, he rode here and there greeting all and sundry, jumping his steed this way and that with great style and control . . ." It seems that everyone, including their highnesses, and especially the young ladies of the queen's court, was captivated by this prancing exhibitionist. "It was a marvel to see such courtliness in a knight bred so far from Castilian circles."

The camp was no place for the unassuming. Martial or devout, the pretensions of its members were constantly publicized, often in a package combining the two elements. Bishops rode in gleaming armor at the head of its squadrons; churchmen of top rank attended its battle councils. Ferdinand, no drab himself in red doublet and yellow satin breeches, now bowed three times to the queen in formal reverence while Isabella, having returned the compliment in kind, removed her hat and allowed him to kiss her. In the royal pavilion, where the sovereigns and their advisers would complete their latest plans, stood a large holy cross in massive silver. Arrangements had been made to transmit news of the triumphal progress of the crusade to its donor, the pope, whose blessing, together with aid of a more tangible sort, had been carefully solicited by the promoters. Isabella had also contrived to amass, from various sources, a hoard of sacred treasures to furnish the mosques she intended to have "purified" and consecrated on the trail of conquest. All that was required was the word to move forward.

Eight centuries and more had passed since the Arab invaders, crossing the strait from Africa, had overthrown the last of the old Gothic monarchs near Jerez de la Frontera and swarmed north across the Iberian Peninsula. Since then, through a long and bloody era of reconquest, dominion after dominion had been recovered by Christian princes until a single kingdom in the south remained in the hands of the Muslim. For the last two centuries, Spanish Christianity had gazed with envy and frustration upon the fabled lands of Granada, lacking the cohesion and inspiration completely to dominate the enemy. Two hundred and twenty miles long, and stretching inland at points to upwards of sixty miles, the Moorish kingdom of Granada ran east along the Mediterranean coast from just north of Gibraltar to the Murcian border, including the rich ports of Málaga and Almería. Protected from the interior by formidable mountain ranges, whose cascading streams provided water for a broad network of irrigation, it had red soil and luxuriant green vegas that abounded in cattle, fruit, sugar cane, olives, and cereals; its mineral deposits were copious beyond measure. Granadine metalwork was world-famed, as were its silk stuffs. This had long been one of the most prosperous realms in the Arab empire, with more than a dozen busy cities and several times as many well-fortified towns. At its heart stood perhaps the most exotic metropolis in Europe.

Christians and Muslims alike regarded the city of Granada with a kind of sensuous exaltation which has not altogether cooled down the years. Arabic literature descants the praises of its marble turrets and metal cornices, glittering, in the imagery of the poets, like stars through the foliage of the orange groves: an enameled vase of a city, sparkling with hyacinths and emeralds. Indeed, to the traveler from the roads of the arid outer world, coming on the Granadine vega, with its vines and orchards, its fountains and water mills, shady farmsteads and cool country houses, must have seemed like approaching the oasis of oases. Rising in terraces from the level of

the River Darro, set against the rugged, white-capped sierra, the
medieval city was strongly Moroccan in atmosphere. The houses
were small and dark, enclosed within the various quarters of the
town by an intricate system of walls. So narrow were the streets,
declared a writer of the period, that "from a window on one side
a person could touch the other side simply by stretching out his
arm. There were places where it was impossible for mounted men
carrying lances to pass." The market quarters, in particular, involved warrens of little lanes, often vaulted, where the aroma of
spices and ripe fruits filled the shadows, and where shafts of sunlight might reveal costlier wares, silks, gold brocades or delicate
Moorish jewelery. Here the well-to-do farmers of the surrounding
countryside rubbed shoulders with the merchants of the Mediterranean, buying trappings for their showy ponies or gifts for their
favorite wives. The women, veiled and trousered, delighted in fancy
adornment. According to an early visitor to the city, small graceful
shoes, plaited stockings and high hair combs could be discerned
beneath the light drapes of their robing. It was written, doubtless
with some exaggeration, that Granada had thirty thousand inhabitants and thirteen hundred towers, and that, on top of its regular
garrison of mounted warriors and footmen, "three days sufficed to
assemble there fifty thousand men-at-arms from the Alpujarra, the
Sierra and the Granadine valleys and countryside." Most certainly
it was a bustling conurbation. In relative tranquillity amid the
clamor of the guard posts and markets stood such public buildings
as hospitals, Koranic schools, and mosques, while, above all, aloof
and sequestered, towered the crowning glory of the city, the Alhambra.

Since the ninth century, a royal palace had dominated Granada
from its stately hilltop situation. Though always a stronghold, the
magic of the setting and the scope of the interior gave it an Arabian
Nights splendor which had reached its peak in the fourteenth century at the hands of inspired craftsmen of the Nasride dynasty. The
crux of their achievement was a brilliant marriage of artifice and
nature. Perched breathtakingly over the gorges of the Darro, with
splendid views of the multipatterned vega, the Alhambra ("Me-
dinat al-hambrâ," i.e. "the red town" after the color of the building
stone) was a masterpiece of refined opulence designed less to com-
pete with the surrounding attractions than to woo them into

aesthetic submission. In common with other Moorish secular buildings, this lofty, roseate citadel was externally rugged. Inside, by contrast, the effect was delicate and enchanting, full of decorative *entrelacs*, arabesques, honeycomb vaulting and long inscriptions in tribute to Allah. Around a courtyard graced with an elegant pool, the Court of Myrtles, lay the rooms of the royal residence proper, the Divan. Around the Court of Lions, another yard centered by a fountain and statuary, were the women's apartments, the Harim, while a third section of the palace, the Mexuar, was built for public assemblies and meetings of justice. Neither in scale nor material was the architecture pretentious. Much of the decoration was in wood, molded brick and plaster. In truth, removed from their environment, such components as the Court of Lions and the Court of Myrtles would have been dimmed by the sidelights of many a northern palace; the gardens, by European standards, were puny. Yet such were the subtlety and harmony of the whole creation that each modest individual attraction—a bright dome, a vividly colored ceiling, the tinkle of a fountain, the scent of roses and jessamines amid an array of glazed pantiles or porcelain, a small archway framing a dazzling vista—breathed the essence of Sybaritic genius. Lightness and charm touched everything in the palace. Here, down the years, remarkable in turn for their cruelty and cultural refinement, the kings of Granada had held court, read poetry, studied the stars, passed their cushioned, unlonely nights. From here they had gone forth by day to protect their dominions, to raid those of their neighbors, or simply to assert their inimitable horsemanship. When it suited them, they had paid tribute to the advance guards of Christendom, but even toward the end of the fifteenth century they could still feel too strong and independent to accord the monarchs of Castile much respect. Aery, reposeful, perfumed, and delicious, the Alhambra had glowed tantalizingly in the dreams of generations of Christian kings, a symbol of the final crusading challenge in Spain.

Isabella and Ferdinand planned to translate the dream into action by aiming their first crucial blow of the war not at the city of Granada itself but at Málaga, the main supply port of the Saracen realm and capital of its western province—the theater nearest the Christian bases of Seville and Córdoba. Accordingly, in the spring of 1487, the knights of the cross packed their sumptuous chattels and, to the rumbling overture of a local earthquake, struck the road to the coast. In column of march, the full diversity of Christian arms became apparent. Behind twelve thousand horsemen trooped forty thousand foot, predominantly feudal retainers of the lords, but including a hard core of professional soldiers. The value of steady infantry as against erratic peasant levies had been clearly marked in earlier engagements. A Spanish writer, reporting how the English footmen had led an advance on one Moorish town, battling stoically forward shoulder to shoulder, admitted that his countrymen watched in amazement. Even the flamboyant Woodville had dismounted to command them, having his front teeth knocked out in the process. For all their glamor and gorgeous accouterment, the Spanish chivalry could learn a lesson from such plebeian warriors, and the sovereigns had been at some pains to reinforce the traditional element of their army with the rugged as well as the romantic.

Tramping doughtily amid the thoroughbred squadrons surrounding Ferdinand were tough Spanish mountaineers from the distant northern regions of Galicia and Asturias, men well suited to campaigning in the Granadine highlands. Then there were contingents from Isabella's own royal police force, the so-called Hermandad, specially mobilized for war service. From beyond the peninsula came a number of hirelings of pugnacious reputation, notably a body of crack Swiss mercenaries proud of wearing armor only on their front. They were among the finest infantry in Europe, and their example was to prove more than an immediate asset—it helped set a new pattern of skilled and dedicated soldiering that was to bring world fame to the Spanish arms of the future. And trundling at the rear of this remarkable war train came Ferdinand's master stroke, the *enfant terrible* of the campaign, the ordnance.

For long preparatory months, the agents of Isabella and her husband had scoured Christendom for gunsmiths and powder. From Italy, France, and Germany had come the former; from Portugal, Sicily, Flanders the latter. Workshops had been set up at bases and camp, and the whole project of artillery, then radical and controversial, placed in the hands of an ingenious engineer from Madrid, Francisco Ramírez. As the crusading army had grown daily more diverse and spectacular, Ramírez and his team of international mechanics had set to work to produce a battery of giant cannon that were to startle an already incredulous knighthood. The lombards, as they were known, consisted of iron bars, some two inches wide, fixed in rings to form barrels about twelve feet in length, immovably bolted to carriages of extraordinary weight and clumsiness. The projectiles designed to be hurled from these contraptions were up to fourteen inches in diameter, weighed as much as a hundred and seventy pounds, and were variously carved from marble or forged in metal. By heating the metal ammunition to a semimolten state, it could be thrown in the form of a glutinous fire. Unfortunately, the transport problem presented by the lombards, and numerous smaller pieces turned out by the workshops, was so great that a special corps of six thousand pioneers had to be created to build suitable roads and bridges, and now, despite the constant efforts of these sappers, the artillery fell steadily behind the main column. In some parts of the sierras, progress averaged less than a half mile a day.

It was a rough trip for all concerned. The passes were craggy, the hills crippling, and the rivers swollen by recent rains. On top of which, there was the constant fear of Moorish ambush, especially for the stragglers. Though unsophisticated by Christian standards, the Muslim forces were by no means contemptible. Traveling light, uncluttered by the excessive trappings of their enemy, they specialized in the lightning raid, the swift, unexpected foray. Their breakneck charges on horseback could be both bewildering and damaging. When a troop of Moorish horsemen and a Christian cavalcade had inadvertently crossed paths on an earlier occasion, it was the Moors, with ferocious verve and fine riding, who had come off best, returning home with Christian heads dangling from their saddles. Nor were they less formidable in defense. Of their fortitude under siege, Pulgar wrote: "It is impossible not to marvel at the bold heart of these infidels, their ready obedience to their chiefs, their enterprise and patience under privation, the undaunted perseverance behind their purposes." Among their weapons were the knife, the crossbow, and the harquebus. They used the juice of the plant aconite, or wolfsbane, to poison their arrows.

The first round in the struggle for Málaga was fought in the sierra above the seaport, which Ferdinand reached in May, rather more than a month after setting out. Here, commanding the paths with expert crossbow fire from boulder-strewn ridges, the Moors made a strong bid to halt the Christian advance. Deploying his main army in the shelter of valleys, the king threw a corps of Galician hillmen, supported by troops of the royal household, forward in the unenviable uphill assault. The Spanish chroniclers were vivid in their reports of the engagement, telling how the high-pitched battle cries of the Muslim warriors blended with the spontaneous screams of the wounded; how, discarding their bows and lances, the Saracens leaped with flashing daggers on the Christian skirmishers; how mounted warriors, racing sure-footed ponies on the slopes, hurled themselves from the saddle to grapple the attackers, rolling locked in combat down the ravine. Twice, the Christian commando was repelled, and twice reinforced, before the agile enemy, dissolving into the background he knew so well, retired to continue his fight from the city. Ascending the heights, the crusaders peered down on a sight more spectacular than any yet encountered on their journeys.

Nestling like a pearl in the shimmering bay of Málaga, fringed with palm-decked suburbs, brine-washed quays, and sunny vineyards, the second citadel of the Moorish kingdom stretched white and voluptuous below them—the great western gate to Granada. On a smooth sea, effectively blocking enemy communications by water, waited a ready fleet of Christian galleys and caravels—another tribute to the immaculate masterminding of Isabella. While Ferdinand had pushed forward in the field, the queen had calmly shouldered the organizational burden of the war. No general could have asked for a more assiduous entrepreneuse. Now coping with the endless problems of internal government, now at the military bases supervising logistics, now negotiating fresh aid from abroad, Isabella dashed to and fro with a vigor exhausting merely to contemplate. The results she achieved were no less overwhelming. Ferdinand needed mules? Isabella produced sixty thousand. The army needed grain? Isabella had twenty thousand bushels in reserve. The paymaster needed money? She raised the equivalent of half a million dollars on ecclesiastical revenues and persuaded the pope to increase indulgences to crusaders.

And, while her executive genius functioned on a grand scale, her womanly eye missed few details. Knowing the Moors to be distracted by the ringing of bells, an activity forbidden by the Koran, she sent a quantity of these instruments to the front as weapons of psychological warfare. For the sick and wounded, Isabella established the so-called Queen's Hospital, one of the earliest field hospitals noted in military history. So well equipped were its tents, wrote an admiring scribe, that the wealthiest of noblemen could not have bought better attention. Be that as it may, the unit was to provide some comfort for thousands before the war in Granada was over. Nor were those who covered themselves in the blood of the enemy lacking in the queen's dispensations. She created special honors for her heroes, bestowing them in person amid lavish ceremony. Other warriors, less conspicuous, received gracious letters of encouragement bearing her signature. She missed little that went on among the ranks. Notwithstanding Ferdinand's predilections in such matters, her influence curbed the gaming and womanizing prevalent in army camps of the time. Dice and cards were prohibited by her orders along with prostitutes. Blasphemy became a severely punishable offense. Furthermore, she directed a flow of priests and friars to the front to maintain the moral tone she deemed proper in holy war.

Less altruistically, Ferdinand delivered his opening shot at Málaga in the form of a bribe to its commander. The city walls were in good repair; its inner fort, the Gibralfaro, was virtually impregnable; the garrison, including a corps of much-feared African mercenaries, the Gomeres, was resolute. The king's holy ardor was not so fierce that he would not have preferred to buy a deal with the Saracen in cash than in blood. The suggestion was received with disdain, however, by the Moorish general, an inflexible aristocrat named Hamet Zeli, and the Christians had no option but to make good their siege. Luckily for Ferdinand, a relief force hurrying to Hamet's assistance from the east was attacked and dispersed by a rival Moorish faction, leaving the city with little prospect of replenishing its larders. Nevertheless, as summer advanced and the sick and wounded in the siege camp rose to twelve hundred, the Christians still had made no impact on the city walls. To their increasing discomfort, the garrison repeatedly counterattacked, especially at night, keeping the invaders sleepless and jittery. Morale was at a low ebb when Isabella rode coolly over the mountains to inspect the situation for herself. Her presence coincided with a marked renewal of endeavor. The lombards, having now arrived, were heaved into position. Ramírez and his engineers were put to work undermining the defenses, providing tunnels into the city and creating various assault machines, including a number of large wooden towers on rollers, equipped to disgorge troops by drawbridge and ladder across the hostile ramparts.

Boosted by reinforcements to a strength of something like seventy thousand, the Christian army launched an all-out attack on the hungry defenders. With a deafening roar, the lombards erupted in flames and smoke. Amid the scream of caroming missiles and the stench of spent powder, the lumbering assault vehicles moved toward the walls. Tucked behind them, the sunlight glinting on burnished helmets, crouched platoons of stoutly armored troops. In support—a brilliant, banner-toting wave, roared forward by its captains and high priests of the church—came the main line of Spanish infantry. They ran into a withering enfilade of Moorish projectiles. Despite the Christian barrage, the fire from the battlements was uncomfortably accurate. Offensive after offensive was repulsed by the desperate garrison. Hamet's men countermined their attackers, engulfing them in tumbling masonry; they met them in the tunnels, engaging them with ferret-like tenacity; they even pushed out in a flotilla of small boats and chivied the Christian fleet. Some, sweeping suddenly from the gates, succeeded in demolishing the wooden towers assembled by Ramírez. Livid, the chief engineer exploded a hoard of gunpowder alongside one entrance to the city, observing with grim satisfaction that enemy activity in the area promptly ceased. Thus the battle raged, as Pulgar reported it, "with fire and sword, above and below ground, on land and on sea."

Meanwhile, as the Christians struggled to force the latches of Málaga, time itself was forging a master key. Overburdened by refugees and soldiers, the city finally ran out of provisions. Having eaten their horses and oxen, the Malagueños turned in their starvation to the dogs and cats. One last hope of reversing their fortunes glimmered and faded in a wild attempt to assassinate the Spanish sovereigns. According to the chroniclers, a Moorish fanatic actually gained admission to the royal compound in the guise of a wellwisher, only to botch the enterprise at the last minute in a case of mistaken identity. Drawing his knife on the wrong couple, a lady of the queen's court and a Portuguese nobleman, the assailant barely had time to inflict injury before he was hacked to death by the royal guards. His mangled body was flung by catapult into the city. For a while longer, Hamet maintained a hold on the civilian population by threatening summary execution for anyone proposing to surrender, until, by the beginning of August, the incidence of death by starvation and disease had made the threat meaningless. Withdrawing his mercenaries into the Gibralfaro, he left the Malagueños to make the best terms they could with the enemy.

To their dismay, Ferdinand refused to meet their delegation or to demand anything less than unconditional surrender, and, after a vain attempt to extort some promise of personal safety against the lives of their Christian prisoners, the people decided to entrust themselves to the magnanimity of the sovereigns. On August 18, the Christian troops occupied the city. A few days later, hopelessly isolated, Hamet Zeli capitulated, bemoaning his lack of support. It was left for the conquerors to pronounce sentence on Málaga. The entire population, an estimated eleven to fifteen thousand survivors, was condemned to slavery, being consigned largely to members and benefactors of the crusade, though, thanks to the thoughtful intervention of Isabella, a few of the richest were allowed freedom on payment of substantial ransoms to the royal treasury. Of the choicer victims, fifty of the loveliest daughters of Málaga were parcelled to the court of Naples and thirty to the royal house of Portugal. One hundred of the sturdiest Africans, the reputedly fearful Gomeres, were sent as a gift to the pope, who swiftly drafted them into his own guard. Within a year, it seems, they had become "very good Christians."

Good Christians, bad Christians, indifferent Christians! As the sovereigns committed themselves more and more to the war in Granada, weakening the internal resources and safeguards of their realm, the orthodoxy (or otherwise) of their subjects became a matter of increasing concern. Among a following not only lacking the form of patriotism which stems from common pride of territory, but actually steeped in rivalry and separatism, spiritual conformity was the one great hope for the future. The war had already shown that in the chastisement of unbelievers the majority of Spanish subjects could find a common purpose. "One of the advantages neighboring rulers envy you," Pulgar assured the queen, "is having within your frontiers people against whom you can wage not merely just war but holy war, to occupy and exercise the chivalry of your kingdom. Your Highness should not think it a small convenience." Isabella did not. At the same time, she was aware that by no means all her people shared the same animosity. Spain was full of dubious converts to Christianity, people who had switched faith less from conviction than because to do so had become socially expedient. Particularly suspect on the grounds of their racial affinity with the enemy were the Moorish converts, the Moriscos, whose high incidence in Christian Andalusia, the region nearest the theater of war, rated them a special subversive potential. Another suspect minority was formed by converts from the Jewish faith, the Marranos or *conversos,* many of whom had opposed Isabella in her early struggle for power, and whose ancestors were widely regarded as having favored the Spanish Moors.

The disturbing influence of these converts on the rest of the Christians was not eased by their natural astuteness in business. Too often they made making money look easy. For masses of poor, long-suffering Spaniards it seemed as if the rewards of their own faith, their own sweat and loyalty, were being filched by a pack of proselytizing outsiders. "They possess the fat of the land and live in greater prosperity than the natives, though neither tilling and sowing, nor building and fighting, nor engaging in any honest labor." The protest was typical of many leveled at the Jewish population. "By incessant scheming, they carry off the fruits of every man's toil, enjoying power, honor, favor and riches." Envy promoted the wildest complaints. All Moors were the secret agents of Islam. The Jews crucified young Christian boys on Good Friday while their doctors poisoned their Christian patients. Even their cooking was held against them. According to Bernaldez, associating with the Marranos caused many "learned and highly placed" Christians to become "gluttons and big eaters, never losing their Jewish tastes in food . . . stews of onions and garlic and meat cooked in oil . . . a thing which gives a bad smell to the breath. And their houses smelt foul in consequence, while they themselves developed the same malodour as the Jews . . ."

With feeling running high, and the Church demanding action, the sovereigns were well placed for a thorough purge of subversive elements. Their security agency was the Inquisition, a heretic-hunting system approved by the pope and charged, primarily, with stamping out un-Christian activities among converts. At its head was a Dominican prior named Thomas of Torquemada, a pious and achromatic aesthete who happened also to be Isabella's friend and confessor. As a young friar, Torquemada had received the baccalaureate in theology before joining the notably strict priory of Piedrahita. Unlike his worldly contemporary, the Cardinal Mendoza, a married man who campaigned in Granada with great pomp, Torquemada showed little interest in temporal advance, preferring the stern discipline of the monastery. Age imbued him with intolerance of his less devout fellows. Convinced that heresy was undermining the very foundations of the state, Torquemada moved grimly from self-sacrifice to the sacrifice of others. The fall of Málaga found him, at sixty-seven, a slight, brooding figure in the dark robes of his order, immersed with quiet passion in a new and lethal occupation.

It was all done, as Isabella would doubtless have expected, with considerable rectitude. Torquemada furnished his inquisitors with precise and copious articles of guidance. Edicts were published regularly in the churches informing everyone of his sacred duty to lodge evidence, where possible, against heretics. The presumptive proofs of guilt were as clearly defined as they were commonplace. It was enough that a suspect wore his best suit on the Jewish sabbath, that he ate with Jews, that he washed a corpse in warm water, that his children bore Hebrew names, and so on—habits sustained by countless converts, sincere or dishonest. The trials themselves, though substantially secret, threw up some nice touches of superficial justice. Defendants were spared the imposition of irons, a familiar indignity of the times, and permitted the services of counsel. Less hopefully, however, counsel was allowed neither to confer with a client nor confront any witnesses, while the prosecution was authorized to extract evidence by torture. The punishments were phrased with fine condescension. Those found guilty were ordered to be "relaxed"—that is, ceremonially burned alive, in which case the execution became, euphemistically, the "auto da fé" or "act of faith"—or, alternatively, "reconciled," a term signifying anything from denial of civil rights to life imprisonment, and generally involving confiscation of all property.

During Torquemada's regime as Inquisitor General, the agency disposed of something like a hundred thousand cases, executing, it has been estimated, nine thousand people, of whom two thousand were burned under Isabella's authority. Remarkably enough, such activities were not generally regarded as excessive, nor, for that matter, lacking in compassion. "The Church, who is the mother of mercy and the fountain of charity, content with the imposition of penances, generously accords life to many who do not deserve it," wrote Lucio Marineo, an eminent scholar, on what he regarded as the leniency of the Inquisition. "Those who persist obstinately in their errors, having been arrested on the testimony of trusty witnesses, she causes to be tortured and put to the flames. Some perish miserably bewailing their errors and invoking the aid of Christ, while others call upon that of Moses. Yet many more, who sincerely repent, she—notwithstanding the heinousness of their transgressions—merely sentences to perpetual imprisonment." The odor of sanctity dispelled even the stench of charred flesh.

If Isabella ever doubted that these measures had divine approval, she was consoled by the victories granted her crusaders. Besides, the revenue from Torquemada's confiscations had now become important to the war effort. Experience had taught the royal couple that the open sesame to their goal, the legendary Alhambra, lay not in outmoded feudal aids, but in the ready money of their people, the golden fodder of new-style aggression. Gratefully, they snatched up all they could get. For two years, Isabella and Ferdinand prepared for their next major strike in Granada, a great sweep into the eastern province of the land to reduce the Moorish strongholds in the rear of the capital. There were three of vital strategic importance, Guadix, Baza, and Almería, all in the sway of the most dangerous of Saracen generals, the aging and wily chief Abu Abdalla, known as El Zagal, or The Valiant. El Zagal had already ambushed and thrown back a Christian reconnaissance force in his territory, and was firmly settled in Guadix. Almería, the port of the province, was a hopeless march from the Christian bases, and guarded by the uninviting Alpujarras. Ferdinand was left with one initial alternative. In spring, 1489, having moved their forward base east to Jaén, the crusaders headed for Baza—and near-disaster.

The city, surrounded by mountains and screened on one side by thick woodlands, was an ideal base for guerrilla fighters, and the

Moors made the most of their chances. Twenty thousand of them, commanded by a brother-in-law of El Zagal, one Cid Hiaya, a competent tactician, harried the invaders at every opportunity. In the forest, Ferdinand's divisions, reputedly totaling a hundred thousand, were often thrown into confusion. Exploiting a labyrinth of tracks and waterways, the natives surprised the groping crusaders again and again with a tempest of musket fire and arrows, slipping away at the height of combat to renew their ambuscades elsewhere. Ferdinand, endeavoring to keep in touch with the battle from a central position, lost sight of his columns in a tangle of foliage; captains lost touch with their companies; men, with their leaders and banners. After a hectic period of incessant and costly fighting, the king's men broke clear of the forest, only to find the ground on the city side of the cover untenable. After an uneasy night, they withdrew through the same woods. The prospect was gloomy. Nothing short of clearing the timber could enable the Christians to mount an effective blockade, and that in itself would be merely a preliminary. Unlike the defenders of Málaga, Cid Hiaya and his men had an abundance of food. Early warning of the invasion had enabled them to harvest the outlying crops before they fell into the hands of the enemy, and the town was said to possess provisions for fifteen months. On the other hand, a relatively poor cropping season in many parts of the south the previous year had made stores for the crusaders expensive (twice the normal cost, according to Bernaldez) and hard to come by. There was also the problem of the mountain climate. Winter in the eastern highlands would be more severe than in the lowlands to the west. In a meager two months the rains would swell the hill streams to torrents. Bogged down between Cid Hiaya, on one side, and El Zagal on the other, the besiegers might well become the besieged.

Under these circumstances, Ferdinand's lieutenants urged caution. The almost unanimous opinion of his war council was that they should abandon their immediate plans and retire from Baza to a safer place. With discretion very much a part of his own mind, the king reported the facts to his wife. Her reply was swift and characteristic. Of course, *Ferdinand* must make the decision, *but* . . . a reverse at this stage, she had no doubt, might prejudice months, indeed years, of effort. In all probability, they could never resume operations on the same scale. And this, she added, when at last they had the Moors on the hook. If the army did its duty and held on to the end, she would back it with everything it could want, a promise she promptly moved to secure by an impassioned fund-raising campaign in which she went so far as to mortgage the crown jewels. The city of Valencia lent thirty-five thousand florins on her crown itself, a piece studded with fine diamonds, rubies, and pearls. Barcelona advanced money on other items of treasure. Meanwhile, the army dug in.

It took four thousand pioneers seven weeks to clear the woods, while thousands more set about building palisades from the timber to complete the blockade of the city. The Moors contented themselves with desultory and contemptuous sallies, scornfully rejecting appeals to make terms. On this occasion, time was on their side. Winter, their trusted ally, was approaching. It struck early, bringing fresh consternation to the Christian camp. Rain washed out the roads of communication, collapsed improvised barracks, marooned horses and men in a depressingly unfamiliar landscape of mud. Exposure and malnutrition, combined with the effects of enemy action, pushed the casualty list to unprecedented figures. Christian losses at Baza were reported on one count at twenty thousand, a fifth of the entire strength, and, though the statistics are not strictly reliable they well reflect the despondency felt at this point of the crusade. Morale was fading. Talk hinged once more on retreat.

Isabella had seldom faced a more appalling failure. She responded feverishly. Drafting every able-bodied man she could raise in Andalusia, she assembled new pioneer and fighting battalions, and set to work reopening communications. Rivers were bridged, causeways built, old roads repaired, new roads cut. With her diminishing funds, she foraged for fresh provisions, marshaling fourteen thousand mules to transport them across the sierra. Finally, every other effort extended, she set out herself through the mountain passes to Baza. She arrived on November 7, revealing neither the fatigue nor the anxiety of the situation, accompanied by the Cardinal of Spain and, to the delight of the hitherto dejected crusaders, a bevy of charmingly unwarlike ladies-in-waiting. With what apprehension they had followed their mistress through the rains and mountain blizzards can only be guessed. Now, her troupe delivered intact, the queen put on the show of her life.

"She came," in the words of one present in the grim arena, "surrounded by a choir of nymphs, as if to celebrate the wedding of a child." Bernaldez rhapsodized, telling how, as the party emerged from the wintry hills to the strains of lively music, with all the color and spirit of a carnival, the Moors watched amazed from their housetops and battlements. This could hardly be the prelude to a Christian withdrawal; rather, it must have seemed to them, a token of some new enemy triumph. Isabella's psychology confounded the Moorish mind. Her self-assurance hinted at infinite resources. Her serenity brought fresh confidence to her own forces. The spell can have seemed little short of miraculous. Within three days, Cid Hiaya had opened negotiations.

Muslim history brands him a traitor, distastefully noting the gifts and civilities with which the sovereigns deftly lined the path to his eventual surrender. Nevertheless, he saved Baza from the fate of Málaga, using the relative strength of his position to secure terms of safe-conduct for its people and their property. For his own part, Cid Hiaya was treated by the victors like "a great caballero," retaining his castles and land with immunity from taxes and the right to travel where he wished with an armed bodyguard. A further reward of ten thousand reales appears to have been made to him for his part in persuading his brother-in-law, El Zagal, to submit on similar terms. It was a cheap price for converting near-catastrophe to spectacular victory. With Guadix and Almería surrendered peacefully, one capricious gust of good fortune had unfurled the bloodied flag of Christianity across the whole eastern territory. Only Granada itself, and its towering Alhambra, stood out against the brimming tide of reconquest.

The climax was drawing near. After eight tortuous centuries—including a nightmare period when it had seemed that not only the peninsula but the whole continent must fall to the Saracen—Muslim power in Western Europe was on the verge of extinction. For eight centuries the blood and anguish of Spain had served to safeguard millions of more northerly Christians. Now, with the defenders of the faith reaping their reward in heaven-sent victory, pride and self-righteousness blazed in the Spanish breast. An era of frustration was ending. Tomorrow, prince once more in his own palace, the Spaniard visualized himself free at last to fulfill his true destiny; a destiny, among God's legions, of glory and pre-eminence. On April 26, 1491, the crusading army encamped on the vega of Granada, near the fountain of Ojos de Huescar, a mile or so from its long-awaited destination. Serene and lovely to the distant beholder, the great city rose alluringly from the plain, a pink and perfumed Mecca set against hazy mountains. It was a prize too splendid to be taken damaged, and, having ordered their captains to hold their horses, Isabella and Ferdinand severed its lifelines and settled to wait. Contemporary reports tell how, dazzled by the prospect before them, the sovereigns would ride to vantage points overlooking the Moorish capital and gaze acquisitively into the city. Within an ace of her greatest triumph, Isabella regaled an excited and admiring audience with a leisured display of matriarchal magnificence. Superbly mounted on a white Arab charger, and dressed in regal crimson, she made irresistible copy for the descriptive writers of the day. There was time again to relax in the familiar postures of piety and charity. Surrounded by a train of clerics, and the much-traveled ladies of her court, she toured the various sections of the camp with eloquent expressions of praise and sympathy. Even more to the liking of her soldiers, the woman who had refused to contemplate their retirement from Baza could now afford to insist on the minimum of bloodshed.

Each morning, as the sun rose behind the snow-tipped Sierra Nevada, Isabella joined the entire host of troops and camp followers to celebrate Mass with Cardinal Mendoza. It was a fascinating assembly. By now news of the impending triumph had prompted a rare assortment of international opportunists to jump on the royal band wagon for the last lap of its journey. They came from all over Europe—cranks and zealots, astrologers with glowing forecasts, geographers with plans for further conquests, abstruse philosophers and plausible con men—each ready to offer advice to the monarchs, each seeking a trail to self-fulfillment or profit. Unlike the grandees of the court circle, in whose limelight they ventured hopefully, their connections were often tenuous, their fortunes strictly limited. Some, the hot breath of the Inquisition still tingling their necks, were none too anxious to talk of the past.

Among the more notable figures in this circus was Christopher

Columbus, an eccentric traveler in his forties with a flair for histrionic gesture, a stock of tall stories, and some bookish information about distant and uncharted parts. His appearance and style were intriguing. Tall, with a long, florid face, graying hair and beard, Columbus affected, if the general tenor of reports is correct, the grand manner of a noble pedigree he almost certainly did not possess. "Eloquent and high-sounding" with "the mien of a person worthy of all reverence," he emerges from contemporary notices with something of the impact of an early matinee idol fallen on hard times. Bernaldez considered him "a man of high mind but no great knowledge," while another who knew him at the period remarked that "he looked and sounded like a person from another land," adding that Columbus was vague when questioned about his origins.

Absorbed in what he cared to describe as "the secrets of the world," Columbus imagined himself reaching the fabled Asia of Marco Polo by the novel method of traveling west. To this end he had persistently lobbied the Spanish sovereigns for patronage. But with little success. To the campaigners of Granada, his dream realms—the Earthly Paradise, the Spice Islands, King Solomon's Mines—were intriguing but not to be taken too seriously. Columbus might give chapter and verse for a stone which burned with an undying flame, a spring which froze in the sun and became hot at night, a land where gems could be found in the skulls of dragons; for his companions there was a more realistic goal in sight—the Moorish Alhambra. Still, the man added a quixotic touch to camp life. Veteran crusaders, recalling the same odd character at Córdoba, Málaga and Baza, pointed him out to new arrivals as one of the more curious phenomena in an altogether marvelous war.

Meanwhile, Granada, its twisting streets and vaulted alleys a seething mass of Muslim refugees and soldiers, reflected inversely the mounting expectations of its enemies. Reduced to the forlorn hope of intervention by their coreligionists in Africa, its politicians engaged in fierce recriminations. Behind its walls and bastions, the residue of Moorish chivalry awaited with increasing frustration an unforthcoming Christian attack. Finally, more by way of therapy than strategy, groups of Muslim cavalry charged into the open to challenge the enemy to combat. That they found ready takers, despite the royal embargo on such engagements, is as certain as

some of the legendary details of the phase are dubious, and for
some months the no-man's-land between the city walls and the
siege camp seems to have become the arena for many exploits
of individual daring and bravura. But if such tourneying diverted
the noble minority, it did little to ease the tension for the mass of
Granadinos who looked to the Alhambra for something more
decisive.

They looked in vain. Of all things expected of the incumbent
monarch, Boabdil of Granada, decisiveness was the least likely to
be gained. The son of domineering and conflicting parents, Boabdil
had lived from the first between loyalties, developing a devious
and vacillating character. His father, Muley Hacen, emir at the
outbreak of war, had been a tough and implacable hater of Christians to the day of his death. Boabdil's mother, Aixa, apparently
incensed by her husband's addiction in his later years to the
younger members of his harem, had used her own considerable
influence to thwart her rivals and steer her ill-fitted son to the
throne. The resulting pattern of internal strife had involved Boabdil in as much trouble with his own relatives, particularly his uncle
El Zagal, as with the Christians. Indeed, at one stage of the struggle he had actually thrown in his lot with Ferdinand. But, as usual,
his mind had since changed. Now, torn between the threat of the
crusading army at his gates and the angry demands of his own
subjects for action, Boabdil sat in his lovely palace and pleaded
the cruel fortunes of fate.

Whether even the most powerful and dedicated leadership could
have saved Granada at this stage from Christian occupation is
doubtful, but Boabdil neglected at least two marginal chances of
breaking the blockade. On one occasion, Isabella and Ferdinand
rode to the village of Zubia, no great distance from the city, to take
a close look at the conurbation. Though the movement was
screened by a strong section of their army, it seems possible they
might have been cut off by a swift and determined cavalry attack.
As it was, part of the Moorish garrison advanced with a number
of small cannons and aimed some missiles at the enemy lines. But
it lacked organization and leadership and was quickly chased back
to its own defenses. Another time, fire broke out in the Christian
camp at night, spreading rapidly through the closely pitched tents
and pavilions. The confusion was great, Ferdinand seizing his

sword and rushing out in expectation of a Moorish attack while Isabella escaped from the flames with difficulty. Once more, an aggressive Muslim leader might have exploited the situation with success. To the relief of the sovereigns, the disorganized warriors of Granada simply stood on their battlements and gaped. The permanent barracks built by the besiegers on the ashes, a veritable township of substantial dwellings and stables which Isabella devotedly christened Santa Fé, banished Moorish hopes of a Christian withdrawal forever.

On October 28, 1491, his life endangered by a desperate and now openly rebellious populace, Boabdil signed a secret treaty with the Catholic sovereigns agreeing to surrender the capital within sixty days. The liberal terms he obtained for his people (though later dishonored by the victors) represented perhaps the most laudable effort of his reign. Unlike Cid Hiaya, he derived little profit from his enterprise. In December, news of the pact leaked from the Alhambra to the city and Boabdil's subjects rose in revolt against "the traitor." New Year's Day brought an anguished plea from the desolate sultan to the Christians, asking them to occupy Granada at once. Within twenty-four hours, Boabdil had handed over the keys of his stronghold and was riding tearfully toward the Alpujarras and exile, still nagged by his overweening mother. The last Granada saw of its ultimate Muslim ruler was a distant silhouette against the morning sky as he paused with fifty pony-mounted retainers on a craggy eminence to look back on the haunting capital and its red castle, the pride and joy of his forebears. The alleged spot is commemorated in the picturesque sobriquet *El Ultimo Sospiro del Moro*, The Last Sigh of the Moor. The crusade was at an end: the collapse of the Spanish Arab dominions complete. January 1 of 1492, the *annus mirabilis* of Spanish history, dawned not merely on a new year but on an epoch. If the occasion seemed less definitive at the time than it does in retrospect, it was nevertheless one of overwhelming emotion. Next day, as the sun rose on a benumbed and unresisting city, the Christian army was already assembled for its entry. Led by a small standard party of knights and clerics, the now seasoned Spanish infantry moved in to secure the key points, followed in gala cavalcade by the royal court with its cuirassed and brilliant escort. Behind came musicians, the choir of the royal chapel and the whole diverse and glittering war throng. Soon every capital in Christendom would rejoice, but this was a moment created primarily for Spanish hearts. As the banners of Castile and Aragon rose on the Torre de la Vela, the watchtower of the great castle, together with the gleaming silver cross of the crusade, the heralds pealed their exuberance, the royal choir burst into the Te Deum, the entire army dropped to its knees in reverence.

Chapter 2

FROM CAVES TO CASTLES

Physiographically, Spain is a subtle seductress. The exterior she flaunts to the passing traveler—Andalusia, Valencia, and Catalonia on the south and east, and Galicia, Asturias and the Basque Provinces on the north—have an immediate scenic and pastoral charm. Spain has long cherished the image of this rustic idyll. Among the earliest surviving examples of Castilian literature can be found a delightfully enticing passage from the chronicle of the thirteenth-century king, astronomer, and poet Alfonso X, the Learned (an ancestor of Isabella and Ferdinand), postulating a land brimming with milk and honey. "This Spain of which we speak," wrote Alfonso, "is as the paradise of God . . . rich in crops and delicious fruit, with an extravagance of fish, and good milk, and all that is made of it; full of game, large and small, flocks of cattle, noble horses and many mules; secured by numerous castles, convivial in its fine wines, plenteous in its wheat, rich in metals, lead, tin, iron, copper, silver, gold, precious stones and all kinds of marble . . . splendid in shining silks, sweet in sugar and honey, abounding in the wax that gives light, and in oil, and the delectable saffron . . . No land can equal or rival it."

But, once lured by such smiles to her bosom, one discovers in Spain a moodier, altogether more magnificent mistress. Castile, the arid central region of the country, with its barren and wind-swept plateaus, the Paramos or Parameras, is rather akin to the steppes of

North Africa than Alfonso's "paradise." To the southeast, on the
sweltering salt steppe of Murcia, a whole year can pass without
rain. In the west, where the *tomillares*, the rocky heathlands of
Estremadura, degenerate into Las Burdes, an area of virtual desert—
or to the northeast, where the scrubby plains of Aragon stretch
dry and bleak in the summer *calina*, the heat mist—nature's harvest
is minimal. Geologically, upward of half the country's 190,115
square miles is composed of the Meseta, a flat and crusty earth
block reduced in great areas to a state of peneplantation. Climati-
cally, this vast plateau of a land, crowned and imperiously divided
by mountain ranges, is a place of extremes. There is some exaggeration, but more than a little truth, in the familiar Spanish quip
which summarizes life in the dusty central zone of Castile as nine
months of winter and three of hell. Yet here, rather than on her
daintier fringes, is the true fascination of Spain, a harsh, torrid,
inescapably haunting country, whose sunsets have driven countless
pens to turgidity, and whose moons rise with the same purple glow
on her lovers.

In this affecting atmosphere, Isabella had herself passed the
early years of childhood, among other places at Arévalo, an austere
little town at the confluence of two parched rivers on the huge
rocky plain stretching northwest of Madrid and the Sierra de
Guadarrama. Fatherless, the ward of an impoverished and unbal-
anced royal mother, the student princess had turned eagerly from
the stern realities of her environment to the spiritual and intellectual world of her priestly tutors, to the histories and legends of
the early chroniclers, tales which fired her mind as surely as the
surrounding countryside was transformed by those marvelous,
dream-laden skies. If the history on which Isabella based her knowledge of Spain is no longer adequate, the excitement and inspiration
she gained from exploring the past still obtains. Indeed, no understanding of her own and subsequent times can be satisfactory
without tracing the story to its most distant and yet often con-
jectural chapters.

The synthesis of the Spaniard is involved from the start with the
physical duality of his country, the easy appeal of the rich outer
regions and the tempering passions of a harsh and demanding
hinterland. The first of his ancestors to leave their trademarks on
the walls of prehistory were hunters from lands to the north and

south, attracted by the game of those tempting coastal reaches. Because they were hunters, their art re-created the sights of the chase, and, in the thrilling cave paintings of Santander, Asturias and Biscay to the north linger glimpses of scenes more than fifteen thousand years old. Significantly, the same type of cave decoration —line drawings of extraordinary likeness and vivacity—recur in southwestern France, indicating, as far as these survivals are concerned, a primitive culture of Pyrenean orientation. At the same time, rock-shelter paintings occurring in the southeastern quarter of Spain suggest primitive artists with ties in the opposite direction. Though the animals in these pictures have much in common with those of the cave works, they are intermingled with oddly styled human beings, subjects mainly ignored by the artists of the north. Men, often armed with bows and arrows, are shown sometimes with spindly "matchstick" limbs, sometimes with grotesque bulges on the lower or upper leg. Women are depicted in long, flared dresses, some in dancelike postures, others seemingly in conversation. These crudely conventionalized figures bear a striking resemblance to paleolithic rock drawings found in North Africa.

To this evidence of two distinct early societies can be added the fact that ancient writers also distinguished between two basic racial groups in the peninsula: the Basques, living in the region of the Pyrenees, and possibly stemming from a race of aboriginal Pyrenean cave dwellers; and the so-called Iberians, perhaps of Berber origin, who seem gradually to have spread across the country from early stomping grounds in the southeast. To the homelands of these rough and little-known people swarmed the Celtic migrants of the seventh and sixth centuries B.C., refugees from Central Europe, seeking a new and warmer world to the south. In the highlands of the far north, the native stock held its own against this new infusion, as did that of the south and east, but in the west the Celts overran the old tribes, settling in what are now Galicia and Portugal. On the thinly populated central plateau, Celts and Iberians found room to live together, merging to give the Celtiberians of the ancients. About the same time, perhaps a few centuries earlier, the tempting fringes of the old peninsula attracted the first visitors who represented something more than just another folk movement. They came in low galleys, nosing cautiously west along the Mediterranean shore in search of the reputed treasure of Tartessos (the biblical Tarshish), on the Atlantic coast of Andalusia, and found a whole region rich in fruit, livestock and precious metals. These adventurers, the Phoenicians, from Syria, north of Palestine, set up trading posts on the golden strands with their western base at Cádiz, then an island known as Gadir or Agadir, where they built a temple to the god Hercules. With businesslike thoroughness, the costs of its construction were noted on two of its lofty bronze columns. The scouts of commerce had arrived. And with them came a foretaste of civilization; a glimpse of mining techniques, seafaring science, and other accomplishments quite new to the country.

The Greeks who followed, though also primarily traders concerned with shipping out metals, had a profounder influence on native culture. They arrived on the east and south coasts from their Mediterranean base of Marseilles approximately as the last Celtic migrants were crossing the Pyrenees, founding substantial colonies on the seaboard, notably at Ampurias, north of Barcelona, near Denia between Alicante and Valencia, and at the mouth of the Río de Velez by Málaga. Here and elsewhere they built fortified towns or trading posts which they filled with the familiar Greek repertory of arts. Soon, the natives were borrowing ideas from the architecture, statuary and pottery of their visitors. Many surviving items of subsequent Iberian creativity demonstrate Greek influence, perhaps none more strikingly than the so-called Lady of Elche, discovered at the town of that name between Alicante and Murcia, a bust combining classic gravity of feature with some oddly contrasting ornamentation. Likewise, the earliest known coins of Iberian manufacture were directly inspired by Greek money. Even the vine and the olive, symbols of the Spanish way of life centuries before Isabella's time, were introduced to the country by the Greeks.

Neither the Greeks nor the Phoenicians, however, exerted themselves toward the conquest or colonization of the peninsula. As merchants, they were content to maintain trading posts, at the most coastal settlements, at which the iron, copper, lead, silver, gold, and other products in which they were interested could be assembled for shipment overseas. Even so, they had their troubles with the natives, and with each other. In the sixth century B.C., the Phoenicians at Agadir felt themselves so vulnerable that they requested help from their sister people the Carthaginians, who, from their booming capital and naval base near the site of modern Tunis, North Africa, were fast extending their hold on the Mediterranean. Carthage, originally a Phoenician settlement, commenced its intervention by aiding the Agadir colonists and ended by taking over their investment. When Greek interests in southern Spain fell to the same power, the salad days of colonial dabbling in Iberian development were over. Unlike their predecessors, the Carthaginians were soon lusting for more than fringe benefits. This was to prove no desultory flirtation. The seductress had aroused the first of a masterful sequence of conquerors.

The presiding genius of the Carthaginian military machine at the time of its projected conquest of the peninsula, in the second half of the third century B.C., was Hamilcar Barca, one of a celebrated family of generals the fame of which was to be climaxed by the exploits of Hamilcar's own son, Hannibal. Though many of the indigenous people resisted the offensive when it came, ill-organized tribal warriors were a poor match for an army whose recruiting officials scoured North Africa and the Mediterranean for the finest mercenaries, and which maintained an elite corps manned by scions of the highest families in the state as a supply pool of young officers. Intimidated by the odds and tempted by the promises of the enemy, an increasing number of native chiefs, the *caudillos*, went over to the invading commanders as the campaigns proceeded. All the same, the operation dragged on for some nine years, until the death of Hamilcar, by which time the Carthaginians had penetrated the interior to the Castilian plateau and had reached the Ebro in the east.

These gains were consolidated by Hamilcar's son-in-law, Hasdrubal Pulcher, who developed a natural harbor and base in the southeast, New Carthage (later to become Cartagena), as the military and merchant capital of the dominion. Here the Carthaginians held hostages against possible rebellions while, with their customary industry, they exploited the potential of their territories. At Cartagena itself, at Huelva on the Gulf of Cádiz, and elsewhere, they worked mines which are still in existence today. They cultivated saltings and established a fish-curing industry; they produced and exported esparto grass; they stimulated the spread of coinage, no longer of Greek design but bearing the symbols of their own African background; they recruited mercenaries for their armies, teaching the Iberians to campaign in foreign places, by water as well as by land. In short, they subjected many parts of the land and its peoples to the influences of a dynamic and organized state. With time, they might have incorporated all Spain in an African empire. But time, for Carthage, was already running out.

If it is in the nature of things that the main beneficiaries of initiative are seldom the initiators, the Carthaginian contribution to the early unification of Spain is a fair example of the process. What the Carthaginians had begun the Romans completed, so overshadowing their predecessors, as it happened, that it is easy to forget that Carthage not only anticipated Rome's later purpose in the peninsula, but was actually the means of firing her ambition. The Romans arrived in Spain not so much to seize control of a new land as to destroy the power of a feared and long-hated colonial rival. Rome's staggering growth from a petty kingdom to a world-wide empire—to dominate by the first century of the Christian era Italy, Greece, France, Britain, the Netherlands, parts of Germany and many regions of Africa and Asia—had involved inevitable collision with Carthage. The first big crash had come around the middle of the third century B.C., with the two great powers struggling for ascendancy in Sicily and the Tyrrhenian Sea. Though Carthage had suffered heavy losses in this conflict, the First Punic War, her program of expansion in Spain had helped to offset them and Hasdrubal was able to conclude a treaty with Rome in which the Ebro featured as the northernmost line of Carthaginian activity.

But it was an uneasy and short-lived agreement. The Second Punic War, this time a decisive struggle, erupted in 219 B.C., when Hasdrubal's brother-in-law, the celebrated Hannibal, attacked and captured the fortified town of Saguntum (later Sagunto) on the Valencian coast, a place connected by some alliance with Rome. In one of the best-known military campaigns of all time, Hannibal now embarked on the astonishing tour de force which carried him triumphantly through upper Spain, Gaul, and into Italy itself, only to run out of impetus within striking distance of a horrified Rome.

Within an ace of sensational victory, Carthage had floundered. Hannibal had shot his bolt: Hasdrubal, with a relieving army, was defeated at the Metaurus. Purposefully, if with no overwhelming eagerness, the Romans entered Spain to destroy the residue of Carthaginian power there. By the close of the third century B.C. the task was complete and they were able to take stock of what they had inherited.

At first, their impressions were not entirely unfavorable. Passing down the eastern coastal region to seize Cartagena, they turned through the flourishing south on their way to Cádiz, embracing lands of great mineral and horticultural prosperity. Animals roamed in profusion. It seems there was a veritable plague of rabbits. Here, where Greek and Punic influence had been the strongest, the inhabitants had acquired some sophistication. When it came to the rest, however, the outlook was bleak. Mountains, forests, and arid plains, combining with the fierce reputation of many tribes which even the Carthaginians had not disturbed, contributed to a general picture of inhospitality. Roman geographers described the typical Iberians, as they knew the peninsula people of the time, as swarthy and tousle-haired, slight, wiry and pugnacious, practiced horsemen and courageous, often fanatical fighters. Some lived in walled towns, others in more primitive mountain and forest communities. Local pride and overweening independence were placed by many before their own lives and the lives of their families. "Their bodies inured to abstinence and toil, their minds composed against death . . . they prefer war to ease and, should they lack foes without, seek them within. Rather than betray a secret they will often die under torment . . ." declared a Roman commentator. Stories were told of mothers who murdered their children to prevent their falling into enemy hands; of prisoners who killed themselves or slayed grateful companions rather than suffer the indignity of slavedom; of patriots who chanted songs of victory while being crucified by the Romans.

Few needed any introduction to brutality and violence. For many, including the Celtiberian tribes of the interior and the so-called Lusitanians of what is now central Portugal, the normal way of life was warlike and predatory. The Lusitanians, accomplished raiders and guerrillas, practiced a disenchanting habit of gutting their enemies in search of intestinal omens. Among the Galician,

Asturian, Cantabrian and Basque tribes of the north, where the people ate acorn bread and drank beer, prisoners were ceremonially butchered, while social undesirables were dumped over cliffs. Well supplied with horses, trained from childhood to find their mark with javelin and sling, and operating in terrain ideally suited to their bandit tactics, the Iberians posed an awesome problem for the Romans. In the areas of Carthaginian penetration, they had learned military lessons from their former enemies, including, it seems likely, a dawning realization of the advantages of intertribal solidarity in the face of a common invader. At all events, opposition to the new colonizers was to be so widespread and sustained as to diminish anything known in the peninsula before.

A little more than a quarter of a century after the defeat of the Carthaginians, Rome had drafted 150,000 troops to Spain and had been forced to impose permanent conscription at home to meet its requirements. In 151 B.C. reports reached the capital that the armies in Spain were in almost ceaseless combat, that Roman deaths were countless and that the Celtiberians were undefeatable. Officers refused to volunteer for the peninsula, veteran soldiers declined to march with their leaders, while, to the consternation of Roman society, the number of youths evading enlistment was so great that punishment became impossible. Several times, Roman commanders were forced into the unusual and humiliating position of having to sue for peace. It was not a posture which suited their sense of authority. Fearful for their reputations, some resorted to cruelty, some to treachery, to gain their ends. Often the most defiant of their prisoners were crucified, and many Iberian warriors, anticipating their fate if captured, carried poisonous leaves which they swallowed in the final extremity. Where the Romans could not defeat the native leaders in battle, it was not unknown for them to contrive their assassination.

One such victim was the Lusitanian leader Viriatus. In a particularly contemptible ruse to destroy the Lusitanians, then waging remorseless war from their mountain hideouts, the Roman governor, Galba, had pretended to grant an armistice, securing these people in possession of their homes and grazing lands. Taking him at his word, they returned to the plains, where he fell on them by surprise, conducting a pitiless massacre. Viriatus, who reputedly had started life as a shepherd, survived Galba's treachery, using the bitterness of the memory to unite many central and southern tribes under his banner. Dedicated, single-minded, and impassioned, the Celtiberian chief was to become the prototype Spanish hero. His warriors, long hair piled on the top of their heads in battle, were the scourge of the legions. For eight years, Viriatus employed a natural talent for guerrilla warfare and leadership to outwit the best commanders Rome could send against him. In the end, the general Caepio was reduced to plotting his murder by bribery. At the same time, the tribes of Numantia, based on the little Celtiberian town of that name on the Douro above modern Soria, were filling other Roman soldiers with dread. Their epic struggle for independence, like that of Viriatus, was to inspire Spaniards in defense of their country for centuries to come. Roman reluctance to face the Numantians was notorious. The very name of the place became a password to dismay in Italy. For nearly twenty years the Numantians repelled every attempt to subdue them until, in 134 B.C., the renowned Roman general Scipio Aemilianus marched on their capital with sixty thousand men. Even then, he was unable to press home an attack. Outnumbered fifteen to one, the defenders held on for another sixteen months, by which time starvation and lack of water had claimed more victims than the Romans. When Scipio finally entered Numantia, it was to discover a town of smoking ruin and corpses. The last survivors had fired the buildings and committed suicide.

But, moving as such episodes might be, the heroism was touched with despair. Once more, tribal pride and resilience were no match, in the long run, for the resources and perseverance of an organized colonial machine. The fall of Numantia gave the invaders a wide hold on the interior as well as on the east and south. Julius Caesar's governorship (61–60 B.C.) saw the front line pushed to the mouth of the Douro in the west, and forty years later, after some of the most savage fighting the Romans had ever encountered, the Augustan regime completed the job in the far north. In all, it had taken the greatest military power in the world no less than two centuries to master the peninsula, during which time the complexion of both sides had changed. Indeed, so far as much of Spain was concerned, the conquest had long since ceased to be a matter of crude suppression and was well into the assimilatory phase of its evolution.

Though by no means innocent of opportunism in their exploitation of the country, the Romans had their usual advantages to offer the people. For the first time many potentially industrious and productive tribes were secured against jealous and predatory neighbors. Safer travel meant better commercial prospects; a more efficient system of justice swept away many petty tyrannies; the refinements of Roman living gave birth to new social aspirations. Then there was the stimulus of mixed blood. Roman soldiers and colonists were not backward in fraternizing with Spanish women, and the offspring of such relationships, the mestizos, were soon helping to accelerate Romanization. As early as 171 B.C. a whole colony of mestizos existed near Algeciras in the far south. Fifty years later, a Roman leader of mixed blood, Quintus Sertorius, was able to defy Roman political rivals with the enthusiastic aid of an army of already partly Romanized tribesmen. Sertorius, regarded as a champion by a mixed population now agitating for full Roman status, founded a school of languages and civics for the sons of Iberian chiefs. There was to be little looking back in the age of development ahead. Before the first century of the Christian era was over, each of the peninsula's five hundred or more recorded towns, linked by twelve thousand miles of highway, could claim Latin rights, the Roman army there had been reduced to a nominal legion, Hispano-Roman society was wreathed in new peace and prosperity.

As time passed, Spain rewarded Rome for its efforts not merely with the material wealth of its industries but with a good return on its cultural investment. Intellectual circles in the city were besieged by writers and orators from the Iberian provinces. Marcus Seneca and his son Lucius, both popular writers—the latter an influential moralist—came from Córdoba, as did their relative, the poet Marcus Lucanus; Martial, the satirist, hailed from Calatayud, near the northeastern town of Saragossa; Quintilian, the rhetorician, from nearby Calahorra; while two notable orators, the Balbuses, uncle and nephew, came from Cádiz. In the academic field, Columela, regarded as the most learned agronomist of the period, and Pomponius Mela, esteemed as a geographer, were both from the far south of Spain. Though there is no reliable evidence that any of these were of native ancestry, some were certainly born in Spain and all had been domiciled in the Spanish colonies. It seems unlikely that their contacts with the peninsula had failed to make some impression on their characters. The same applied to a number of famous men of action: soldiers, politicians, and emperors. Trajan was born near Seville. Hadrian, Marcus Aurelius, and Theodosius were of Hispano-Roman families.

Appropriately enough in view of his Spanish background, it was Theodosius, the last man to rule the whole Roman Empire, who made Christianity its official religion, thus recognizing an organization more profoundly related to Spain's future than anyone could yet have imagined. Rome was to crumble, its legions to scatter, but the new faith struck responses in the peninsula which were to survive the chaos that followed and impel the nation, in time, to prodigious achievements. At Toledo, central Spain, in the year 400, the Catholic definition of orthodoxy adopted at the first ecumenical council of the Church held at Nicaea, Asia Minor, earlier in the century, was endorsed for the peninsula. It was none too early. Six years later, the first of the barbarians to burst the Rhine frontier of a now perilously distended Roman Empire surged into Gaul and on toward an undefended Spain. Three Germanic peoples, the Vandals, the Suevi, and the Alans, fought each other for lands in the peninsula, the Vandals snatching much of the south where they left their name in Andalusia, the Suevi sheering west to Galicia, the Alans moving mainly to the east. Large areas unsubmerged by the invaders cultivated a new independence. Thus, the centuries of Roman unity broken and the old proclivity to division asserting itself, sudden and dramatic responsibility for the national conscience fell on the one remaining organization with agents throughout the country: the young, resilient, and ambitious society of the Church.

The Church in the peninsula handled its business adroitly. Not only did it nurture its principles through the retrograde years of tribal invasion, but, with a foretaste of the doctrinal intensity that was to characterize Spanish faith in later centuries, actually converted a further wave of invaders, this time Christians, from the Arian heresy to Catholicism. These people, the nomadic Visigoths, or western Goths, once settled in Gaul after a circuitous tour of Europe, had been engaged by a declining Rome to regain the peninsula from the tribes in possession. Like the Carthaginians, they came to help and stayed to take over. By the middle of the sixth century, Toledo had become their capital and they were widely distributed through the land. Though a warlike people, the Visigoths were culturally receptive. They arrived with a Bible in their own language, written laws, and an artistic heritage which, if not polished, reflected something of both the Roman and Byzantine influence encountered in their wanderings. Instead of pressing their Gothic speech on the Spanish Romans, they learned to speak Latin themselves. Their nobles built Roman-style country villas as symbols of their status, and, in time, put aside their rough trappings for something like Roman costume. While Gothic power, then, superseded Roman power in Spain, it became in many respects "Roman" in the process.

But not entirely. The Visigoths introduced two enduring social conceptions to Spain. One was their aristocratic system of serfs and overlords, providing, in war, a military nobility with its own armed retainers. The other was the institution of monarchy. After centuries of subordination to Rome, the peninsula provinces now composed a kingdom in their own right. In 587, the conversion of the Visigothic king Reccared to Catholicism, combining an absolute monarch with the most coherent organization in the country, appeared to presage a period of fresh stability for the royal subjects. It was this Spain, the Visigothic society which persisted slightly more than another century, until the Muslim invasion, that Isabella and other victors of the Christian reconquest were to regard fondly and somewhat superficially as their heritage. The need to identify with a pre-Muslim era of which they knew little beyond colorful legend, eventually gave rise to a charmingly ingenuous picture. Its people, wrote the learned Alfonso X, looking back with hopeful abandon, were "bold, strong, diligent, loyal and studious, courteous in address and perfect in all good." Sadly, such was very far from the truth.

There was at least one fatal flaw in the setup. According to tradition, the king of the Visigoths was elected from the nobles, an arrangement highly conducive among a jealous and self-seeking aristocracy to competition and distrust. Failure to modify the hazard was to prove, in the end, self-destructive. Despite belated attempts to introduce a hereditary system, strongly backed by the more perceptive members of the clergy, internal conflicts accompanied almost every succession. Preoccupied with their own ambitions, the nobles neglected their responsibility to lesser people, whose lot deteriorated in many instances beyond toleration. The Jews, long a numerous and assertive minority, rebelled and were viciously repressed. Serfs went unheeded while their masters indulged an increasing weakness for intrigue and extravagance. By the year 700, two centuries of Visigothic domination in the peninsula were withering through rivalry and decadence. Lords whose rugged ancestors had led their families bravely into Spain clad in armor of leather and rough woolen vests, now flaunted fancy costumes of gold and silver cloth and rode on saddles studded with rubies and pearls. Regardless of ecclesiastical protest, high laymen and clerics alike kept regular harems of concubines. "Perfect in all good" was scarcely the phrase for them. Life devolved on the personal pleasures of the few, to the overwhelming and imminent loss of the state.

Across the Mediterranean, the fall of Carthage to the Arabs in 693 had left Islam triumphant the length of North Africa. Scarcely more than a half century from Mohammed's lifetime, the prophet's followers were ready to carry his teachings to Europe. In 711 an army of twelve thousand Berber tribesmen, commanded by Tarik ibn Ziyad of Tangier, ferried the Strait of Gibraltar on a raiding reconnaissance. They were met, on July 19 of that year, by a numerically superior Spanish force under a bejeweled Visigoth ruler named Roderic. But Roderic's army, riddled with disaffection and defeatism, fell to pieces in an engagement near Algeciras. Amazed and elated, the raiders advanced from one Andalusian town to another, meeting with hardly a blow. In a few places, men actually joined them in arms; in many, it seems, the feeling was one of relief. When Toledo, the capital of the kingdom, opened its gates to the dusty band, their astonishment was complete. Meanwhile, animated by the news, a stronger force under the Arab viceroy in North Africa, Musa ibn Nusair, had sailed from Tangier and was making ground in the wake of Tarik's Berbers. Together, they took Saragossa and, following the valley of the Ebro, continued until they reached France, and beyond. Within seven years the Muslims had consolidated their hold on the entire peninsula save a few small mountainous districts in the far north. To those mountains the reconquest owed its painful birth. But what Islam had captured in less than a decade it was to take Christianity eight bloody and traumatic centuries to win back.

Detonated in Arabia by the prophet Mohammed in the early seventh century, the Muslim explosion which scattered the hordes of North Africa across the peninsula had more in kind with Christianity than subsequent history might suggest. Mohammed, proclaiming a single god, the resurrection of the dead and a final judgment followed by hell or paradise, drove forward a religion which took many of its prophets from the Old and New Testaments and included in its own books the sayings of Christ and the Psalms. Like any religion, however, its converts made of it according to their intellect and temperament. While its propagator the Arab, with his Eastern background and philosophic disposition, invested the ideology with a spirit of subtlety and imagination, many of his proselytes were incapable of matching his insight. Significant among these were the fierce Berber tribesmen of northwest Africa whom the Arabs were pleased to use as soldiers in the northerly extension of their empire. Against Arab idealism, the Berber raised his own fiery brand of the faith: the fanaticism that was to shatter Arab dreams in the peninsula and, by invoking the same fanaticism among Christians, ensure not only his own defeat at their hands but the overthrow of all Muslim Spain.

Broadly speaking, Islam's career in the peninsula proceeded in two phases, one largely controlled by the Arabs, the other in the hands of the Berbers. The first of these began on a note of toleration and acceptance and reached its climax in a period of outstanding cultural enrichment. As the brains and executive of the initial occupation, the Arabs lost little time staking their claim to the lush lands of the south, leaving the Berber contingents, the spear point of the invasion, to hold the wastes of La Mancha and Estramadura. With Córdoba as its capital, the Arab regime set about making the most of its lovely new home in Andalusia. Enterprising schemes of irrigation were embarked on, exotic new crops were introduced from the east, agriculture generally was raised to a new level of efficiency. Arab coffers overflowed with the taxes imposed on the native population, but, too astute to cripple the source of such golden eggs, the Muslim rulers stopped short of ruinous exploitation. For the great majority of Visigothic subjects, the changeover seemed far from calamitous, a point underlined by its generally unhindered progress and the lack of rebellion. Many slaves gained freedom by embracing Islam, the poor classes as a whole found some relief from oppression, while, with a businesslike eye on revenues, the Arabs protected the redevelopment of middle-class commercial interests, particularly of the Jews.

Worse off were the dedicated Christians, who incurred an extra tax and were prohibited from proselytizing or obtrusive demonstrations of faith. Even so, they were not denied the practice of their religion, and many Christian communities, though subdued, remained intact and unmolested under the Arabs. At Córdoba, where half the largest church was taken as a mosque, God and Allah were actually worshiped for some time in the same building. In any case, the masses of the peninsula, still semipagan, were not passionately committed by faith, and large numbers very soon became Muslim converts, *muladíes*. Indeed, the widow of Roderic, the last Visigoth ruler, was among the first to do so. Others, while retaining Christianity as their religion, gradually adopted Arab customs, Arab names and even the Arab language. These were known as *mozárabes*, or "almost Arabs."

At the same time, the Muslim regime in the peninsula was not without its troubles. Rivalry between the Arabs and Berbers was complicated by an influx of Egyptians, Syrians, and others, each with its own sensitivities and antipathies. In the first half-century of the occupation, disunity and strife reached such a pitch that it seemed the Muslim edifice, like that of the Visigoths, was about to be destroyed from inside. It was saved by an even greater upheaval at the heart of the Arab Empire. In 750 the reigning family of the Ommayads, upon which dynasty the peninsula Muslims were theoretically dependent, was violently overthrown in Damascus by a rival family, the Abbassides, and its members massacred. To the orthodox Muslims of the west, the Abbasside coup was an impiety, and when, after many personal adventures, a lone survivor of the old royal family turned up in Spain, there was at last a chance of touching a common sentiment among the rival Muslim elements in that country. In his early twenties, Abd al-Rahman was

young enough and sufficiently determined to pull it off. Surrounded
first by family partisans in the peninsula, and later by a great army
of mercenaries, largely Berbers, he fought ceaselessly for more than
two decades to establish a respectful and independent Spanish
emirate. The social disciplines of Abd al-Rahman I and his successors, often achieved at the price of appalling butchery, paid
dividends, these reaching an economic and cultural zenith in the
reign of the first emir's namesake, Abd al-Rahman III (912–61),
who expressed his disregard for the eastern dynasty by assuming
the ultimate title of caliph.

To Abd al-Rahman's so-called Caliphate of Córdoba, and its inheritance, belonged the finest years of the Spanish Arabs: the brief
flowering of a civilization beside which the Europe of the Vikings,
the Franks, and the Anglo-Saxons seemed, rather than in fact contemporary, to belong to a darker and bygone age. Mining, textiles,
and leatherwork boomed. Marble, glass, and crystal ware flowed
to eager markets overseas. From Seville, Málaga, Almería and
other ports, the Arab merchant fleet, among the largest and most
ubiquitous of its period, sailed regularly to North Africa, Egypt,
Byzantium and Palestine. Goods from Arab Spain, the Muslim al-
Andalus, traveled as far as India and Central Asia, while Arab
traders imported many Oriental products. Some idea of the scale
of Arab trading can be gained from the fact that export and import
taxes formed the largest single source of the great Abd al-Rahman's
revenue. At the same time, such inland cities as Toledo and
Granada spread their renown through the clattering mouths of the
seaports.

Córdoba itself, lying on a gentle slope between the Sierra Morena and the Guadalquivir, was among the largest and richest capitals in the world. Arab writers told ecstatically of its 200,000
residences, including magnificent palaces and numerous mansions;
of its 600 mosques and 900 public baths. Captivated by the element
so elusive and precious in their history, the Arabs piped the pre-
cincts for water, or made good the Roman systems, reveling in an
orgy of ablution and the joy of countless fountains. The streets, it
appears, were paved, while the immaculately whitewashed ex-
teriors of the buildings gave the city that glistening, sugary aspect
still preserved among Spain's southern towns. Inside, the larger
dwellings and public structures were appointed with a sense of

elegance and color unrivaled in the lands to either the north or the south. The great mosque of Córdoba (now the cathedral), though today a defaced relic of its former glory, has survived with the Alhambra as a reminder of the beauty of Islamic architecture in Europe. Its low roof flown on a forest of marble columns and mesmeric perspectives, its complex of double-banked horseshoe arches, its graceful mihrabs (the prayer niches) facing Mecca, its pulpit of exotic woods lit by hundreds of lamps, its wealth of porphyr, jasper, and mosaic once made it the veritable magnet of Muslims in the west. And not only Muslims found Córdoba alluring. Among travelers from many parts of Europe, Asia, and Africa, the reputation enjoyed by the city attracted a fair share of Christians. It was by no means uncommon to see foreign monks wandering its streets.

The Arab rulers loved learning. When the Emperor of Byzantium sent Abd al-Rahman a Greek treatise on medicinal herbs, the caliph was disconsolate to discover that no one in Córdoba could understand it. Refusing to be cheated of the knowledge it contained, Abd al-Rahman appealed to the emperor for a translator. The arrival of such a person two years later opened new fields of botany and medicine to Córdoba and, in due course, to much of the west. Similarly, a whole range of Greek and Roman works, especially the former, channeled to the caliphate by Arab agents and scholars, was eventually disseminated through medieval Europe. Arab Spain, resuscitating not only classic culture but also wisdom from the Far East, spread the fame of Aristotle, gave the Western world Arabic numerals, algebra, and alchemy, and, among other subjects, taught its visitors astronomy, geometry, and mechanics. The art of manufacturing paper, imported by the Arabs from China and flourishing in Spain three centuries before it spread north of the Pyrenees, did much to facilitate learning in the area. Linked with the speed of Arabic script, and a growing army of professional copyists, it contributed to the creation of a remarkable system of libraries of which the most renowned, that of the caliph himself, reputedly numbered no less than 600,000 volumes. Fifty public libraries existed in al-Andalus, where the widespread teaching of reading and writing ensured their good use.

All of which had a most depressing effect on the more ardent among Christians in southern Spain. "My coreligionists," bemoaned one, "delight in reading the poems and romances of the Arabs. They study the works of Muslim theologians and philosophers not to refute them, but to acquire good Arabic themselves . . . Alas! all the young Christians with a reputation for talent know only the language and literature of the Arabs. They read and study Arabic books with the greatest enthusiasm. At considerable expense they assemble extensive libraries of them, proclaiming on all sides that this literature is admirable." To the better satisfaction of the militants, however, there were regions adjacent to the caliphate where such compromising enlightenment had not reared its skeptical head. In the north of the peninsula a new and aggressive breed of Spanish princes, descendants of the Christian Visigoths, toughened by years of exile in the Cantabrian mountains, was edging south in a no-holds-barred scrimmage for power and land.

To regard the movement, at this stage, as a crusade would be wildly romantic. The primary motivation of these people was acquisitiveness, and if this not infrequently involved fighting Muslims, they gave as much energy and malice to killing each other. The effect, nevertheless, was one of gradual reconquest. It had started with a simple oversight on the part of the original African invaders. Fleeing north before the first wave of Muslims, a small band of Visigothic Spaniards had holed-up in the hills of Asturias to wait for the high tide of the conquest to subside. Under a former dignitary of the court of Toledo, a man named Pelayo, they had actually repulsed a scouting party of the enemy at Covadonga in 718. In the years to come, many a Muslim would curse his forefathers for having allowed Pelayo and his desperadoes to survive, but at the time they had seemed of little consequence and the invaders had turned from the mountains to settle on more promising land. In fact, they withdrew the whole length of the uninviting plateau of the northwest to a line running somewhat north of the Tejo.

Elsewhere, another portion of the country was secured against the Muslims by a different agency. Having failed in one crossing of the Pyrenees to repay the Saracens for their earlier incursion in France, the northern emperor Charlemagne returned with his son Louis at the end of the eighth century and cleared Catalonia, the extreme northeastern region of the peninsula, of Arab domination.

For a long time to come, Catalonia would reflect Frankish influence, remaining singularly independent of the rest of Christian Spain. Meanwhile, left to their own devices in the Asturian highlands, the original core of fugitives had established a kingdom with its capital at Oviedo, reaching east and west to Santander and Galicia. From Oviedo, the focus of reconquest moved down to Leon, and from Leon to Burgos, capital of a new domain named (after its bristling frontier forts or castillos) Castile, which became a monarchy under Ferdinand I (1035–65). Ferdinand had received Castile from his father, Sancho "the Great" of Navarre, a state lying to the east on the north coast and then enjoying a brief ascendancy among the newly emergent kingdoms. At the same time, another of Sancho's sons, Ramiro, was developing his own inheritance, Aragon, between Castile and Catalonia. These two, Castile and Aragon, pioneered politically by the same family, would eventually share the domination of all Spain until their ultimate fusion created the modern nation.

While the Ommayads maintained the caliphate as a unity, however, the northern kingdoms were still torn by the rival ambitions of their rulers. This condition was aggravated by an increasingly prevalent habit of succession in which the Christian kings divided their realms piecemeal among their sons, a system fraught with hardly less disunity and competitiveness than the old Visigothic method of electing their monarchs. In the feuds which repeatedly followed, the only certain beneficiaries were the Muslims. When, in the eleventh century, the great caliphate itself began to disintegrate, undermined by a succession of improvident rulers, the situation became even more redolent of anarchy. The resulting over-all pattern of the peninsula, a jigsaw of small states, Christian kingdoms and Muslim taifas, with constantly shifting hostilities and alliances, tended to blur the form of reconquest even further. So far, the ideology that would finally set the Christians aflame was only smoldering, a secondary, in a sense half-conscious incentive. On the Muslim side, the relative tolerance of Arab religion had yet to be swept aside by the Berbers. Embattled Christian lords gratefully struck alliance with Muslim neighbors while Christian knights commonly fought for Arab rulers. It was every man for himself, and perhaps none better illustrates the ethics of this medieval free-for-all than the most famous of early Spanish heroes, the Cid.

Roderic or Ruy Díaz, known as the Cid after his Arabic title of Sidi (Lord), was born of noble Castilian parentage at Bivar, a village on the desolate plain of that name near Burgos, about 1043, and brought up at the court of Ferdinand I. Hairy and muscular, according to the slender evidence that has survived of his appearance, Roderic distinguished himself as a soldier at an early age, content at first to obey his royal masters. The death of Ferdinand, resulting in the customary discord between the king's sons, found him leading the troops of the eldest, Sancho of Castile, against Sancho's younger brother, Alfonso of Leon. When, in 1072, Sancho was killed and Alfonso (VI) became king of both Leon and Castile, the shaggy young general seems to have switched masters without too much trouble, marrying Alfonso's niece Jimena a couple of years later and soldiering energetically for his former enemy. If there was a hint already that he loved overlords less than battle and booty, his freebooting instincts were soon plainly to the fore.

In 1079, on a mission to Alfonso's tributary, the Arab king of Seville, Roderic the Cid appears to have taken it upon his own initiative to join a local war against the king of Granada. Unfortunately for the swashbuckling Castilian, his profits from the engagement included the capture of one Count García Ordóñez, who, while fighting on the Granadine side, turned out, with a perversity all too typical of the times, to be a good friend of Alfonso. The regal disfavor which resulted for Roderic was not helped by García's reluctance to forgive and forget, nor by the Cid's own disinclination to swallow pride and initiative. Two years later, riding roughshod over already tender sensibilities, he launched an unauthorized raid on the Muslim kingdom of Toledo, which Alfonso fondly regarded as his protectorate. It was more than the king could stand. The Cid was banished from Castile.

With what regrets he turned his back on the countryside of his birth can only be guessed. Banishment involved humiliation as well as material deprivation, yet the sentence enriched him in the long run and may have brought a sense of liberation to a born soldier of fortune. Perhaps he considered himself lucky to have a future at all, for there were more drastic ways of dealing with troublesome vassals. Certainly he made the most of his assets. His first move was to offer his services to the powerful Count Berenguer of Barcelona, then at war with Muslim Saragossa. When Berenguer snubbed him, the Cid took the obvious alternative. Saragossa, threatened not only by Berenguer's Catalans, but by two other neighbors into the bargain (Christian Aragon and Muslim Lérida), proved less indifferent to the rugged adventurer. The city, at the junction of the Ebro and its northern tributary, the Gallego, was among the most Islamized in the peninsula. The ramparts of its palace, the Aljaferia, standing to the west of the old conurbation, looked down on a glistening sprawl of tufa masonry, chalky walls, domes, shady alleys and minarets. The royal court, both cultured and wealthy, abounded with philosophers, poets, and scientists. The Cid, surveying it all with calculating interest, must have decided he had found a good billet. It remained to make terms with the Saragossan ruler, Moctadir.

Moctadir was not disappointed with his hired man. For several years, the Cid fought the battles of the Muslim king and his successors with every distinction. At Almenara, near Lérida, his band of eager mercenaries and their Saragossan fellows-at-arms beat the Catalans so substantially that the Cid was able to return to his employers with the Count of Barcelona his prisoner. Delighted, the people of Saragossa loaded him with presents, investing him with the rank of chief adviser to the king. Riding now against Aragon, the Castilian outcast scattered the Christian king's army, enriching himself and his knights with Aragonese booty before homing triumphantly to his Muslim citadel. Linked with a new sobriquet, Campeador, or Challenger, the name of Roderic Díaz became synonymous with panache and audacity throughout the country. No authority was so powerful that it overawed him, and his raiding spread to new and increasingly profitable boundaries. The already legendary figure of the Cid Campeador, sword flailing, cloak flying from broad, armored shoulders, struck terror impartially among Muslims and Christians, fighting and plundering as opportunity offered—ostensibly still in the name of Saragossa, but more and more to the personal advantage of the Cid.

Success attracted men to his banner. Inspired by the prospect of battle and by stories of fabulous loot, the restive knights of the time came forward to enroll among his mercenaries. Wrote an

Arab contemporary of the Cid: "His power grew enormous, nor was there a district he did not ravage. Nevertheless, this man, the scourge of his day, was in his love of splendor, boldness of character and dauntless courage one of the marvels of the Lord." At the height of his buccaneering career, Roderic Díaz drew an inestimable fortune in tribute or protection money from Valencia, Albarracín, Alpuente, Segorbe, Jérica, Almenara, and elsewhere. Individual treasure troves were often stupendous. When he captured the palace of the Muslim prince of Denia, between Valencia and Alicante, he is reputed to have discovered a complete Ali-Baba's cave of gold, silver, gem stones and costly merchandise concealed in a hillside by the ruler. But, if rapacious, the Cid was no mere hedonist. The court of Saragossa provided intellectual stimulation. Here he acquired, among other things, a sound knowledge of Islamic law and customs, an education that was to prove invaluable in achieving the political aspirations which, with time, brought a new turn to his career. For maturity, in its skeptical fashion, had diminished the appeal of a predatory, uncommitted existence. The scourge of kings himself felt the urge for a kingdom.

His choice, the broad and tempting domain based on the eastern port of Valencia, was not exclusive to the desire of the Cid. Three major rivals contested his ambition to possess this fine city. One was his old suzerain, Alfonso, with whom he had renewed an uneasy contact. Another was Moctadir's grandson, Mostain of Saragossa, to whose power the Cid still offered, if with increasing independence, his service. The third was a new and threatening element in the peninsula. This force, a fanatical Muslim sect of North African origin, known in Spain as the Avowed to God, the Almoravides, was of great significance, for it was to alter the whole complexion of the reconquest. The Almoravides resulted from the conversion to Muslimism of a number of Berber tribes in the Sahara, fierce, uncompromising people who, under their king and prophet Abdulla, had rapidly spread their brand of sacred intolerance through the Atlas region of Morocco. With primitive ardor, the Almoravides sought their converts with the sword, exulting in a form of baptism by lash. Abdulla's empire, passing to the female saint Zainab, and hence to her widower, Yusef ibn Tashfin, had now been extended to stretch from Senegal to Algeria. Comparing the dynamism of this movement with the decline of the

Cordoban caliphate and the waning power of the *taifas*, the *al-faquies*, or juristic priests, of Spain had sniffed the breezes from Africa and caught an intoxicating promise of renewed religious influence. For a while the Arab princes, steeped in a tradition of conflict with the Berbers, had held out against an alliance with Yusef, but their power was fading, their voices growing weaker. With the loss of Muslim Toledo to Alfonso in 1085, the cries of the *alfaquies* finally overwhelmed them. Between the devil and the deep blue sea, a number of taifa rulers invited the Almoravides to help them.

It was the end of Arab power in the peninsula. One by one the Arab states were overrun by the rampaging Berbers until practically all al-Andalus had been claimed for Yusef's African empire. From now on the Berbers, hitherto the soldiers and subordinates of the Arabs, would dominate Muslim Spain. Indeed, but for that subtle old seductress the land itself, with its ineffably mellowing qualities, they might well have gone on to annihilate the Christian rulers whose eyes scanned the south with growing alarm. It was in the teeth of this dramatic Almoravide expansion that Roderic Díaz, the Cid Campeador, made his bid for Valencia.

His methods, as the time demanded, were ruthless and cunning. They revealed a talent for systematic intrigue hardly less remarkable than his accomplishments in the field of generalship. So thorough were they that, at one time or another, almost all the rival factions seeking control of Valencia seem to have been convinced that the Cid was on their side. He had a face for each camp. Before the Saragossans, he was their champion for possession of the city. Before Alfonso, he was the spirit of Castile and Christianity. Before the Valencians themselves, he was a would-be protector, ready to defend them against all comers if only they let him enter their walls. But everybody's friend was nobody's ally. By an unfortunate oversight, he managed to forget Saragossa's interests in the heat of the fracas, while, when Alfonso appeared to be doing too well on his own account, the rogue Castilian promptly caused a diversion by invading the king's lands and burning the town of Logrono to the ground. As for the Muslim defenders of Valencia, their stubbornness, though admirable, was more than a nuisance. Tired of waiting outside, the Cid eventually hastened their decision to hand him the keys by roasting a few of their number on his campfires and coursing others with his dogs.

The capitulation of Valencia to the Cid revealed his true allegiance once and forever. Within a few months he had broken the terms of his treaty with the Muslim defender Ibn Yehaf, burned him alive, and was established at last as a ruler in his own right, a man who, in the depths of his Castilian heart, had perhaps never served anyone but himself. Legend has it that among the treasures he forced Ibn Yehaf to disgorge before killing him was a bewitched necklace of immense value known as the Scorpion's Sting for the misfortune it allegedly brought its possessors. If so, Roderic Díaz climaxed his amazing career by defying not only human adversaries but the supernatural, for, throughout the last phase of his life at Valencia he held the Almoravides at bay with characteristic tenacity, defeating them at Cuarte (1094) and Bairén (1097). The extent of his prestige was well reflected in the careers of his daughters, who made brilliant marriages within the ruling houses of Barcelona and Aragon.

For three years after the Cid's death in 1099, his wife Jimena continued to hold Valencia against the hordes of Yusuf until, forced to retire before the sheer volume of the enemy, she set out for Burgos, the hefty body of her warrior lord embalmed in spices and strapped to his favorite war horse. With his burial at the monastery of San Pedro de Cardeña near the old Castilian capital, a great individualist passed out of history into legend—a legend whose mounting overtones of idolatry he would surely have dismissed with a belly-laugh. By the reign of Isabella, the Cid was a chivalrous Christian hero. One Spanish monarch actually tried to persuade the pope to pronounce him a saint. Diverse societies cloaked him in their own aspirations. To the romantics Roderic Díaz became a knight-errant, to the poor a sort of Spanish Robin Hood, to royalists an unruly but ever-loyal vassal, to republicans a fiery antimonarchist. So wonderful grew the posthumous career of the Cid that at least two serious later-day historians declared their doubts that he ever existed. Yet, when all such mantles are lifted, the stature of the man remains. He would have done equally well for himself, one suspects, in the Normandy of William the Conqueror's youth or on the Viking austrvegr. As it happened, he was born a Castilian, an outstanding but nonetheless plausible example of the type of self-assertive pragmatist without whom Catholic Spain might never have flowered and flourished.

During the years of Arab rule in the peninsula, Christian faith had been catching hold in the north. From the start, the kings of Asturias, with varying sincerity, had cultivated the ecclesiastics they found among their subjects, quick to harness priestly persuasion to royal ambitions. This spiritual aspect of the northern system had received a big boost in the first part of the ninth century when the discovery was proclaimed from western Galicia of the sepulcher and body of the apostle James in the countryside near the modern town of Padrón. The spot underwent the metamorphosis customary to the resting places of saints. The relics, with their wonder-working potential, demanded a church, the church and its ancillary buildings gave rise to a township which, helping to promote the fame of the precious find, very soon became a city. Since popular belief held that a star had revealed the site, this city became known as St. James of the Field of the Star, or Santiago de Compostela. The shrine was to have far-reaching effects on the reconquest, for, attracting a stream of pilgrims from other parts of Europe, it not only brought new cultural influences to bear on northern Spain, but helped in turn to put the cause of Spanish Christianity on a larger map, eventually engaging the interest and sympathy of the pope. It also gave Spain a new slogan. Prompt to endow their patron saint with a soldierly image, the warriors of the north evolved the rallying cry "St. James and close in, Spain!" ("*Santiago y cierra España.*")—a cry that, in due course, would ring around the world.

For all that, religious motive was not conspicuous among the Christian magnates of pre-Almoravide Spain, as the career of the Cid, among others, attested. It was not until the Berber threat raised the stark alternatives of uniting or perishing that the Christian rulers began to admit a common purpose, utilizing the religion they shared as a welding power. Moorish fanaticism provoked a corresponding zeal among the Christians. At last the reconquest could properly be termed a holy war, a conflict, however lingering, to the death. In this, however, the Muslims were to suffer the handicap of one more major revolution. Not even the uncompromising Almoravides could withstand the seductions of Andalusia for long. Transplanted from the harsh sands, the intellectual vacuum of the Sahara, to the mild valleys and knowledgeable courts of al-Andalus, the puritan Berber, yielding to temptation, began to sample the Arab way of life. From the court of the formidable Yusuf himself blossomed perhaps the most celebrated of all Muslim philosophers, Ibn Roch, alias Averroës. Amid the blandishments of Andalusia's bold-eyed women and warm, scented nights, many a stern follower of Abdulla turned poet, harem master, and lettered skeptic. The mellowing provoked a further African reaction. In 1146 the Almoravides in Morocco were overthrown by a fresh tide of Berber fanatics, the Almohades, who proceeded to force their dynasty on Muslim Spain.

But the Almohades faced a tougher proposition than their forerunners. The Christian rulers, strengthened by thousands of Mozárabes who had fled from Moorish oppression, were pressing steadily south. Early in the thirteenth century, Alfonso VIII of Castile, an outstanding warrior whose power had already been felt by Leon and Navarre, persuaded the pope to pronounce a full-blooded crusade against the Almohades. Assembling a great army on his southern border, including many Christian troops from outside the peninsula as well as forces from Castile, Leon, Aragon, and Navarre, he advanced into Andalusia to challenge the enemy. In the event, the Leonese contingent and the majority of the non-Spanish volunteers opted out before the fighting started; nevertheless, Alfonso retained sufficient strength to carry through the engagement. On 16 July, 1212, near the village of Las Navas de Tolosa, on the slopes of the Sierra Morena, the Christians dealt the Almohades a blow from which they never recovered.

Alfonso's example was followed by two ardent, and contemporaneous, crusading monarchs, Ferdinand III of Castile and Leon, and James I of Aragon. Between them, they took the main honors in demolishing the now rickety edifice of Muslim power in the peninsula. Ferdinand, employing among other arms a squadron of warships on the Guadalquivir, conquered the whole of northern and western Andalusia, including Córdoba, Seville, and Jaén, and his son Alfonso (later Alfonso X, the Learned) occupied Murcia. At the same time, James, aided by the marine-minded lords of Catalonia, conquered the Balearic Isles and took Valencia. Refreshingly enough, the galloping expansion of Castile and Aragon under these dynamic monarchs stopped short of war with each other. Elated by successes against the Muslims, they seem to have been too concerned with pressing their advantages overseas to fall out over mutual boundaries. Having concluded a treaty with France to regulate his northern borders, James equipped an armada to attack Palestine, but was thwarted by stormy waters. Ferdinand died planning a major invasion of North Africa. With his death, the reconquest puffed at last to a tired halt—almost, but not quite, completed. In the far south, the hilly Muslim kingdom of Granada, thrown up in 1238 from the shipwreck of the Almohade dominion, had survived the Christian onslaught. One more offensive might have finished the job, but Ferdinand's successors, gazing up at the fastnesses of the Granadine Sierra, decided it was time for a breather. That breather lasted upward of two hundred years.

Six centuries of Muslim occupation had left a profound influence on Spanish character. Along with something of the spasmodic violence of the Berber—a case history of severed heads and vicious massacre—Christian Spain had inherited much of the poetic fancy and erudition of the Arab. Toledo, quickly becoming the "Christian Córdoba," had preserved the continuity of academic interests personified in the conquering Ferdinand's son, Alfonso X. Alfonso, with his rare and cerebral attitude to life's problems, reflected the intellectual bias of a host of Muslim rulers. At the same time, the shift of emphasis from a warlike regime to the peaceful administration of much-expanded Christian territories brought many new social developments.

For the military-minded aristocracy, accustomed to the smash-and-grab freedoms of war, it meant frustration and restlessness. On the other hand, an economy based increasingly on labor and trade rather than on the fortunes of battle meant greater prosperity for the so-called bourgeoisie, the middle classes who, banded mainly in the towns and cities, became distinctly less amenable to the highhanded ways of the nobles. In many such communities, brotherhoods, or *hermandades* were formed with the purpose of municipal defense, in general against the lawlessness residual to war but particularly as protection against the grasping and domineering magnates. The political import of this new force, "the people," was not lost on the kings. Recognizing it as a check on the turbulent nobility, not to mention a now landed and powerful Church, the crown helped to promote the stabilizing potential of the middle class by the liberal granting of bills of municipal rights, the *feuros*, and by welcoming the towns to the national assembly, the Cortes. Encouraged by these stirrings of emancipation, and occasionally by active rebellion on their own part, the servile classes of the countryside eased the centuries-old burden on their shoulders, moving a little closer to personal freedom.

More spectacular, if less central to Spanish development, was the blaze of Catalan enterprise which rose and died on the blue eastern waters of the period. James I's conquest of the Balearics had been much indebted to the adventurous knights of Catalonia, who later sailed to many other parts of the Mediterranean. By the early fourteenth century, Aragon's influence to the east included the possession of Sicily, where a strong contingent of Catalan mercenaries, having played a leading role in securing the island for their employer, were ready to accept a new hirer. Their adventure began with a call for help from the Emperor of Constantinople, Andronicus, then hard-pressed by the warlike Turks and badly in need of reinforcements. Under the leadership of one Roger de Flor, six and a half thousand men sailed to the rescue from Sicily to receive a rapturous welcome in the Byzantine capital. Roger de Flor was given the title of megaduke and the King of Bulgaria's daughter as his wife. Fighting lightly armed but with great vivacity, the newcomers scored brilliantly against the Turks, gaining such fame back home that they were duly strengthened by further expeditions of Catalan and Aragonese adventurers. Between them, they saved the day for Andronicus. Transported with relief, the emperor upgraded Roger from megaduke to caesar, granting the whole of Anatolia (modern Turkey) to his saviors.

But such generosity proved too much for the emperor's subjects. Led by the heir-apparent, Prince Michael, a group of them successfully plotted the murder of Roger de Flor and his lieutenants at a banquet. Simultaneously, hundreds of Roger's unwary followers were surprised and massacred. The remainder of the Spaniards—now reduced to some three and a half thousand men—turning on the Byzantines in a spate of revenge, sacked a number of towns then decamped in disgust. From Greece had come a new

SOS. It was the Duke of Athens, beset by political enemies, who now sought the aid of the roving Spaniards. Again, their military accomplishments well justified their employment. Again, their reward was sourly seasoned with treachery. They were learning the lesson familiar in time to all mercenaries, namely that the welcome seldom outlives the cause of the hiring. This time, however, they were not outmaneuvered. Seizing Athens by force, the dwindling band took control of the duchy where they and their descendants wrote an end to the adventure, ruling the city for about sixty years.

By 1394 Athens had fallen to the old eastern enemy, the Turk, but the days of Aragonese adventuring were not done. During the first half of the fifteenth century the King of Aragon personally took possession of Naples in circumstances which begin to sound vaguely repetitious. Having been invited by the queen of that city to assist in fighting her enemy the Duke of Anjou, the Aragonese monarch was brazenly sold out in a last-minute pact between the queen and her erstwhile antagonist. After years of campaigning and many setbacks, including a period of captivity, the victim eventually forced his sovereignty on Naples—an act of rough if not entirely admirable justice, since the queen had enticed him with a promise of the throne in the first place. At all events, the outcome was mightier than the motive, for by establishing a link with the Italy of the early Renaissance, Aragon sowed the seeds of a cultural harvest that was to enrich Spanish art, indeed the creative impetus of the whole peninsula, beyond measure.

While the braves of eastern Spain followed fortune in the Mediterranean, the home scene had been lashed by fresh storms of dissension. Reverting to their old form, the nobles thundered for power and action; the kings struggled with varying success to restrain them. Repeatedly teetering on the brink of anarchy, this conflict clouded the remainder of Spain's Middle Ages. The breather had turned into a howl of bitterness. At the depths of the depression, Portugal—born itself amid Castilian disunity in the twelfth century—France, and even England sallied advantageously within the Spanish borders, while Muslim Granada looked on with renewed hopes. Revitalized by its connections with North Africa, the Moorish state lost few chances to exploit the troubles of its Christian neighbors, snatching ground when it could and inflicting sharp military defeats. The lengths to which Spanish kings of the period were forced to go to survive the web of plot and counterplot which surrounded them were dramatically evinced by Peter I of Castile (1350–69), who murdered nobles, churchmen, relatives—even, it was claimed, his own wife—in a nightmare of distrust and desperation. His dual epithets, "the Cruel" and "the Dispenser of Justice," were eloquent of the divided nature of the country. Castilian fought Castilian, Aragonese fought Aragonese, and, for good measure, Castile and Aragon lambasted each other.

By the early fifteenth century Castilian politics were in a state of near disaster. Two kings made it complete. John II, a dedicated aesthete but a futile politician, pinned his hopes on his favorite, Alvaro de Luna, but Alvaro was executed at the behest of the queen. Henry IV, succeeding John, his father, introduced a new level of hopelessness to the proceedings. His own favorite, a ne'er-do-well courtier, was not executed by Henry's queen; instead, she took him as her lover. With an incompetent and a cuckold on the throne, the court fell into contempt. Political chaos was matched by social disorder. Crime and immorality became widespread and brazen. Knights ran amuck, churchmen guzzled and rutted, law keepers turned a blind eye or joined in the game. Wrote a despairing contemporary of the result: "Cities and towns were undermined by thieves, murderers, adulterers and all manner of delinquents . . . Some, contemptuous of any law, divine or manmade, took justice into their own hands. Others, gluttons and layabouts, shamelessly violated wives, virgins and nuns . . . Yet more robbed and assaulted tradesmen, travelers and people on their way to the fairs. Some, with greater power and folly, seized lands and castles belonging to the Crown, using their advantage to plunder and violate their neighbors. They also kidnapped many people, whose relatives were obliged to pay as much in ransom as if they had been captured by Moors and barbarians."

If there was one consolation, it was that things could hardly get worse. In fact, a glimmer of hope lit the horizon. The reputation of Henry and his voluptuous wife inspired the barons who opposed them to brand their heir, the princess Joan, illegitimate and to promote Henry's young half-sister Isabella as their candidate for the succession. Isabella was an altogether new proposition. The daughter of John's late second marriage to a highly strung

Portuguese princess, she had scarcely known her father. His death in her infancy, plunging her mother into a state of morbid religious obsession which led in time to outright lunacy, left the child poorly protected. But Isabella had sufficient force of mind to turn her mother's weakness into her own strength. Piety, reacting to the soullessness of Henry's menage, gave her a sense of purpose, and, though she was still an adolescent when approached by the rebel barons, her precocious intellect jumped at the challenge. Her first master-stroke was the offer of marriage to Ferdinand, a youthful but battle-tested heir to the throne of Aragon. Ferdinand shrewdly accepted. Thus, her fortunes aligned with the east, Isabella awaited the moment of action. Joan, looking to the west for support, became the bride of the king of Portugal. Henry's death quickly threw their plans to the test. It took five years of bitter civil war to prove Isabella's foresight, but her triumph in the end was twofold. By the peace of Trujillo, forced on Joan and Portugal in 1479, Isabella was acknowledged Queen of Castile. In the same year, Ferdinand inherited his father's crown. Suddenly, Isabella and her husband were all-powerful. Between them they ruled a greater area of the peninsula than had been united in centuries.

It remained to ensure that the old forces of disunity did not once more tear it apart. Switching their attentions with unexpected alacrity on the recuperating barons of Castile, the sovereigns tackled their strongholds and powers one by one. A central law court was established to deal with the intransigent; new regulations were made to stamp out lawlessness; punishments were applied with merciless vigor, often under Isabella's own eagle eye. In the royal councils, the influence of both nobility and bourgeoisie was diminished by the introduction of professional civil servants. Everywhere, the reins of the Crown were tightened on its subjects. For many, such measures were intensely unpopular, particularly in Aragon, where the magnates and the Cortes had a strong tradition of independence. Isabella forced the field with another master-stroke.

Weaned on the evangelic mythology of the reconquest, she had long sensed the dramatic appeal of a new holy war. If the crusaders of old could unite against the Muslims, why not invoke the spirit of common purpose afresh—complete the job left unfinished two hundred years earlier? All the signs pointed to the kingdom of Granada. Its possession was desirable, its rulers were a nuisance, its chastisement would divert the Spanish lords from other mischief, its conquest redound to the prestige of Spain and its monarchs throughout Christendom. The cause was both righteous and expedient. With some misgivings, for his own ambitions lay to the north, Ferdinand agreed to the enterprise and, two years after the peace of Trujillo, war was enjoined with Granada.

Chapter 3

THE EXPLORERS

Halfway round the Gulf of Cádiz, that sweeping indentation on southern Spain's wild Atlantic coast, lies the Río Saltes, a broad estuary between the sea and two rivers, the Odiel and the Tinto. At the time of the war with Granada, the Saltes was the gateway to a cluster of thriving ports. Following its course, the incoming voyager passed among a vast expanse of sandbanks, salt flats, and marshes before arriving at the parting of the waters: left for the Odiel and the harbor of Huelva, right for the Tinto and its ports, Palos and Moguer. Overlooking the confluence of these rivers, and their swampy surroundings, stood a lone Franciscan monastery, La Rábida, linked by land along a hilly ridge to Palos. La Rábida, tuned to the voices of the sea, poised at this junction of marine communication, provided its studious occupants with a constant stream of worldly information. From Spanish ports to the east came news of the crusade in Granada; from Italy, word of the latest developments in that fashionable pursuit of learning and beauty that marked the flowering of what would later be known as the Renaissance. Voyagers from Germany, where a child named Martin Luther was still squalling and kicking in the cradle, talked of a new invention, the printing press, while French captains abused a teenage degenerate, Charles VIII, their king since the recent death of Louis XI. The English, long enmeshed in their wars of "the Roses," were reportedly still busy slaughtering each other.

No news was more avidly received on the Saltes than that of its Portuguese neighbors. Along the shore to the west of La Rábida, beyond the little white ports of the Algarve, Portugal's craggy Cape St. Vincent pointed a compelling finger at the uncharted regions of the Atlantic. Here, the Portuguese visionary Prince Henry, known as the Navigator, had founded his celebrated academy of hydrographic and marine intelligence earlier in the century, leaving behind on his death in 1460 a tradition of systematic inquiry that had given his country a flying start on her rivals in maritime exploration. While the Spanish were still struggling to take Moorish Granada, the Portuguese, rid of the invaders earlier, had already colonized the Azores (a third of the way to America), discovered the Cape Verde Islands off northwest Africa, and set up trading posts on the African coast as far south as the Gulf of Guinea. The result was not only a fund of navigational experience, but an increasing turnover in material wealth. Vessels sailing south with gaudy cloths and trinkets returned laden with ivory, slaves, and gold. And, as each new source was established, the discoverers ventured farther afield to find others. Successful pilots became popular heroes, the idols of their time, winning noble titles and considerable riches. Their exploits, the talk of the Atlantic coast, provoked a rash of mercantile speculation. In the ports of southwest Spain, shipowners watched and listened attentively, weighing their own prospects of discovery, of pulling off one audacious gamble, against the relative security of routine sailing.

Such men were not unknown to the monks of La Rábida, where the subject was of more than academic interest. For, from the pope down, the Church was concerned and involved with discovery. New lands posed a proselytizing challenge, the chance of multitudinous conversion to the faith, while participation in their detection and colonization meant a stake in their worldly resources. The papal archives contained centuries-old reports of exploration, and Rome kept a keen eye on new developments. Of all its outposts, the ocean-minded house of La Rábida was not unconscious of such farsighted politics. It was with some excitement, therefore, that one day in 1484 the Saltes Franciscans received at their door two strangers, a tall, imposing man and a small boy, the former claiming connections with high Portuguese society. The man gave his name as Christopher Columbus, son-in-law of Bartholomew Perestrello, a noble late of the service of Henry the Navigator. Columbus, with his son, Diego, had arrived at Palos from Portugal on a personal mission concerned with ocean enterprise and, being unfamiliar with Spain, begged advice and introductions of the learned brothers.

In turn, the monks inquired of the visitor's history. Born about 1446, probably in Genoa and possibly of Jewish extraction, Columbus had first gone to sea at fourteen as an apprentice dealer in wool and silks, later joining his father in the latter's textile business. But Columbus had not been cut out for business. Resuming his journeys at a more mature age, he had taken ship for northern waters, calling at England among other places, before settling eventually in Portugal, where his brother Bartholomew had a map-making and bookselling concern. Here, cultivating the society of Bartholomew's clientele, Columbus had been able to meet and marry Felipa Perestrello, daughter of the well-to-do mariner. Felipa had given him both a son, Diego, and the entree to a new world. Mixing now as the social equal of the eminent sea explorers of the day, he had become increasingly absorbed in their interests, on one occasion accompanying the admiral Azambuja to the Gold Coast. Inspired also by the Eastern writings of the traveler Marco Polo and the imaginative Cardinal Pierre d'Ailly of the Sorbonne, Columbus had gradually become obsessed with the idea of reaching the Orient by traveling west.

In fact, the concept had not been new. With the growing acceptance of the round-earth theory, seamen and theoreticians had been mooting the prospect for at least half a century. That it seemed more practicable to Columbus than others was in some part due to an error in his reckoning. Overestimating the size of the Asian continent, he had placed its eastern extremities optimistically close to Western Europe, a misapprehension prompting him to seek backing for a voyage of exploration. For the moment, his chief assets—self-conviction, a commanding façade, and the gift of rhetoric—had made an impression on the young Portuguese king, John II. But they had not beguiled the king's experts. To the shrewd and experienced Portuguese pilots, Columbus had seemed a pretentious upstart. Navigationally, he was a novice; academically, he was an ignoramus; socially, he was a climber of dubious origin. Professionalism is a harsh critic. The pilots had drubbed him. The politicians, for their part, had been no easier. Already committed to proving a passage to the East around Africa, they had their own incentive to discourage rival projects. Perhaps to this end, perhaps simply to hedge the existing bet, they had agreed that a single ship should be dispatched to the west, but that its command should not go to Columbus. Predictably, the reported findings of its voyage had been negative. By 1484, disgusted with John and his advisers, Columbus had persuaded his brother Bartholomew to sound English and French reactions to his project. Meanwhile, hard-pressed for money, his wife now dead, the would-be explorer had skipped Portugal and his creditors to confer his ill-used talents on Spain.

That not all of this was revealed to his hosts at La Rábida is obvious. Conscious of the shortcomings of his background in relation to ambition, Columbus resorted throughout his career to a discreet veil of mystery where his past was concerned, embellished occasionally by romantic misrepresentation. There was enough in his manner and ideas, however, to persuade the best judge of his abilities at the monastery, a student of cosmography and navigation named Antonio de Marchena, that the visitor deserved further consideration. To Marchena, the broad case for western exploration was credible. The legend of some sort of land to the west was deep-rooted in European history. Plato and his fellow Greek, Theopompus, had hinted at it; the Romans and the Arabs had been aware of it; stories of Norse enterprise in Greenland and Vinland (North America), spreading through Europe by the late eleventh century had aroused fresh interest. Well before the birth of Columbus, world maps were depicting land to the far west of the Atlantic, and if this took the form of fanciful islands with such names as St. Brendan and Antilia, the concept of a global earth gave them a new significance. It was known, for instance, that the easternmost extremity of the Orient, Cipangu (Japan), was an island.

There was also a mounting body of contemporary evidence. Stories popular along the Atlantic coast of the peninsula in the fifteenth century told of strange items of flotsam found in the ocean after westerly gales: a piece of unidentifiable wood wrought in a hitherto unknown fashion, bamboos of astonishing circumference and, off the Azores, the bodies of two men "broad of feature and differing in other aspects from Christians." Was it not reasonable that their origin, the substance behind the whole legend, was eastern Asia? And, if the concept were plausible, what of the man himself? Ostentatiously pious, engaging in a somewhat histrionic fashion, a "big" personality, Columbus made a hit with the monks. After all, men who had sailed to the Gold Coast and could speak of their dealings with the King of Portugal did not arrive at La Rábida every day. After some negotiation, its occupants agreed to take the boy Diego into their care and to furnish his father with useful introductions.

For the moment, prospects looked brighter. Christian Spain, on the surge of its own great adventure in Granada, was not without sympathy for one who echoed the go-getting mood, albeit in extremity, and the traveler gained new and influential friends together with a modest but encouraging subsistence from the government. He also gained a mistress, one Beatrice Enriques, who bore him a second son, Fernando. But, beyond this, results were more elusive. Applause for his good intentions was one thing—the chimerical notion of a passport to unlimited riches, plus the possibility of taking Islam in the rear, appealed at once to the cupidity and prejudice of the Spanish Christians. Hard and fast backing was something quite different. Isabella, who many imagined would prove susceptible to his presence, was too preoccupied with the crusade to succumb to the blandishments of Columbus. Instead, she passed him to one of her close advisers, Fernando de Talavera, prior of Prado and a man of integrity, who raised a committee to consider the matter. Columbus could hardly have asked for a fairer examiner. Unfortunately for the visitor, Talavera's impartiality was matched by his taste for learning. The council he convened was uncommonly well informed.

If Portugal exposed Columbus to the judgment of practical men, Spain threw him to the scholars. Unerringly, they reached for the fault in his argument. Columbus, founding his calculations indirectly on the conclusions of the second-century geographer Marinus of Tyre, appears to have reckoned 78 degrees of longitude between the meridian of the Canary Isles reached by the Catalans in the preceeding century and that of Japan, each degree representing rather less than 57 miles at the equator, 50 on the loxodrome of his projected route. From the westernmost point of Spanish territory, therefore, he contended, the distance to the Orient was in the order of 3900 miles. Not so, declared the scholars. The number of degrees involved was nearer 200 than 100, at least 180. They preferred the mathematics of Eratosthenes, the ancient Greek scientist, to the calculations of Marinus. Eratosthenes made the equatorial degree 87½ miles. Thus, by their computation, the distance would be more like 14,500 miles, a voyage of hopeless magnitude. There were, of course, other arguments, theological as well as scientific, and the council, which took an unconscionable time to reach a decision, was not unanimous. Nevertheless, its verdict, that the west-to-the-Orient plan as propounded by Columbus was vain and impractical, was substantially correct. Columbus was two-thirds short in his estimate.

Rejection of the plan was profoundly disturbing to its author, the more so since Bartholomew had failed to produce good news in England, and Columbus refused to seek fault in himself. Victimization, a recurring theme of his letters and journals, was the excuse for his crisis. Ecclesiastics and aristocrats had befriended him, the government had maintained him, a council of eminent scholars had given his ill-presented scheme its closest attention and, even then, there was a sympathetic promise that the subject would be reviewed when the war in Granada was over. But to Columbus, a self-styled "victim of opposition and aversion," it was all an elaborate torment. "Everyone to whom I spoke of my enterprise considered it a mere jest." To many, in fact, he had ceased to be amusing. Columbus, with his grand airs, his naïveté, and his petulance, had become the despair of his supporters and his own worst enemy. For all that, well-wishers persisted in backing his project.

The closing months of 1491 offered another chance. Two new factors were involved: 1, the imminent fall of Granada, now a foregone conclusion, had at last produced a favorable atmosphere at court. 2, a fresh wave of westing interest was sweeping the Atlantic ports. Far from rejecting this sphere, it seems, the Portuguese had dwelt on it with mounting fascination. Since Columbus had left Portugal, two men, Fernam Dulmo, a crown official of the Azores, and João Estreito, a wealthy merchant of Madeira, had actually mounted an exploration of the southwest. Two others, the German cosmographer Martin Behain and a fellow countryman named Muntzer, were rumored to be advancing plans for the western discovery of China. In Palos itself, at the very door of La Rábida, a Spanish shipowner, Martín-Alonso Pinzón, was seriously considering the prospect of an Atlantic exploration at his own expense. Here was an argument more galvanizing, politically, than a decade of scientific discourse, and the Columbus lobby had no intention of allowing its protégé to hash the issue. This time, his supporters handled its presentation themselves.

The consequences were prompt. Columbus, sheltering once again with the Franciscans, received a command to return to the royal court, where his arrival, in time to witness the fall of Granada, was noted by the queen with quickening interest. The crusaders were *en fête*. All endeavor appeared to them blessed with success. Yet Isabella was too familiar with history to view the future complacently. Bereft of the common purpose of holy war, Christian Spain had once turned upon its crown and its kin with appalling results, and what had happened two centuries before could well repeat itself. Already there were signs. Persecution of the Jews, to lead within months to the dismal expulsion from the country of some 200,000 or more for refusing Catholic baptism, was rapidly superseding reconquest as a national pastime. And after the Jews, who next? A new and constructive direction for the aggressive energy of Isabella's people was needed, and, in Columbus, she began to see a prophet of hope. If there were really a short cut to the East by sailing west, then the ideological struggle embodied in the reconquest could be extended to the very heart of Islam. Better still, if the Orient were as richly endowed as many held, then such a campaign would pay for itself, perhaps even recoup the distressing financial outlay on the war in Granada.

As a prophet, Columbus was back in his element. Wish fulfillment was his speciality. From the medieval geographies in his satchel he could give chapter and verse not only for the riches of the Orient but for the very dimensions of paradise. Again and again in his copies of Marco Polo and d'Ailly's Ymago Mundi he had underscored references to gem stones, gold, and other precious metals; an obsession repeated in his marginal notes. God willing, he would lead Spain to a land where the very houses were roofed with gold and whose mythical ruler, the Grand Khan, only awaited the persuasions of Columbus to lend his resources to a great new crusade. Let the sovereigns prepare to take no less than the Holy Tabernacle—"for I declare to Your Highnesses that the gains of my enterprise must facilitate the conquest of Jerusalem." If Ferdinand viewed the prospect skeptically, the nagging thought of being scooped by the Portuguese helped to temper his judgment. The outcome was a new council of inquiry, now seemingly prejudiced by royal favor for the project. The only stumbling block remained the form of contract.

Flushed with confidence, Columbus held out for princely terms. In the first place, he demanded the ennoblement so incomprehensibly denied him by birthright, plus the title of admiral, an appellation of the grandest esteem in Spain. In the second place, he demanded the effective viceroyship of all the territories he should discover, that is to say, the absolute right of appointment over administration and justice in any continent or island his efforts might bring under Spanish sway. In the third place, apart from the salaries attaching to such posts and functions, he demanded a tenth of all profits, trading and otherwise, which might result from his enterprise. Finally, he demanded these privileges not only for himself but for his heirs and successors in perpetuity. By comparison, the cost of equipping the three ships he asked for—two million maravedis (say 100,000 dollars at present value)—was a modest requirement. To the privilege-conscious nobility of the day, still smarting under the restraint imposed on personal aggrandizement by their monarchs, his arrogance was astonishing. On the evidence of his early biographers, this impoverished adventurer was deemed to behave as though he held the world in his hand.

At least the royal council was convinced, for on April 17, 1492, after some halfhearted bargaining, Isabella and Ferdinand signed an agreement, the so-called "capitulation," acceding to the exactments of Columbus, who was also provided with credentials in Latin to the unknown potentate he was hoping to visit. "To the Most Serene Prince . . . [blank], our very dear friend," wrote the sovereigns, "greetings and wishes of prosperity and success. From the reports of certain of our subjects, and others who have come from your realms and countries to us, we have learned joyfully of the good will you bear toward us and our kingdom, and how eagerly you desire to be informed of our prosperity. For this reason we have decided to send you our noble captain Christopher Columbus, bearer of these tidings, from whom you will learn, among other things we have commanded him to tell you, of our good health and happiness. We beg that you give us the extreme pleasure of putting as much faith in his words as you would in ourselves. Personally, we declare the inclination and preparedness to do all we can to please you. From our city of Granada, 30th April of the year of the Lord 1492." Signed Ferdinand and Isabella.

"I left the City of Granada May 12, 1492, a Saturday," Columbus informed the sovereigns in a journal of his first voyage, "coming to the seaport of Palos where I equipped three suitable vessels and, having made ample provision for the necessary stores and seamen, set sail on Friday, August 3, half an hour before sunrise, steering for the Canary Islands of your highnesses, thence to proceed till I arrive in the Indies [eastern Asia] and fulfil the embassy of your highnesses to the Princes there . . . my plans involve such close attention to navigation and hard work that, considering all, I shall have to forget about sleep."

A charming simplification. Despite his royal commands, despite the untiring support of the Saltes Franciscans and even an official promise of freedom for convicts willing to risk sailing with him, Columbus originally failed in his efforts to recruit an expedition. For seven years he had not set foot on shipboard: before that, his sailing record was dubious. The men of the Atlantic ports knew it. Apart from attracting a handful of riffraff and some sharp dealers who would have fobbed him off with a number of old hulks, the grand explorer could get nowhere. By the end of June he had been forced, reluctantly, to do a deal with the Palos shipping "magnate" Martín Pinzón. The nature of their agreement is unknown, but some form of profit-sharing basis is indicated. Tough, accomplished, and independent, Pinzón had the respect of the seafaring people of the Saltes and all the practical authority Columbus lacked. It was Pinzón who found and equipped the vessels; Pinzón who persuaded good seamen to man them.

Indeed, the influence exerted by Pinzón from the start was evident in the make-up of the expedition. Martín Pinzón and his brother Vincent captained the two best ships in the flotilla, the fast caravels *Pinta* (about fifty tons) and the *Niña* (about forty tons), while another brother, Francisco Pinzón, sailed with Martín as a pilot. Though Columbus was content to take the largest and most imposing vessel, the hundred-ton *Santa María*, she was, he declared later, "a dull sailer and unfit for discovery." Moreover, though her owner, Juan de la Cosa, an experienced navigator, sailed with Columbus, the crew of the flagship proved the least reliable of the three vessels. This might have been partly the fault of her captain, but seems also to reflect on Pinzón's knowing, if not impartial, selection. In all, about a hundred men were picked for the exploration, largely from Palos and neighboring Huelva and Moguer, but also from Seville, Córdoba and elsewhere in Andalusia. Among the specialists in the party were three "surgeons," one for each ship, an official secretary to record discoveries, a royal controller to keep an eye on the gold they expected to pick up, and an interpreter who spoke Arabic, the language hopefully attributed to Japan and China.

Four days out on the week's run to their starting point proper, the Canaries, Columbus was already recording his suspicion of other members of the expedition. Martín Pinzón had reported trouble with the rudder of the *Pinta*, which was either loose or unshipped. This misfortune was weirdly rationalized in the admiral's journal as an act of sabotage on the part of the ship's owners, Rascón and Quintero, "because the voyage was not to their liking." What Rascón and Quintero hoped to gain by imperiling their own vessel Columbus did not explain, and his reasoning was the more mysterious since both men were on board the *Pinta*. At the Canaries, where, thanks to Pinzón's masterful handling, the crippled ship was put in for repairs, Columbus heard that three Portuguese caravels had been sighted in the area. This time, he concluded, it was the King of Portugal who was out to wreck his chances, envious because Columbus had left Lisbon for Spain. At all events, the small convoy of explorers duly sailed unimpeded into the uncharted Atlantic, having left the Canary Isle of Gomera on the morning of September 6.

The whole voyage was blessed with near-perfect conditions. Catching the northern edge of the northeasterly trade wind, the

three ships clipped along briskly on a smooth sea. It was, wrote
Columbus, "like April in Andalusia . . . only lacking the song of
nightingales." With celestial navigation still in its infancy, the
pilots worked mainly by dead reckoning, using the compass for direction, a half-hour sandglass suspended from a beam for time-
keeping, and pure guesswork for estimating speed. Like many
simple procedures, it proved surprisingly effective. Each day,
Columbus logged the distance he reckoned they had traveled, reducing this slightly in his announcements to the crew as an insur-
ance against the voyage proving longer than expected. As it turned
out, the fake estimate was more nearly accurate than the "true"
one. Columbus was overgenerous in his judgment of progress.

Nevertheless, after ten days' sailing the expedition had made
an admirable headway of over 1100 nautical miles westing, and
had experienced only one uneasy moment—on discovering the
westerly variation of the compass. On this occasion, Columbus
checked the dismay of his crew by declaring that the Pole Star
moved "like other stars," whereas the compass needle "always tells
the truth." The mood of optimism continued. During the five days
following September 16, the wind gradually decreased, dropping on
the twenty-first to a dead calm. During this period they made a
modest progress of some 230 miles, but were bucked to discover
sargasso, which they took to be drifting river weed. It was, they
considered, the first signal of land, and they actually tried to
measure the depth of the ocean, here getting on for 2500 fathoms,
with a 200-fathom line. A series of false zoological assumptions
now drew them excitedly on, each vessel vying to outsail the others. At first, they found a live crab in the sargasso and spotted a
boatswain bird, neither of which would be likely, they considered,
to venture far to sea. On September 20, hopes were further raised
by the capture of "a bird like a tern," while, on the following day, a
whale was sighted. Both these creatures were assumed to stay close
to land. On the evening of the twenty-fifth, their mounting hopes
reached a climax. A cloud bank on the western horizon was hailed
from the leading vessel, the *Pinta,* as an island, whereupon the
crews roared a lusty Gloria in Excelsis Deo and Columbus fell to
his knees in gratitude.

Disillusionment was harsh. Depressed by the anticlimax, the
men of the *Santa María* now regarded the freshly stirring trade

wind less as an ally than as an enemy carrying them ever farther from home. By October 6, a month from leaving the Canaries, they had made another thousand miles or so without new encouragement and, though the sea remained calm, some members of the crew were not so. On October 7, Martín Pinzón maneuvered the *Pinta* close to the flagship and shouted his opinion that they should alter course toward the southwest, perhaps on the evidence of migratory bird flight. Columbus resisted the suggestion, holding steady through the coming night. At sunrise, to his delight, the *Niña*, now leading, hoisted a flag at her masthead and fired a cannon to indicate the sighting of land. As the day wore on, however, it failed to materialize, and, by evening, had become just another banished hope. On second thoughts, Columbus altered to west-southwest. By this time, his crew was sadly demoralized. Unlike the men of the *Pinta* and *Niña*, commanded by mariners of a type they knew well and respected, those of the *Santa María* had spent long enough cheek to jowl with the "foreigner" Columbus to draw some disturbing conclusions. On the evidence of his own journal, Columbus was a dissembling captain as well as a fanatic. Such qualities were not easily hidden on a small ship.

On Wednesday, October 10, there was a move toward mutiny. The journal of Columbus (partially preserved in the form of an abstract made by his admirer, Bishop Las Casas) dealt briefly with the matter. "Here the men could bear it no longer, complaining of the length of the voyage. But the Admiral enheartened them to the best of his ability, reiterating the favours they stood to gain and pointing to the futility of their complaints since, God willing, he intended to continue until he found the Indies." The real troubleshooters, it seems likely, were the Pinzóns. According to one of their followers, Martín Pinzón responded to the news by bawling across the water to Columbus, "Hang half a dozen . . . or throw them overboard! If you dare not, my brothers and I will come and do it," to which Columbus, now able to pose as the guardian of the dissenters, allegedly replied, "Martín Alonso, let's remain friendly with these good fellows and proceed for a few more days, then if we haven't sighted land we'll take other dispositions." The dialogue is contentious, but there can be little doubt where the realistic deterrent to further trouble on the *Santa María* lay. In fact, "a few more days" proved longer than enough.

At two o'clock on the morning of October 12, a sailor named Rodrigo de Triana unmistakably sighted land—a tongue of sand shining in the moonlight—from the *Pinta* and, the signal given, the crews shortened sail and waited for the dawn. Thoughts of mutiny vanished in the excitement. For the watchful Rodrigo it was a doubly thrilling night, for Isabella had promised a small annuity to the first man to sight land. The poor man reckoned without the cupidity of his admiral. Columbus, asserting he had spotted "a light" a few hours prior to Rodrigo's sighting, duly claimed the income for himself, utilizing it to pension his mistress. Daylight revealed the *Pinta*'s find as a small island, generally identified today as Watling Island in the Bahamas, but christened by Columbus San Salvador, or Holy Savior. Having landed with the Pinzóns in an armed boat, ceremonially taking possession in the name of Isabella and Ferdinand, Columbus spent a couple of days exploring the island. He found it a pretty place, covered with tropical hardwood and occupied by a simple pastoral people, the Tainos —the Spaniards regarded them as Indians—who had superseded a more primitive race, the Siboney, in the Bahamas and much of Cuba.

For their part, the natives thought the Spaniards had descended from the sky. Despite their friendliness and immediate generosity, Columbus was disappointed. They were a far cry from the rich orientals he expected—"on the whole, it seems to me, a very poor people. They all go as naked as their mothers bore them." There were, however, compensations. "They are bright and should become good servants . . . and I believe they would readily become Christians, for they seem to have no religion." One observation dominated the admiral's sanguinity. "I investigated carefully to discover if they possessed gold. Noting that some had small pieces of this metal attached to holes in their noses, I extracted from them by signs the information that by traveling south, or circumnavigating the island in that direction, there might be found a monarch with vast quantities of gold, including huge vessels wrought from it." That was good enough for Columbus. Taking six natives on board as guides, he left San Salvador on October 14.

For the next fortnight, the explorers examined a succession of islands with much the same results as before. At Rum Cay (christened Santa María de la Concepcion), Long Island (Fernandina),

Crooked Island (Isabella) and others, the natives happily turned
out to barter spun cotton, parrots and fruit for Spanish trinkets
and, when asked about gold, glibly assured their strange visitors
there was plenty—somewhere else. One island in particular was
mentioned for its large size. "From what I can make out from the
Indians on board, I believe this to be Cipangu [Japan]," wrote
Columbus. "They call the island Colba . . . I am determined to
go on from there to the mainland, deliver the letters of your highnesses to the Great Khan and return home with an answer." With
Japan and the Chinese mainland in mind, Columbus set out for
"Colba," following the direction of his guides. Passing to the south
of Long Island by Crooked Island Passage, the flotilla crossed the
foot of the Great Bahama Bank near Ragged Island and struck
south for their destination, the "big island."

On the morning of October 28 the explorers arrived at Bahía
Bariay, Cuba. It was another disappointment. The beauty of the
harbor was undeniable, but the welcome was no more "Oriental"
than it had been on the other islands. The same natives in the
same canoes, the same offering of spun cotton, the same willingness to humor the visitors by copying the sign of the cross or re-
peating the Salve and Ave Maria, but not a golden-roofed temple
nor a mandarin in sight. Farther along the coast, the Tainos indicated a place of some importance in the interior, and Columbus
sent an embassy of two men armed with the diplomatic portfolio
to ascertain the nature of its ruler. The two men, the official interpreter and a seaman from Ayamonte who qualified as an expert
on pagan royalty, having once met a Negro king in Africa, were
conducted by guides up the Cacoyuguin valley to the present site
of Holguín. There they discovered a simple village of some fifty
huts. Still, Columbus was convinced that eastern riches and civilization were close to hand. Fresh calculations, combined with a
limited exploration of the north coast of Cuba, had now persuaded
him that this was not Japan but the southeastern corner of the
mainland, a peninsula shown on the maps of the time as a Chinese
province named Mangi. By his reckoning, the eastern extremity
of Cuba, Cape Maisí, was the "Land's End" of Asia.

Accordingly, a collection of "Oriental" specimens was assembled
for the purposes of proof and display on returning to Spain. Various species of Cuban flora were stored on the ships, among them

specimens quite wrongly assumed to be coconuts, cinnamon, gum-mastic, aloes, and other curiosities popularly associated with the East. A surgeon named Sánchez actually identified some roots as Chinese rhubarb. Since specimens of the population were also needed, and the guides taken earlier had begun escaping, Columbus made a number of prisoners. "Yesterday six young men visited the ship in a canoe. I ordered five to be detained and I have them with me. Later I sent men to one of the dwellings ashore and took seven head of women big and small, and three little boys. My reasoning is that the Indian men will behave better in Spain in the company of women of their own land than without them . . ." The same evening, the distraught husband of one of the women paddled out to the *Santa María* and begged to be allowed to stay with his wife. He was granted the privilege.

Having failed to find gold in Cuba, the Spaniards turned their interest to other islands, gleaning what intelligence they could from the Cuban Tainos. Not all of it was encouraging. Tribal elders warned Columbus that some of the people across the sea were hostile. They spoke of a race of men with only one eye apiece; others with noses like dogs who beheaded and castrated their pris-oners, drinking their blood. But they spoke also of an island which raised the hopes of Columbus. It lay to the southeast of Cuba and they called it Bohio. It was, they said, the repository of infinite quantities of gold which the people there wore on their necks, arms and legs together with pearls. Martín Pinzón heard of an-other island called Babeque, to the northwest, a romantic wonder-land where the natives reputedly gathered gold on the beaches by candlelight. For the first time on the voyage the ships parted com-pany. On November 21 Martín Pinzón in the *Pinta* sailed in search of Babeque, to discover in fact Great Inagua Island before moving on to rejoin Columbus off Bohio. Columbus, who much resented his partner's display of independence, made southeast with Vin-cent Pinzón and the *Niña*, following the course indicated by the Tainos for Bohio, arriving at Môle St. Nicolas, Haiti. Haiti charmed him so greatly that he paid it the tribute of naming it La Isla Española, the Spanish Isle. Having decided that Cuba was a province of China, Columbus felt certain that Española was Japan.

During December, he explored the north coast of the island,

landing at Moustique Bay, the mouth of the Trois Rivières and Acul Bay, at each of which he found the inhabitants enchanting. Often, his descriptions were fulsome. He could not believe that anyone had ever discovered "people of such good heart and so ready to give of their own . . . they are people of love, devoid of cupidity . . . they love their neighbour as themselves and have the softest and gentlest speech in the world." Predictably, however, the Europeans mistook peacefulness and trust for lack of resolution. "They have no weapons, going naked, and are very cowardly with no spirit for arms, for a thousand of them would not stand up to three of us, hence they are fit to be ordered and made to work, sow and do all that we need . . ." Though Columbus had the sense to maintain a benevolent front, the continuing insistence of the Tainos on the remoteness of gold sources suggested that they were not entirely taken in by the visitors. One elderly sage, telling of an island formed entirely of gold at more than a hundred leagues distance, seems to have expressed the situation succinctly.

But Columbus believed he was nearer to treasure than that. The Haitian caciques and their people displayed a greater number of golden nose plugs and other ornaments than he had seen hitherto. "Lord in your piety," beseeched the admiral in his journal, December 23, "guide me that I may find the gold, that is to say their mine." Considered as a rejoinder, the events of the next day were exemplary. Leaving Acul for Marien in the northwest of Haiti, where Columbus hoped to hear more of the mines, the *Santa María* and the *Niña* were becalmed near Cape Haitien. As evening drew on, the sea "as smooth as a plate," the tired crew of the flagship settled to rest before the dawn of Christmas day. Columbus was asleep. The helmsman, lulled by the calm, had handed the tiller to an inexperienced youth. Gently, the vessel settled on a coral reef. As usual in adversity, Columbus blamed everyone but himself, including the absent Martín Pinzón, using the ship's master and owner La Cosa as his chief scapegoat. La Cosa appears to have put out in a boat with members of the crew to enlist the aid of the *Niña* in hauling the *María* from her grounding. He was an experienced captain and, while there was no danger to life in such equable conditions, his own ship was at stake. According to Columbus, however, La Cosa was fleeing to save his skin. The slander was imaginative even by the admiral's standards. At all events, the *Santa María* was beyond saving, and Christmas was spent salvaging stores and equipment with the generous assistance of the local populace and their chieftain, one Guacanagari.

Calm again after the crisis, Columbus proclaimed the wreck a stroke of good fortune predestined by God. Clearly, it was intended, he declared, that he should found a colony on that sunny strand (possibly the sandspit Limonade Bord-de-Mer), and that the crew and timbers of the *Santa María* should form its nucleus. About forty Spaniards were left at the camp, called Villa de la Navidad, Christmas Town, under a Cordoban named Diego de Arana. Columbus left them food for a year, cannon and powder, the flagship's boat and a large quantity of beads and other trinkets to trade with the natives. Their instructions were to consolidate the friendship established with Guacanagari and his people, to search for gold mines and, if possible, to find a site for a permanent town with a good harbor. On the second day of 1493, the first Spanish colonists in the New World attended a farewell feast with Columbus, Guacanagari and the crew of the *Niña* at which an artillery demonstration was given to impress the Tainos. At sunrise on January 4, Columbus set sail in the *Niña* for the homeward passage.

Two days later, he sighted the *Pinta* coming to find him and the two ships beat against the trades through the rest of January gradually edging north until, on the latitude of Bermuda, a strong westerly caught them, spinning them toward the Azores at eleven to twelve knots. The *Niña* reached the Portuguese islands on February 18, having again lost contact with the *Pinta* during a storm a few nights earlier. At first, the Portuguese were suspicious of the *Niña's* activities and a number of her crew, offering thanks for their deliverance in the chapel of a little fishing village, were set on by the inhabitants and thrown into jail. Eventually, Columbus persuaded the governor to give him clearance for Spain, but a further storm encountered after leaving the Azores forced him to seek shelter at Lisbon. The malicious motives attributed to John of Portugal by Columbus at the outset of his voyage were now ridiculed by his reception, for the king and queen of Portugal treated him with great honor before assisting the little ship on her way. On March 13, the *Niña* put out from the Tagus on the last lap of her voyage home to the Saltes.

Meanwhile, Martín Pinzón, who had been blown to the north and had made landfall near Vigo in Galicia, was also heading south for Cape St. Vincent and Palos. Curiously enough, though neither sighted the other until reaching harbor, the *Pinta* followed the *Niña* across the bar of the Saltes on the same tide of March 15, two hundred and twenty-four days after setting out. Of the two remarkably intrepid commanders, fate arbitrarily bestowed the whole of the ensuing triumph on Columbus, for Pinzón, already a sick man on reaching Palos, took directly to bed and was dead within the month. It is a sad commentary on the pathological egotism of Columbus, in other ways a brave and endearing man, that he never found the grace to pay tribute to Pinzón's role in the enterprise, rather exploiting the man's death to discredit him. At the same time, he spared no efforts to justify his own success. On two points he was clearly vulnerable to skepticism: the loss of the *Santa María*, and his failure to locate the source of gold or other treasure in any bulk. These he dealt with, 1, by denigrating his subordinates, and, 2, by presenting speculation as fact. In a circular letter dispatched to members of the Spanish court on his return, he stated categorically that in Española (Haiti) "there are numerous spices, large mines of gold and other minerals."

The letter, a tempting confusion of native hearsay, conjecture, and established fact, told, among other things, of a region in Haiti where people were born with tails and of an island exclusively inhabited by weapon-toting women. In it Columbus was at pains to emphasize the wealth and beauty of the places discovered, their proximity to the realm of the Grand Khan and the exploitation potential of the "Indians." "In conclusion," he wrote, "taking account of no more than has been accomplished on this rapid voyage, it will be evident to Their Highnesses that I have assured them as much gold as They wish, as many spices and as much cotton as they desire and as much gum of the mastic-tree as they care to load, gum so far found only in the Greek island of Chio and which their Lordships can sell at the price of their asking. Furthermore, I shall make available as many aloes and devoted slaves as they wish to embark. I believe, also, that I have found rhubarb and cinnamon, not to mention the valuable products which will come to light through the investigations of the men I have left behind in

Espanola. I myself have not done much detailed exploration since, while the wind was favourable, I did not settle anywhere, except at Villa de la Navidad where I paused to set up a sound and orderly establishment. Indeed, I would have done a lot more had my ships served me as well as might reasonably have been expected . . . Since Our Redeemer has given this triumph to our Most Illustrious King and Queen and to their realms which will accordingly become famous, all Christianity ought to rejoice and celebrate, ardently offering thanks in prayer to the Holy Trinity for the exaltation that will result from the conversion of so many tribes to the holy faith, also for the material benefits to come, for not only Spain but all Christians will find happiness and profit in it."

If this oblique piece of trumpet blowing brought smiles in high places, the implications of the news were not lost. Before the month was out, Isabella and Ferdinand, then at Barcelona, had written Columbus to come to them at once, but not before arrangements had been set in motion "for your return to the lands you have discovered." At the same time, fearful of Portuguese rivalry, the sovereigns applied to the pope for confirmation of their rights. Pope Alexander VI, a Spaniard, hastened to oblige, issuing two bulls Inter Cetera on May 3 and a third on May 4. This restricted all future Portuguese discoveries to the east of a line along the meridian one hundred leagues west of "the islands known as the Azores and Cape Verde," likewise limiting Spanish discoveries to the west of the line. A more precise ruling was agreed shortly afterward between Spain and Portugal. John had first proposed dividing the unexplored world into north and south, based on a horizontal line through the Canaries, Spain to take the north, Portugal the south. Under the so-called Treaty of Tordesillas, however, he now agreed to a modified version of the east-west division, the line adjusted to the meridian 370 leagues west of the Cape Verde Islands. The sublime presumption underlying the treaty was dryly observed later by the King of France (Francis I) who expressed an interest to see the clause in Adam's will authorizing such a share-out.

On the last day of March, Columbus staged a suitably colorful entry to Seville on his way to the court at Barcelona. With his West Indians, his parrots, his exotic plants and other souvenirs displayed around him, it must have been rather like the grand parade of a circus. All along his route, people deserted their homes and fields to line the road in an excited and curious throng. At Barcelona itself, the crowd was so thick that it hindered progress. For Isabella, his arrival marked the end of a period of great personal tension. Shortly before Christmas, Ferdinand had been struck down in the city by a would-be assassin. The weapon used had narrowly missed splitting his skull, grazing the side of his head and striking his shoulder. "I had no heart to see the wound," wrote the queen, "it was four fingers deep and so long that my hand trembles at the thought of it." It had been a chilling aftermath to the triumph of Granada and a vivid reminder of her fears of unrest. Now, with Ferdinand recovered, came the harbinger of a new and reassuring success. The sovereigns received Columbus with an esteem he can hardly have exceeded himself. Not only did they confirm all the honors they had promised, they bestowed others of which the noblest of their courtiers had cause to be envious. They rose to greet him from their thrones in public state, they offered him a seat at their side, and, when an emotional ceremony was over, they ordered the whole court to escort the admiral to his billet. Columbus rode in the midst of the royal family.

That evening, Cardinal Mendoza, the grandest personage in the land after their royal highnesses, invited Columbus to dine at his residence, "and, bidding him sit at the most pre-eminent seat, that next to him, had him served in a covered dish and his food tasted for poison, and that was the first time that his food was so tested . . ." It was indeed a convincing recognition of success.

The first voyage had been delayed by a shortage of recruits; the second suffered from no such problem. The impression that fortune awaited everyone in the Indies provoked a minor gold rush in which the organizers were confronted with an excess of volunteers. Of some 1500 picked, all male, a good proportion owed their selection to social influence. Ambitious young noblemen, aristocratic adventurers, black sheep with fancy pedigrees, many whose qualifications were less impressive than their sponsors, took their place beside a determined covey of monks, a range of earnest scientists, and the hard core of seamen and artisans. Each was obliged to swear an oath of allegiance to the sovereigns, who were at some pains to emphasize that all colonial decisions, orders, and patents given by Columbus were to be written in their own names.

Columbus chose a number of old friends and accomplices to go with him, including a brother, Diego, who had turned up in Spain, Marchena, his original ally from La Rábida, and, despite the admiral's earlier imputations, La Cosa of the *Santa María*. On the fitting of the fleet, organized by Juan de Fonseca, an administrator who later founded the Royal House of the Indies, Columbus brought a number of complaints. The wine was so poorly casked that it ran to waste on the ships, he declared. Twenty horsemen signed after producing fine chargers for inspection, sold them afterward, embarking a string of scrawny hacks. All the same, Fonseca appears to have done a fair job. Working through the summer at Cádiz, the base for the voyage, he bought or chartered seventeen ships, victualed them for a round voyage of six months, stored enough arms and ammunition for a considerable campaign, assembled the personnel, rounded up sufficient domestic animals of all descriptions to stock the new settlements, and stacked aboard those inevitable quantities of cheap beads and trinkets with which European civilization was so frequently to seduce peoples all too readily susceptible to delight.

The fleet sailed at sunrise, September 25, the admiral commanding from a big transporter known as the *Marigalante*. In attendance were two other large vessels of similar type, perhaps a dozen caravels approaching the size of the *Niña*, once more under commission, and one or two small barks for use in shoal water. They made a brave sight. Each ship flew the royal standard and was dressed with colorful banners, some bearing the arms of their noble passengers. A ceremonial send-off included music and the firing of cannon, while a fleet of Venetian galleys which was visiting Cádiz escorted the colonists from the harbor. As before, Columbus made first for the Canaries, thereafter setting a course somewhat to the south of that followed on his maiden voyage, catching the full benefit of the trade wind. With this advantage, the heavily laden caracks made the crossing in the admirable time of twenty days, striking land at Dominica in the Lesser Antilles. Turning north in search of the small colony left earlier at La Navidad, the fleet found a succession of islands in the Leeward group, commencing with Marigalante, named in honor of the flagship. Most were christened after Spanish monasteries or saints.

The first intimation that the natives here were of a less hospitable disposition than those of Cuba and Haiti came at the volcanic island of Guadeloupe, where the satisfaction of commandeering twelve buxom Taino girls in a deserted village was rather spoiled by the information that the locals, who had captured the girls on Española, were predatory and cannibalistic. Known as Caribs, and probably originating from the Matto Grosso of southwest Brazil, these people had filtered north through the jungle lands of the Amazon, established themselves in the Guineas and Venezuela and, in comparatively recent times, pushed their invasion seaward through the Lesser Antilles. Though their general culture stood comparison with that of their Caribbean neighbors, they were distinctly more aggressive and warlike. Confirmation of Carib hostility was encountered at St. Croix, the island named Santa Cruz by Columbus, where an armed Spanish boat reconnoitering the estuary of Salt River Bay ran into a Carib dugout. Its occupants, four men and two women, defied the Spanish party, numbering twenty-five, with a volley of poisoned arrows. By the time the Carib craft had been rammed and its survivors overcome, two Spaniards were wounded, one fatally. Even in hopeless adversity, the Caribs were tenacious. One prisoner, appallingly wounded in the stomach, was thrown into the sea. He struck hard for the shore. Recaptured, bound hand and foot, then thrown back, he still managed to swim until a flight of Spanish arrows scuttled him. Another, a naked woman, was captured by a friend of Columbus, Michele de Cuneo, one of three members of the armada to leave a detailed account of the voyage. Taken to his cabin, she fought off his advances with a determination Isabella would have found highly commendable. Unfortunately, the thrashing her resistance earned reduced her to such a state that, as Cuneo boasted, "I can tell you she behaved as if she had been brought up in a school of harlots."

Shocked by the revelations of Guadeloupe and the incident at St. Croix, Columbus promptly departed the latter island, traveling via the Virgins and Puerto Rico (the Spanish called it San Juan Bautista) to Española and the camp at Navidad. Here, the admiral received an even greater shock. The strongpost was in ruins and its garrison had perished. Timidly, the local natives gave their version of what had happened. Encouraged by the awe in which the chief Guacanagari and his people held them, the men of Navidad apparently commenced their stay by making free with tribal possessions and women. An easy, self-indulgent life had soon undermined discipline, giving rise to factions and fights among the Spaniards themselves. Eventually, a small group had set out to seek gold in a region ruled by a cacique, reputedly of Carib origin, known as Caonabo. Resentful of the intrusion, Caonabo had killed them, then, in alliance with another chief, Mayreni, descended on Guacanagari's village and Navidad. According to Guacanagari, he and his people had tried to defend the Spaniards, but, with the exception of a few who had fled into the sea and drowned, these had been massacred by the attackers. To substantiate his statement, he pointed out that several of his people were wounded. A Spanish doctor, Diego Chanca, who examined their wounds, decided these had in fact been inflicted by native weapons.

Nevertheless, the story met with considerable skepticism among the admiral's followers, many of whom, including the senior priest, Friar Buyl, strongly advocated Guacanagari's execution. They were none the happier when most of the native girls on the ships escaped shortly afterward and disappeared along with the mistrusted chief. Still, Columbus cherished the good will of the Tainos. At the same time, he did not feel disposed to renew settlement at Navidad, moving instead some thirty miles to the east, to the point of Monte Cristi, where the Spaniards founded Isabella, their first town in the New World. (The capital was moved again before long to San Domingo.) The fleet had reached Navidad at the end of November. By the beginning of next February several hundred men were sick, Chanca and the other doctors were out of drugs, and the general logistical situation was becoming desperate. On February 2 Columbus sent most of the ships home under his flag captain, Antonio de Torres, with an urgent request for provisions.

While the settlement awaited the arrival of fresh supplies, Columbus left his younger brother Diego in charge and set off with three caravels to pursue his search for the realm of the Grand Khan. In five months of sailing, he discovered Jamaica, explored the south coast of Cuba from the Jardines de la Reina to the Isla de Pinos, cruised the south coast of Española, and found the island of

Mona, then returned by the north coast to the settlement. His exploration of the long Cuban coastline, which he had discontinued somewhere short of its western extremity, encouraged Columbus in his belief that this was the Asian mainland, a conclusion duly noted in a document witnessed by his crews on June 12. The voyage, however, was ill-timed. The departure of the admiral at such a crucial moment in the life of the newly founded colony had a retrograde effect on developments. Diego Columbus, a mild fellow whose ambition was to take holy orders, was no match for the frustrated adventurers of Isabella. Many, no less rugged and assertive than most pioneer colonists, had kicked from the start against a policy of wooing the native powers. Bad fortune increased their misgivings. Nor were trading and husbandry suited to the style of Spanish nobles, especially since neither occupation showed much sign of alleviating their troubles. There was, moreover, a growing feeling that the promised gold mines were fictitious.

Feeling veered toward a more aggressive exploitation of the country, deriving inspiration from the dashing, but so far limited, exploits of two intrepid adventurers, Columbus's military chief, Pedro Margarit, and a lively Andalusian named Alonso de Ojeda. Backed by the aggressive Friar Buyl, these had already gone a fair way toward offending and alienating the caciques of Española by the admiral's return. The situation was now critical. Though the arrival of some supplies under the command of Bartholomew Columbus, who had reached Spain too late to join the main voyage, helped a little, mutiny seethed among the settlers. To add to the problem, the admiral was indisposed for several months by sickness. By the time he recovered, drastic action was imperative. Margarit and Buyl had commandeered ships and deserted to Spain. Fearful of the picture of failure they might paint, Columbus proceeded to round up the neighboring Tainos, five hundred of whom he shipped off in the wake of the deserters as a token of his potency, placating the settlers by offering them as many slaves as they wished. He then turned to the job of suppressing the chiefs. Among the most hostile were Caonabo, the man responsible for the attack on Navidad, and one Guatiguana, who had been captured in the earlier roundup but had gnawed through his bonds and escaped. Luckily for the Spaniards, the caciques of Española were not united. Some, still remote from the Europeans, were apathetic.

At least one, the formerly helpful Guacanagari, nursed a lingering respect for Columbus. Divided, they were conquered.

At Puerto de los Hidalgos, March 1495, in the first pitched battle between the Spanish and the people of the New World, rather more than two hundred settlers led by Columbus, Bartholomew, and Ojeda routed a native horde under Guatiguana. Dismayed by the effect, rather than the efficiency, of the discharge of several score harquebuses, confused by a pack of dogs set upon them, the Tainos fell easy prey to Ojeda and twenty men mounted on weedy horses. Next, Caonabo was tricked into paying a ceremonial visit to the town of Isabella, where he was thrown into jail. With the chiefs subdued, Columbus and his lieutenants built forts at strategic points on the island and forced the natives to pay tribute. By now it was clear that the only sure way of producing gold was to denude the Tainos of the modest quantity they had accumulated, and to force them into the laborious and uneconomical process of panning for dust on the surface. Accordingly every Indian of fourteen or upward was obliged to pay an annual or monthly tribute of gold dust according to his rank, an imposition later modified to the system of *repartimientos*. The economic consequences for the indigenous people of Española were disastrous. Driven by forced labor from their normal way of life, thousands fell victim to broken health and its consequences. Others fled to the hills where they were hunted down by the Spaniards. In rather more than a decade, less than a quarter of their original number survived. Half a century later, they were close to extinction.

Meanwhile, by the beginning of 1496 the number of Spaniards on the island had itself fallen to less than 650, most of whom were disillusioned and heartily homesick. "Nobody," wrote Cuneo, "wants to live in these countries." To the increased discomfort of Columbus, the reports of Margarit and Buyl had resulted in a royal commissioner being sent out from Spain to investigate the state of the colony. Columbus decided to circumvent further reports by returning and stating his own case. In March 1496 he sailed for Cádiz in the *Niña*, accompanied by one other caravel, both vessels being greatly overloaded by passengers. According to Oviedo, "they came back so enfeebled, disease-worn and ill-visaged that they appeared more like dead men than living." The homecoming was indeed a dismal sequel to the grand departure two years and nine months earlier, but Columbus at least made the most of it. Exchanging his admiral's finery for the austere habit of a Franciscan monk, he gave an emotional and dramatic rendering of his religious mission in the Indies. Now entirely white-haired and of a strikingly biblical appearance, he had begun to sign himself Xtoferens, or Christ-bearer, insistent in his claim that a whole continent of potential converts was almost within his grasp. Granted one more expedition, he would discover no less than the "Terrestrial Paradise." Fortuitously, since his reception by the court was not enthusiastic, it was known that the Portuguese were themselves equipping a strong fleet for a secret voyage of discovery. Fear of its outcome prompted the Spanish sovereigns to give Columbus another chance.

In fact, though he made two more trips to the Indies, the admiral was embarked on a declining worldly career. From the first of these voyages, on which he discovered Trinidad and several points on the north Venezuelan coast—which he regarded as islands leading to the mythical paradise on earth—he was shipped home from Española in irons. The persistent failure of Indians to survive transplantation in Spain had now confirmed the queen as a fierce opponent of this form of exploitation, thus depriving the island of its last hopeful export. Amid renewed colonial mutiny, violence, and despair, another royal commissioner had arrived at Española and arrested the Columbus brothers. But the admiral was not finished. Playing on the sympathies of the Spanish public with histrionic and heart-rending eloquence, he again managed to raise humiliation to triumph. On a surge of new popular favor, he was once more honored and rewarded. Isabella reputedly wept at the admiral's account of his ill-treatment. Nevertheless, his days as viceroy and governor of the Indies had ended.

On May 8, 1502, he left Cádiz with four caravels on his last attempt to find the world of his dreams. Instead, he spent more than a year stranded on the coast of Jamaica, beset by mutiny and disease, his calls for help belatedly and grudgingly answered from Española. After a sequence of further mishaps, he limped into Spain, November 1504, his ships and his own health broken. Renting lodgings in Seville, the once flamboyant adventurer, now approaching old age, enervated and gout-ridden, faced the final price of eccentricity. His affairs were in chaos. For all his extravagant demands in the past, he had kept no proper accounts of the moneys owing to him, he had borrowed on all sides, his enemies in the Indies had no inclination to help, and repeated letters to the Spanish authorities brought little encouragement. His real deprivation, however, went deeper, clouding his enforced retirement with the urge to vindicate his global concepts. For while La Cosa, Ojeda, and others who followed went on to proclaim a new continent to the world, Columbus, seeker of Cipangu, Cathay, Mangi, the Grand Khan and the Earthly Paradise, had always failed in what he set out to discover.

Chapter 4

A NEW POWER IN EUROPE

In the summer of 1504, while Columbus was struggling for the last time with a hostile Atlantic, Isabella fell ill at Medina del Campo, on the broad, stony plains of her childhood. Here, in a grimly turreted fifteenth-century palace, the Castillo de la Mota, she did her best to keep abreast of affairs from her sickbed while her health became worse. By autumn, the court was seriously apprehensive about her fate. In a letter to the Count of Tendilla on October 7, Pietro Martire, an Italian scholar and one of the queen's favorites, wrote gloomily of the prospects. "Her whole system is subjected to a dissipating fever. She abhors food of any kind, is tormented by incessant thirst and the disorder has every appearance of terminating in a dropsy." Things were not made any easier by Isabella's reluctance to be thoroughly examined by male physicians. By October 15, all doubts of the outcome were gone. "We sit sadly in the palace all day," reported Martire, "tremulously awaiting the hour when faith and virtue shall depart the earth with her. Let us pray we may be permitted to follow later where she must soon go. So utterly does she transcend all human excellence that there is little of mortality about her. She can scarcely be said to be dying, merely passing to a nobler environment, a matter for our envy rather than sorrow. She leaves a world filled with her renown, to enjoy eternal life with God in heaven.

I write this between hope and fear, while the breath is still fluttering within her."

The thoughts of all Castile were centered on the woman. At fifty-four, a queen for thirty years, Isabella had acquired such remarkable authority in Spanish life that, for many, it was hard to imagine it continuing without her. Harder still to recall their misgivings, three decades earlier, when a young gentlewoman had inherited half a century of lawlessness and anarchy. Spain had had much to learn then of its bright-eyed innocent. Ironists still relished the first sharp twist of the social scalpel: the disbelief of the ubiquitous, free-ranging outlaw suddenly faced by the sharpshooting archers of the youthful Isabella. Dragged back to the scene of his crime, he had been lashed to a wooden framework and pinioned with arrows. The new justice had been violent and expeditious. Revitalized law courts, often dignified by the young queen's presence, had issued a spate of mutilations and beheadings —"terrifying and appalling vivisections," an eminent doctor of the time described them with professional indignation. Ferdinand, the queen's partner in wedlock, war, and politics—but always the junior where Castile was concerned—must sometimes have regarded the soft and dutifully acquiescent companion of his bedchamber with an icy tremor of the spine. Yet, for the first time in their lives, women and children had been able to travel unprotected.

In bringing the great entrenched institutions of aristocratic and clerical privilege to their knees, Isabella's methods had been more complex but no less impressive. She had flattered the pride of the nobles with gracious but trivial concessions. One by which they set much store was that of keeping their hats on in the royal presence. She had played on their rivalries to divide and isolate. She had undermined them on their own ground by encouraging the emancipation of the peasants who had become a free laboring and renting class by the end of her reign. And she had undermined them in government by giving key posts to bourgeois professionals trained in the academies she sponsored. In short, it had been relatively painless. They had surrendered their teeth but kept their fancy hats. Not that the queen had been moved by democratic principles. On the contrary, she had stifled the political outlets of the lower orders as effectively as she had tamed the aristocracy. During the sixteen momentous years from 1482 to 1498, she had failed to assemble the Cortes even once. Against the receding influence of the representative body she had raised a new and dominant Royal Council, overwhelmingly composed of bureaucrats. Each was solemnly sworn to secrecy. Masterfully, she had engineered her omnipotence.

Few could reflect more clearly than Martire, now keeping vigil in the hushed palace, on the keenness and versatility of the dying woman's intellect. A proven wizard of logistics, Isabella had been strong, too, on peaceful communications. Her reign had seen a great improvement in roads, a sharp stimulation of the shipping that was to bear directly on the future fortunes of the Spanish Empire, and a brisk trade in exports, particularly the wools of Seville and Toledo. In the financial sphere, she had left few stones, however muddy, unturned. Though the war in Granada had ravaged the profits, Castilian revenues had increased sensationally since her accession. In 1474 the figure had been 885,000 reales. Thirty years later it was more than 26,000,000. And, withal, she had not neglected her cultural heritage. An ardent and fashionable champion of scholarship, Isabella had provided not only her children—a son, John, and four daughters, Isabella, Joanna, María, and Katherine —but her entire entourage with opportunities for a polished education. Antonio de Lebrija, one of the most eminent scholars of the day, had written his Grammatica Castillana especially for the ladies of her court. Resolving to learn Latin in the full flood of her queenly duties, Isabella had decorously employed a woman teacher, Beatrice Galindo, familiarly known in royal circles as La Latina. According to another intellectual, Marineo, the queen had acquired a working knowledge of the language within a year.

Martire could recall all too vividly her efforts to divert aimless soldiers to academic pursuits when the war in Granada was over. Requested by the queen to open a school for young aristocrats, he had been dubious. "Like their ancestors," he had protested, "they consider letters of slight importance, an obstacle to military success." He had reckoned without Isabella's influence. "The whole day," he had soon been able to report delightedly, "my establishment swarms with noble youths converted from unworthy occupations . . . I sincerely impress on them that true excellence in any field, whether in peace or war, is unattainable without science." With Isabella's encouragement, foreign books had appeared everywhere, printing presses were established in the principal cities, universities prospered at Salamanca, Toledo, Seville, Granada, and elsewhere. Her ancestor, Alfonso the Learned, would have been proud. During the two centuries and more since Alfonso's time, the language and thinking of Castile had strongly influenced the rest of Spain. Under Isabella, Castile became the dynamo of the Spanish Empire.

The last decade of her reign had been dominated at home by two massive achievements, Church reform and the conversion of her Moorish subjects in Granada. The changing face of the Church during Isabella's time was illustrated vividly by the image of her primates, Mendoza and Jiménez. Pedro Gonzalez de Mendoza, sometimes known as the "Great Cardinal" or the "third monarch of Spain," had been very much the aristocratic and full-blooded prelate of the fifteenth century. Fighting for Isabella while she was still a princess, he had played a prominent part in bringing her to the throne and remained a powerful partisan and adviser of the queen to his death in 1496. A big, expansive man of generous faults and virtues, Mendoza tended rudely to capsize his critics, and Isabella had been too shrewd not to overlook the less priestly of his habits. If he spent lavishly on worldly pomp and magnificence, he had also dispensed largesse with pleasing abandon. If he ate and drank liberally, he had also the diplomatic asset of easy hospitality. And if his mistresses, who had included at least one lady-in-waiting of the queen, bore him bountiful offspring, it had been tempting to attribute his brood to the same warmth that had prompted him to spend ten years building a home for foundlings at Toledo. Though, in the heat of the moment, Mendoza had been as violent as most leaders of his day, he seems to have exhibited little of the malice or spiritual bitterness that was to sustain and increasingly pervert the Inquisition. When an indiscreet priest once complained obliquely in a sermon of the cardinal's self-indulgence, Mendoza had riposted generously by sending the man a rich gift of game and gold doblas.

He had died, however, undeluded by his bluff attachment to the past. Aware of the changing pattern of society, he had left a large slice of his fortune to the endowment of education, nominating as his successor a rabid ascetic. Francisco Jiménez, a scholar and monk of humble origin who had first tasted power on joining the privileged club of Isabella's confessors, was in almost all respects the inversion of his earthy predecessor. A man who carried the principles of elevation through self-denial to near masochistic limits, Jiménez reputedly wore the rough frock of a monk beneath his cardinal's robes, kept a bed of plain boards under the ceremonial trappings of his couch and refused to ride, or allow his aides to do so, whenever it was possible to walk. Limited to himself, such austerity could have brought little but admiration, for its profound benefits to the soul were widely accepted. With inflexible integrity, however, Jiménez had set himself to impose proper discipline and standards on the clergy as a whole, particularly on members of religious orders who had habitually flouted rules denying them worldly possessions. Thrust upon them by Jiménez, such spiritual benefits had been bitterly resented by the monks. Only after a prolonged tussle with Rome, in which Isabella had schemed tirelessly for her dour cardinal, had his program of reform become effective.

Together, they had turned to the outstanding politico-religious problem of the state: the conversion to Christianity of the conquered Granadinos. Manifestly, the retention of a predominantly Muslim populace, even a subject one, on the vital southeast coast of the peninsula had been dangerous; a free license to the Barbaresque pirates who harbored there as well as an invitation to invasion from Africa. Yet, under the terms of the treaty of Granada, attempts to convert by coercion were forbidden; the Moors were to retain their own property, customs, laws, and religion. For five years after the conquest, the new archbishop of Granada, Talavera, the man who had supervised the original examination of Columbus, had worked to convert by reasonable methods. Setting himself and his priests to learn Arabic, he had succeeded in earning the respect and ear of many of the people. But results had been neither fast enough nor sufficiently dramatic to satisfy the requirements of politics. Accordingly, in 1499, the sovereigns had agreed with an impatient Jiménez that he should join Talavera in his efforts. Jiménez had scarcely arrived in Granada before his implacable zeal had dominated the whole tenor of proceedings.

Beginning by bribing the Moorish *alfaquies*, he had soon extended his range of persuasion to compulsion and terror. Unco-operative chiefs were thrown into irons while countless copies of the Koran and other Arabic works, the surviving legacy of the great libraries of the caliphate, had been burned in the streets. Impelled by the logic of the reconquest, Spanish Islam had moved to its inevitable, and now graceless, end. When the cardinal's measures provoked Moorish rebellion, Jiménez had come out with his ultimate plan. Like the Jews before them, the Moors must be presented with the choice of baptism or departure. On February 12, 1502, Isabella had issued an edict of expulsion on all unconverted adult Moors in her peninsula realms. Thousands, assembling to be christened en masse by aspersion, had preferred to risk inquisition than to face the perils and doubts of expatriation. For Isabella, perhaps her dearest ambition had been realized. She had lived to rule an entirely Christian kingdom.

But the queen's health had already shown signs of failing. The strain of constant and prodigious public efforts had been aggravated by a tragic sequence of personal grief. Through the diplomatic marriage of their five children, Isabella and Ferdinand had anticipated glittering European prospects for Spain. Two of their offspring, the only son and a daughter, were married to the Habsburgs, two other daughters to Portugal, and the remaining daughter to England. It was indeed a formidable castle of wedding cards. In 1496, however, the death of Isabella's deranged but long-cherished mother had appeared to send a shudder through the pack. In 1497, the death of the queen's son John, heir to the thrones of both Castile and Aragon, had been closely followed by that of his own posthumous child, who perished at birth. In 1498, the next in line, the queen's favorite daughter Isabella, wife of Manuel of Portugal, had herself died in childbirth. Her infant, a son, hopefully acclaimed by Portugal, Castile, and Aragon as heir to the entire peninsula, had died at the age of two. To make matters worse, the princess Joanna, now married to Philip the Handsome of Burgundy and the senior of the remaining daughters, had inherited her grandmother's mental instability. If there had been any doubts about this earlier, they had been sadly diminished in the spring of 1504 when, incensed by her husband's admiration for one of the ladies of her suite, Joanna had jumped on the woman in a paroxysm of hysteria and shorn the victim of a substantial quantity of hair.

The resulting scandal did nothing to improve Isabella's health. In October, soon after receiving the news, she put a feeble hand to her last will and testament. The succession was settled on Joanna, but with a significant rider. In the event of Joanna's "incapacity," Ferdinand was to become sole regent of Castile until the majority of Joanna's young son, Charles. The queen thus left her husband a strong chance of picking up the reins of her realm. She also left him a fixed income of ten million maravedis annually and half the net profits of whatever might proceed from the new lands in the west. Her last words to him—tender yet with a businesslike reminder at the end—were pure Isabella. "I beseech the King my Lord," she declared, "that he be pleased to accept my jewels and belongings, or such as he likes best, that seeing them he will be reminded of the singular love I always felt for his lordship; and even so, that he may ever bear in mind that he is to die and that I am waiting for him in the other life, with which memory he may live more purely and justly." Shortly before noon on Wednesday, November 26, 1504, Isabella the Catholic died, modestly declining to expose her feet as was customary on receiving the extreme unction.

"My hand falls powerless to my side in sorrow," wrote Martire that day. "The world has lost its most exalted ornament; a loss to be mourned not only in Spain, whose cause she has advanced so gloriously, but by every nation in Christendom . . . I am conscious of no other member of her sex, in ancient times or modern, worthy in my judgement to be named with this incomparable woman." In accordance with Isabella's wishes, her body was transported unembalmed to Granada and entombed in the Alhambra, the symbol so long of her ambition, where it was to remain until the death of Ferdinand. As the funeral cortege had wound its slow and comfortless way across the wintry countryside, a bedridden mariner in Seville was writing to his son with quivering impatience: "It is strongly rumoured here that the Queen, who is with God, has willed that I be restored in possession of the Indies," and, again, a week later, "it is necessary to discover if the Queen, who is with God, said anything about me in her will." But the queen had not mentioned Columbus. The tide of events sweeping Spain to imperial pre-eminence had already swamped his usefulness. Sick, lonely, now living on borrowed money, the man who had unknowingly altered the whole course of Spanish history lingered on with his dreams for one more round of the seasons, then followed Isabella to rest.

At a time when European thought was only beginning to regard politics as a subject for detached observation, Ferdinand of Aragon's talents were often underrated, usually to the cost of somebody else. His genius, unlike the queen's, was not cast before the masses. Ferdinand tended to appeal to the connoisseur. Such a connoisseur was the Florentine statesman and political philosopher Niccolò Machiavelli, whose concept of power and the modern state has been taken to mark the end of the Middle Ages and to herald a new phase of European development. For the first time since Aristotle, Machiavelli detached political consciousness from divine institution, drawing aside the curtains of medieval tradition to seek conclusions in "natural causes" and events. His view of statesmanship, placing an enhanced value on intellect, brought politics into step with the renaissance and placed a new premium on the science of diplomacy. His opinion of Ferdinand, therefore, is significant. In his most famous work, *The Prince*, a dissertation on the acquisition of sovereign power, Machiavelli observed of the late Isabella's husband: "One may almost consider him as a new prince, to the extent that from being a king of limited influence his successes have raised him to the status of first monarch of Christendom. If you consider his actions, you will find them all great and some of them extraordinary." Extraordinary, perhaps, was the less contentious term.

Absorbed not only with internal affairs but with the Indies and the constant menace of Islam, Isabella had left Ferdinand to deal, in the main, with the rest of Europe. It was the most sophisticated field of Spanish affairs and one which challenged the utmost political dexterity. Everywhere, the pattern of power was changing. By the close of the fifteenth century a continent once tumultuous with independent aristocrats was hardening into a conclave of great central authorities, each taking the measure of the other, each suspicious of its neighbor, each seeking alliance while grinding the knife. In England and France the Spanish monarchy had its counterpart in Henry VII and Louis XI, both of whom had emerged from violent backgrounds of civil strife. To the east, Maximilian I, ruler of the Germanic Roman Empire, had thrown the Hungarians from his Austrian dominions and extended his territories by marriage to include the Netherlands, Artois, and the French Comté. For Spain, these powers threw a shadow in the north as grim and potentially disastrous as the Barbary lightning flashing in the south.

Above all, France, closest to the peninsula and traditionally hostile to Aragon, loomed black and charged with rivalry. Not only were there frontier disputes between the two nations in the form of Navarre, Cerdagne, and Roussillon; trouble rumbled over the distant Kingdom of Naples, to which Aragon and France had debatable rights. Naples, held in turn in the past by both Anjou and the crown of Aragon, was now ruled by neither. Instead Ferdinand's uncle, Alfonso, came to power in defiance of his nephew. The French gazed on his kingdom greedily. For Charles VIII of France, Louis XI's young and impetuous successor, Italy was the key to all worldly ambition. Indeed, many statesmen acknowledged the concept. By the ultimate decade of the fifteenth century, when the storm burst, Italy was regarded with a desire that reflected more than the glittering treasures of her culture and commerce. The advisers of a sixteenth-century emperor could tell him: "Italy occupied and reduced to subjection is the true seat and sceptre for dominating the entire world." Neither Ferdinand nor Charles could afford to ignore it. For if Spain extended her possessions to Italy she would dominate the eastern Mediterranean and complete the encirclement of France by her enemies on land and on sea. On the other hand, if France took Italy, the tables would be considerably reversed. As well as having a hostile Africa to the south, Spain could look forward to being blockaded to the north and east; France would gain the ports to challenge Spanish maritime power and would very soon supplant Aragon as possessor of Sicily.

All of which might have been dismissed as idle speculation had Italy herself conformed to the changing structure of other nations and seemed at all likely to defend herself with resolution and unity. In fact, though she had led Europe to new levels of social cultivation, was commercially enterprising and generally prosperous, she had not come near to a concord of government. Italy, at the time, consisted of a number of small states—principally the Republics of Venice and Florence, the Duchy of Milan, the Kingdom of Naples and the papal see—none of which was strong enough to overthrow the others, though the plotting and intrigue between them was formidable. A determined invasion by a great power seemed unlikely to fail. At least, such was the opinion of Charles of France and his advisers.

Though French pretensions had some backing in Naples, Charles's cover for a move on Italy was more elaborate. He was initiating, he declared, a new crusade against the Turks. From Naples he would attack Constantinople itself, striking a telling blow for Christendom. This, though hardly an original excuse for aggression, was a useful argument in the handling of Spain and Italy, both of whom lived in fear of Turkish expansion. To further assure the success of his plan, Charles sought to buy Ferdinand's neutrality by offering to relinquish the disputed territories of Cerdagne and Roussillon, occupied by Louis XI, in return for a promise of Spanish nonintervention. Having made suitable terms with his other neighbors, Charles now felt ready to march.

If Ferdinand's strategy in the circumstances was not touched with greatness, it was certainly, to use Machiavelli's alternative description, extraordinary. With the costly war in Granada barely over, Spain's immediate resources were slender. Yet Ferdinand sat down to mastermind an operation that would not only give him Cerdagne and Roussillon, but bring ruin to Charles in Italy and, in the end, place Naples once more in the hands of Spain. The whole was to be achieved with a minimum of expense and manpower. For a start, no army at all was needed. The first step was easy. Accepting the offer of Cerdagne and Roussillon, Ferdinand entered into the so-called Peace of Barcelona with France, convincing Charles that he was free to go ahead with his game. At the same time, the Spanish king embarked on a program of international intrigue designed to turn the alluring leg of Italy into a fatal trap for the gathering French invaders. In essence, the scheme was to promote an armed alliance against Charles between Spain, the emperor, and a number of the northern Italian states. Even to this extent, the problems of bringing together a complex of traditional rivals were enormous, and Ferdinand spared few means of persuasion. To add to the difficulties, each diplomatic maneuver had to be conducted in the deepest secrecy lest the French caught wind of developments. Above all, the extent of ultimate Spanish success depended on judging the pace of events. Ferdinand's talent was to be evinced most clearly in their timing.

In August 1494 there commenced the most spectacular Alpine raid on Italy since Hannibal. Charles, a flamboyant, acquisitive fellow only just in his twenties, led a massive army out of Vienne, on the Rhone, and crossed the mountainous border. His force, which contained a strong body of Swiss mercenaries, reputedly numbered more than twenty thousand infantry plus many hundreds of mounted knights and a powerful train of artillery. French ordnance, then second to none in Europe, was horse-drawn and well fitted for swift movement. Lightly mounted, its eight-foot bronze cannons fired iron ammunition with relative rapidity and precision. By comparison, Italian artillery was risible. Ponderously hauled by oxen, it projected small stone balls at such a slow rate of fire that, when used against battlements, it was said that the enemy had time to make good the damage between discharges. Nor were Italian arms as a whole a better match for the French. Compared with their northern neighbors, the Italian fighting classes of the time were effete; their wars conducted in an eminently refined manner. Two Italian battles described by Machiavelli appear to have produced no more than one fatality: and he was suffocated by the weight of his armor, having fallen from his horse into mud. The French approach was watched with feelings of impotence and horror.

On the last day of December, Charles and his legions swaggered into Rome, where the pope and his cardinals had taken refuge in the castle of St. Angelo. Within a few more weeks, the French were at the gates of Naples. Alfonso had scuttled while they were still in Rome, abdicating the kingdom to his son Ferrante, who now fled to the isle of Ischia. So far, though voicing dramatic protestations on behalf of the pope and issuing threatening warnings about Naples, Ferdinand had carefully concealed his hand from Charles. His plans were very well suited by allowing the French king to evict the ruling family of Naples. It was not until the invaders had had a week or so to explore the treasures of the city and thoroughly upset its people by their greed and rapacity, that Charles received the devastating news from the north. On March 31, 1495, an alliance had been signed in Venice between Spain, the emperor, the pope, the Venetians, and the Duke of Milan. Known in its own terminology as the League of Venice, its immediate intentions were all too apparent. The trap had sprung on Charles with a vengeance. He had the choice of trying to hold Naples in isolation from France, or of running the gauntlet of the coalition in order to reach home and safety. With more spirit than discretion, he decided to attempt both. Shipping off a large consignment of looted treasure by sea, Charles left half his army to defend his new possession and made a break for France, by land, with the other half. His treasure ships were seized by a Spanish and Italian fleet in the Ligurian Sea. Charles himself was challenged by an allied army on the bank of the Taro, between the Po and the Levante, but eventually managed to complete his retirement after a fierce action in which he fought with verve and desperation.

So much had been achieved at negligible expense to Ferdinand. There remained half the French army between the Spanish king and Naples, and Ferdinand knew just the man to deal with it cheaply and effectively. Charles had left Naples in May. That same month, a dapper and quietly authoritarian Castilian general landed with a modest following in Calabria, the southernmost region of Italy. Gonzalo Fernández de Córdoba, son of the Count of Aguila and already, at forty-two, a veteran of the Portuguese and Granada wars, was poised for the campaigns that would inspire historians to write of him as the first of Europe's "modern" generals. Both as a man and a military leader, he stood apart from the traditions of medieval soldiering. In person, he was composed and abstemious, displaying none of the cruelty and licentiousness so common to power in the era of chivalry. To the end of his life, he remained singularly devoted to his wife, María, and their daughter Elvira, his heir and the apple of his eye. Even when campaigning, he took his daughter with him. As a soldier, he was prudent and cerebral, opposed to the bravado which often passed for fine leadership among his contemporaries. Though immensely aggressive once committed to engagement, Gonzalo was careful to avoid fighting in conditions of tactical disadvantage.

Above all, he understood and exploited the nature of his men.

In the Spanish recruit, Gonzalo recognized the stubbornness and sobriety, the capacity to endure prolonged privation, that derived from a normal livelihood of the utmost frugality in grueling climatic contrasts. He recognized, too, the profound sense of superiority, that form of spiritual arrogance, which the Spanish soldier had inherited from the reconquest. It was fundamental to the general's achievement that he direct this potential to the greatest utility: the production of a superb long-range infantryman. To some extent, the development had been foreshadowed in Granada. In Italy Gonzalo defined the ideal.

His first steps were to rearm and reorganize the forces available to him. The lightly equipped soldiers who had fought effectively against Muslim skirmishers in the Andalusian highlands were no answer to the solid and heavily armored legions of France. Under Gonzalo (and, to a lesser extent, under the Generals Gonzalo de Ayora, who was also influenced by warfare in Italy, and Enríquez de Guzmán, who fought the French in the Pyrenees) Spanish troops began to take on the appearance so familiar to followers of sixteenth-century adventure. From their French and Swiss adversaries, they borrowed the pike and the concept of regular defensive armor for footmen. This included a light metal helmet with brim, a cuirass, gorget, and brassarts. Half the men in each infantry regiment, or *escuadrón*, were given long, double-handed pikes, a third swords and spears, and the remainder harquebuses. New battle formations were standardized. The front presented to an enemy was usually a bristling phalanx of pikes covered by harquebusiers and artillery, behind which lay the more agile swordsmen awaiting their chance to duck under the pikes and create confusion among the engaged ranks of the foe. So successful was this simple tactic that it soon became a classic Spanish maneuver. Cavalry, the omnipotent arm of medieval peninsula warfare, was now reduced gradually to a supporting role. The balance eventually achieved was an army substantial enough in armament to withstand onslaught by the best troops of Europe, yet sufficiently nimble to outmaneuver and outmarch them.

For the moment, however, there was one deficiency Gonzalo could do nothing to remedy: a deficiency of numbers. Determined to achieve his ends with the maximum economy, Ferdinand had provided the general with something less like an army in size than a raiding force. The plan was to augment it with Italian levies, but these scarcely met the exacting standards of the commander, and Gonzalo began his campaign in Calabria with a force of Spaniards less than half the size of the army left behind by Charles. The general's first battle in the toe of Italy was very nearly disastrous. Joining up with Ferrante of Naples, who had returned from exile in Ischia, he met a powerful French force near the small Calabrian town of Seminara. Ferrante's men fled before the iron ranks from the north, leaving Gonzalo to fight a desperate delaying action. The great coolness and tenacity with which he held off the French advance and, at length, withdrew his troops from danger, distinguished him even in defeat. With no great regret he watched Ferrante depart by ship to try his luck elsewhere, then, having reformed his small task force, started again.

This time there were no mistakes. In a brilliant and relentless march through southern Calabria, the general won outpost after outpost from a surprised and infuriated enemy. Carefully avoiding the head-on collision he could ill afford with his meager numbers (diminished further by the need to leave garrisons behind him), he concentrated on surprise tactics, nocturnal attacks and ambushes, whittling the French resistance piecemeal. Decisive and unruffled, an immaculate will-o-the-wisp at the head of his loping raiders, Gonzalo de Córdoba became a figure of fear among every enemy garrison south of the Gulf of Taranto. By the end of the year, his power was uncontested in lower Calabria. Only Ferdinand's continued austerity delayed further progress north. Reinforcements badly needed to compensate for garrison commitments arrived late and only at token strength, while funds were so short that Gonzalo remained at a standstill in the central Calabrian town of Nicastro until February 1496, unable to pay his small band of men. For all that, he had resumed his campaign in the Lucano hills before winter was out, mastering most of upper Calabria by spring.

In a devastating climax to his progress through Calabria, Gonzalo took the mountain pass via Morano to attack a key enemy stronghold at Laino, a town on the northeast border of the province. Laino, occupied by an impressive array of Frenchmen and Italo-Angevin lords, lay across the adjacent river Lao from a formidable fortress. Once inside the fort, the French and their allies could defy the Spaniards with impunity. Gonzalo did not intend that they should make it. In the Morano valley a horde of Calabrian levies with Angevin sympathies lay in ambush for his hard-marching column. Dividing his men to right and left, the general surrounded and destroyed the ambushers before pressing forward to his objective. He reached the town at dawn after an all-night march, quietly taking command of the bridge on the Lao while the locals were still asleep. The Spaniards then stormed the streets. Caught napping, the French and their allies did not stand a chance. Those who managed to get clear of their billets, rushing for the safety of the castle, found the intervening bridge in Spanish hands. Many fought bravely, but it was a battle between a confused defense and a cool and eminently collected attack. By the time the Spaniards had wiped the blood from their pikes, the commander of Laino was dead and no less than twenty Angevin barons stood among the prisoners. It was a demoralizing blow for the French in southern Italy. Gonzalo de Córdoba, the "Great Captain," as writers were beginning to call him, seemed invincible.

After Laino, he was left with less than three thousand Spaniards, but no soldiers were so respected in Italy. Linking forces with a now well-supported Ferrante to the north, Gonzalo continued to enhance his reputation until, by the end of summer, the remnants of the mighty army Charles VIII had led to Naples were straggling desperately homeward in the retiring footsteps of their master. It was a pathetic evacuation. "They made their way back through Italy," wrote a contemporary, "in a state of appalling destitution and suffering . . . a sad example of the caprice of fortune." Of the ten thousand or so men Charles had left behind on his withdrawal, only a few hundred ever saw their homelands again. Meanwhile, the interests of the members of the League of Venice had begun to diverge. It had served the wily Ferdinand's purpose. Thanks to the astuteness of his own diplomacy, and the military efficiency of Gonzalo, he had witnessed the humiliation of his French rival at a trifling expense. Only in one respect had the outcome denied him satisfaction. Naples had yet eluded his grasp. For, aided by popular disaffection for the French, Ferrante had re-established himself dramatically in his capital and was asserting his rights with vigor throughout the Campanian kingdom. Ferdinand's work was not finished in Italy.

Three years later, with subtle prompting, history appeared about to repeat itself. Charles of France had died in an accident, and, in November 1500, his successor, Louis XII, concluded an agreement with Spain. By summer of the following year, a French army of upward of twelve thousand was marching once more on Naples. Louis's intentions were clear. France was asserting her familiar ambitions in southern Italy. But, as usual, few knew just what Ferdinand was up to. In Rome, that listening post of European politics, a worried pope questioned the Spanish ambassador. The ambassador was as much in the dark as the next man. In Naples itself, where Ferrante had been succeeded by his uncle, a peaceful ruler named Frederic, fear was unbounded. Desperately, Frederic appealed to Ferdinand for Spanish help. Gonzalo was in Sicily ready to move. But Ferdinand held his orders. Finally, early in July, the French army crossed the Neapolitan border and advanced on the sunny capital amid a welter of lust and savagery. If Charles's occupation had done little for French repute, the behavior of Louis's army was by all accounts incorrigible. At one town, Capua, it completely ran riot, slaughtering several thousand citizens and wantonly assaulting their womenfolk. Almost simultaneously with the French crossing of the frontier, Ferdinand ordered Gonzalo into Calabria from Sicily. The secret was now out, for Ferdinand moved not to save Naples but as Louis's ally. They had agreed to share Frederic's kingdom between them.

It took Gonzalo, with rather less than five thousand men, no more than a month to occupy most of the territory assigned to the Spaniards—Calabria and Apulia—though a number of snags remained to ruffle the customary orderliness of his progress. For one thing, Ferdinand's financial economies led once more to arrears in the pay of the soldiers, finally proving critical to discipline. Led by a contingent of rugged Biscayans, strong-willed individualists from the Basque country, Gonzalo's penniless troops marched on his quarters in a grim mood. With at least one pike slanted purposefully at his chest, the "Great Captain" coolly detailed his own difficulties, assuring the men he was doing all he could to obtain funds. When a Biscayan spokesman loudly averred that it would prove more remunerative to send the general's daughter, Elvira, to a brothel, Gonzalo merely repeated his quiet assurance, prevailing in the end on the crowd to disperse. To ease the situation, he contrived to seize a friendly cargo ship in nearby waters, distributing the proceeds of its freight among his troops. "A general," he was quoted by a contemporary biographer, "must secure victory at all costs, right or wrong; this done, he can compensate those he has made suffer with ten-fold benefits." He was not thinking of loudmouthed insurgents. The morning after the scene of mutiny, the brothel-minded Biscayan was found outside his billet, hanging by the neck.

The Italian defense of Taranto, coinciding with these incidents, proved of considerable nuisance value to Gonzalo. Occupied, among others, by Frederic's son, the Duke of Calabria, the port resisted the general throughout the ensuing winter, capitulating only after the Spaniards had manhandled a number of ships across land from the sea to an inner basin, where they were able to threaten the most vulnerable quarter of the town. As a condition of the garrison's surrender, Gonzalo pledged on oath to allow the young Duke of Calabria and his suite to depart unmolested. Ferdinand, however, had other ideas. Shortly after the party had gone, orders arrived from the King of Aragon that the duke was to be detained and sent to Spain as a prisoner. It throws an interesting light on the soldierly reflexes of Gonzalo, a man of honor and good faith in most things, that he promptly sent after the duke and arrested him. It was not the last *volte-face* to be demanded of the general, for, with Machiavellian logic, Ferdinand was already preparing the final move of his strategy. With its king a prisoner in France, and his son held by Spain, Naples lay leaderless and submissive beneath the arms of those nations. Only his allies-in-occupation, the French, stood between Ferdinand and the crown of the whole Neapolitan kingdom.

Gonzalo, having once fought to expel the French from Naples, then joined them in the name of his sovereigns to retake it, was now expected to expel them for the last time. Even of Gonzalo, it was asking a lot. He had received no fresh troops since landing from Sicily; his small army was already spread thinly and provocatively beyond the boundaries agreed with Louis; he was destitute of funds, supplies, and equipment. To make matters worse, the reinforcements duly consigned to him by Ferdinand were intercepted in Calabria and overwhelmed in a shrewdly anticipatory move by the French. The latter, with getting on for eight thousand of their best troops and mercenaries in Naples, as well as those of the Angevin lords of the kingdom, were scarcely dismayed by the modest band of ill-supported Spaniards. Under the French commander, the Duke of Nemours, a young aristocrat from one of the loftiest houses of France, rode some of the most celebrated warriors of his nation, including the redoubtable Pierre de Bayard, the knight "*sans peur et sans reproche*" of legend. Louis himself, resolved not to be cheated of his gains by Ferdinand, crossed the Alps and established a headquarters at Asti, near Turin, the better to keep in touch with operations. Prospects can seldom have looked less hopeful for the "Great Captain." Indeed, it is indicative of the unenviable position of the Spanish force that Gonzalo, by habit an attacking general, drew off to Barletta, on the Adriatic, where, though still a menace to the French, he could at worst pull his troops out by sea.

With Gonzalo on the defensive, there followed a period of stalemate in which action reverted to the outmoded pattern of chivalrous challenges which still decorated the fringes of war. On September 20, 1502, the Italian population of Trani, near Barletta, turned out en masse to watch eleven French knights, among them the chevalier Bayard, engage the same number of Spaniards in formal combat. Though the champions, armed to the teeth and splendidly mounted and caparisoned, fought until dusk brought an end to the contest, neither side was judged to have won by the referees. More decisive was a duel between Bayard and a Spaniard named Alonso de Sotomayor. French chroniclers described it with relish. Sotomayor, a big man who claimed a grievance against the French champion, apparently had the choice of fighting mounted or on foot. Picking the latter alternative, he joined the Frenchman in the customary prayer, crossed himself and moved to grips. Each man carried sword and dagger and was heavily armored. Bayard, the lighter of the two and inferior in strength, depended on agility to avoid the powerful blows of the Spaniard. He moved, in the words of a Frenchman, "as lightly as if he would lead a fair lady to the dance." Doggedly, Sotomayor slashed at the metalled bantam, attempting by sheer strength to force him down, but Bayard, striking with more science, pierced the Spaniard's gorget to draw first blood. A moment later, Sotomayor was on him, bearing him to the ground in a ponderous bear's hug.

According to the story, the crowd waited for the Spaniard to end it. But Sotomayor lay still. Bayard's poniard had pierced his eye to the brain.

For Gonzalo, such amateur escapades held little satisfaction save that they gained him badly needed time. Within the strong walls of Barletta, he continued to wait impatiently for the sea-borne supplies and reinforcements without which he had no chance of mounting a decisive offensive. Outside, the Duke of Nemours, multiplumed and surrounded by glittering lieutenants, waited with equal impatience. At last, early in 1503, the duke challenged the Spanish general to settle matters once and for all in pitched battle. It was the imperious gesture of a materially stronger commander, and Gonzalo promptly taught him a lesson. Replying that he would fight when he was ready and not before, the "Grand Captain" allowed his snubbed enemies time to retire a few miles towards their various quarters then dispatched a flying column of cavalry and infantry to overhaul their tail companies. So completely was the French rear guard surprised that the Spaniards had overwhelmed it and returned to Barletta before Nemours himself discovered what had happened. It was a painful reminder of Gonzalo's reputation, and the young French commander cannot have been sorry to know that fresh troops were mustering for embarkation at Genoa to swell his forces in Naples. He was not, however, destined to receive them. At about the same time, Louis was entertaining a messenger of peace at Lyons. That messenger was Ferdinand's son-in-law, the Archduke Philip who, mindful of his wife's inheritance, had volunteered to arrange a settlement between the warring countries. The terms he put forward, and which were met with much rejoicing at the French court, seemed so favorable to France that Louis not only canceled the embarkation at Genoa but sent orders to Nemours to cease operations. The result was fatal for the French forces in Naples.

Having gained time for the provisioning and reinforcement of Barletta, Ferdinand refused to ratify the so-called treaty of Lyons. On April 28, a Friday, Gonzalo marched out of his stronghold at the head of a revivified army and headed across country toward Naples, by-passing a livid Nemours en route. Declining as usual to fight at a place of the enemy's choosing, the general had left the French army arrayed at Canosa, a small town on the south bank of the river Ofanto, crossing the stream with his own troops and forcing the pace to Cerignola, which lay some sixteen miles from Barletta. And, by mounting as many men as possible two to a horse, Gonzalo reached it in time to prepare his lines before the French could catch up. They found the Spanish army sited on a gentle slope covered with vineyards and protected by a deceptively innocent-looking ditch. On a hastily built rampart of earth stood Gonzalo's small train of artillery, thirteen guns strong. The evening sun glinted on metal-tipped pikes. Very shortly that sun would set, and, after some hesitation, Nemours decided on an immediate attack. Numbers were roughly equal at between six and seven thousand men a side, but behind the French commander rode the finest heavy cavalry in Italy, eager to prove itself against a predominantly pedestrian army. As the champing horses strained forward, a shattering explosion, followed by a dense pall of black smoke, announced that Gonzalo's artillery magazine had blown up. Elated by their luck, the French riders spurred in a cheering mass toward the ditch that covered the Spanish front. Only at the last minute did they discover the true nature of the obstacle. Excavated at some depth by Gonzalo's laboring footmen, its interior bristled with hastily, but all too effectively, sharpened stakes.

Loath to withdraw, Nemours wheeled his horsemen along the line of the barrier, irritably seeking somewhere to cross. Gonzalo would have considered it an elementary mistake. To the gratification of the Spanish harquebusiers, the pride of the French army was crossing their front at close range, its flank presenting a perfect target. Among the riders who fell to the forthcoming gunfire was Nemours himself, blasted from the saddle by the contents of three pieces, to die swiftly and grimly mutilated. By now, the French infantry, moving in behind the cavalry, was attempting to force the Spanish entrenchment. The troops stumbled and slid on the loose earth. Those who managed to scramble from the ditch met a steady line of pikes, and wavered. The commander urging them forward was dropped by a Spanish ball. Leaderless and peppered by gunfire, the attack degenerated into a confusion of milling horses and footmen. Clinically, Gonzalo unloosed his own cavalry from the wings, at the same time ordering an advance of his infantry. The ensuing rout of the French army resulted in appalling massacre. Their own writers put their losses at not less than three thousand (some, substantially higher), while nowhere were Spanish losses placed at more than a hundred. Even allowing for exaggeration, the victory was remarkable. The whole engagement was over within an hour. Among other spoils, Nemour's personal pavilion, set for a triumphant feast in the French encampment, was taken intact, providing a gratuitous banquet for its captors. Gonzalo could hardly have hoped to inflict a more thorough defeat. To complete his triumph, he heard next day that one of his lieutenants had routed the French in Calabria. Just over a fortnight later, on May 14, the Spanish general entered the city of Naples.

For the rest of the year, Louis of France tried desperately to reverse his ill fortune. Mounting a diversionary offensive against the Spanish in Cerdagne and Roussillon, he sent yet another army south through Italy in an attempt to retake his lost possessions in Naples. Gonzalo met it at the river Garigliano, to the north of the capital, where, after a campaign of several months, he put the new French force to flight in a decisive night attack. By the beginning of 1504, Louis was ready to recognize Spain as the lawful possessor of the whole Neapolitan theater. For Ferdinand, ten years of outstanding political dexterity had paid off. At a fraction of the cost incurred by France, the Spanish king had frustrated his rivals on all counts, and richly extended Spain's empire to boot. Not only Machiavelli would note his virtuosity. At fifty-two, a now bulging and heavy-jowled Ferdinand had added a new dimension to peninsula influence. No longer the back-door prodigy of Europe, Spain sat squarely at the top table of international politics.

Isabella's death, however, had exposed old weaknesses. With Castile's partner in the royal marriage gone, resentment of her Aragonese survivor became ripe for exploitation in Castilian circles. Joanna, heir and elder of Isabella's two surviving daughters, though duly proclaimed queen while absent in Flanders, had now become highly unstable in behavior and was in no condition to bear the responsibility of power. Her husband, on the other hand, was only too willing. For this moment the comely and ambitious Philip of Burgundy had suffered the scandals and torments of life with his Spanish wife. Extravagant and affable, born to the good things becoming the son of an emperor, the blond archduke relished the idea of a warm and splendid court in the south. Nevertheless, he was not precipitate in leaving Flanders. Theoretically, his position was strong, but only a fool would have ignored Ferdinand's reputation, and Philip was not prone to the delusions of his wife. Acutely conscious of the dangers implicit in tangling with so wily an operator as his father-in-law, the Habsburg heir took good care to prepare his descent on Spain with generous promises to the Castilian grandees and assurances of good will in other quarters of Europe. He even contacted Gonzalo de Córdoba in Naples in an attempt to win the "Great Captain" to his side.

Fate, in its premature call on Isabella, had plunged Ferdinand abruptly from triumph to crisis. His immediate action was to forestall French assistance to Philip by making things up with Louis. This time, the diplomatic somersault involved, among a number of less pressing undertakings, his marriage to the French king's niece, a volatile beauty of eighteen named Germaine de Foix. Though the wedding, celebrated in March 1506 at Dueñas in the heart of the Tierra de Campos, the great plain of Old Castile, pleased those who still wished a specific heir to the throne of Aragon, it produced a further spasm of anti-Ferdinand feeling in Isabella's country. It did not help that Dueñas, a pretty village on a small hill some eighteen miles north of Valladolid, had played a prominent part in the first meeting of the Catholic monarchs. "It seemed hard," wrote Martire, "that this wedding should take place so soon, and in Isabella's own kingdom of Castile . . . where she is still venerated as she was while living." But Ferdinand had no illusions on the score of popularity. Ill-equipped to beat the bush of Castilian sentiment, he had settled, doubtless shrewdly, for the bird in the hand.

Six weeks later, Philip and Joanna landed at La Coruña in the northwest corner of the peninsula. Though they had been refused permission to cross France, Philip had contrived to assemble a formidable guard of German infantry around him, which, to his delight, was soon joined by a force of several thousand Spaniards. The eagerness with which the Castilian nobility responded to the enticements and glamour of the young northern prince more than justified Ferdinand's forebodings. A year earlier, he had persuaded the Castilian Cortes to ratify him as regent in his daughter's absence. Now, a number of towns went so far as to obstruct his admittance. To make matters worse, Philip's advisers, frightened of the Catholic king's astute influence, refused all requests to let Ferdinand contact his daughter. At last, after a circuitous advance inland to avoid his father-in-law, Philip reluctantly agreed to a meeting with the rival camp.

The confrontation, at Puebla de Senabria, near the southeast boundary of Galicia, was fraught both with tension and humor. Convinced that the aging wizard of Aragon would try to pull a fast one on him, the archduke approached the rendezvous tucked cautiously behind the armed companies of his Castilian adherents. Around him bristled the spears of a heavy bodyguard. Many of the Spanish nobles wore mail beneath their costumes as a precaution against surprise attack. To the front of them ranged three thousand Germans in full fighting order; to the rear, bowmen and a host of light cavalry. Surrounded by upwards of ten thousand men, Philip prepared for the worst. To his immediate relief, but subsequent embarrassment, Ferdinand appeared in a casual black cloak and soft hat accompanied by a few score supporters on mules. Sheepishly, the deflated lords of Philip's party were presented to the king and paid their respects. Ferdinand received them blandly, a quick word and a smile for those he knew best. Loyal accounts of the incident told with malicious glee how, observing the warlike turnout of a particularly vain Castilian noble, the Duke of Najara, Ferdinand exclaimed sardonically, "Still as conscientious as ever, I see!" Then, embracing his former minister in Rome, Garcilaso de la Vega, and feeling the armor under his dress: "Well done, Garcilaso! You've improved your physique since last we met."

The negotiations which followed dispelled Philip's apprehensions. In the first of two treaties signed at the meeting, Ferdinand unequivocally promised to withdraw to Aragon and leave the government of Castile to his "beloved children." The second, seemingly underlining Philip's victory, deprived Joanna of power on grounds of "her infirmities and sufferings," leaving no room to doubt which of the "children" intended to do the governing. Complacently, Philip signed and relaxed. He should have known his father-in-law better. The ink was barely dry on the documents before Ferdinand had pronounced them invalid, declaring that his part had been forced on him under duress. Too late, Philip must have cursed his ostentatious show of strength at the encounter. Never, added Ferdinand, would he agree "that his daughter should be deprived of her liberty or rights as hereditary proprietress of this kingdom." Thus, having deftly stigmatized his son-in-law as the usurper of Isabella's realm and the jailer of her daughter, the King of Aragon hastily retired and left time and Castile to do the rest. The outcome was unexpectedly dramatic. Within a few weeks, Philip lay dead at Burgos. Contemporary physicians proclaimed natural causes; others have considered the verdict problematic.

The event had a tragic effect on Joanna. While hitherto deplorably eccentric, she now lost interest in life altogether, venturing from a darkened apartment only to gaze morbidly on the decomposing remains of her husband, whose coffin she insisted on opening for the purpose. It remained for a stunned Castilian aristocracy to repent its brief Habsburg honeymoon, and for Ferdinand to be confirmed administrator in his daughter's name. The king's victory was complete, yet not without an understandable residue of bitterness. The affair served markedly to heighten his distrust of his late wife's subjects. In the popularity of Gonzalo, whom he consigned to retirement from Naples, Ferdinand now found grounds for suspicion and jealousy. For the tireless Jiménez he conceived an even greater antipathy. In the zealous cardinal he saw a continuation of Isabella's most fanatical and domineering attributes, offset by none of her saving graces. If Ferdinand were devious, deceptive, and ruthless in conducting the affairs of his office, he had often shown a degree of worldly tolerance toward the affairs of others that had been notably lacking in his first wife. He had, for instance, never matched her enthusiasm for the Inquisition, while Aragon alone of the peninsula authorities had yet to order the expulsion of its Muslims. For Ferdinand, the struggle to maintain Spain's new position in international politics was a matter of wit and discretion. He wanted none of the cardinal's crusading projects to upset the balance.

It was with considerable reservations, therefore, that he gave his blessing in 1509 to a Jiménez-inspired attack of unprecedented strength in North Africa. For some years, the Kingdom of Fez, immediately across the strait, had been assigned by treaty to

Portugal. Spain held Melilla, and, in 1505, thanks largely to the energy and determination of the cardinal, had captured Mers-el-Kebir, to the east. The advantage of holding the North African ports as a first line of defense against renewed Moorish invasion and Barbary pirates was obvious, but Jiménez had greater ambitions than that. Isabella's will had begged her successors "that they will devote themselves unremittingly to the conquest of Africa and the war of faith against the Moors." Fired with religious ardor, her cardinal dreamed of a Christian empire extending south to the Sahara. Ferdinand, on the other hand, preferred to leave the North African hinterland to its own metaphysical devices. With his resources already stretched to their limits, a full-scale crusade in Africa struck him as potentially ruinous to the whole edifice of the new Spanish Empire. Accordingly, he had not only delayed the cardinal's projected expedition until his own immediate problems in Europe were settled, but he had taken good care to ensure that his own ends were served by it.

For one thing, he had refused Jiménez the services of Gonzalo de Córdoba, appointing instead Pedro Navarro as the military commander. While Navarro, a subordinate to Gonzalo in the Italian wars, was a resourceful soldier, he was also a trusty pawn of the king in his scheme to restrain Jiménez. For another thing, the cardinal had been obliged to provide a substantial sum toward the cost of the expedition, thus unwittingly subsidizing a venture no longer his own but Ferdinand's. On May 16, 1509, with the seventy-three-year-old primate bravely on board, an army of upwards of fourteen thousand embarked in a great armada of warships for North Africa accompanied by a shoal of transports. The greater part of the force was put ashore at Mers-el-Kebir, a short march from its primary objective, Oran. Mounted on a mule, and preceded by the archiepiscopal cross of Toledo, Jiménez spared no eloquence to spur the troops for battle. Alternately preaching hatred of the Muslims and dwelling lavishly on the rich spoils ahead, he commended the awed pikemen to the cause of the faithful and avowed his own readiness to die in the struggle for Africa. By all accounts, his harangue ranks among the great battle speeches of history and, though the men themselves dissuaded the fiery but somewhat infirm orator from actually joining the impending action, there is little doubt that his inspiration dominated its outcome.

Warned by watch beacons of the threat to their great seaport, the Moors had lined the high ground between Mers-el-Kebir and Oran in large numbers, and the uphill advance was an unnerving maneuver for the Spaniards. Helped by a screening evening mist, however, the close ranks of infantry survived a flurry of Moorish missiles and charges to reach the summit in time to see the Kasbah and minarets of the city, the pride of the sultans of Tlemcen, aglow in the dying sun. For a while, the Moors continued to dispute the advance until the steady pikes of the Spaniards, together with a battery of cannon which Navarro had brought to bear from a flank, induced them to seek the safety of their walls. Meanwhile, the Spanish fleet was covering the landing of a smaller assault force by engaging the Moorish coastal artillery with cannon fire. Taking advantage of the momentary confusion of the defenders, the leading Spanish detachments rushed the fortifications and, thrusting their pikeheads into cracks between the stones, scrambled rapidly onto the ramparts. Jubilantly, their approaching compatriots watched the primate's standard unfurled on the battlements before the scaling party, hacking its way to the gate, threw the city open to the invaders. Inflamed by victory and the cardinal's fervor, the troops ran amuck. By morning, a third of the population of Oran, irrespective of age or sex, had been massacred and weary Spaniards, their arms full of loot, stumbled through streets made grotesque by the dead.

Discipline resumed and the city cleaned up, Jiménez was escorted in and presented with the keys of the alcázar, from whose dungeons a large party of captive Christians was liberated. For a start, Jiménez claimed rights in Oran for the see of Toledo by way of compensation for the financial aid he had already provided (and in accordance with an earlier understanding with Ferdinand), then urged the march inland on Tlemcen. But the cardinal's usefulness was over. Now Navarro showed his true colors. Scorning the see of Toledo, the military commander proclaimed Oran for the crown, suggested that Jiménez should rest on his laurels, and made it clear that his (Navarro's) commission under the primate had terminated with the city's capture. If this were not enough to disabuse the tough old man, his followers intercepted a letter from

Ferdinand to Navarro urging that the cardinal should be delayed abroad on some pretext, as his presence was not greatly desired in Spain. Within a week of landing at Mers-el-Kebir, Jiménez re-embarked in disgust for his homeland, where, disdaining an audience with Ferdinand, he proceeded to his favorite seat at Alcalá accompanied by a small train of camels and slaves bearing Muslim treasures. For the rest of the reign, he haggled unsuccessfully for the rights to Oran.

Ferdinand had yet to complete his strategic triumphs. While Navarro pursued their intended policy of taming the Mediterranean ports of Africa (taking Algiers, Ténès, Dellys, then Tripoli), the king added yet another twist to his relationship with Louis by joining the Holy League, an alliance of European powers formed under Pope Julius II in 1510 with the intention of ejecting the French from northern Italy. With France fighting desperately to retain the one link she still held in the chain of rivalry that otherwise surrounded her borders, Ferdinand exploited Louis's preoccupation to achieve the culminating conquest of his career. In the western Pyrenees, a vital gateway between Spain and France, the small kingdom of Navarre had clung perilously to her independence through the first decade of the sixteenth century by playing her bigger neighbors against each other. Sooner or later she was bound to fall to one side, and Ferdinand had long determined to have her. In the summer of 1512, the Spanish king acted. Having talked Henry VIII of England, now his son by marriage to Katherine of Aragon, into menacing the adjacent region of Guyenne, thus further diverting the French command, Ferdinand pushed an army of seventeen thousand into Navarre from Castile. Hardly had the Navarrese recovered from the first shock, when a further Spanish force marched in from Aragon. The invasion, dubiously legalized by the pope on the grounds that the Navarrese were heretics and schismatics, was a pushover. It was said that the normally undemonstrative Ferdinand wept with joy at news of its success. The last chink in Spain's national armor was covered. It was a fitting conclusion to a reign of extraordinary strategic enterprise, and at sixty Ferdinand gave it a rest.

Of the famed adversaries he had outwitted, few were still alive. Louis XII of France, one of the last, and perhaps the most long-suffering, died in 1514, having seen his forces expelled from Milan.

Next year, Spain lost her venerated Gonzalo de Córdoba, the "Great Captain." Weakened by quartan fever, he died peacefully at Granada in the arms of his wife and his daughter, Elvira, without a single battle-scar on his body. By this time, Ferdinand, despairing of an heir by the lively Germaine, had taken to medicines to boost his virility. If anything, they seem to have had the opposite effect. In autumn 1515, suffering from a bad heart and respiratory trouble, he set out for the warmth of Andalusia. He never made it. On reaching the village of Madrigalejo, near Trujillo in Estremadura, he became too ill to move further. At last, all the astuteness in the world was no use to him. Nothing could now alter the fact that his eldest grandchild, Charles of Flanders, son of Joanna and the hated Philip, was next in line for Castile. With Aragon heirless, the king reconciled himself to the ironic prospect that the first monarch to rule a united Spain in his own right should be a foreigner. Equally inescapable was the realization that the only feasible choice of regent meanwhile was Jiménez. Thus resigned, Ferdinand passed from the world in the early hours of the morning of January 23, 1516, sixty-four years after he had entered it.

With a foresight the king himself might have respected, many of his courtiers abstained from following the cortege for fear of stepping off on the wrong foot with his successors. Ferdinand's remains were placed beside those of Isabella in the Alhambra, both being removed soon afterward to a specially built chapel (the Capilla Real, or Chapel of Kings) beside the present cathedral of Granada, where Domenico Fancelli of Florence sculpted their effigies in white marble. Between them, Isabella and Ferdinand had taken a Spain ravaged with dissent and futility and led it to the threshold of undreamed opportunity. To the rich potential of her national resources and skills, they had contributed stable administration, progressive academic development, and an unprecedented complex of territorial security. To the north, the Pyrenees, once feared for their paths of invasion, had been turned into a formidable barrier of defense. To the east, command of Naples as well as Sicily and the Balearics had provided new depths of assurance. In the south, the Christianization of Granada and the establishment of coastal bastions in North Africa had diminished the old threat from Islam. To the west, a friendly Portugal, as Spain herself, was preoccupied with transoceanic exploration, and, here

again, the sovereigns had secured unrivaled prospects in the New
World. Above all, they had engendered the concept of unity. At
last Spain had perfected a formula to synthesize the collective
drives of her long and anguished evolution. The result was a sense
of common destiny, a national soul, a race of men that felt equal
to all things. Ahead lay the era generally regarded as Spain's golden
age.

Part 2

THE AGE OF PRESUMPTION

"To God, I speak Spanish . . ."
The Emperor Charles V

Chapter 5

THE CONQUISTADORS

Charles I of Spain, son of Joanna and Philip, and grandson of Ferdinand, had a notoriously plain face, but in many ways an appealing character. He was amused by jesters, in whose ranks his large Punch-like lower jaw was not out of place, and could display a self-deprecating sense of humor. He once declared that since artists often exaggerated his ugliness, people meeting him in person tended to be agreeably disappointed. Charles adored children, animals, and flowers, was knowledgeable about music, and liked fine painting, especially the work of Titian. Though inclined to self-righteousness and obstinacy, he was an adaptable as well as purposeful administrator, eschewing favorites, getting the best from his ministers and less ready than some of his contemporaries to accept that ends justified the worst possible means. As a military leader, he had a high reputation. Though frightened of mice and spiders, and sometimes gripped by fits of nervous trembling, his behavior amid danger and crisis was exemplary. He possessed that pure form of courage which transcends a naturally timid disposition. In all, Charles—the first person to be crowned king of both Castile and Aragon, thus making the union at last a legal fact—might have been as great a boon to Spain as his maternal grandparents. Unfortunately, his talents were diverted almost from the start.

Born at Ghent, 1500, and brought up in Flanders, Charles did not arrive in Spain until nearly two years after Ferdinand's death, during which time the country was held for him by Jiménez. But Jiménez died a few weeks later in his eighty-second year, and the king was left surrounded by Flemish advisers. He had made only the briefest acquaintance with his new realm when another death, this time of his paternal grandfather, the Emperor Maximilian, pitched him straight back into northern affairs. To the discomfort of Spain, not to mention his rivals for the imperial crown, Francis I of France and Henry VIII of England, Charles not only contested the succession but duly won it. Suddenly, as the Emperor Charles V, the young Fleming possessed the greatest empire in Christendom. To some ten million subjects in Spain, plus populations in Italy, North Africa and the Indies, were added countless millions in Germany, Austria, the Netherlands and the French Comté. Among such responsibilities, Spain could expect no more than the divided attention of her monarch. The long and demanding reign of the new Habsburg colossus was to belong less to Spanish than European history.

Resentful at first, Spain gradually grew accustomed to the absences of her king and the constant demands on her resources as he toiled to secure his mammoth holdings. Indeed, long before his reign of thirty-nine years was over, the Spanish people had come to be identified closely with his cause throughout Europe. For his own part, Charles, who had arrived a foreigner unable even to understand the Castilian language, learned to regard his peninsula dominion with new eyes, to accept many of her ideals and concepts and, in the end, to find in her a haven from a thankless and overbearing world. In the foreign service of the emperor, Spanish arms added new brilliance and glory to the prestige they had established under Gonzalo de Córdoba. In Italy and the west, the main enemy was France, whose king waged bitter wars of rivalry on Charles. At the battle of Pavia (1525) a resounding triumph for the emperor, Spanish troops contributed substantially to the victory, carrying Francis himself to Madrid as their prisoner. To the east, they followed Charles in wars against the Turks, who threatened Vienna and the ports of North Africa. In a memorable assault on Tunis (1535), the haunt of the powerful Turkish pirate Barbarossa, their mettle matched that of the emperor, who led them in person. Against the greatest of all threats to imperial stability, however, it was already too late for armed force to prevail. To the fatal detriment of Charles's ambitions, his accession to the German throne had coincided with the rise to prominence of a contumacious Augustinian monk, Martin Luther. Luther, exploding an ideological bombshell at the very feet of the new emperor, triggered that chain of repercussions known as the Reformation, from which the empire never recovered.

The Reformation was the result of lingering and widespread dissatisfaction with conduct at Rome and throughout broad sections of the clergy. Preaching to an audience already sickened by the blatant materialism that riddled its church, Luther picked the cynical sale of indulgences by Catholic priests as his principal target, combining with his attack theological views of his own unacceptable to Rome. For these views, the pope formally condemned him in 1520. Much of Germany, on the other hand, came out on Luther's side. For Charles, the implications were enormous. While Luther's protest was not directly political, religious authority and imperialism were too closely intertwined for defiance of one to be ignored by the other. From the beginning, Lutheranism, or Protestantism, as it came to be termed, held a strong political appeal for Germany's anti-imperial elements. At the Diet of Worms in 1521, Charles tried to temporize in the matter, but Luther's zeal was implacable and Spanish troops were soon being called to fight rebellion in Germany. For years the issue remained unresolved. Threatened now by France and now by the Turks, Charles was forced repeatedly to compromise with the religious problem in order to keep the empire intact. Meanwhile, Protestantism gathered force in other parts of Europe. In Geneva, and later Holland and Scotland, it took the form of Calvinism, after the French preacher John Calvin; in many parts of the Netherlands it gave rise to Anabaptism; in England, where Henry VIII broke with Rome to form his own national church, the new ideology was soon winning converts; in Scandinavia the King of Sweden and his court endorsed it. In France, Lutheranism was seized as a royal weapon against an old rival, French might being thrown in on the side of the Protestants when Charles, all attempts to promote a doctrinal rapprochement failing, was forced eventually into a showdown. In the end, neither the Catholic troops of Spain nor those of the pope could prevent the empire, indeed Christendom, from splitting. At the battle of Innsbruck, 1552, Charles was decisively beaten by the Protestant forces. Three years later, the Diet of Augsburg conceded the equality of both religious persuasions.

Through all this, Spain remained spiritually untrammeled. After all, on the score of moral reform, Jiménez had anticipated Luther by many years without raising any problems of doctrine. As far as heresy was concerned, the Inquisition, excelling amid the general religious intolerance which swept Europe at the time, was as capable of dealing with Protestants as with others. Not that there were many in the peninsula. The vast body of Spaniards was too profoundly Catholic to be other than confirmed in its creed by the troubles in Germany and elsewhere. Born in defense of the faith against the south, the modern Spaniard was quite prepared to turn his spiritual passion on the north. Spain, as orthodox as Rome itself and frequently more fervent, was the natural hothouse for a new Catholic offensive in the battle of ideas waging outside her borders. No one better personified the Spanish lead in this urge to reaffirmation than a Basque soldier named Iñigo López de Loyola, once a page at the court of Isabella and Ferdinand. Renouncing his sword for an intellectual and spiritual armory, Loyola founded in 1539 the Society of Jesus, to become famous as the nonviolent commando of the counter-reformation.

At the same time, a less aesthetic offensive was well under way in the west. While Charles and his imperial armies struggled to hold an old empire together, an Homeric band of Spanish adventurers was carving a new one from uncharted expanses in America. At the accession of Charles, Spanish settlements on the American mainland had been few and little developed. For a while after the death of Columbus, initiative in the Indies had faltered. Various islands had been explored and culled for slaves, while the admiral's fellow campaigners Ojeda and Juan de la Cosa had made superficial contact with the Venezuelan coast. For the most part, however, interest concentrated on the original base, Haiti, or Española, as the whole island was known, where the survivors of the early expeditions got down to some serious colonization. Planting, especially sugar cane, flourished, as did pig rearing, and Negro slaves from Africa were imported as a labor force. Unlike the indigenous population, which, failing to adapt to the impositions of its conquerors, rapidly perished, the resilient Negro survived. As the seat of the viceroy and home of administrators and planters, Española soon evolved a relatively secure society. The arrival of a number of Castilian ladies, wives and attendants of the governing officials, added an aura of decorum and culture.

By the end of the first decade of the century, the more restless and adventurous element had departed to try its luck in the larger of the neighboring islands. Puerto Rico was entered in 1508, and Jamaica a year later. After the pacification of the local tribes, towns were founded and the natives divided among the settlers in a manner approximating to the fiefs of feudal Europe, such divisions being known in general as *repartimientos*, or allotments. Though the Spanish crown, in the persons of Isabella and Ferdinand, and later Charles, was insistent that the unfortunate serfs should be treated and worked with moderation, such sentiments were too remote, the needs of the Indian too little appreciated, to allay the pattern of depopulation. As the natives disappeared, more Negro slaves were imported; in turn, the *repartimientos* system faded. Meanwhile, Cuba, the largest and most westerly of the Caribbean islands, was claimed in a succession of expeditions, for the most part under another old companion of Columbus, Diego Velásquez, who came to govern the island. From Cuba, the Spaniards turned seriously to the business of exploring and colonizing the mainland.

To this end, licences were granted in 1509 to two men: Ojeda, who was assigned rights on the north coast of what is now Colombia, and a courtier named Diego de Nicuesa, whose field embraced roughly the Caribbean shores of Panama, Costa Rica, and Nicaragua. The dangers and discomforts before them were intense. Of Nicuesa's original force of seven hundred men, only forty survived the ensuing expedition in his company. "Emaciated through hunger, filthy and awful to behold," Nicuesa was charged after rescue with abusing authority, cast afloat in a decrepit ship with few provisions, and was never seen again. Ojeda fared little better. Sailing with three hundred men, including the navigator La Cosa, he had lost all but sixty of his followers when the chance appearance of a lone pirate ship near the Gulf of Urabá, where he was stranded, enabled him to reach Española before dying. The bulk of his party had succumbed to starvation or the poisoned arrows of the natives they encountered, including La Cosa, who died raving from poison. In an attempt to relieve the small and desperate band of survivors left behind on the Colombian coast, a lawyer named Enciso now sailed from Española with provisions and fresh men. On board was a stowaway, a man named Balboa, who had hidden in a barrel to escape his creditors on the island. Unfortunately, by the time Enciso had contacted the despairing residue of Ojeda's force, the rescuers themselves were in no state to help. To make matters worse, the well-meaning lawyer was lacking in the rugged qualities of leadership vital to survival.

Instead, circumstances threw up a natural leader in the person of the bankrupt stowaway. A tough, resourceful man in his thirties, Vasco Núñez de Balboa utilized a vague knowledge of the coast acquired in an earlier reconnaissance to lead the party to a more hospitable point to the west, known as Darién. Here a settlement was founded of which Balboa, by general consent, became commander. For some time, the Spaniards explored the Central American isthmus, subordinating the tribes of the Caribbean coast by the diplomatic cultivation of native allies who, in return for assistance in their tribal battles, helped Balboa in his conquests. In one case, he accepted the daughter of a chief as his wife, inducing his new father-in-law to accept baptism and a Spanish name. In reports to Spain, the commander of Darién pointedly contrasted his humane attitude toward the Indians with the cruelties of other captains. Yet, if the contrast were valid, he was certainly no angel of mercy. Boasting that he had learned secrets of "gold and wealth with which a great part of the world can be conquered," he went on to describe his methods as "putting some to torture . . . treating some with love."

It was among Indians of a friendly tribe that Balboa first heard of a hitherto unsuspected sea, bounded by a fabulous province of gold, in the south. Following the directions of his native guides, he set out to find it, leading a company of some 190 Spaniards across the narrowest part of the isthmus. On September 25, 1513, having overcome jungle, swamps, and hostile tribes on his path, Balboa reached an eminence from which could be seen the silver sheen of the Gulf of Panama. By sighting the Pacific, the former desperado and bankrupt had not only established the greatest landmark in Spanish discovery since the first voyage of Columbus, he had simultaneously confounded the dearest of the admiral's theories. Gone forever was the chimera of an oriental landfall to the Atlantic. There was, after all, another ocean between the Spanish Main and the Asiatic continent. With the sublime confidence of the true conquistador, Balboa waded chest-deep into the water brandishing his sword and called witnesses that he took possession of the south sea in the name of Castile and its monarchs.

In Spain, news of the discovery, combined with evidence in the shape of pearls and gold from the gulf, provoked a fresh emigration rush. Indeed, so many volunteered to join Balboa that the crown had to limit the number to fifteen hundred, while the historian Oviedo, who sailed with the expedition, wrote of its brilliance in terms matching the second sailing of Columbus. People traveled in their finest silks and brocades as if bound for the courts of Lisbon or Venice. Balboa, it was fondly expected, would receive them splendidly amid the gala trappings of colonial wealth and stateliness. It was a rude shock to find him stripped to the waist like an Indian, helping to thatch a house on a rough-and-ready pioneer settlement. Within a short while of reaching Darién, more than a third of the newcomers had expired from malnutrition or sickness. Among those of tougher stuff was a veteran captain named Pedro Arias de Avila, otherwise Pedrarias. Pedrarias had been sent out to take over the administration of Darién for, though the king was pleased to appoint Balboa admiral of the south sea, the lawyer Enciso had turned up in Spain with some jealous tales of the stowaway who had usurped his leadership, and it was thought wise to put a proven trusty in charge of the settlement.

In many ways, Pedrarias set the tone of cruelty that was to characterize the exploration and conquest of the south. Colonial life seems to have brought out the worst in his nature, and Balboa was soon protesting against the indiscriminate oppression of the Indians under the new regime. For a few years the two men coexisted on edgy terms, then, on the verge of setting out to navigate the sea he had discovered, Balboa was arrested on the orders of Pedrarias, tried on a nebulous charge of planning treason, and beheaded. The man who arrested him was an ambitious ruffian named Francisco Pizarro; the judge who sentenced him, one Gaspar de Espinosa. Each was to acquire notoriety of a greater order in due course. As for Pedrarias, sixteen years of vicious government in the Indies earned him the nickname Old Fury. By the time he died in 1531, having founded Panama and supervised the penetration of Nicaragua and Honduras, humane opinion in Spain held him responsible for a history of murder and slavery as inexcusable as it was unsavory.

Among other reactions to the tyranny of Pedrarias, and the hell of Darién, was the decision of a small body of men from the settlement to seize a ship and sail in search of better lands. Their enterprise, gaining the aid of Velásquez of Cuba, cast them in the year of Charles's arrival in Spain upon the shores of the broad, flat promontory of Yucatán. What they found there was to quicken the imagination of all Europe. For instead of the customary naked Indians of the new lands, Yucatán revealed people in brightly colored cotton clothes, cultivating corn fields, worshiping elaborately conceived gods, and possessing cities of towering masonry so marvelous to Spanish eyes that the visitors named the first they encountered Great Cairo. They were on the fringe of a civilization whose calendar dated from 3000 B.C. and of which the Christian world had never heard.

The golden age of the Maya had spanned from the fourth to tenth centuries, A.D. Centered in the south of the Yucatán peninsula and spreading to Chiapas, Guatemala and parts of Honduras, the old empire had represented the most brilliant pre-Columbian civilization in America. Its city states, politically independent and based on the flourishing production of corn, encouraged such intellectual activities as writing, mathematics, architecture, astronomy, chronology, sculpture, and painting, often marked by notable perception and grace. While the abundance of corn around the cities lasted, the Mayan people had pursued their lively and creative culture under a free-and-easy system of government. But the time came when the soil, exhausted by erosion and lack of replenishment, failed to meet the needs of the society. From the tenth century, a harsher economy, attended by intensified competition and civil wars, led to a deterioration of Mayan life. By the arrival of the Spaniards, it had lost its intellectual momentum, the cities were depopulated, their communities fragmented and leading a more rustic existence.

In the early thirteenth century, a band of migrants from the northern continent, moving south toward the regions of the Mayas, had settled on the islands of Lake Texcoco, Mexico, in the mountain valley of Anáhuac. According to legend, these people, the Aztecs, had found the little carved idol of a god on their travels, and taken it as their own. Inspired by the god, Huitzilopochtli, and their own questing energy, the Aztecs soon dominated the established powers of their adopted land, pushing south and east in two centuries of imperial expansion until they lapped the borders of the old Mayan Empire. Unlike the declining Mayas, their Aztec neighbors were a dynamic force when the Spanish first landed in Yucatán. Less imaginative than the Mayas in their heyday, the more aggressive and doctrinaire Aztecs surpassed them in state organization. Life was meticulously ordered from the cradle to the grave. Child education and discipline were rigorous. Boys were trained as soldiers, priests, or laborers; girls carefully indoctrinated in marital and domestic duties. Unswerving respect and obedience were demanded by a supreme council of divisional representatives whose elected leader, or emperor, assumed ultimate authority on all matters, religious or secular. Deities were lavishly propitiated with sacrificial victims, usually in the persons of captured enemies.

By the reign of their fifteenth-century emperor Moctezuma I, Aztec armies had fought victoriously on all sides, and, in 1487, the guiding spirit of Huitzilopochtli had been memorably recognized by the deification of a great temple in the lake capital of Tenochtitlán (now a site in Mexico City), where thousands of prisoners from the south were ritually sacrificed. In 1502, Moctezuma II succeeded to the throne of the Aztec Empire. He was a lightly built young man of walnut complexion with shoulder-length black hair, a skimpy beard and a grave but not entirely humorless countenance. "He spoke well and wittily when there was occasion for it, yet prudently," wrote Cervantes de Salazar, a Spaniard who later knew him. "Towards his own people, he maintained a lofty majesty. With the exception of a few great lords of royal blood, he allowed no one to gaze upon his face, or to wear shoes or sit down in his presence. He was smart in appearance and richly dressed, scrupulously clean (taking two baths a day), seldom left his chamber other than to eat, received few visitors and conducted the bulk of his business through the members of his council. Even they contacted him through intermediaries. For the sacrifices at the temple of Huitzilopochtli, where he displayed great devotion, he made his way through his own quarters, remaining at some distance from the rest of the hierarchy, and returning downcast, deep in thought, speaking to no one."

Religiosity was to be the downfall of Moctezuma, and through him the state, for, while invested with over-all powers of decision, he seems to have been unduly impressed by the more mystical element in his following, prophets of the priesthood whose authority was well served by encouraging fear and superstition. Thus, when news first reached him that strange people had landed among the Mayas with unheard-of animals and fire-breathing weapons, he withheld from alerting his generals, relying instead on the advice of men who sought portents in the stars and the twittering of birds. They are said to have informed him that the strangers were disciples of Quetzalcoatl, the Feathered Serpent, god of learning and god of the wind.

Hernando Cortes, leader of the Spanish invasion of Mexico, was substantially mortal and scarcely the personification of scholarship. The son of a former infantry captain and a mother of noble connections, Cortes had spent his childhood at Medellín, a small town on the Guadiana in Estremadura, before being sent to Salamanca University at fourteen. Two years were more than enough to convince him he was not cut out for an academic life, and at sixteen he was back in Medellín, a wild, headstrong youth, rowdy and troublesome with girls. Determined now on a career of action and adventure, he spent some time trying to join Gonzalo's forces in Italy, but, failing to get a passage east, turned about and set his sights on the Indies, obtaining a berth in 1504. The more mature for having sown his wild oats early, Cortes soon made a name as a promising junior to Velásquez and, despite one or two scandals with the ladies of Cuba, was eventually appointed alcalde, or mayor, of the settlement at Santiago. In 1519, preliminary reconnaissance in Yucatán having suggested immense riches for the taking in Mexico, Velásquez named Cortes to raise an expedition.

At thirty-two, the commander designate had a somewhat delicate face and ashen complexion, contrasting with broad shoulders and a muscular, barrel-chested frame. To a confident faith in his own capabilities, he brought the power to instill that faith in others, plus a reputation for cool, decisive thinking and stubborn independence. It was apparently the latter quality which caused Velásquez, on reflection, to change his mind about the appointment. Characteristically, however, Cortes had sailed before the aging governor got around to naming a more compliant commander. Since Hernando Cortes is perhaps the outstanding example of the conquistador, the conqueror, in the history of Latin America—certainly, the best known—he provides a valuable study in the psychology of the species. Acquisitive of treasure, domain, and power, he believed devoutly at the same time in his evangelical mission. A law unto himself once free of Cuba and Velásquez, recognizing no earthly master save Charles the emperor, he saw God as his one great and indispensable ally. In the first of a number of rules Cortes laid down for his followers, he made it clear that in destroying idolatry and bringing Christianity to the Indians, "we shall not only be winning eternal glory for our souls but also ensuring the assistance of God in our worldly endeavours." Cortes was taking no risk of offending his ally. "Since God is much displeased by swearing and blasphemy," he added, "I command that nobody of any rank shall dare to say 'I don't believe in God,' or 'Damn it,' or 'God has no power.' The same goes for Our Lady and all the saints." A vital difference between Cortes and Moctezuma, as it turned out, was that while the Aztec declined to presume the favor of his gods, the Spaniard had no doubt that his own was fundamentally on the right side.

The first call of the little armada—eleven ships, five hundred and fifty men and sixteen precious horses—was on the island of Cozumel, off the north of Yucatán. Here Cortes came across two Spaniards, stranded from earlier voyages, who had been living with the natives. One of these, a sailor from Palos named Guerro, was happily settled with three young sons and their Indian mother, and had no wish to join the expedition. The other, Aguilar, having narrowly escaped being sacrificed at a tribal feast, was pleased to rejoin his countrymen. Since he had acquired a fair knowledge of the Mayan language, he was a considerable asset to Cortes. Before moving on, the commander engaged in an earnest dissertation with a black-robed Indian priest who was haranguing the Spaniards from a nearby temple. Cortes answered with a long exposition of the Creation, the authority granted St. Peter and his successors, and the pope's allocation of the Indies to the Castilian sovereigns. This formula, a standard opening gambit of the conquistadors on first meeting Indians, was known as the requisition, the *requerimiento*. Rendered doubly meaningless to its audience by rudimentary interpretation, the ceremony gradually became a mockery to its performers. Cortes, however, never lost heart, and the bizarre discourse was repeated countless times in his conquests.

From Yucatán, Cortes sailed on to Tabasco, in the Gulf of Campeche, where a landing led to the expedition's first skirmish with the natives. Jealous of intrusion, the Tabascans turned out in some force to oppose the invaders. Their warriors, armed with bows, spears and lances, wore feathered headdresses and quilted jackets thick enough to turn an arrow. But they were no match for Spanish guns and cannons, which, like the horses, amazed them. "I remember," recalled one member of the expedition, "that when we fired the field-pieces the Indians yelled and whistled noisily, throwing up dust and grass to prevent our seeing the damage inflicted . . . so absorbed were they that they failed to notice our horsemen coming in from their rear. The ground was flat, the horses fast, the riders skilled. They lanced at pleasure. Never having seen horses before, the Indians thought rider and mount were one body. After routing them . . . we fell out under a group of trees and gave thanks to God and His Blessed Mother." Eight horses and five riders were wounded in the fight, together with several dozen Spanish footmen. Dead Indians were everywhere, and the Spaniards cut some open to obtain grease to treat the wounds of the horses. As a peace offering, the frightened natives offered Cortes twenty girls, whom he promptly preached to, baptized, and allocated among his captains. One of the girls, Malinche, the daughter of an Aztec cacique sold into slavery with the Mayas, became Cortes's mistress and Aztec interpreter.

From Malinche, Cortes heard about Quetzalcoatl, and how the priests feared that the white-winged ships of the Spaniards might be part of his forces. Later, Cortes would do his best to exploit those fears. Meanwhile, he set about establishing a base on the west coast of the Gulf of Campeche, from where he could penetrate the mountainous lands of the Aztecs. Everyone, including the commander, joined in the labor, and the resulting town, complete down to whipping posts and gallows, was named Villa Rica de la Vera Cruz, the Rich City of the True Cross. By forming a municipal government, which duly elected him governor and commander of "New Spain," Cortes shrewdly placed himself under the direct protection of the king, thus proclaiming independence from Velásquez. Before long, Moctezuma's envoys were on the scene. They brought rich gifts of gold and fabrics, and burned incense in honor of the Spaniards. At the same time, they were insistent that the invaders should decamp and sail away. Cortes countered with a picturesque show of strength. The fit horses were brought out and galloped in a mock charge. Then there was a demonstration of cannon fire. It was a bright, still day, and the proceedings had an incongruous air of pageantry. "We could trace the balls as they went singing through the woods," wrote Bernal Díaz, a witness. Conscientiously, the Aztec envoys made pictures of the scene, sketching horses and cannons for the information of their ruler.

If the Aztecs were impressed by the quality of the Spanish forces, the Spaniards were by no means unfearful of the numbers ranged against them—Moctezuma was said to have tens of thousands of warriors—and a faction of the expedition strongly advocated taking the gifts and departing. Cortes reacted with dramatic finality. Literally burning his boats, he left no option but to stagnate in Veracruz or go on. "My intention," he wrote with characteristic lack of equivocation, "was to confront Moctezuma wherever he might be found . . . for I promised that I would have him dead or in chains if he would not submit to the Crown."

Leaving a hundred and fifty men to garrison Veracruz, Cortes set out with the rest of his band on the mountain trail toward the fabled Aztec capital of Tenochtitlán, accompanied by a motley array of native allies. A good deal of rough campaign humor emerges from the annals of the march. The Indian girls, repeatedly pressed on Cortes as gifts of peace in wayside villages, were often a matter for embarrassment. The Spaniards were greatly amused, for instance, by the diplomatic predicament of their leader when invited by one chief to marry his immensely fat daughter. Another time, Cortes, intent on promoting the myth of Spanish immortality, got his own back by assuring a rugged Biscayan: "You're so ugly they'll take you for an idol." But there was always a strong element of discipline. Though widely admired by his men, Cortes demanded strict obedience, and inflicted flogging, hanging, and sometimes mutilation as punishments. One recorded incident told how a soldier who got out of line on the march received such a sharp lance-thrust from his officer that he remained maimed for life. The faithful and long-suffering nature of the junior ranks was well personified in a bluff Castilian infantryman, Bernal Díaz, whose matter-of-fact memoirs were to provide a fascinating account of the conquest.

Higher on the social scale than the stocky, phlegmatic Díaz, who became a special trusty in the eyes of Cortes, was an ebullient and impetuous aristocrat, Pedro de Alvarado, whose laughing face, loquacity, and brilliant rig-out earned him the Indian nickname Tonatio, the Sun. In a spectrum of colorful personalities, Díaz and Alvarado went some way in marking the diversity of temperament and breeding harnessed to the driving ambition of Cortes. Díaz, hurt twice in the first major conflict of the advance, made light of his wounds, but not of his apprehensions and fear. The enemy, it seemed to him, was so numerous "that they might have defeated us by throwing earth on us." So close did death seem, he confided, that he and his comrades spent the whole of one night confessing and praying to God for help. The situation was all the more dismaying to the Spaniards since the warriors opposing them belonged to the region of Tlaxcala, which was hostile to Moctezuma, and had been looked to rather for help than hindrance. The Tlaxcalans, however, were fiercely possessive of their freedom and liked Spanish intrusion no better than Aztec. Standing bravely before the Spanish horses, they managed to kill and make off with one animal in an early engagement, and, having severed its head, displayed it in their villages as proof that the monsters were mortal. Thus heartened, they returned day by day to the attack.

At night, the Spaniards huddled in the bitter winds of the sierra, lacking adequate clothing for the unexpected drop in temperature and short of dressings for their wounds. The thought of reaching Tenochtitlán took on the proportions of a grim joke. "When the Tlaxcalans had brought us to such a pass, we asked ourselves, what hope had we against the armies of Moctezuma?" Díaz reported. But the Tlaxcalans themselves were not tireless, and, though some younger men would have continued the fighting, wiser council prevailed and the sides opened negotiations. "Just in time," commented Díaz, "for we were all-in and sick of battles, never thinking we'd see the end of them." Cortes was invited into the town of Tlaxcala, which he described for the Emperor Charles as "much larger than Granada and much better fortified. Its houses are as fine and its inhabitants more numerous than those of Granada when that city was captured . . . there is a market as well arranged as any in the world and shops in all quarters of the city . . . there are booths for hair-washing, barbers for shaving you and public baths. Finally, good law and order are maintained among the people, who behave with sense and reason. The foremost city of Africa cannot equal this."

During a rest of some two or three weeks in Tlaxcala, Cortes did his customary preaching, received the allegiance of the chiefs on behalf of the emperor and distributed more girls, after their baptism, to his followers. One of the prettiest, christened Luisa, was given to the dashing bachelor Alvarado, by whom she eventually had a son and a daughter, the latter marrying a cousin of the Duke of Albuquerque. Indian blood was not long in trickling into the rich mixture already established in Spanish veins. Despite further visits from Moctezuma's envoys, and repeated warnings that the Spaniards should turn back, Cortes now persuaded the Tlaxcalans to join him in his march to the Aztec capital. Failing to create dissension between the new allies, Moctezuma's agents retired to Cholula, the next town on the trail, to prepare an ambush. The plan was that the people of Cholula should welcome the invaders who would then be attacked by an army of warriors lurking in the streets. To this end, trenches had been dug and walls built to hinder the Spanish horses. Arrows and other missiles would be unleashed from the flat roofs of the houses.

Cortes was saved from disaster by his mistress. Mistakenly pitying Malinche in her plight, the wife of one of the Cholulan chiefs volunteered to help her escape from the Spaniards, indiscreetly hinting at the fate which awaited them. Malinche revealed the plot to her master, who swiftly and catastrophically turned the tables. Falling on the city next day, the Spaniards proceeded with the wholesale slaughter of its inhabitants, enlisting the enthusiastic aid of the Tlaxcalans. The gods themselves could not have wrought a more terrible vengeance. Several thousand Cholulans were butch-

ered in perhaps the most appalling massacre of the conquest. At
last the horror was more than anyone could stand. "Cortes, his
captains and soldiers had pity on them, and we stopped the Tlaxcalans from doing more damage." The road lay open to Tenochtitlán and Moctezuma.

Cortes had marveled at Tlaxcala and Cholula—the latter as fine
to look at, he declared, as any city in Spain—but what lay ahead
was infinitely more wonderful to Spanish eyes. For a few days the
trail was arduous, snaking through stony passes sprinkled with
snow and ice. Cortes picked his way warily, cross-examining Indians they met on the road and sending his scouts well ahead. Alvarado rode jauntily on a racy bay mare. Díaz trudged doggedly
after them on foot. They slept in Indian mountain shelters,
mesones, lighting fires with straw and posting strong guards. At
one of these shelters, they were accosted by yet another deputation
from Moctezuma, bearing exotic bribes and imploring them to
travel no further, ostensibly on account of the bad roads and the
lack of provisions. But already the scenery was changing intri-
guingly, luring them on. From a descending trail they now caught
sight of the Mexican lakes, a new country of towns, temples and
towers set on water, of pond-fringed fields and scented shrub-
gardens against a background of snow-capped volcanoes. Soon they
were marching on long causeways between islands, watched by
countless thousands of Indians from canoes, the shores and their
urban dwellings. The danger was awesome, but the sheer spectacle
more so. Flocks of water fowl bobbed on the water and heady perfumes issued from flowers and trees. Wrote Díaz: "How can I
recount such wonders . . . so many things never seen, heard or
dreamed of before that day."

Having spent a night near one of the satellite towns of the
Aztec capital, the little column of Spaniards, footsore and smudged
with the congealed blood of their battles, embarked on the last lap
of the journey. "After half a mile," wrote Cortes, "we entered on a
causeway which crosses the middle of the lake arriving finally at
Tenochtitlán, which is at its centre. This causeway is as broad as
two lances and stoutly constructed . . . quite close to the city is a
wooden bridge about ten paces in length beneath which the water
flows through the causeway as the level on either side changes:
moreover, it serves as a defense for the city, for they can remove

the beams whenever they desire." As they crossed the bridge, the Spaniards could see a dense crowd in the streets ahead; streets which contained "very beautiful, large houses, private dwellings and temples." Through the crowd approached two lines of barefoot but richly clad noblemen, some two hundred in all, each line keeping close to one side of the street. In the middle was borne a litter, bright green and decorated with silver, pearls, emeralds and feathers worked in gold. This was preceded by a group of officials sweeping the ground it would pass over and laying cloths where its occupant might wish to walk. The whole pageant, wreathed in mist from the lake and touched with morning sunlight, left the Spaniards breathless. Cortes was about to meet Moctezuma.

Moctezuma's welcoming address was a classic of caution. He and his people, he said, had deduced from the histories that their ancestors had come from distant parts, led by a great god-king who had then returned to his old domains. Ever since, the Aztecs had believed that sooner or later one of this lord's descendants would send agents to claim his title to the land. Now, if it were true, as Cortes had said, that a great and distant ruler had sent him to Mexico, and that this ruler had preknowledge of the Aztecs, then their land must truly be his land, in which case the Spaniards would do nothing remiss or disrespectful. Rather should they rejoice in the comforts he would provide and rest from the fatigues of their journeys and battles. At the same time, he should point out that if the enemies of the Aztecs had told the Spaniards that his land was rich in gold and treasures, then his visitors had been deceived. An examination of the houses, streets and chattels of the city would reveal that they were not of gold but of stone and wood and earth. "True, I have a few articles of gold handed down from my forefathers, and these shall be yours if you desire it. Beyond that, you will see that my enemies have lied. I am now going to retire to my palace. You will be provided with what is necessary for you and your men. Make yourselves at home, and don't misbehave." It would be hard to imagine a more prudent speech from one yet uncertain if his visitors were the agents of gods or mortals.

Moctezuma was as good as his word. The provisions he arranged for the Spaniards were excellent, and to Cortes he gave a number of generous presents including one of his own daughters and a necklace of shells and shrimps worked in gold. Beneath the courtesy, however, the confrontation was clearly a test of nerves. Impossibly outnumbered, short of powder and hopelessly distant from help, the intruders were soon in a bad state of jitters. A few days after their arrival, four of their captains approached Cortes and expressed the strength of their fears. They were in such terror, declared Díaz, "that the food turned to poison in their stomachs." The plan Cortes proposed was scarcely reassuring. Yet, on deliberation, they agreed it was the only gainful way out of their predicament. The scheme was to seize Moctezuma and hold him hostage in his own capital. At the best they might win a tractable puppet, at the worst the waiting would be at an end. It was all or nothing, and Díaz related that "having decided the day before to take Moctezuma prisoner, we passed the night in prayer, beseeching God to let it turn out well in His holy service."

It turned out better than any dared expect. Making a deft excuse of some trouble among the ruler's distant vassals, Cortes invited Moctezuma to move to the Spanish headquarters, a strong and defensible building, whence he might continue to rule in all safety. "I begged him not to be upset," wrote Cortes, "for he should not be there as a prisoner but in perfect liberty, with no impediment to the government and command of his dominions." Nonetheless, in the event of Moctezuma resisting, one of the Spanish officers was ready to run him through with a sword while the rest attempted to resolve the crisis by force. But the Aztec seemed resigned to the idea from the first, entirely delighting the Spaniards by his behavior. Díaz, who was one of his guards, made a point of saluting him and removing his helmet in his presence, and even plucked up courage later to ask him for a girl, having so far drawn a blank in the share-out. Moctezuma promised to obtain him a pretty one, and told him to treat her kindly. "I thanked him with great respect for so great a favour and hoped that God would prosper him." Alvarado, too, got on well with Moctezuma, who had a quiet sense of humor. Sharing a penchant for gaming, they spent many hours playing *totoloque* together, sometimes with Cortes, and Moctezuma amused everyone by chiding Alvarado for cheating.

Though the Spaniards still slept booted and armed, sway over the Aztec king gave them great influence, and, but for an unfortunate coincidence, Cortes might well have consolidated his hold on the country in relative peace. During the winter of 1519–20 the Spaniards extended their knowledge of Tenochtitlán and the outlying districts. Cortes described the city as comparable in size to Seville or Córdoba and wrote to Charles at great length of its booming and varied commerce and the general sophistication of society. "One square in particular is twice as big as that of Salamanca and completely surrounded by arcades where more than sixty thousand people buy and sell daily." Like Venice, it was liberally laced with waterways "along which pass many canoes." Only the blood-splattered temples struck him as obnoxious, and the Spaniards lost no time in building their own church. In May, however, disturbing news arrived from the coast. A fleet of ships had anchored at Veracruz from Cuba with almost nine hundred troops, a tenth of them mounted. Their leader, Pánfilo de Narváez, had orders from Velásquez to depose Cortes in Mexico.

Cortes had to act quickly, and without upsetting the calm in Tenochtitlán. Announcing the arrival as a welcome reinforcement, he left Alvarado in charge of Moctezuma and the city, setting out himself with some two hundred and seventy men for Veracruz. Díaz, who was with him, told how they force-marched the sierras, following the rivers toward the coast, sleeping without shelter and stopping only when absolutely necessary. Two factors at least were in their favor. Narváez was overconfident and careless in his guard. And his men, though far more numerous, were less experienced than the veterans of Cortes. The sides clashed at a small town named Cempoal, where Narváez had stationed his force. It was raining and the men from Tenochtitlán had no food. Waiting for dusk to cover their attack, they simply sat and thought of the odds against them. When finally they moved in, a sentry raised the alarm. Díaz, in a party assigned to take the artillery, found himself splashing across sodden ground toward the guns. One went off and three men fell dead. But the match holes on the pieces had been closed against the rain, and most of the crews, fumbling in the dark, took panic. Overrunning them, the attackers charged on. Díaz arrived in a courtyard among a number of the enemy. "We fought some time with our pikes, then suddenly heard the voice of Narvaez shouting, 'Santa Maria! They've got me! In the eye!'" He had taken refuge on the roof of a building with some of his bodyguard. When the thatch was fired, wrote Díaz, "they all came rolling down on us."

With Narváez captured, his men gave up the fight and soon joined the persuasive Cortes. Thus, reinforced and replenished, the conquistadores set forth once more for Tenochtitlán. But they had overcome one crisis to be faced with another. Alone in command of the capital, unsure of the fate of his leader, the impetuous Alvarado had lost his head. Convinced the populace was plotting against him, he had sallied from the Spanish stronghold in the absence of Cortes and murdered two hundred Aztec nobles. The result had been to turn the people not only against the Spaniards but against their own ruler, whom they now had every reason to regard as ineffective. Cortes arrived to find the city seething with hostility. After a furious scene with Alvarado, he arranged for Moctezuma to appeal for order from the balcony of his residence. The response was a flight of missiles. Struck by stones and arrows, Moctezuma declined to have his wounds dressed or to take food or drink from the Spaniards. He died three days later, refusing to repudiate his faith.

Deprived of their royal trump, the Spaniards were in an untenable position. Many of them were wounded or sick, they could no longer rely on supplies, their Tlaxcalan allies were swept by an epidemic of smallpox brought in by the Narváez expedition, the city swarmed with thousands of armed and vengeful Aztecs. Dividing what gold and treasure he could assemble among his forces, Cortes ordered the retreat. After some fierce preliminary skirmishing, it took place on the night of June 30, 1520, the famous "noche triste," and proved disastrous. The withdrawal had barely commenced when the Spaniards were surrounded by Aztecs and had to fight every foot of the way through the city. Reaching the causeway, they found that the bridges had been destroyed to bar their passage. All order gave way to confusion. Men swimming for their lives were intercepted by Aztec canoists who swarmed on either side of the escape route. Others drowned under the weight of armor and treasure. Somehow, Díaz struggled to the far end of the causeway with Cortes and the exhausted remnants of the vanguard, only to learn that Alvarado and the rear guard were

trapped on the far side of the last bridge. Less than a dozen infan-
trymen and a few captains had the heart to attempt a rescue. Díaz
recalled that it was very dark and drizzling with rain. "Soon they
came on Pedro de Alvarado, badly wounded and on foot. His
horse had been killed but he still carried his lance. With him were
seven soldiers all wounded, and eight Tlaxcalans streaming with
blood." According to some accounts, Alvarado had vaulted the last
gap on his lance. His news was that the rest of the rear guard was
lost.

Cortes put the Spaniards killed that night at a hundred and fifty,
but his concern was to minimize his defeat and others put the
number more reliably at three hundred. Two thousand Tlaxcalans
in Spanish service were estimated to have died. "God knows what
fatigue and toil we suffered," wrote the commander, "for not a
horse of the twenty-four remaining could run, nor a horseman
raise his arm, nor was there an infantryman unwounded or fit to
fight." After suffering more losses in a hazardous retreat across the
mountains, they eventually reached friendly Tlaxcala. Here Cortes
licked his wounds and planned a return match. Within six months,
he was on his way back to Tenochtitlán. He had mustered nearly
six hundred Spaniards (forty mounted), eight guns and several
thousand Tlaxcalans. This time, however, he had an additional asset; boats. Cortes had learned expensively that command of the
capital lay on its waters. Fetching rigging and equipment from
Veracruz, he built thirteen small vessels in detachable sections,
each section capable of being humped across the hills.

Unlike the original march on Tenochtitlán, the new advance
was hotly contested. The Aztecs had manned outposts in the
mountains and hurled boulders on the Spaniards as they climbed
through the passes. Eight men were smashed to death by these
missiles in a single attack on a hill the Spaniards called El Penol.
On another occasion, Cortes's horse collapsed in the middle of a
hand-to-hand tussle and he was narrowly rescued by Alvarado,
among others. The invaders were not cheered to find the desiccated
heads of former comrades in wayside temples, and a friar who had
arrived by sea on a mission from Charles did a brisk trade with a
stock of reassuring papal messages. According to Díaz, he returned
home in a few months, a rich man. In particular, the Aztecs were
drawn to the boats. Three times during the period of assembly on

the lakeside, they attempted to burn them, though not with success. By April 1521, Cortes was ready to press home the attack. In each boat he placed twelve oarsmen and twelve men armed with crossbow or harquebus. Supported by this fleet, the rest advanced across the causeways. The tactic served until they reached the center of the city, where sheer weight of the numbers against them forced them to fall back with heavy casualties. The camp they made on a nearby island was close enough to provide a view of captured comrades being sacrificed before a statue of Huitzilopochtli. For ten days they watched and listened despairingly as the temple drums beat the death ritual, and groups of helpless Spaniards were dragged to the knife.

Hope of capturing the city intact had now vanished. After a vain appeal to its new ruler, Cuauhtémoc, to surrender, Cortes resolved to break the Aztecs by a campaign of sheer destruction. Having cut the water supply to the capital and deployed his boats to intercept provisions, he began a systematic harrying and firing of the suburbs. It was a long and costly task. As they captured the bridges on the causeways, the Spaniards filled them in to facilitate their advances. But by night the Aztecs descended in hordes and reopened them. "For three and ninety days," wrote Díaz, "we were in front of the city, and not a day passed without we had to fight." The wounded turned out with the rest. "Had they all remained in camp, no captain would have had more than a handful of men to support him." Díaz was hit by an arrow while struggling against Aztec canoists. The more prominent Spaniards were singled out as special targets. "Every day we had to get another ensign to lead us and carry the flag." But every day, too, a little more of Tenochtitlán was devastated. With the boats to support them, the Spaniards made fearful use of their superior fire power, while their Tlaxcalan allies contributed fiercely to the damage. After four months, three-quarters of the city which Cortes had described as "the most beautiful in the world" was in rubble or ashes. The remaining inhabitants were plagued by thirst and hunger. On August 13, Cuauhtémoc and his family were captured crossing the lake by canoe. His first words to Cortes, according to Díaz, epitomized the whole spirit of the Aztec defense: " 'I have done my duty . . . I could do no more. Take your dagger and strike me dead.' "

At first Cuauhtémoc was treated with courtesy. Later he was

tortured in an attempt to discover the whereabouts of the reputed Aztec treasure trove. But he revealed nothing, and, indeed, the companions of Díaz who had boasted in victory that "they would buy horses with golden saddles and arrows of gold" were sadly disillusioned. The wealth of Mexico was not lying around for the picking. It had to be won from the ground. With the city in his hands, Cortes rapidly extended his power in the country, promoting many enterprises, including mining. Land and sea communications were opened and an early start made on the rebuilding of Tenochtitlán as the Spanish capital of "New Spain of the Ocean Sea." In 1529, the conqueror was received with great honors at home, where he joined Charles in planning the extended education and religious conversion of the Mexicans. But, though he returned to the scene of his triumph for a few years, he was soon superseded, along with others, by a new wave of administrators from the homeland. During the declining years of his career, he became involved with expensive and fruitless expeditions in the South Seas, a near-disastrous voyage up the Gulf of California, and an abortive attempt to capture Algiers with Charles. Like Columbus, he ended his life burdened with litigation and debt, the victim of his own willfulness and the jealousy of less adventurous government officials.

When Cortes died in 1547, aged sixty-two, his last letter to the emperor had reposed in the government files for three years. "I am old, poor and in debt," it read. "Again and again I have begged your Majesty to convoke the judges of the Council of the Indies and other royal councils that they may decide on the deed by which your Majesty was pleased to grant this servant a small part of all he had won for your Majesty . . . and without delay, for should the matter drag on much longer I shall be forced to retire in ruin. I am past the age to be knocking from pillar to post, and must settle down to make my account with God. It is a long one, and I have little time to balance it . . ." On the back of the letter someone had scrawled: *"Nay que responder"*—"No need to reply." Already, his achievement in Mexico had been dated by its numerous offshoots. In 1540, his successor in "New Spain," the viceroy Antonio de Mendoza, had promoted an expedition to Arizona and New Mexico, fragments of which penetrated Colorado, Texas, Oklahoma, and Kansas. Narváez, recovered from his earlier mauling, had previously struck the Floridan coast, and in 1539 Hernando de Soto had marched northwest from Florida to find the Mississippi. Another figure from the great days of Cortes, the reckless Alvarado, had blazed a fiery trail south to Guatemala, where, after much trouble with both the natives and his own men, he founded the capital of that region. It was in Guatemala that Díaz spent the last years of his life, a poor but engagingly philosophical old soldier. Alvarado found no such contentment. Cheated once more by a lack of gold and silver, he sailed for Ecuador to try his luck among the Incas, a race reputedly rich in treasure. A fortune-hunter named Pizarro had beaten him to it.

The conquest of Peru was in many ways a brutal parody of the conquest of Mexico. Francisco Pizarro, already in his fifties at its outset, was an older and coarser version of Cortes. Though unquestionably fearless in pursuit of aggrandizement, he was also sickeningly unscrupulous and lacking in honor. The illegitimate son of a poor Estremaduran farmer, he had never learned to read or write and could not sign his name. He had, however, a keen eye for the main chance, and a strong arm to back it. Such attributes gained him some substance in the Indies, where stories of Inca wealth drew him south on a series of exploratory probes from Panama. Cortes had chased the illusion of fabulous treasure; Pizarro, with his baser instincts, was to strike the real thing bang on the nose. The Inca court at Cuzco, in the Peruvian Cordillera, exceeded the wildest Spanish dreams in its brilliance. For the monarchs of an empire comprising large parts of what are now Ecuador, Peru, Bolivia, and northern Chile, gold and silver were commonplace materials. Their household utensils were of these metals, the walls of their famous Temple of the Sun were covered with sheets of gold studded with jewels, their gardens contained not only an abundance of real flowers but replicas of them in gold and silver.

The cradle of Inca civilization lay in the great plateau from Lake Titicaca south between the eastern and western Cordillera of Peru and Bolivia. From this rarefied kingdom, guarded by peaks rising above twenty thousand feet, the Incas had extended their empire in the four centuries preceding the arrival of the Spaniards north up the Andean chain to Quito, descending east and west to the adjacent lowlands and the Pacific coast. By and large, it was an orderly and stable empire, linked by sweeping roads and ingenious alpine bridges, and held together as much by understanding as coercion. Less bellicose than the warlike Mexicans, industrious and submissive to their rulers—the revered Children of the Sun— the Incas were nevertheless plentiful in warriors. Their weapons included battle-axes of copper and spiked maces of copper or silver.

Pizarro's intention to brave these warriors in their Andean fast-nesses met with derision in Panama, and, in 1528, unable to raise capital for a major expedition, he sailed to Spain to seek the sup-port of the emperor. The moment was propitious. A few sum-mers earlier, eighteen exhausted seamen had reached Seville in a weather-beaten ship named the *Vittoria* after the most remarkable voyage then on record. More than three years earlier, a Portuguese exile, Ferdinand Magellan, naturalized as a Spaniard, had left Se-ville in command of five vessels to try to find a passage around the south of America. After many adventures, he indeed found the strait named after him, sailing on through immense hardship across the ocean he christened the Pacific, only to be killed by natives in what were later known as the Philippines. The survivors sailed on to Borneo, intent on following the Portuguese route back to Eu-rope round the Cape of Good Hope. Only two ships now re-mained, and one of these had to be abandoned as unseaworthy before reaching the Indian Ocean. Cursed by disease, starvation, contrary winds, and storms, the *Vittoria* finally reached her desti-nation, the first known vessel to circumnavigate the globe. The court was still savoring this staggering achievement when Cortes had arrived with reports and evidence of his own outlandish tri-umphs. No project seemed too bizarre in the mood that prevailed, and Charles happily appointed Pizarro his advance agent and com-mander in Peru, especially since the salary agreed was to be col-lected from the Incas themselves.

In 1531, Pizarro returned to Panama with four brothers and a cousin to reunite with an earlier partner in his enterprise, Diego de Almagro. Like Pizarro, Almagro was aging, illiterate, rough and dynamic. Fleeing to the Indies to escape Spanish justice, this ugly and stocky son of Castilian peasants had joined Pizarro and others in a number of profitable ventures, the proposed conquest of Peru being the latest and biggest. Leaving Almagro to continue the difficult task of recruiting, Pizarro now set out with some two hundred men for Ecuador, whence, after some hard jungle marching and a great deal of sickness, he reached the southern shores of the Gulf of Guayaquil and took the Inca town of Tumbès. To his considerable advantage, the Incas had just emerged from a rare and debilitating war among themselves. Two princes, Huascar and Atahualpa, fighting for the dominions of their dead father, the emperor Huayna Capac, had thrown the customarily united Inca Empire into confusion. Atahualpa, gaining victory, was at Cajamarca in the central cordillera, when Pizarro, having moved down the Peruvian coast, struck at him across the intervening mountains.

Though less than two hundred strong, the Spanish expedition had a high proportion of horsemen—more than sixty—and some cannons. Leaving the coast in October 1532, it reached Cajamarca in a little under nine weeks to find the city deserted. Terrified by the nature of the intruders, its inhabitants had joined Atahualpa and his warriors, reputedly thirty thousand in number, at a nearby camp. On learning the size of the Inca force, the Spaniards in turn were terrified. Pizarro, mindful of the ruse used by Cortes, decided to lure Atahualpa into a trap. Inviting the Inca to return peacefully to the city for talks, the Spanish leader concealed his troops and cannons in ambush. Surrounded by his court and a guard of several thousand warriors, Atahualpa was carried into the main square on a golden litter to be confronted by a single Spanish priest who proclaimed the usual *requerimiento*. Perplexed by the reception, the ruler waved him aside. From the nearby buildings, the Spanish guns now opened fire on the dumfounded Inca masses. As they broke in disorder, the waiting horsemen charged without mercy. Hundreds were slaughtered and Atahualpa was captured. By the time Almagro arrived on the scene with reinforcements, Pizarro and his men were in complete command. Not one Spaniard had been lost amid the horrors of Cajamarca.

Almagro also fround the conquerors rich, for in return for a written promise of freedom, Atahualpa had provided a massive ransom in Inca possessions, priceless treasures which, melted and beaten down, amounted in weight to thirteen thousand pounds of gold and twice as much silver. Instead of keeping his part of the bargain, Pizarro had Atahualpa baptized and immediately strangled. With scant attempts to conceal their gold lust, Pizarro and Almagro now proceeded to ransack the rest of the Inca Empire. In the north, Quito and Guayaquil were captured with the help of fresh recruits tempted by the glittering pickings, and Almagro arrived in Ecuador in time to buy off the free-lance invasion of Alvarado. To the south, Pizarro seized Cuzco, stripping the Sun Temple and every other likely edifice of treasure, then murdering and torturing in the hope of finding more loot. In 1535 Pizarro marked the apparent completion of his conquests by founding a triumphal monument to his achievements in the form of a royal city, soon to be called Lima, roughly halfway along the Peruvian coast. From here he was to command for the next six years—years which saw increasing Spanish penetration in Chile, Colombia, and the lowlands of the Amazon and Rio de la Plata—and here he would lie on his death in 1541. His greed had paid dividends of bloody justice. Incensed by his cruelties, the Incas and their native allies repeatedly harassed his cities and settlements. Almagro, discontented with his share of the profits, challenged his partner with mounting jealousy until defeated by Pizarro at the battle of Las Salinas and executed. Even then, Pizarro was not free from vengeance. Three years later he was assassinated in a plot led by Almagro's son, one so-called "Almagro the Lad." By an apt stroke of fate the "Lad" was a half-caste.

In 1551 the redoubtable viceroy Antonio de Mendoza moved from Mexico to bring Peru a more ordered and stable government. The initial Spanish conquest of America—"the most brilliant feat of imperial expansion the world had ever known" in the words of Hubert Herring—was drawing to a close, achieved by the audacity of a few thousand men. From the Gulf of California to Santiago, the colonial period, with its equally remarkable impress of language, faith, and commercial and political patterns, was beginning. Throughout the main centers of settlement, Spanish culture was already showing vivid expression. Thanks to the zeal of the Church and the sweat of Indian and Negro labor, religious buildings of fine quality were springing up everywhere. For the most part, as with the secular architecture rising beside them, the style was contemporaneous with that of the homeland, though local skills and materials sometimes produced intriguing variations. Across the vast span of some seven thousand miles, communications and administration blossomed with amazing rapidity. Industry, notably the mining of precious and other metals, grew apace. At first the colonists concentrated on gold, but before the halfway mark of the century production had swung emphatically to silver. Between 1505 and the end of the century, the turnover in precious metals had risen more than twenty-eightfold.

In Spain, the House of Trade, the Casa de Contratación, was quickly expanded not only to govern imports, emigration, and the legalities of most matters involving New World commerce, but to provide nautical training for the officers of a growing Atlantic fleet. To aid the authorities and hinder revenue evasion, all American trade since 1503 had been limited to the port of Seville. At about the same time, the royal share of the proceeds from American mining enterprise had been fixed at a fifth, the familiar "royal quinto." Charles needed every penny he could get. Indeed, so great were the expenses incurred in his attempts to manage his turbulent German Empire that he even seized private remittances from the Indies as compulsory loans. In 1526 he had married a Portuguese princess, Isabella, primarily for her excellent dowry. A year later he was still in debt, but had, additionally, a son and heir, Philip. As his mortgages mounted, so the interest demanded grew with them. Flemish and Italian bankers charged him up to forty-three percent. He was forced to give a large part of Venezuela to his German financiers. Still he continued to strive for European unity, spending more and more Spanish money. "I say it once and three times: I want peace, I want peace, I want peace," Charles insisted. He got French wars, Turkish wars, and religious rebellion to boot.

By 1555 Spanish revenue was mortgaged five years ahead and a weary Charles wanted nothing better than to abdicate his formidable inheritance and retire. "Nine times," he declared in Brussels that year, "I have seen upper Germany, six Spain, seven Italy, ten Flanders, four France, twice England and twice Africa—forty trips altogether, in peace and in war, apart from travelling within my dominions. I have sailed the Mediterranean eight times, and three times the Atlantic between here and Spain. Now will be the fourth, when I return there to die." Within three years he had abdicated the German throne in favor of his younger brother, Ferdinand, passing Spain, with the Low Countries and the Italian dependencies, to his son Philip. A few months after divesting himself of his burdens, Charles was dead. He spent his sadly short respite at the monastery of Yuste, above the Rio Tietar and its peaceful valley in Estremadura. It has been said of Charles that he was the first great European, but it was not true, as his rivals claimed, that he sought universal domination. The man they would more properly fear was to come. For, under Philip, Spain reached the very peak of her world-shaking power.

Chapter 6

OF PRINCES AND POETS

In the first week of October 1571, two great fleets, one Christian, one Turkish, prepared to meet in what would rank among the bloodiest sea conflicts in history, the Battle of Lepanto in the gulf of that name near Corinth. Amid three hundred other Christian vessels making for Lepanto rode the Spanish ship *Marquesa*, in whose hold lay a singularly unbloodthirsty young Spaniard. Ill with fever, Miguel de Cervantes wanted nothing more than to be left in peace with his sickness. The leanness of his cheeks and the length and angularity of his nose were emphasized by his feverish pallor; his thin body, deprived of its customary energy, adhered sweatily to the vivid uniform of the "rooster," the Spanish infantry soldier. Each pitch of the ship increased his discomfort. Already, he felt like death, and the battle had not yet started. The irony of the situation cannot have been lost on one who aspired to success as a poet.

Born twenty-four years earlier at Alcalá de Henares, the second son of an impoverished doctor, Cervantes had recently published a number of unexceptional verses in Madrid. Impelled by a quest for greater achievement, he had then set out for Italy and Rome, the inspiration of many a literary fledgling before him. But the scope for unknown writers was depressing, and, consoled perhaps by the thought that the fashionable Garcilaso de la Vega, "prince of Castilian poets," had been a professional soldier until his death earlier in the century, Cervantes had enlisted in the army. His prompt posting to Messina to join the fleet there fitting to challenge the Ottoman navy introduced him to an amazing series of adventures in which was forged the philosophy that would eventually bequeath Spain the first, and perhaps greatest ever, "modern" novel of world literature.

The development of Spanish letters had been complex. The transformation of Latin into Romance, commencing in the peninsula before the Muslim invasion and continuing through the reconquest, had resulted in a number of regional languages of which three, Castilian, Catalan and Galician (the latter to develop as Portuguese), were to retain more than dialectal status, along with the much older Basque. By the end of the fifteenth century, Castilian had achieved sufficient dominance to be equated to "Spanish." The evolution of Castilian literature alone—through the heroic poetry of the eleventh and twelfth centuries, through the beginnings of prose and the quest for erudition blessed by Alfonso the Learned in the thirteenth, through the imaginative blossoming of the fourteenth and the new worldliness of the fifteenth—had been involved with thoughts and techniques beyond elucidation in any simple pattern or summary. Muslim influence, evident for example in the blend of eroticism and devotion prominent in some Spanish writing, had been just one of its complications.

The first known masterpiece of Castilian literature, the epic *Poema de mio Cid*, by an anonymous twelfth century writer, had set a precedent of earthy realism that would have gratified its hero himself. Likewise, the first universal masterpiece of Spanish prose, the *Tragicomedia de Calixto y Melibea* (c. 1499), an unactable dialogue by the converso Fernando de Rojas, had produced a character of such dominant realism, Celestina, that the work had been popularly renamed after her. Indeed, when Spanish writers had set aside their tendency to idealize long enough to look closely at life as it existed, their standards had been of the best. However, the advent of the printing press, creating an avid and not always discriminating public, had encouraged much that was less admirable in Spanish writing. The sentimentalized hangover from medieval chivalry, striking a responsive chord in the national breast, had provided the printers of the sixteenth century with a readily salable fund of romance. Interminable novels of the chivalresque genre flooded the markets. Idealism was debased to escapism, heroism to mere wishfulness, in their pages.

One reaction to these fanciful tales of knight-errantry had been the vogue of the pastoral novel, initiated in the peninsula about 1559 by Jorge de Montemayor's Diana, after the style of the Italian Sannagaro. The pastoral novel did not deflate the knight-errant so much as elevate the peasant. Shepherds became aesthetes in the terms of its lyricism; goatherds behaved like courtiers. Meanwhile, a more direct challenge to the chivalresque had appeared in the so-called picaresque novel of around the same period. The picaro, or antihero, took a backstairs view of life, living on his wits, unencumbered by ideals, happy enough to have dodged the latest blow of a cruel master or fickle fate. As a corrective to the romantic knight, he served his purpose, but had added little of positive value to Spanish letters. With the sixteenth century passing, Castile awaited a literary monument above merely this or that vogue, a pen educated not only in physical reality but gifted with poetic vision and psychological insight, a writer capable of facing contemporary life at its cruelest and still finding warmth and delight in the Spaniard and his countryside.

Miguel de Cervantes lapsed into fitful sleep. The Christian fleet plunged steadily toward Lepanto. With it went the prayers of a great deal of Europe. The Ottoman Empire, straddling the Middle East from the borders of India to the Aegean, its sights set on central Europe and control of the Mediterranean, had made use of the constant conflicts among the Christian nations to press its advantage in the west. Along the coasts of Italy, Spain, and North Africa, countless small communities lived in peril and dread of the free-ranging Muslim pirates. Now, under its overlord the Sultan Selim II, the naval strength of Turkey was second to none of its rivals. At Algiers, the Turks had overwhelmingly defeated the Emperor Charles, whose escape had been made good only by the extreme competence of the great Genoese admiral Andrea Doria. In the very year of the accession of Charles's son Philip II, the enemy had wrested Tripoli from its Christian garrison, annihilating a strong force subsequently dispatched to evict them. Boldly, the Turkish galleys had swept the Adriatic, ravaging the coastlands, slaughtering, and enslaving, until they threatened

Venice itself. Finally, with Cyprus, the most easterly Catholic stronghold, on the verge of succumbing entirely to their onslaught, the pope had entreated Philip to join a Holy League against "the Infidel." The Christian forces had assembled in Sicily, where, on September 20, 1571, the resulting fleet, laden with some twenty-eight thousand men, had weighed anchor at Messina and headed east to meet the enemy.

Its main squadrons, from Spain and Venice, were commanded by the Marquis of Santa Cruz and the Venetian admirals Barbarigo and Veniero. From the papal states came a small fleet under Marc Antonio Colonna, a scion of one of the oldest and most powerful Roman houses, and from Genoa another under Giovanni Andrea Doria, a great nephew of the Andrea Doria who had fought the Turks with Charles. The whole force was commanded by a young man no older than Cervantes, John of Austria, generally known as Don John. John was an illegitimate child of the late emperor and a Flemish dancer named Barbara Blomberg. Reared in Spain in the household of the king's chamberlain, Luis Quijada, the boy had much impressed Charles during his retirement at Yuste, where he had prevailed upon Philip to recognize the lad as his brother. Philip had conferred upon his half brother the title John of Austria. John's first big chance to prove his worth in command had occurred toward the end of the sixties in what came to be known as the Alpujarras rising. This throwback to the old Moorish problem in Granada had been linked with the increasing aggressiveness of the Turks. More directly, it had resulted from the failure of Granada's Morisco population to integrate with established Catholic society. Half a century and more after their forced conversion, the Moriscos were still wearing Moorish dress, speaking Arabic, and strongly influenced by the ways of their old faith. Not surprisingly, they had been accused of sinister understandings with the Turks.

Philip, driven by a burning belief in the Catholic cause and the need for absolute peninsula unity, had lost little time in strengthening the Inquisition against Protestant ideas from the north and the hard-dying Muslim traits in Granada. When, in 1567, he had directed his attentions more closely on the Moriscos, they had shown their resentment by taking to arms. The rebellion had centered on that old trouble spot, the Alpujarras. With Islam watching greedily, Philip had had to move fast, especially since Spain's military strength was widely dispersed through her empire, and none too powerfully at home. Rushing troops back from Italy, the king had placed Don John in charge of operations. John had not let him down. In a campaign notable for both cruelty and personal bravery, Philip's twenty-year-old half brother had obliterated every sign of resistance in the hilly southern sierras. The Moriscos had been dispersed forcibly throughout the rest of Spain and twelve thousand northern families settled on their now ravaged lands. John had barely completed his mission when the pope had sounded his call of alarm.

The plash of wood on water, monotonously regular as the armada crossed the Ionian Sea, was interrupted by a signal shot and the clatter of kettledrums. The Turkish fleet had been sighted in the Gulf of Lepanto. The cross-emblazoned banner of the Holy League rose challengingly on the Christian flagship. As the allied squadrons deployed to face the enemy, their crews received a graphic lesson in the proportions of Ottoman sea strength. The waiting navy, scarcely fewer in ships than the combined force under Don John, stretched almost from shore to shore in the mouth of the gulf. Cervantes, climbing weakly to the deck of the *Marquesa*, faced a spectacle unique in its time and thereafter. For, with the major strength of each fleet represented in galleys, Lepanto would go down on record as the last great naval engagement between oar-propelled vessels. In a Turkish force of three hundred ships, more than two hundred and fifty were galleys. Of a similar number of Christian vessels, at least two-thirds were oar-propelled. Now, amid the sound of drums and trumpets, the rattle of scimitars on shields and the thud of the first ranging cannon shots, the contestants drew laboriously together. It was October 7, a Sunday. By noon, the Christian fleet was poised for battle. Don John, in the center of the line, spent a few last minutes on his knees in prayer on the poop of the flagship before urging his men to the slaughter. Around him were the largest Christian vessels. To the left of the line, the Venetian Agostino Barbarigo cheered forward his squadron. The first to be engaged by the Turks, Barbarigo received a mortal wound from an arrow. On the right wing sailed Andrea Doria. Santa Cruz, the Spaniard, lay back in reserve.

On the *Marquesa*, a pale and shivering Cervantes, striking his captain, Francisco de San Pedro, as an ill man and a liability, was ordered to return to the hold. But when the feverish soldier protested, San Pedro did not bother to argue. The Turks were too close. Their commander, Ali Pasha, resplendent in white adorned with silver, and a turban studded with gem stones, was conspicuous at their center, beneath the banner of the sultan. On his right flank, engaging Barbarigo's squadron, fought a commander named Mohammed Sirocco; on his left, Uluch Ali, a formidable and enterprising Turkish admiral. Uluch Ali was quick to display his resourcefulness. Moving as if to outflank the Christian wing, he induced Andrea Doria to part company with the main force, then promptly switched direction and isolated the Genoese squadron. The situation was saved by the alertness of Santa Cruz, who checked the dangerous Turkish maneuver with his reserves. In the center, Don John's Spaniards fought ferociously with Ali Pasha's own galleys, the big Spanish vessels gaining successes.

The *Marquesa* struggled at the thick of the contest. Cervantes found himself in charge of a section of harquebusiers in a ship's boat alongside the galley, a position affording a frightening perspective of the conflict. On all sides, ships towered above the small skiff. Smoke hung everywhere, from the cannons and from vessels in flames. Below decks, galley slaves winced as they hauled on the heavy oars. Ships rammed, were rammed in turn, boarded, captured, or sunk. Cervantes heard the chanting of priests among the bellowing and moaning of the wounded. His captain, San Pedro, had fallen. Barbarigo had expired in a pool of his own blood. Fainting with sickness and injury, Cervantes had little option but to stick to his post, where he received three gunshot wounds, two in the chest and one in the left hand, the latter to maim him for life. The sea was littered with bodies and debris. But the Christians were slowly getting the best of the fight. The severed head of Ali Pasha, displayed on a pike, augured ill for Turkish fortunes. His flagship had been captured and its immediate companion ships beaten. As the news spread, many of the Turkish captains panicked. By evening, most of their ships were destroyed or captured. Uluch Ali alone among the Ottoman leaders remained sufficiently capable to retrieve a few crews from the slaughter. He was lucky, for a gale springing up soon after the battle ruled out the possibility of Christian pursuit.

It remained to assess the losses, which were onerous. A probable thirty-three thousand men had died at Lepanto (eight thousand Christians and twenty-five thousand Turks), while the number wounded was forever inestimable. More happily, some fifteen thousand Christian oarsmen had been liberated from slavery on the Turkish vessels. News of so dramatic a victory filled Catholic Europe with relief and elation. Few cared that the triumph of Lepanto was not measurable in territorial gain, wealth or governmental submission. Struggles of greater material significance might come and go; Lepanto, believed the faithful, would live forever— "the noblest occasion that past or present ages have seen or future ones may hope to see," wrote Cervantes. Indeed, it was less a victory than a moment of truth. Divine providence had granted the true cause its sanction. Declared a tearfully grateful pope with a play on the Gospel: "There was a man chosen by God, and his name was John." In Spain, the Andalusian poet Herrera, a follower of Garcilaso, wrote in verse of the battle. In Italy, Tintoretto and Veronese painted it. Don John, overnight a hero of international proportions, returned to a jubilant and festive Messina, where the little-known soldier Cervantes began his recovery in a hospital. For a while longer, the careers of the two men were connected. In 1573, Don John took Tunis from the Turks. A year later, when they recaptured it, he mounted an unsuccessful expedition to relieve the Christian garrison. On both occasions Cervantes served under him. In return, John provided his literary-minded follower with a testimonial addressed to Philip, supporting Cervantes in a bid for promotion.

On September 20, 1575, Cervantes left Naples, his most recent posting, in the galley *Sol*, the *Sun*, bound for Spain and Madrid. He traveled in high hopes. Since chance had diverted his path from poesy to soldiering with such well-noticed results, his intention was to make the most of it. Don John's recommendation would assure him a captaincy; natural talent and finesse would take care of the rest. Already, he had the air of a true leader of men. The small, pointed beard he affected lent verve to an aesthetic face. He bore his thin figure with an elegance which did justice to the testimonial secreted in his uniform. His maimed hand, the prized badge of Lepanto, gave him a certain poignant distinction. In Sicily, he had won the interest of the viceroy, the

Duke of Sesa, who, like John, had furnished him with a good reference. In Naples, his romantic confidence had gained him a mistress of a quality more than usually memorable among the run of garrison liaisons. It remained only for his caliber to be discerned beyond the water: a hope all too perversely translated, as it happened, by fate. Six days after leaving Naples, the *Sol* and her companion ships, the *Higuera* and *Mendoza*, ran into a flotilla of Barbary corsairs off the French coast near Marseilles. After a brisk fight, the *Sol* was overrun and her survivors taken prisoner to Algiers. They were a sorry-looking lot, but their captor, a renegade Greek captain named Dali Mami, had a shrewd eye for value. One victim in particular attracted his notice: the man who possessed letters from the great Christian leader John of Austria, and the Viceroy of Sicily. Cervantes was soon chained in the strongest of Mami's dungeons.

At the time of Lepanto, Philip II of Spain, the most handsome, powerful and industrious monarch in Europe, had seen eight years' work on his favorite personal project, the construction of a remarkable palace-cum-mausoleum and monastery at Escorial, a small hill village thirty miles northwest of Madrid. Still the largest building in the country, the Escorial, or more properly the Monasterio de San Lorenzo del Escorial, forms a revealing monument to the man and his reign. The immense granite pile, rising gray and somber from the bare Sierra de Guadarrama, is 680 feet long and 530 feet wide, the forbidding rectangle of its outer walls comprising huge blocks of local stone, some of which had to be dragged from the quarries by up to fifty yoke of oxen. There are in the Escorial a hundred miles of corridor, 2673 windows, 1200 doors, 88 fountains and 86 stairways, while the original keys weighed half a ton. Philip intended it as a burial place for his father, Charles, and as his own retreat from Madrid and the outer world.

Everything about the Escorial, from its lofty and remote situation to the Titians on its walls, reflected Philip's taste. In the twenty years it took to complete, its original designer, Juan Bautisto de Toledo, died, and the work was finished by his pupil, Juan de Herrera. But Philip, a keen amateur architect, supervised all details. Toledo, trained in Italy, had based the style on the severe Italian classicism of the time, which the king much approved. If the outward impression were austere, however, the interior was in many ways lavish. Jasper from Burgo, bronze and ironwork from Saragossa, and marble from various parts of the south, mingled with embellishments from all over the Spanish Empire: richly colored woods from the forests of America, splendid tapestries from Flanders, gold and silver work from Milan. Ornate silver reliquaries containing the bones of saints and martyrs by the hundred filled the halls. Four thousand books in a variety of languages, particularly the Oriental, were selected as the basis of a library. Statues and murals commissioned from Europe's finest artists came under the king's most stringent observation. Only the best, as Philip saw it, was good enough for the Escorial. The Italian painter Zuccaro was paid up and sent home for not meeting the necessary standards. In all, the cost of construction and decoration was estimated by the prior of the monastery at about six million gold pieces. And the prior was concerned with stressing the value of the bargain.

For the warm and intimate delights of the southern Alhambra, Isabella and her grateful followers had praised God. For the vast, impersonal pile in the Guadarrama mountains, at least one rapturous Spanish priest was to declare that God owed a debt of gratitude to Philip. Though the king himself was not unduly arrogant, security at home and power abroad had gone to the heads of other Spaniards. In 1557, a Spanish victory over the French at St. Quentin had led to France repudiating her designs on Italy and accepting peace terms with her successful neighbor. Following that, the triumph of Lepanto, under Spanish leadership, had not only appeared to diminish the Ottoman threat but to confirm Spain in the role she had coveted since the reconquest: supreme exponent and champion among the great nations of Catholicism. Only the glittering treasure of the New World was needed to complete the illusion of grandeur.

Since Philip had made it his permanent capital, Madrid sparkled in season with the glossy horses, coaches, liveries and other finery of a nobility intoxicated by the riches of the Indies. Their palaces and chapels were magnificent; their households proliferated with gentlemen-in-waiting, equerries, bodyguards, and retainers; their wives assumed the manner of queens. Though often heavily burdened, the revenues of many Spanish grandees were the envy of Europe. The income of the Duke of Medina Sidonia was reckoned at a hundred and thirty-five thousand ducats a year. Incomes from fifty thousand to a hundred thousand ducats were common among the top nobility, whose attitude to lesser mortals was not tempered, on the whole, with modesty. "The arrogance of the great lords is beyond belief," it was reported abroad. "When they meet a foreign ambassador, even the nuncio of his holiness, rarely do they condescend to salute him . . . all affect that imperturbable hauteur, or indifference, which they term sosiego (quietude)."

Stimulated by the wealth of the Indies, Spanish industry had brought new prosperity to many of the nation's cities. Saragossa, Valladolid, Segovia, Granada, Valencia, and others provided good work for the skilled and diligent in all manner of occupations from arms production to art crafts, cabinetmaking to tanning, the provision of salt, silkworms, soap, and ceramics. Above all, Spanish textiles flourished as never before. The Concejo de la Mesta, a great corporation of livestock producers, raised millions of sheep whose wool, especially the merino variety native to Spain, was renowned the world over. In Seville, three thousand looms kept some thirty thousand operators busy, while a profusion of silversmiths, jewelers, and other dealers in luxuries attested to the general affluence of the city. In Toledo, the home of fifty thousand silk looms alone, business was so buoyant that on one occasion nearly six hundred members of a hatters' guild paraded in costumes of satin and velvet embroidered in silver and gold thread. Many smaller towns, such as Ocaña, to the south of Madrid, which was famed throughout Europe for the manufacture of gloves, enjoyed their share of prosperity.

Linked with this mood of industrial vigor went the building of new roads and bridges, the opening of hitherto unnavigable stretches of the Tagus and other rivers, the digging of canals and irrigation reservoirs, and the improvement of facilities at a dozen and more ports from Barcelona round the coast to Cádiz. It stimulated, too, a fresh interest in scientific values. Among the many cultural developments fostered by the king were an Academy of Sciences and an Academy of Mathematics and Engineering, each catering both for civilians and officers of the armed services. In the field of natural science, a botanical garden was established at Aranjuez, the royal summer residence on the Tagus south of Madrid, and a scientific expedition sent to the Americas to collect specimens. The climate generated a whole range of fine scientists, artists, and men of letters, among them the architect and engineer Juan de Herrera of Escorial fame, the naturalists Francisco Hernández and Antonio Nardo, and the erudite Aria Montano, who, true to the spirit underlying so much Spanish endeavor, supervised the publishing of a monumental polyglot Bible. It was the era that promoted the painting of El Greco and gave birth to the even greater Velásquez. Over all, the apex of empire, the living symbol of what would come to be known as Spain's Golden Age, presided a royal court of such lofty style and ostentation that even the prosperous burghers of Castile complained of its extravagance. From the greatest of its major-domos to the most junior of its pages, the royal household comprised not less than fifteen hundred members and cost as much to maintain, according to a reflective Cortes at Valladolid, "as would be needed to conquer a kingdom."

Yet, if the king considered such display consistent with imperial dignity, he was not as a person rash or flamboyant. His good looks—thoughtful, wide-set eyes, straight nose, and generous mouth—augmented by an upright, soldierly carriage, were almost always offset by dark, funereal garments. Portraits of him in his prime, by Sancho Coello, and in his sixties, by Juan Pantoja de la Cruz, showed him with the same erect bearing, trim beard and black clothing. He looked, and to some extent behaved, like a princely librarian. In his father, he had seen the fate of the traveling, battling monarch, and was not inclined to repeat it. In a reign of four decades, he would scarcely move outside his own country, and for the greater part of the time ruled from the confines of an office. Even at the Escorial, Philip was most at home in his so-called cell, his inner sanctum, where, it was his boast, "with a bit of paper" he governed two hemispheres. Spain had never known a more aloof and self-possessed authority, nor had the affairs of her dominions been supervised so minutely from one desk. Tireless in the bureaucratic arts of drafting, annotating, and creating committees, Philip preferred to pore all night over memos rather than relinquish the slightest power of decision. Unawed either by the nobles or the

Cortes, he took all things on their merit in his own eyes, deliberated laboriously and acted firmly, as he thought for the best. Frustrating as his methods sometimes proved to those around him, most Spaniards respected his unstinting labor. Elsewhere in Europe, he was distrusted and feared like the devil.

But to the energetic Don John, among the country's more adventurous gentlemen, there seemed some truth in the nervous foreign jibe that, if death were to come from the Spain of Philip, people would be a long time dying. In particular, John found his sequestered half-brother's reaction to Lepanto dull and unimaginative. Philip not only restrained John's elated impulse to fall on Constantinople and carve out an eastern empire, he poured equally cold water on an even more romantic scheme to rescue Mary, the Catholic Queen of Scots, from a Protestant prison in England and place her on the throne of that kingdom. The king was conserving his strength for a move neither to the north nor the east, but in a direction at once less expected and more obvious. Meanwhile, he plowed through the routine administration of empire, and waited in patience. "Time and I," he was pleased to assure his detractors, "are a match for any other two." Not all Spaniards had so much time to spare. Many, left stranded by the changing tide of politics, deteriorated hopelessly in Barbary dungeons. In the Netherlands, the one portion of the strife-ridden Roman Empire remaining to Spain, others fought a messy battle against mounting nationalist sentiments. Riots fomented there a decade earlier by the Calvinists had provoked retributive brutality from the Catholic authority, leaving a legacy of civil war, hatred, intrigue, and treachery which was very little to Philip's tidy and methodical taste.

In 1576, Don John was appointed governor-general of the Flemish provinces. The hero of Lepanto had wanted action; Philip granted it—not in England, but at least on the doorstep of the island. It was a far cry from the sunny waters of John's greatest success, and his response reached home in increasingly despondent letters. He had arrived to find the Spanish forces of occupation in mutiny and Antwerp sacked in defiance of their commanders. The whole bleak country was embroiled in violence and disorder. No loyalties could be trusted. "I feel desperate," he wrote. "I have fallen into a hellish pit and can see no way out." Two years later

John lay ill with fever amid the mud of Flanders. The fight had gone out of him. In the winter of 1578, a brief communique, from Francisco de Orientes, one of John's captains, lay among the papers on Philip's desk. "He died in the garret of a Flemish farmhouse like a simple soldier, thus following our Lord Jesus Christ."

The king was preoccupied with news from other quarters. At last the chance he awaited in the west was arriving, materializing in a maelstrom of drama. Not even the patient Philip could have believed time would prove so consummate an ally. Portugal, long associated with Spain through a sequence of royal marriages and a joint monopoly of colonial enterprises, had experienced a progressive decline in the caliber of her monarchs. The line which had begun auspiciously in John I, the outstanding Portuguese patriarch, had now reached absurdity in a misguided young man named Sebastian. Had Sebastian merely been impelled by devotional lunacy, he would not have been unique in peninsula pedigree: what distinguished him was his power to deny all restraint. It was his mission, he deemed, to cross to Morocco and wage all-out holy war on the Muslim. This intention he detailed to Philip, who was sufficiently impressed by the disastrous possibilities of the project to offer some help. The gesture, though predictably lacking in fulfillment, contributed to Sebastian's resolve to defy his own counselors. In June 1578, while John of Austria was succumbing to the ardors of the Netherlands, the headstrong Portuguese crusader bade farewell to a country creamed of its wealth and chivalry and sailed from Lisbon on his mad and ruinous venture.

Five hundred ships accompanied Sebastian to North Africa, bearing some seventeen thousand soldiers and getting on for ten thousand noncombatants. So certain was the king of Moroccan submission that he had brought his own crowd of spectators to witness the triumphal procession. A large number were women, among them many adventurous young beauties. More astonished than dismayed, the Emperor of Morocco allowed them to proceed. For five days he let them march inland beneath an unsparing sun, then, their strength and enthusiasm drained in the hot sand, he turned his warriors on the invaders. With the treatment of their Morisco brethren across the straits still rankling, the Muslims did a thorough job. In four hours, the flower of Portuguese chivalry was strewn in the dust of Alcázar-Kebir. Thousands of the invaders lay dead and mutilated, presumably including Sebastian, who was never heard of again. Thousands more were herded into captivity and slavedom. For many an excitement-seeking Portuguese spectator, the day ended all too dramatically. Less than a hundred of Sebastian's followers reached the ships and safety.

The news stunned Madrid as well as Lisbon, but the former was quicker to recover. Spain buzzed with the implications. Not only was Portugal virtually defenseless; Philip, son of a Portuguese princess and son-in-law of a Portuguese king, could fairly bid to become her sovereign and protector. The most imperturbable of Castilian nobles was hard put to uphold the "sosiego." For the first time in almost a thousand years, the whole peninsula was within the grasp of a single Spanish monarch. With Europe's second-largest colonial empire merged with the largest, Spain would dominate the trade routes to the east as well as the west and rule possessions from China around the world to America. The average mind boggled, but already Philip had the step measured, the plan neatly filed in his head. His anticipation was completed by military preparedness. The army, as it happened, was confronted by no problems. Overwhelmed by Sebastian's disaster, the remnants of Portugal's nobility and her clergy were easily coerced. By December 1580 Lisbon was Philip's. For the first time in twenty-one years, he left Spain to celebrate the occasion, actually discarding his black costume for a suit of festive brocade to make a gala entry of the city.

Muslim Algiers, so persistently a thorn in the flesh of Christendom, basked with deceptive charm beside the bright sea. Against its mosques and chalky flat-roofed houses fell the shadows of palms and the softer outline of cypresses, laurels and orange trees. In the cooling evening, its narrow streets, with their perfumiers and sellers of spices and sweet drinks, echoed scents and sounds vividly implanted in Spanish consciousness. Guitars played, fountains splashed, and the ritual chanting of an ever-watchful religion wafted on gusts of warm desert air. There were many Spaniards in Algiers. Some came and went freely as traders and ambassadors, but most were prisoners or slaves: simple fishermen and peasants snatched by corsairs from the coasts of Andalusia, Valencia, and Catalonia, or soldiers taken at Tunis and elsewhere. Many were used to row the galleys of their captors; others sold as menials into Muslim houses and palaces. Cowed into passivity by privation and brutal punishment, the majority had little hope of regaining freedom. Only the wealthy, or those with influential home connections, dared look forward to a purchased release, and even then the wrangling over terms frequently proved dishearteningly protracted.

For a while, Cervantes had languished grimly in Mami's dungeon. With no outside contact save the regular intoning of the muezzins, he sickened and grew alarmingly weak. At last, fearing the loss of an extravagant ransom through overzealous security, his captors permitted the bearer of Don John's letter to mix with less closeted prisoners. Among the ransom-worthy Spaniards held in Algiers on the arrival of Cervantes were such men as Juan de Lanuza, a son of the chief justice of Aragon; Antonio de Toledo, a brother of the current duke of the illustrious house of Alba; and Francisco de Valencia, knight of the militant order of St. John. To be classified as a potentially valuable property, albeit by an avaricious renegade like Mami, gave Cervantes a prestige with his fellow prisoners beyond his rank, if not his pretensions. Soon his immediate circle of friends included captains and aristocrats, among whom the newcomer saw himself as a figure of hope and fresh initiative. By the beginning of 1576 he was at the center of a small group planning its escape from the city, and had personally induced a Moorish guide to aid the venture. But the plan, to set out on foot for Spanish-held Oran to the west, was optimistic. The journey, well over two hundred miles, would involve a good deal of trackless, unwatered terrain, and the chances of finding the way safely were poor regardless of further hazards. These included apprehension or pursuit in the region of Algiers, attack by lions which infested the neighboring hills, and the likelihood of encountering tribesmen in the wastelands, hostile nomads whose attitude to prisoners was less sentimental than that of the Algerians themselves.

The small gang of desperadoes, among them a Spanish sergeant who had already been deprived of his ears for an earlier escape bid, need not have worried about such eventualities. On their first day out, the guide provided by Cervantes deserted them and they were left with no option but to retrace their tracks. For his part in the fiasco, Cervantes was treated with increased severity by Mami. But his hopes were not crushed. The following spring, two priests of the Order of Mercy arrived in Algiers with money to ransom a number of prisoners. With them they brought three hundred crowns provided by the parents of Cervantes. To raise it, his father had pawned his modest belongings, while the mother had masqueraded in widow's weeds and begged from door to door in Madrid. Since the sum was insufficient to free Cervantes, it was spent instead on ransoming his brother Rodrigo, also a prisoner at Algiers. The release of Rodrigo inspired Cervantes with a second, and more ambitious, escape plan. On his return to Christendom, Rodrigo should procure and brief a rescue ship to rendezvous with his brother at a quiet beach to the east of the city. Through a fellow prisoner who was gardener to the *caid*, or city governor, Cervantes had access to a quiet plot of land bordering the shore a small distance from the town. On this secluded section of the *caid's* estate existed a little-known cave, well hidden by thickets. Here, an escape party could await the arrival of the boat.

Cervantes lost no time in bestowing his inventiveness upon the more important of his associates, two of whom provided letters of recommendation for Rodrigo to take to the Spanish authorities, each urging the loan of a frigate. At the same time, another Spaniard ransomed by the priests, a sailor named Viana, who knew the Algerian coast, pledged himself to navigate the rescue vessel. Viana was as good as his word. Some four months later, he set sail for Algiers from Majorca. News of the sailing, reaching the escapees on the Christian "grapevine," caused a burst of excitement. Some had been hiding in the cave for months, supplied with food by Cervantes, the gardener, and a Spanish renegade nicknamed El Dorador, the Gilder, whom, like the guide of the first instance, the master planner had somewhat sanguinely trusted. Cautiously, Viana approached the shore under cover of darkness and put down a boat. With equal caution, the prisoners crept from their hiding place. Suddenly there were shouts, and a scuffle of feet in the distance. By sheer coincidence, it seems, a party of Moors had been passing along the beach at the time. As they now made off in alarm for the city, the boatmen hastily retreated to the frigate which immediately stood out to safer waters. Cervantes later accused the sailors of "lacking in spirit," but they could hardly have been blamed had they suspected a trap. In fact, that was yet to come. Under pressure, the weakest link in the escape system cracked. Fearful that the prisoners would be discovered, the renegade El Dorador promptly put himself right by betraying the cave and its inmates to the Ottoman viceroy of Algiers, Hassan Pasha.

Not only were Cervantes and his fellow fugitives apprehended, but Viana's boatmen, returning for a second rescue attempt when the coast appeared to have quietened, rowed straight into ambush and were captured as well. With patriarchal resignation, Cervantes took the entire blame upon himself. At first the viceroy threatened him with death, but since, having remitted the sentence, he then bought Cervantes for five hundred crowns from Mami, the threat was possibly a ploy to reduce the purchase price. It seems that the romancer with the crippled hand was still regarded as a lucrative property in Algiers, a delusion his lofty if incompetent role as escape hero had done nothing to diminish. At all events, the viceroy, Hassan, a former Venetian who had formed an alliance with the admiral Uluch Ali, conceived a desire to preserve his intriguing captive; a desire which was to persist, rather oddly, despite repeated provocation. Cervantes had been spared, but the Spanish gardener was hung by the feet until killed by his own blood while other unco-operative captives continued to be burned, flogged to death, or impaled on hooks to perish in unspeakable agony. Undeterred, Cervantes pursued his mission, the tireless agent of hope and freedom.

The same year, he dispatched to the Spanish secretary of state, Mateo Vázquez, a smuggled letter addressed to King Philip. A less exceptional champion of the oppressed might have been content to let the facts speak plainly for themselves. Cervantes wrote in verse, parading an elaborate and pretentious command of language. Again, a less exceptional champion might have feared to presume to advise the Spanish king. Cervantes suggested that an expedition should be mounted to seize Algiers and end the misery of the captive Christians. Moreover, confident that an armada would result from his request, he outlined to the closest of his associates a plan to assist the expected squadrons by fomenting revolt among the prisoners. "The very thought of your approach," he assured the sovereign, "will so terrorize the foe that I predict his rout and perdition." But the state office had more important matters to attend to than the predictions of an obscure poet in Muslim Africa, and the idea of acting on such a letter was never entertained. Despairing at length of help from Madrid, Cervantes turned his thoughts once more to the objective of his original project, Oran. If he could not reach Oran, at least the governor of that city, Martín de Córdoba, himself a former captive in Algiers, might be persuaded to send help. In 1578, Cervantes wrote to governor Córdoba, entrusting the letter to a Moor who promised to return with a reply. The Moor never got out of Algiers. Apprehended on the outskirts, he was duly impaled for his trouble, while Cervantes, hauled again before Hassan, was sentenced to two thousand strokes. Such a sentence implied the equivalent of being killed several times over, and the viceroy, having relished his joke, did not proceed with its execution.

Meanwhile, Cervantes' father and mother had remained active in Spain on their son's behalf. Apart from presenting petitions and testimonials in his favor, they had applied for leave to export goods to Algiers and, in the summer of 1579, paid another sum of money toward a ransom to two Trinitarian monks who were bound for North Africa. The monks moved slowly, however, and before the end of the year Cervantes was implicated in yet another escape scheme. This time no less than sixty prisoners were promised their freedom. The enterprise depended on striking a deal with a pair of men of very different persuasions. One was a Spanish renegade from a reputable Andalusian family, Girón, who had taken the name of Abderraman. Abderraman-Girón was desirous of returning to the land and faith of his fathers, and Cervantes, having cautiously won his confidence, hit on a plan to their mutual advantage. The other man was a wealthy Valencian merchant named Exarque, who did a thriving trade between Spain and Algiers. Exarque, with homes on both sides of the sea, was happy talking business with either Christians or Muslims. The proposition was simple. To Exarque, Cervantes spoke of his many influential associates in Algiers, men capable of bringing rich support to the Valencian's business house should they manage to gain their freedom. All that was required to guarantee their good will, he maintained, was a cash advance on future trading: say, enough to buy an armed frigate. To Abderraman-Girón, Cervantes promised the money to buy a ship that would sail him to Spain. All Girón had to do in return was to take a shipload of prisoners with him. The method was that Exarque would give the money to Cervantes, Cervantes would pass it to the renegade who would then purchase the ship, ostensibly to set himself up as a Muslim privateer. Of the three principals, none but Cervantes knew the identity of both the others. It was Cervantes, too, who chose and instructed his fellow escapees. But, as usual, there was a snag. To his misfortune, he had excluded from his choice a Dominican monk named Juan Blanco de Paz, who appears to have borne Cervantes an excessively bitter grudge. So much so, in fact, that he warned Hassan that the poet was involved in a new escape plot. Cervantes was forced to call off the operation and give himself up. Though he refused to name any of the other conspirators, the viceroy once more spared his life. So long as he had Cervantes in his charge, he is said to have asserted dryly, his Christians, his ships and his city were safe.

Whether Hassan regarded Cervantes as an engaging risk or a form of human escape alarm, it is certain that the captive now owed his life more than once to the reputedly heartless viceroy, whom he regarded as his archenemy. By the late summer of 1580, Hassan's turn of office in Algiers was at an end and Cervantes was embarked for Constantinople along with other Christians owned by the Ottoman official. But the Trinitarian monks from Spain, having arrived in Algiers in April, had not been inactive. Even as the ship prepared to sail, they were bargaining for a release. Hassan had persistently refused less than five hundred gold ducats in ransom, and, since the money available was substantially less, the final hope remained in raising the difference from the Christian merchants in the city. Eventually, Exarque and two other Valencians paid up. On September 19 the monks triumphantly produced the required sum and Cervantes was put off the ship a free man. By Christmas he was in Madrid. After the first elation of homecoming, his impressions were depressing. To a capital preoccupied with Portugal, acquisition, and affluence, one more ex-prisoner of war among the disabled "heroes" and paupers on the streets was not an appreciable embarrassment. In Algiers, he had passed as somebody; in Madrid, he was a nobody. His sole wealth consisted of a small charitable payment made by the Church out of its collections for prisoners from North Africa. His parents, now old and ailing, had given their all to raise the ransom. Don John, his hero and great hope, was dead.

Many changes had occurred in political circles since Miguel de Cervantes had left Spain, and the stories which surrounded some of them did not inspire him. There was, for instance, a bitter note in the accounts he heard of the end of a great man of his younger days, Espinosa. A cleric of relatively humble origin whose worldly capabilities and energies had commended him to Philip, Espinosa had lived to be one of the country's most versatile men of affairs: president of the councils of Castile and the Indies, minister of state, and, to the great distaste of his enemies, Inquisitor General. He also had held the bishopric of a very rich see, Sigüenca. Regarding the tireless churchman as a useful check on the ambitions of certain nobles, the king had even applied to Rome to have Espinosa capped as a cardinal. But, as the pundits not unhappily related, so much so quickly had proved the man's downfall. Intoxicated by success, the fine cardinal had begun to encroach tactlessly on the king's own prerogatives. That had spelled the end. In a somewhat theatrical scene during a ministerial debate, Philip had smashed the power he had promoted, furiously denouncing Espinosa as a liar. His stunned protégé had plunged swiftly through crisis to a quick death (1572).

Gossip had been the more pungent for the king's uncharacteristic display of emotion. Philip rarely took his seat in the council of state, preferring to receive written reports of proceedings which, in the privacy of his closet, he could embellish at length with his tightly scrawled comments. It was his contention that his ministers would debate more freely in his absence, while the resulting acridity often served his purpose. He was a master at playing the more assertive elements of his government one against the other. Among the most powerful of these before the time of Cervantes' departure had been the Duke of Alba, an aggressive militarist, and a more pacific and liberal grandee, Ruy Gómez da Silva. Both had many followers, but after initiating a disgraceful campaign of terror in Flanders in 1567, substantially worsening the situation in that country, Alba had lost ground, allowing Ruy Gómez to further his own cause. Close to the king's ear, he had been a sage and moderating influence, but he was not then a young man and his death in 1573 had set the stage for another scandal, which, when Cervantes returned, was hot on the lips of Spanish society.

Ruy Gómez da Silva had enhanced his estate by marrying a much younger woman, Anna de Mendoza, Princess of Eboli, rich, vivacious, and gallante. Blind in one eye, a notorious glint in the other, Anna had taken as her lover one Antonio Pérez, an underling of her late husband. To add sauce to the situation, Pérez, an astute and dedicated careerist, had soon replaced the deceased lord as a favored minister to Philip. Indeed, as head of the *despacho universal*, the private bureau from which the king issued his dominion correspondence, Pércz became Philip's most intimate assistant, a man uniquely responsible and trusted. The more sensational, then, his arrest in 1579 for instigating the murder of another of the king's secretaries, Juan de Escobedo, whose friends laid the charge with inescapable credibility. The victim, well known for his blunt and tactless advocacy of Don John's ill-favored post-Lepanto strategies, had been found dead of knife wounds in a Madrid back street after surprising Pérez with his mistress and berating them, it seems, for their disreputable behavior. So much was sensational, yet more was to come. For Pérez, forced into a corner, claimed Philip's complicity in Escobedo's murder.

Like Espinosa, however, he was to find the king unrelenting toward protégés who overstepped the mark, and was lucky to escape eventually to France with his life. As it happened, Philip, though unquestionably behind Escobedo's removal, went on to turn the affair to good advantage. Pérez fled first to Aragon, which still insisted on its traditions of independence and was often obstructive to the crown. When the king demanded that the prisoner be turned over by the authorities who held him in Saragossa, the people of that city took arms to prevent it. Philip had the perfect excuse to deploy troops. Not only was he quick to restore order, he also took the opportunity of ridding himself of a number of leading Aragonese nobles and citizens. The constitutional changes he subsequently inflicted on the government of Aragon, though moderate, gave the mass of people greater protection under the crown than before and restricted the more tyrannical activities of their masters. Nevertheless, the original scandal had been unsavory, and Cervantes, returning to Madrid in the earlier stages of the episode, must have been shocked by the slander and defamation on all sides. After the simple values and ideals that had sustained him through his hard times abroad, the high-powered intrigue and competition of the capital, with its seeming cynicism and lack of charity, provided a harsh revelation.

For the next few years, Cervantes tried hard to earn a living by writing. His major project, La Galatea, a pastoral novel in the fashion of the moment, was at least a vehicle in which to escape into a kinder and better-ordered world. Arcadian in concept, prolix and ornamental in treatment, it satisfied the requirements of its type and, on publication in 1585, gained its author a measure of notice. It did not, however, bring fame or fortune. "It proposes something and concludes nothing," he wrote himself. Meanwhile, his first love, the poetry he continued to write with fluency and facility, contributed even less toward his security. Instead, he turned a hungry eye to the world of theater. A decade or two earlier, a traveling player named Lope de Rueda, from Seville, had raised the curtain on popular theater in Madrid and other Spanish cities by writing and performing a series of verse plays interspersed with short, racy sketches, or pasos, in everyday Spanish. These sketches, involving such stock characters of commedia del arte as the servant, doctor, Negress, rustic, and so forth, took place on crude, improvised stages and met with such success that other companies had soon followed Rueda's lead. Before long, regular theaters were built. By 1584, there were three permanent theaters in Madrid, while "fine weather" performances took place in gardens and courtyards. It was not unlike the Elizabethan stage of England with the additional attraction that actresses took part. One result of this rapid new development in entertainment was a lack of suitable writers. Plays written by poets and novelists tended to be too slow, too literary in form to satisfy an audience stimulated by Rueda's intuitively visual studies. It seems that Cervantes was no exception.

Though he considered several of his own plays "worthy of

praise," and at least one as "good among the best," he failed to grasp the opportunities waiting in the theater. With such themes as Jerusalem and the Battle of Lepanto he aimed at a virtuous and patriotic note, but he lacked the temperament to write uninhibitedly to a public. Neither was failure made any the easier by the rise of a rival, fifteen years his junior, who offered his audiences everything they had been looking for. If it is a remarkable coincidence that the two greatest names in Spanish literature should have lived at the same time, it is also remarkable how little their lives resembled each other. Lope de Vega, or more precisely Lope Félix de Vega Carpio, had been born at Madrid in 1562, the son of an amateur poet from Santander, and educated at a Jesuit college and Alcalá university. From the first he had shown the precocious versatility that would lead in time to the production of no less than fifteen hundred plays and inestimable poems, not to mention an endless series of involved love affairs, all sorts of business interests and a diary brimming with social activities. Agile and comely, stylish in all things, Lope was one of nature's favorites, a privileged being for whom all endeavor was blessed with success. At five, he had dictated verse to older children, at ten he had already written plays, by the time he left school he was accomplished at music, dancing, and swordsmanship. Confidence and impetuosity led to mischief in his youth. At twelve, Lope had run away "to see the world," hiking across half Spain before returning. At seventeen, now given to theatrical company, he fell passionately and boastfully in love with a Madrid beauty named Elena Osorio, the separated wife of an actor and the daughter of a prominent actor-manager, Jerónimo Velásquez, the producer of a number of plays by Cervantes. On his own count, Lope wrote some two thousand verses extolling the charms of Elena, but, falling out with her parents, apparently added one or two others in a different vein. From these vitriolic little satires one might have decided that the fair Elena was merely a bawd, her mother a procuress, while her father and brother lived on her earnings. The outcome was a libel action, conviction and Lope's proscription from Madrid for several years. Little abashed, he soon returned to the capital in defiance of the order and eloped with the daughter of one of the king's heralds.

Lope de Vega's great zest for life, his highly impressionable mind and quick impulse to transform emotion into action, admirably equipped him for the job of writing popular plays. By the mid-eighties, when an impoverished Cervantes was ready to abandon the theater and writing in general as a livelihood, Lope was beginning to be talked about as the brilliant new playwright. Already he was aware of the facility that would enable him, later, to maintain a regular production of two plays a week and complete some in no more than a couple of days. Though given to disparaging the audience that adored him—"the vehemence of the seated Spaniard," he wrote, "is not appeased unless he is shown in the space of two hours everything from Genesis to the Last Judgement"—he catered for its demands and receptive limitations with astute professionalism. Describing his method of working, he asserted the necessity of first "locking up" the classics in order that their "truthful voices" might not distract him. He favored a three-act formula, concerning himself in the first with exposition, in the second with advancing the action and adding complication, and in the third with a satisfying resolution of the plot. He knew well that his audience lost interest after the denouement and took pains to conceal it until the middle of the last act. He was also cynically conversant with the psychology of popular conceits, and took care to flatter his public accordingly. The finished product, fast-moving, elegant, and entrancing, was illumined always by the vividness and variety of an incredibly alert perception.

Forced to admit the younger man's genius, Cervantes found nothing in the other to draw them together. While Lope de Vega, with his brilliant and glancing sketches of life, proceeded rapidly to wealth and prominence, Cervantes, searching ponderously within for a viewpoint, trod a path of repeated humility and misfortune. With a seedy eye on the dowry of her propertied family, he sought at one stage to alleviate his poverty by marrying a seemingly dreary maiden of nineteen. The dowry—"some household furniture, an orchard, five vines, four beehives, forty-five hens, one cock and a crucible"—proved scarcely sustaining, and within a few months the couple had parted. In 1587, he went to Seville in search of employment. After living for a while on the generosity of a former actor who had taken an inn there, he got a job as a commissary with the fleet. There was little pay attached, but the opportunities for a dishonest man were obvious. According to royal decree, the duties were to requistion grain "from whoever has it in his possession, regardless of station or office, whether ecclesiastical or otherwise." Unfortunately for Cervantes, he was honest to the point of recklessness. At Ecija, in the Genil valley, he requisitioned a supply of corn belonging, in part, to the dean and chapter of Seville. The outcry was immediate. With the Church behind them, the people saw their chance to vent their fury on one of Seville's detested commissaries. Cervantes left the town hurriedly, but the archbishop of Seville's steward excommunicated him and the church at Ecija carried news of his disgrace on its notice board. "How can they talk so much about God and act so much like the Devil?" Cervantes would write later. He put the words in the mouth of a dog.

Chapter 7

SPAIN "INVINCIBLE"

Few cities are more spectacular on approach than Cádiz, shimmering off the Atlantic coast of Andalusia like *"una taza de plata,"* as the Spanish have it; like a dish of silver. On this lump of shell-limestone rock, with its rim of white water, the Phoenicians founded their trading base of Gadir, later Gades. Here, the Greeks first studied a phenomenon new to them in the rise and fall of Atlantic tides. And here, the Romans, full of praise for the cuisine, observed another phenomenon, the port's famous dancing girls. From the beginning, Cádiz catered for the tastes of its visitors, and when the Indies fleets began to use its harbor, the place enjoyed added prosperity and liveliness. As a shipping rendezvous at the gate between east and west, the anchorage served every type of vessel, from little Mediterranean coasters to the towering treasure carracks of the Spanish main. Toward the end of April 1587, something like five dozen seagoing craft packed the harbor, among them some big ocean traders. To their crews, Cádiz in spring, with canaries singing beside white-framed doors and windows, and the distant sierra covered in wild flowers, must have seemed an enviable station. It is known that on the afternoon of the twenty-ninth of that month, a Wednesday, a company of strolling players presented a *comedia*, a play, at the seaport. In the town square, a professional acrobat went through his paces. For those seeking headier diversions, the bold wines and the bold wenches of the town promised evanescent pleasure. The evening might bring trouble; but only from jealous husbands and sportive drunks.

There was no immediate anxiety, therefore, when a line of un-identifiable sailing vessels was spotted standing in for the harbor at about four o'clock. Only as the line drew closer, and the form of the ships became evident, did curiosity turn to consternation. Seven powerful galleons, bristling with guns, were followed by a similar number of lighter men-of-war and a dozen or so frigates and pinnaces. Spain had no fleet of such proportions in home waters. In fact, her defense squadrons consisted mainly not of sail-ing galleons but of galleys, the standard oar-propelled warships of the Mediterranean. Six or seven of these now lay in Cádiz, long, low craft armed largely with antipersonnel weapons. Any one of the approaching galleons had more fire power in a broadside than all the galleys in Cádiz together, and when one of the latter, mov-ing sprucely forward to hail the oncomers, was stopped short by a barrage of flying metal, the consternation took a turn toward panic.

Many women, hustling children and old folk before them, fled for the shelter of the town fortress, fearing a prompt landing and the sack of their homes. The commander of the fort, loath to be impeded by noncombatants, closed the gates against them, where-upon a score or more were crushed to death in the narrow streets outside. There was scarcely less confusion in the harbor itself. Many of the ships, immobilized by repairs or short of crew, were doomed from the first to a passive acceptance of the crisis. Others, scrambling on sail as the enemy drew closer, fouled each other in the race to escape. Only the smaller craft, able to navigate the shoals to the harbor extremities, had better luck. Here, they re-ceived a measure of cover from land batteries intended against Moorish invasion. But such guns were not sited to range the bay, and the intruders bore in with alarming precision. On the attack-ing flagship, the *Elizabeth Bonaventure* of England, a professional corsair named Francis Drake ran a practiced eye around the anchor-age. Drake, small and fiery, with an old grudge against Spaniards, had become the most feared pirate from Gibraltar to the Carib-bean. So keen was his nose for plunder that superstitious seamen, marveling at his shrewdly calculated interceptions, swore that he worked with a magic mirror in his cabin. But not even El Draque had been looked to for so outrageous an affront as that now taking place.

Backed with ships and resources by the English government, Drake had planned this, his most audacious raid to date, where the prospects seemed fattest and a strike least expected. As the great line of warships moved menacingly into the harbor, it seemed once more as though the "mirror" had been right. Only the small flotilla of painted galleys barred the way to the town and its shipping. Swinging their broadsides into action, the English galleons swept the low decks of the defenders with missiles. Shaken, the galleys sheered off, wheeled, and came in from a different quarter. Again, the English gunners stopped them at a distance. It was a fascinating if grim engagement, confirming with utmost clarity the obsolescence of the galley after centuries of naval supremacy, and the new omnipotence of the heavily armed sailing vessel. For all their elegance, darting speed and independence of wind, the oar-propelled warships that had inflicted such fearful damage to each other at Lepanto were futile against the floating fortresses that had evolved from the quest for ocean riches. Bravely as the defenders of Cádiz snapped and barked at the aggressors, it took no more than an occasional side kick to repel them. Drake swept on, an intruder confronted with toy dogs. Perhaps inspired by the courage of the smaller ships, a heavy trader, waiting to clear the harbor for Genoa with a cargo of hides, wool, and logwood, joined the one-sided contest. She was a huge vessel, armed for the corsair-ridden waters of Italy, and she opened up on the leading galleons with everything she had. Her cannons were still discharging as she began to sink, shattered by English broadsides.

Eventually, while the battered galleys pulled off to land their casualties, the raiders settled to the task of capture and destruction. As dusk thickened, the first of the doomed ships were set ablaze, their flames providing a light by which Drake worked into the night. By morning, the demolition was almost over, one of the last vessels to burn being a splendid Spanish galleon in dock for the installation of new cannons. At dawn, a company of Spanish infantry marched in from neighboring Jerez. Soon afterward, a larger force arrived under the Duke of Medina Sidonia, captain-general of Andalusia. A massive bronze cannon with almost eighteen feet of barrel was now manhandled from one of the town gates to an eminence above the harbor, where it proceeded to lob balls at the enemy fleet. Though frustratingly inaccurate at the given range, it threw a potentially dangerous missile and succeeded in holing one English galleon near the waterline. Meanwhile, the Spanish galleys kept up their harassing tactics, darting out from sheltered points in the bay and sprinting away again before the broadsides could straddle them. Their vigilance at least limited the activities of the smaller English ships.

By noon, Drake was ready, even eager, to depart. His main weapon, surprise, was blunted, and the Spaniards were beginning to take the initiative. At the water's edge, squads of men filled light vessels with combustibles, setting them alight and towing or drifting them toward the English squadron. But the tactic, like Drake's exit, was marred by a drop in the wind. Doggedly, the Spaniards lugged another heavy cannon to the foreshore to join its erratic companion in a largely harmless bombardment. To those with no clear view of the drama, the spasmodic booming of the two pieces provided its audible finale. The calm continued until around midnight, when a breeze sprang up from the land. By dawn, Drake had gone. He had, at his own estimate, depleted the shipping in Cádiz by thirty-seven vessels, destroyed or captured. The Spanish put the figure at twenty-four, to the value of a hundred and seventy-two thousand ducats. Perhaps mindful that the damage was shared by foreign owners, Philip declared it to be "not a very great loss," adding, however, that "the audacity was very great indeed." Certainly, few Spaniards cared to swallow the insult, and action against El Draque and his country became urgent. Drake himself had no doubt that repercussions would follow. What he had been able to glean in Cádiz and elsewhere on the coast confirmed the general impression already obtaining in Europe that Spain intended another march of expansion, and that this time the objective could be none other than England. "I dare not almost write of the great forces we hear the king of Spain hath," the Devon captain warned in breathless syntax. "Prepare in England strongly and most by sea!" The queen of that country was heedful of the warning. None knew better than Elizabeth the provocation her brother-in-law Philip had suffered.

"Never lose the friendship of England!" Philip, raised on the
maxim by his father, had responded as far back as 1554 by marrying Mary Tudor, thus furthering union with that country against
France. In 1558, however, her death had left him with a more
complex view of alliances. In Mary he had wed both England and
a Catholic; in her self-possessed sister and successor, Elizabeth,
he was faced with the chosen ruler of heretics, a queen much of
Europe regarded as illegitimate. When, into the bargain, she
played hard to get, coyly demurring on his dutiful offer of marriage,
he had felt free to turn to another Elizabeth: Elizabeth Valois of
France. If, in deciding to cement the peace with France which
followed St. Quentin, Philip married into a new field of alliance,
he by no means neglected the old one. Indeed, to many observers
it seemed that Philip had adjusted his father's dictum to read
"Never lose the friendship of Elizabeth Tudor!" When a Protestant plot to put her on the throne in the place of her sister had
been uncovered during Mary's reign, he had intervened in her
favor and doubtless saved her life. He had backed her accession,
using his influence with the pope to ward off the excommunication
that threatened. He had tolerated her most cynical and capricious
behavior while Catholics throughout Christendom urged him to
have done with her. He was open to charges of weakness.

Not for love did Philip suffer his late wife's sister. His main
concern was to forestall the pretensions of her rival, Mary Stuart,
"Queen of Scots," who, apart from being the Catholic heroine of
the period, was the wife of the dauphin of France and an intimate
ally of that country's most powerful family, the Guises. Little as
Philip relished dealing with English heretics, the prospect of an
Anglo-French alliance under Mary Stuart and the Guises was even
less palatable. In due course, he believed, Catholicism must rise
again in England, but not for Mary—at his own pleasure. Meanwhile, Elizabeth exploited his compulsory restraint to the utmost.
Nowhere was the virility of her aggressive, up and coming nation
more evident than at sea, where the robbery of Spanish shipping
became a highly lucrative profession. With sardonic satisfaction,
Elizabeth sponsored and shared in the profits of such activities

while disowning them to Philip as acts of private piracy. For Drake and his kind the situation was perfect. English galleons preyed on the plate fleets and spice ships not only off the peninsula and the Azores, but in the very ports of the New World itself. Others pounced on transporters in the Channel, capturing supplies and equipment bound for the Netherlands. Here again, with the ready connivance of Elizabeth, Englishmen were confronting Spaniards as volunteers for the rebel Prince William of Orange.

For every Spanish complaint, the Queen of England had an answer; with every fresh outrage came declarations of her good will. It was enough to exhaust even Philip's patience, but he needed time to co-ordinate his strategy. Two lines of development were especially important. In a France increasingly committed to counterreformation, his agents were working cautiously but successfully toward an understanding with the Guises, an understanding that would end Elizabeth's diplomatic immunity and, coincidentally, render Mary Stuart expendable. At the same time, Spanish fortune in the Netherlands was at last in the ascendant. Don John's death had seen things at their lowest ebb, with all but two of the seventeen Low Countries provinces virtually beyond Spain's control. In the north, the seven "United Provinces" (modern Holland) had actually proclaimed formal independence. Then something had happened to raise Catholic spirits. In the south, John's nephew and successor, Alexander Farnese, had taken the initiative with remarkable brilliance.

Alexander, Duke of Parma, the new governor-general of the Netherlands, was a soldier in the tradition of Gonzalo de Córdoba. Like the Great Captain, he commanded with his brain, outthinking his enemies as much as outfighting them. Like Gonzalo, he had a fine sense of terrain, turning land to his advantage, winning victories with dykes and ditches as well as with pikes and cannon balls. Like Gonzalo, too, he had great tenacity, dash, and bodily endurance. He was also a diplomat and politician of talent. In short, Spain at last had a leader in the Netherlands with the intellectual and physical equipment to grasp the situation in all its complexity and pursue an effective plan of action. Restored to confidence after years of despair, the army of occupation began to recover its function. One by one, the towns of Flanders and Brabant conceded to Parma until he had regained the whole of the south. In 1584, William of Orange was assassinated at his house in Delft. A year later, Antwerp submitted to the Spanish. With the irresistible Parma a short hop across the water, it was Elizabeth's turn to be worried. The same year, determined at least to deny Philip the Dutch invasion ports, she dropped her earlier pretenses and openly sent an army to Holland. It was a brawling, untrained, and ill-armed mob of six thousand, but it had enough English pugnacity to stand its ground against Parma's pikemen, and it enabled the Dutch to hold the Spaniards at bay.

Elizabeth's overt intervention in the Netherlands urged Philip to think in detail of a conquest of England. With England inside the Spanish Empire, all would be order again: in the Netherlands, on the high seas, throughout Western Europe. It was, as one of his ambassadors put it, "God's obvious design." The settlement of Portugal had helped to make it evident. Here, with customary discretion and moderation, Philip had left the laws, privileges, and administration largely undisturbed, setting up among his many other boards and committees a council of Portuguese nationals to deal with matters of their land in Madrid. The resulting good will in Portuguese circles was as important to what came to be known as the "England enterprise" as Portuguese vessels and ports. Spain's premier admiral, the Marquis of Santa Cruz, an aging hero of Lepanto, was particularly impressed by the Portuguese sea force. In contemplating the new enterprise, however, neither he nor Philip underestimated the English fleet. Verging on his sixties, a cataract dimming one eye and a hand shot with gout, the still-handsome Philip was not blind to the danger of Drake and his compatriots, nor inhibited in correcting the over-optimistic. Time and again, bent over the desk in his inner sanctum, the king had scrawled "impossible" or "nonsense" against memos from gentlemen who regarded as easy the conquest of so small a nation as Elizabeth's. Santa Cruz estimated that he would need about five hundred sailing vessels to do it, a hundred and fifty of them galleons or big armed merchantmen, with thirty thousand mariners and sixty thousand soldiers. On the other hand, Parma intimated that he could land an adequate army in barges from Flanders by night without naval assistance. His scheme, however, was conditional upon an element which, to Philip, seemed as impossible of attainment as the old admiral's dream of five hundred ships. Parma stipulated the need for absolute surprise.

The strategy Philip himself conceived, a modified combination of the methods outlined by the two men, was more truly related to realities. 1, Santa Cruz would collect an armada at Lisbon (an armada less impractical in size than the admiral's estimate, but still larger than anything yet floated by the nation). 2, This armada would sail up the English Channel and rendezvous with Parma's barges off Flanders. 3, The combined force would proceed to a landing point on the southeast coast of England, the bigger ships deploying as necessary to beat off the English navy and to maintain a line of communication with the Netherlands. Assuming a safe landing, Philip relied heavily in his calculations on the backing of English Catholics who, so their activists assured him, awaited only a signal to rise against their government. This was the most dubious aspect of the project. As it happened, with that insular phlegm that had frustrated so many foreign missionaries, Englishmen were ill-disposed toward a civil war of ideologies. Too many, irrespective of religion, had hitched their fortunes to Elizabeth's regime to want them upset by a Spaniard who already, as they saw it, owned more than a fair share of the world. Especially was this true of the southeast, the projected Spanish beachhead, where London, among other places, was stoutly for Elizabeth. Suitably horrific stories were spread to further the queen's cause. The Spaniards, it was said, would bring cargoes of torture implements for use by the Inquisition in a conquered England. Accompanying them, another tale had it, would sail thousands of wet nurses to take charge of the babies of murdered English parents.

When, in February 1587, Mary Stuart was led before a chilly audience in Fotheringhay Hall, England, and beheaded on a velvet-covered chopping block, the apparent apathy of the island's Catholics was scarcely an omen the invader might have relished. Even her son, James VI of Scotland, was satisfied by the public tears of Elizabeth, the woman who had signed his mother's death warrant. Elsewhere in Europe, however, there was fierce indignation. Spaniards were still discussing Elizabeth's villainy when Drake sailed into Cádiz and put a torch to the whole inflammable situation. In the clamor for war that immediately swept Spain, the silence of England's Catholics went unheeded. Philip, having once written that in so important a project as the conquest of England "it is appropriate to move with leaden feet," was eager of a sudden for action. The mood of his people, he appreciated, was well suited to the by no means enviable business of amphibious invasion. "Hurry!" he was soon urging his subordinates, "Success depends mostly on speed." There were yet to be months of frustration. At first, the wave of chauvinism that followed Cádiz did little but illumine earlier apathy. The corruption and resistance Cervantes had met in his requisitioning duties at Seville were only part of the general confusion that had surrounded armada preparations. Procrastination, incompetence, and profiteering had dogged Santa Cruz from the beginning. Merchants exploited him with faulty goods; workmen delayed or extended their jobs. The marquis himself was near the age of retiring, wearied by a hard and unsparing life. To Philip's dismay, a special commissioner sent to check progress toward the appointed time of sailing found stores and ordnance in chaos. The ships themselves, less than a hundred discounting auxiliaries, were mostly slow and decrepit, rejects from every sea in the Spanish orbit. Some were frankly unsailable. A mere dozen could be classified as first-line fighting galleons, and even these needed attention. To cap everything, with sailing due in a few days, Santa Cruz died.

His successor took command with the greatest reluctance. Alonso de Guzmán el Bueno, Duke of Medina Sidonia and head of one of the most illustrious houses in Castile, had been endowed at birth with as much eminence as his mild and sensitive temperament desired. Of average stature, with benign, rather fragile features, the illustrious duke was both acutely conscious of the problems facing the armada's commander and unimpressed by what others might have deemed the private glory. "Since I lack experience either of the sea or of war," he wrote on receiving news of the appointment, "I do not feel I should command so important an enterprise. Being ignorant of the Marquis of Santa Cruz's activities, and his knowledge of England, I believe I should give but a poor account of myself." Such modesty, all too readily accepted at face value later, did not deceive Philip. Rather must it have confirmed the very qualities of honesty and directness so badly needed to pull the project together. Nor were these the only attributes equipping the duke for the venture. His sense of duty to Spain and the Church was impeccable. His social distinction was such that the touchiest of nobles would not be offended to serve under him. His tact and affability enabled him to get on with most men. By and large, he seems to have been an intelligent, clear-minded, and honorable gentleman. At all events, Philip, holding to his commission, was rewarded by prompt improvements at Lisbon.

If Medina Sidonia lacked the warlike experience and nature of Santa Cruz, he proved no sluggard in organization. Once in office, he briefed himself rapidly and systematically, establishing a harmonious team to assist him. For most, he represented a change for the better. Talented officers who had sulked irritably under the dogmatic veteran of Lepanto lent themselves with fresh enthusiasm to this quietly attentive aristocrat. In the new mood of cooperation his methods engendered, Medina Sidonia set carpenters to work on the ships in the harbors, replacing rotten timbers, and building additional fighting decks. Obtaining fresh help from the government, he assembled new squadrons, completed the equipment of the infantry, brought crews up to strength, and called in foreign experts to advise on ordnance. Though a shortage of heavy guns remained a nagging weakness, he greatly strengthened the armaments put in hand by Santa Cruz. Where thirty cannon balls to a gun had been aimed at for the heavier pieces, Medina Sidonia raised it to fifty, with a total at all weights of nearly one hundred and twenty-four thousand. He was careful to acquire the best powder. Nor did he neglect more humane points of detail: good Portuguese and Spanish wines for the store ships, a medical corps to take care of the injured, one hundred and eighty priests to add spiritual comfort. Durable provisions such as biscuit, dried fish, bacon, and beans were loaded in hundreds of tons.

Santa Cruz had died in February. By the end of April, Medina Sidonia had transformed a scene of confusion into a force of such impressive order that officials were talking of "*la felicíssima armada*," the fortunate armada. Others called it "*la invencible.*" In its final state, the fleet comprised 130 vessels, including 20 galleons, 44 big armed merchantmen, 4 galleasses (armed sailing vessels supplemented with oars) and an assortment of victualers, transports, and lighter craft. Aboard this fleet were some 7000 sailors and upward of 17,000 troops. The whole, drawn from all parts of the Spanish Empire, was a remarkable feat of organization. Not only were there differences of language and procedure to contend with among Spaniards, Portuguese, and Italians, but even among these there were regional variations. Apart from the galleons (ten Portuguese, ten Castilian), regarded as a force in their own right, the fighting squadrons were detailed on a provincial basis. Among the officers, Juan Martínez de Recalde, commanding Biscayans, Miguel de Oquendo with Guipuzcoans of the Basque region, and Pedro de Valdés with Andalusians were leading members of the admiral's war council. The galleasses, from Naples, were under Hugo de Moncada. As his chief of staff, Medina Sidonia had an ambitious and talented Spaniard, Diego Flores de Valdés, who would operate during action from the flagship *San Martín*.

As the day for sailing approached, Spain gave herself to a spate of prayer, processions, and austerities designed to proclaim her service and surrender to God. In Lisbon, the duke received his last instructions from Philip. The English fleet would be faster and better gunned than his own. After a successful landing, he might choose to seek its destruction; till then he was not to be distracted from his primary objective, the vital rendezvous with Parma. On April 25, Medina Sidonia knelt quietly in Lisbon Cathedral. The holy banner of the expedition was carried from the altar to the harbor. Every man of the expedition, from the country squires and city bloods who had flocked for adventure to the humblest deck hands pressed into service, had confessed and communicated. On the galleon *San Juan*, the playwright Lope de Vega, ever game for new excitement, watched the womenfolk on the quayside and, perhaps thinking of his latest love, caught the mood for one of his finest ballads.

> Gazing on the mighty vessels
> Which for England now are sailing,
> With her sad tears fair Belisa
> There augments the gleaming waters
> For the love who sails and leaves her . . .

In May, the armada raised sail and moved off, "all ablaze with banners," as the poet put it, "pennants fluttering on each spar."

Medina Sidonia expected the English to strike in the Channel. That long, tapering strip of water with its western point of entry between the Lizard and Ushant, its narrow eastern neck between Dover and Calais, was home-from-home to the enemy navy. And Philip had been giving no secrets when he warned of the strength of the English ships. Though the number of galleons and armed merchantmen in Elizabeth's defense was no greater than its counterpart in the armada, the best English vessels were unmatched for their fighting qualities by any in Europe. The pride of the queen's navy, eighteen galleons upward of three hundred tons apiece, had been fashioned during the preceding ten years by a radical naval architect named John Hawkins, who, contrary to the conventional practice of the time, believed in fighting at artillery range rather than closing and boarding. To the consternation of many an old-school captain, Hawkins had cut down the familiar bow and stern castles on the English warships, decked over the sheltered waists and generally reduced the protective aspect of design. By streamlining and clearing the decks for a greater number of heavy guns, he had improved both sailing performance and striking power. Unlike the stubby, inaccurate cannons which provided the heavy armament in most navies of the day, the long guns the English favored were objective and damaging at well over half a mile. No one had any delusions about England's naval power. Medina Sidonia faced the fastest, most weatherly and best-armed ships on the high seas.

The admiral of the English fleet was Charles Lord Howard of Effingham, a tall scrawny aristocrat in his fifties whose long neck, big nose, and receding forehead gave him something of the appearance of a buzzard. He now hovered watchfully on the south coast of England, where a great chain of bonfires was ready to blaze as a warning when the armada approached. At Plymouth, toward the western extremity of the Channel, lay Drake, newly appointed vice-admiral to Howard, and with him Hawkins and ninety ships, large and small. At the other end of the Channel, thirty-five English sail under Howard's nephew, Lord Henry Seymour, lurked around the heel of Kent on lookout for Parma. Plans to challenge the Spanish force on its own coast had been circumvented by a summer storm, with adverse winds following, and the Plymouth fleet could only stand by with mounting tension. Delay raised many problems. It overtaxed the resources of the small town, reducing stores to a scant level, while ships grew unhealthy for want of rummaging and cleaning. Fretfully, Howard appealed more than once for fresh food and recruits. He would have been glad to know that his adversary was faring no better. Beating slowly north from Lisbon, Medina Sidonia had encountered the same storm that had landlocked the English fleet. Part of his force was scattered; the rest ran into La Coruña for shelter. From here, in June, he wrote in somber tones to Philip. Some of his best ships were missing; others were battered and leaking; his supplies were spoiling; many soldiers and sailors were sick. Facts had to be faced. If the "invincible" armada proceeded, he warned frankly, the outcome must be open to grave doubts.

His misgivings conveyed to the king, the duke systematically set about improving his position. A hospital was established ashore to check the spread of sickness, neighboring ports were scoured for provisions, repair and maintenance work was put in hand on the ships. A month later, when most of the missing vessels had returned to the fold, the armada was back to fair shape. On July 22, having received no alteration of his original orders, Medina Sidonia sailed on. He reached the Scilly Isles, off the toe of Cornwall, before being spotted by the enemy. On the morning of Friday, July 29 (by the new calendar then in use by the Spaniards; July 19 by the old one still favored by the English), one of Howard's light ships, patrolling the mouth of the Channel, ran into the vanguard of the armada. Racing for base, the Englishman was able to give Howard just enough warning to get his fleet to sea before the Spaniards were off Plymouth. Cautiously, Medina Sidonia skirted the port, leading his host at the marching speed of its slowest member into the narrowing funnel that led toward the North Sea and Parma. English observers were staggered by the sight of the armada. With its towering poops, its forest of masts and flags, its scarcely perceptible movement, it looked like a floating city. Nowhere in the world had anyone ever beheld such an array of hostile sailing ships.

As they came in sight of the coast, palls of smoke began to rise from the warning beacons, but, if this were the moment Philip had counted on to bestir the English Catholics, it brought him no luck. Those thought likely to rejoice in the approach of the Spaniards were either under house arrest or in prison. Elizabeth was

taking no risks. Her commanders had been chosen for their unquestioned loyalty, none more fervently Protestant than the lofty
Howard, none more callous of Spanish interests than his small
lieutenant, Drake. With the Plymouth fleet behind them, these
two were now maneuvering to windward of the armada for the
lethal game of tag that was to range the Channel in the next week.
Since the wind, with brief exceptions, favored Medina Sidonia's
aim to reach his rendezvous with the minimum of digressions,
Howard's strategy was to use the superior sailing performance and
firing-range of his ships to harass from the rear, thus holding the
weather gauge. There were surprises in store for both sides. As the
English galleons swept in to make their first pass, a signal cannon
boomed on the *San Martín* and the great armada moved ponderously into defensive formation: a sweeping half-moon, victualers
and other vulnerable craft at the thickest part, sturdy warships at
the points which curved back toward the enemy. The maneuver
was remarkable both for the skill of its execution and the cunning
of its conception. The only Spanish vessels open to attack without
great danger of the English being lured into the pincer-like arms of
the crescent, or losing the weather gauge, were the big, tough ships
at the tips.

On the left wing of the formation was a massive Levanter, the
Rata Coronada, and another huge carrack, the *Regazona.* Howard,
in the English flagship *Ark Royal,* led part of his fleet against
them, line ahead, exchanging broadsides but warily remaining at
long range. On the right wing, Juan Martínez de Recalde in a
powerful galleon, the *San Juan de Portugal,* met a similar attack led
by Drake in the queen's ship *Revenge.* Swinging to meet the
enemy, Recalde invited the English to come to grips. Joined by
Hawkins in the galleon *Victory,* and another English captain,
Martin Frobisher in the *Triumph,* Drake pounded the Spaniard
from a respectful distance. Even when the *San Juan* stood alone
against his whole squadron, Drake disdained to mix it, withdrawing
as the rest of the Biscayans turned to support their bruised leader.
The affray involved little damage, but confirmed the broad tactics
on either side: the Spaniards advancing up-Channel in steady military order, the English pounding with impunity, but no great
effect, from long range. The prospect was fraught with frustration.
"Their ships are so swift and sprightly," it was noted in the Spanish

log, "that they can do as they like with them." Observed Howard
with equal exasperation: "we durst not adventure to put in among
them, their fleet being so strong."

The first losses of any magnitude in what came to be known as
the Battle of the Narrow Waters were the result not of action but
of accident. It was early evening, and the English had fallen back,
when the flagship of the Guipuzcoan squadron, the *San Salvador*,
was torn by explosion. The powder store at her stern had blown up.
Medina Sidonia halted the fleet and supervised the transfer of
injured men while their unharmed comrades fought a fire that
raged on the stricken ship. The sea was already rough, and with
squally clouds and darkness looming ahead, it was a risky business
standing by in the tight crescent formation. The duke, who had
been on deck all day and had not eaten since breakfast, watched
anxiously as the flames were subdued and the *San Salvador* brought
in tow by a brace of galleasses. He had scarcely given the order to
proceed when the flagship of the Andalusian squadron, the *Nuestra Señora del Rosario*, took a nasty plunge and lost her foremast.
Once more, the duke stopped the armada; once again, cables were
brought out. This time, the *San Martín* herself prepared to give
tow. But the *Rosario* was pitching violently and the line came
adrift. By dusk, all efforts to pass another had failed. Diego Flores
de Valdés, the duke's chief of staff and a cousin of Pedro de
Valdés, captain of the *Rosario*, had no doubt that every moment of
further delay was one of peril for the whole fleet. The risk, he
urged, was out of all proportion to the safety of a single ship.
Reluctantly, Medina Sidonia agreed. Ordering one or two lighter
craft to stay and do what they could, he gave the signal to resume
course. The wallowing *Rosario* fell behind in the fading light.

The Spaniards were now off Start Point, Devon, about to cross
the wide bay which reaches to Portland Bill, Dorset. Behind them,
Howard had deputed the lead for the night to Drake and had settled the *Ark Royal* comfortably in the wake of his subordinate,
prepared to follow the *Revenge*'s big poop light. When the *Rosario*
was sighted, she seemed to be deserted, but the boom of a big
gun aboard her soon belied the impression. Her small escort had
sped away on the approach of the English fleet, and Howard, noting
the position of the crippled ship, gave orders that his force should
press on without stopping. In Howard's judgment, it was vital to

keep every vessel he had in touch with the armada. Drake, however, had other ideas. In the course of the night, the *Ark Royal* lost sight of the *Revenge's* lantern. Fearing he was falling behind, Howard ordered more sail and the English flagship plunged forward until the glimmer of a light once more offered guide. Not until the first streaks of dawn lit the Channel did it occur to the admiral that the lantern he was following belonged to the *San Martín*. He was almost in the jaws of the Spanish pincer. Two other English ships had made the same mistake. The rest, confused by the disappearance of the *Revenge's* light, had dropped far behind, "not knowing whom to follow" as one report had it.

As Howard hastened to pull back from the armada, Drake was calmly talking terms with the *Rosario's* captain. Overwhelmed by his privateering instincts, the English vice-admiral had doused his light deliberately and turned back in the darkness. Now, in return for a pledge of good treatment for the men of Pedro de Valdés, Drake won what transpired to be the fairest prize of the whole action. Apart from the value of the *Rosario* herself, more than fifty thousand gold ducats were stashed aboard her. If the incident as a whole had any greater significance for the two fleets, it was that the English could learn a lesson about co-ordination from the Spaniards. They were to do so very shortly. Off Portland, a surprise change in the wind gave Medina Sidonia the weather gauge, and Howard, bent on regaining the advantage, set out to haul between the armada and the coast. With prompt accord, a squadron of the duke's galleons moved to intercept. Switching tack, Howard made to pass instead to seaward. Another Spanish squadron peeled off to cut his new line. Try as he would, the English admiral was unable to weather the flank of the well-drilled armada. Indeed, on several occasions Medina Sidonia was able to bring the faster but more haphazard English fleet to close range. At one time, the largest of its vessels, Frobisher's *Triumph*, was in danger of being cut off and captured. Through all this, the vulnerable, slow-moving core of the armada maintained safety and solidarity with deft precision. When the wind returned to its original quarter, the English had withdrawn. The armada moved on in its great arc.

On August 3, Howard somewhat imitatively reorganized his fleet in four squadrons. He had been reinforced by some volunteers from the Channel ports, and the admiral, vice-admiral,

Hawkins, and Frobisher each took a group of about twenty-five ships. Medina Sidonia encountered this new grouping in battle on Thursday off the Isle of Wight. This time, the day began in dead calm. Frobisher's squadron was positioned between the armada and the English coast, the *Triumph* herself well to the front, that is the easternmost station. Howard's other squadrons were to the rear of the Spanish fleet, where a number of his galleons put down boats and began towing into firing range. Some desultory shots had been loosed from either side when a breeze sprang up from the southwest, placing Frobisher's squadron in a tricky leeward situation. Perceiving his advantage, Medina Sidonia attacked. Most of the Englishmen managed to scramble back to the rear of the armada, but the *Triumph* was once more in trouble. Caught in an onshore wind with no room to maneuver, it seemed she could scarcely escape the grappling irons of the Spaniards. Frantically, her boats tried to tow her from danger. Other boats arrived from the English fleet to help. The *San Martín* drew nearer. Then, suddenly, the wind veered and the *Triumph* was clear.

The duke had little time to dwell on his misfortune. Drake was now pressing hard on the seaward tip of the crescent, repeatedly pounding the wing ship, a Portuguese galleon. She took it for a while, then changed places with another vessel. Distracted by the action, the duke himself had a near escape. To the east of the Isle of Wight, off Selsey Bill, lies a reef of jagged rocks, the Owers. The armada was almost on top of it when the pilots noticed the changing color of the water and spotted the first crags nosing the surface. Immediately, Medina Sidonia alerted his fleet and veered away from the English coast toward the center of the Channel. He was now drawing near to the eastern straits and Parma, and wished to gain the Continental side of the sea, anyway. At the same time, seeing the Spaniards stand out toward France, Howard's force broke off the engagement, content to shadow the ponderous but still orderly armada. Howard had his own rendezvous to keep in the straits. Here, he would link up with his nephew, Seymour, gaining strong reinforcements.

Friday, calm and peaceful, gave time for stocktaking and reflection. If the English believed they had diverted an attempted landing on their south coast, then the honors Howard dispensed among his officers that morning expressed a mood of understandable, though misconceived, elation. Judged in relation to Philip's intent, Medina Sidonia's performance was worthy, in a truer sense, of commendation. Not only had he pursued his task to the letter of instructions, he had done so at a cost which, by any objective pre-estimate of the hazards (not least his own), must have seemed mercifully slight. During a week of nerve-racking campaigning in the Channel, seldom out of touch with the English fleet, the duke had lost two of his original one hundred and thirty ships, and both these by ill-luck. The *Rosario*, representing the greatest part of his losses both in men and equipment, could be counted an inexplicable gift of God to the enemy. The *San Salvador*, taken in tow after her explosion and fire, had later been evacuated and cut loose in a sinking state. According to the official returns of his captains, the duke had lost a hundred and sixty-seven killed, and two hundred and forty-one disabled in action. Though undoubtedly a low estimate of the dead (captains on both sides faked their muster roles in order to draw the pay of dead men), the figures did not suggest a high toll for four vigorous battles in which the duke commanded upward of twenty-five thousand men. When it was additionally considered that slow and highly vulnerable hulks comprised something like half his fleet, that his progress up the Channel was ordered by the slowest of these to an average two knots, and that he was campaigning in foreign waters with a miscellaneous fleet of provincials against a national fleet of superior warships closely backed by its own ports, Medina Sidonia had little cause to rebuke himself. Bemoaned one English veteran of the outcome to date: ". . . so much powder and shot spent and so long time in fight, and, in comparison thereof, so little harm." It was meant as an admission of error on the part of English gunners. It could as well have been a tribute to the handling of the armada.

On Saturday, the Spanish fleet anchored beneath the cliffs of Calais, the first stage of its assignment completed. The time had come for Parma to show his hand. Several times during the advance Medina Sidonia had sent fast pinnaces ahead to keep the general appraised of his position, but, so far, had nothing by return. Now, with his big ships as close as he dared to take them to the banks and shallows of the invasion ports, the duke sent another messenger to ask when Parma's men were coming out to meet him. Next day, he received some disturbing intelligence. It came from a captain named Rodrigo Tello, whom the duke had dispatched to Parma over a week ago. Tello brought greetings from the general and the promise of a sailing at the earliest moment consistent with the completion of some final preparations. What those preparations were the duke could only guess from the observations of his messenger. According to Tello, who had visited both the main embarkation ports, Nieuport and Dunkirk, the invasion arrangements were hopelessly belated. Barges were inadequate in quality and number, stores had not been loaded, and Parma himself was not even on the coast. The messenger had left him at Bruges. There was a further complication. The shallow waters from Gravelines to the Scheldt were firmly monopolized by the coastal gunboats of the Netherlands rebels, the Dutch. Even if Parma could float his invasion force, there was no knowing when he could get it out.

The whole situation was so uncharacteristic of the vaunted Alexander, Duke of Parma, as to seem unbelievable. Perhaps he had never expected the armada to reach Calais. Perhaps, with Holland still flouting his authority, he had better uses for the reinforcements Philip had sent for the English project. Perhaps . . . Medina Sidonia had little time to ponder. Howard had now been joined by Seymour and the English fleet was anchored close to windward of the armada. Already, they would be planning their next attack, and, though the duke had plenty of ammunition in hand for the land operations of his troops, rounds for his ships' guns were dangerously low. Of the English advantage, he wrote sharply to Parma, "They can bombard me when they like; I shall be powerless to answer effectively." To another form of attack, the duke was even more vulnerable. Wind and tide made the closely anchored armada a perfect target for fire ships, a favorite device of the Spaniards themselves. That Sunday, the duke posted a screen of light craft between his fleet and the English to ward off incendiaries. The precaution, it seemed, was well taken. Before many hours had passed, the lookouts on the Spanish vessels reported activity in the English fleet. Shortly before midnight, lights were seen flickering in the distance. Soon eight points of fire detached themselves from the enemy lines and grew bigger. Dutifully, the screening craft moved to intercept.

The factors between anticipated danger and sudden crisis were

not individually catastrophic. It was the unforeseen combination
that proved ruinous. Howard, no less impressed with the obvious
tactic than the Spaniards, had sent to England for combustibles
and suitably expendable vessels. Long before these could arrive,
however, the fear of a change in conditions had persuaded his
command to obviate further delay by sacrificing a number of its
own ships. Thus, while the men of the Spanish screen expected to
grapple with fishing smacks or drifting hulks, they found themselves facing fully sailed warships, guns primed to blast off in the
mounting heat, blazing and erupting like engines from inferno. To
this peril was added a freshening wind and a strong tide, impelling
the incendiaries at a pace altogether disconcerting. Though the
guard boats fought bravely to close with the sparking monsters, all
but two of the latter swept by on a true course. Within a few
minutes, they would be amid the Spanish fleet: a fleet, like any
of its time, as inflammable as tinder. Even so, Medina Sidonia had
prepared further action. According to his earlier orders, should
fire ships elude the protective screen, the armada was to slip cables,
stand briefly to sea while the danger passed, then, at daylight,
resume its former anchorage. Given a more ordinary drift to the
incendiaries, and the normally fastidious drill of his captains, the
maneuver was feasible. But these were no ordinary fire ships. Indeed, at the very moment cool thinking was essential, they brought
to mind an unpleasant rumor, in fact unfounded, that the English
possessed a weapon of unprecedented destruction, a bomb which
could be mounted in just such vessels. (The Italian engineer and
bomb expert Giambelli was then working for Elizabeth, but in a
purely civil connection.) For the first time since the armada had
entered the Channel, its officers failed to co-ordinate.

Most cut their cables in the scramble to clear the anchorage.
With a blustery wind, and cloud obscuring the moon, anxiety to
avoid the fire ships was quickly heightened by anxiety to avoid one
another. By daybreak, almost all had been swept away through the
straits toward the sandbanks of Flanders, borne on a rising sea
and a powerful current. Moncada's galleass, the San Lorenzo, lay
aground with a broken rudder, to be claimed by the governor of
Calais. Only the San Martín herself, with Recalde's San Juan and
two or three other galleons, had adhered to the authorized maneuver and stood now between a scattered flock and the whole

English fleet. Medina Sidonia had little choice of duty. To win time for the armada to re-form beyond the straits, he would be obliged to fight a rear-guard action against the joint forces of Howard and Seymour, something in the order of a hundred and fifty ships. Accordingly, he set his small convoy for the North Sea, the *San Martín* in the rearmost and challenging situation. As the English fleet overhauled her, she swung her broadside to meet it and lay to defiantly. The first of the pursuers to come plunging up was the *Revenge*, closely followed by the rest of Drake's squadron. The *Revenge* opened the exchange at closer range than anything yet ventured by the home fleet. The *San Martín* shuddered and belched smoke in reply. One by one, the ships of Drake's squadron unleashed their broadsides and passed on, while the Spanish flagship made the most of her scant ammunition.

Next came Frobisher's squadron led by the *Triumph*, the great vessel that had so narrowly escaped capture earlier. Now she rode boastfully alongside the Spaniard, lashing out with her heaviest armament. Behind the splintered bulwarks of the *San Martín*, the duke's men struggled to reload broiling cannons or answered the English long guns with musket fire. By the time Hawkins and his squadron came up, Medina Sidonia had stopped trying to keep count of the enemy. But his stand was not thankless. Amid the mass of the queen's sail there began to appear an occasional Spanish flag. The more weatherly craft of the shattered armada were starting to rally on their admiral. For a while there were just a few, perhaps half-a-dozen, then the number grew to thirty or so, and the disposition of the vessels assumed a ragged pattern. Stubbornly, with almost instinctive deliberation, the Spaniards were rebuilding their battle crescent.

It was a stirring gesture, a demonstration of immense skill and resilience on those hostile waters, but it was to take more than a formation at this stage to discourage the English. The paucity of Spanish gunfire, even at close range, was a clear admission the duke's ships were starved of ammunition. Relentlessly, Howard's squadrons pitched in, hurling broadside after broadside at decks already smashed and littered. This time, the armada was really taking a beating. Most of the ships with Medina Sidonia were heavily damaged; one or two were sinking. To what extent the English might have pressed their advantage it is difficult to say, for their own ammunition was all but expended when a squall stopped the action. That night the weather increased in fury and Tuesday morning saw the Spaniards in danger of being driven onto the Zeeland sands north of Ostend. "We saw ourselves lost," wrote one member of the armada, "either caught by the enemy or wrecked on the shoals. It was the most terrible day of all. The men had despaired of the outcome and were sure they would die." Plumb lines were showing a mere six fathoms. Some vessels had not rigged spare anchors since Calais. Those that had found them dragging in the loose sands. The English fleet hovered to windward. Then, on the absolute verge of catastrophe, the wind shifted, and the duke was able to lead his ships back to deep water.

At a meeting on the *San Martín* afterwards, the duke's war council decided unanimously that, if the wind favored, they should try to seize a port in the south of England. If, on the other hand, the present southwesterly persisted, they would have to run north to Scotland and try to reach home by an anticlockwise turn round the top of the British Isles. At all events, they could not afford to waste time. Provisions and water were frighteningly low. As it happened, the weather decreed the second of the alternatives and, nursing his crippled fleet as best he could, Medina Sidonia started on the long and circuitous return trip to Spain. The English followed to the Firth of Forth, then gave up the exercise. Howard, himself short of food and anxious to land casualties, was satisfied the danger of invasion was over. He had achieved his objective at remarkably small cost in life and damage. The armada had yet to pay the full bill of its voyage. Lashed by gales, thwarted by head winds, it struggled on, its crews depleted and weary. The duke cut the daily ration to eight ounces of biscuit and ordered horses and mules to be dumped to save water. Day after day, one crippled ship or another would succumb to the waves, or sheer away, sinking, in search of a neutral harbor. Many were wrecked on the coast of Ireland, where hundreds of Spaniards drowned. Their companions, floundering ashore exhausted, were hounded and killed by the English lord deputy.

The English fleet had parted company with the armada on August 12. On September 23, the *San Martín* limped into Santander. Nearly two hundred of her men were dead from privation besides the many killed and injured in action. Of the sixty-five other ships which reached Spain in the next few days, plenty were worse off. Some were almost unnavigable due to damage. Others ran aground, their crews too depleted or weary to trim them. At least one sank after entering harbor. Medina Sidonia, carried ashore semiconscious, sent immediately to the authorities for help, but the nation was not prepared for the disaster. Weeks afterwards, men were still dying for want of attention in ports quite unfitted to receive them. Among those beyond help on arrival were the commanders Recalde and Oquendo. Weak and delirious, the duke struggled to organize emergency facilities, insistently blaming himself for everything. If most of Spain, in her horror, was all too ready to believe him, perhaps Philip knew better. In October, having granted his sick commander leave to recuperate in the peace of his Andalusian estate, the king told his bishops: "Our duty is to praise God whatever his pleasure. At this time, I offer thanks for His mercy. In the storms which beset the Armada it might have suffered a worse fate . . ." It might easily have had a worse leader. The fact that forty-four of its original sixty-eight major fighting ships ever got home was a tribute to the duke's dedication. But Spain never forgave him. Hardly a village in the country was without its bereaved, and the nation demanded a scapegoat. Posterity was to perpetuate the error. In retrospect, the failure by no means diminished. Despite a number of abortive expeditions at a later date, mainly aimed at the Irish coast, the defeat of the armada was never reversed. Spain had made her bid for unchallenged world supremacy. The moment was lost.

Not the least of Philip's armada reckonings was the cost in hard money. The expense of Spain's ceaseless campaigns, especially in the Netherlands, had been more than even the treasure of America could defray: the economy had long since burst the limits of prudence. From the beginning of his reign, Philip had been haunted by the huge debts incurred by his father. At first, he reckoned he owed seven times the national revenue. Soon, the annual interest owing to foreign bankers exceeded income. He had tried repudiating interest payments and confiscating private bullion from America, but neither had lasting effect. The international bankers merely threatened to blacklist him; confiscation of imports was fiercely opposed by the Cortes and the merchants involved. Like Charles, he fell back on heavy taxes. "The common people who have to pay the taxes," Philip had once written to his absent father, "are reduced to such extremes of calamity and misery that many go naked . . ." Yet he himself could not avoid increasing the taxation. Vast as the wealth of the New World proved, it was forever mortgaged in advance, while the scramble to import more and more silver blinded Spain to a fundamental weakness in her position, the depression of agriculture at home. Many parts had never recovered from the ravages of the peasant rebellions that had greeted Charles's reign. On top of this, large sections of the rural population had joined the rush to the New World or migrated to industries where the prospects seemed better. Deprived of its more enterprising sons, that part which remained was often apathetic to progress. Plans to develop agriculture, albeit inadequate, were hindered by inept officials and the innate conservatism of the peasants. If God wished them better, held many, he would see to it himself.

Meanwhile, Philip was forced to temporize with piecemeal enactments which tended to show sympathy rather than a solution. Some indeed brought a measure of relief in isolated circles; others, designed to placate the Cortes by restraining the ostentation of the well-to-do, were merely negative. In a typically fussy "pragmatic" denouncing sartorial opulence, the king dwelt on details of apparel, male and female, with a thoroughness that would have done credit to a professional costumier. On the same theme of austerity, he discouraged the use of coaches, regarded by the Cortes as symbols of soft living and decadence. By way of a more direct palliative, he sponsored a revival of bullfighting, once the sport of aristocrats, now a popular spectacle. As a politician, Philip operated deeply, sometimes drastically; as an economist, he dabbed ineffectually at symptoms. The result was that while Spain, like the armada, sailed forward bedecked in the full glory of her "golden age," her course led closer and closer to ruin. The English enterprise, costing ten million ducats, led to a new tax on the basic necessities of life and a new level of poverty among the mass of people. Even industries hitherto flourishing by contrast with agriculture, began to go out of business. The effect of defeat was profound. If God had reasons for hurling disaster at the faithful crusaders, to Spain they were anything but evident. The militant spirit faltered. Disillusion and skepticism became prevalent attitudes, scorn attaching to many an ideal of the old life.

Eight years after the armada, Elizabeth's ships again raided Cádiz with impunity, carrying their depredations this time to the city. Now Spain vented her bitterness not only at the enemy but on the "defenders." For many Spaniards, the national militiamen who marched resplendently but belatedly to relieve the already ruined port were figures of derision. Like the effigies carried in procession during Holy Week, they impressed the mob, it was remarked, but did not scare the English. In the grandeur of his palace at Madrid, a sick and bankrupt Philip counted his blessings. He had thwarted an English attempt to put a puppet on the Portuguese throne after the armada. He had preserved a strong force under Parma in the Netherlands. He still ruled, if tenuously, the largest empire possessed by any European nation. To the north, France, though a dubious ally, at least remained Catholic. But so much more had been expected. Like his father before him, he approached his end wearily: a man, in his way, of almost superhuman effort, overcome in the long run by a superhuman task—and a debt now running at a hundred million ducats.

In June 1598, aged seventy-two, he was carried sick and dying from the capital to the Escorial, where he planned to spend his last hours. The roads were lined with beggars and adventurers, and what might have been fields was a wilderness around him. At least he was far from the seas now controlled by his enemies. With final thoroughness, he issued detailed orders for his funeral, then settled to await a painful and protracted end. He spent the next few weeks tortured by disease and his doctors, who, among other futile measures, forbade him the water he craved to drink. He never complained. His patience was to hold to the end. In August, the doctors gave up, appalled that life persisted in a body so far gone. At the close of the month he was thought to be dead, but the touch of a relic revived him. Still he had the strength and dignity to comfort those near him. He died eventually on September 13, clasping the crucifix Charles had held in his last hour. According to his own instructions, Philip's body was sealed in a metal inner case for reasons of hygiene, then placed in a coffin, white-lined but showing a somber exterior. The chapel of the Escorial was hung with the same black cloth that the king had worn most of his life. For nine days and nights, bells tolled unceasingly throughout Spain while the people reflected on so much that now seemed a fading mirage. When the bells stopped, more than Philip was dead.

A few years later, there was published in Madrid a book which not only buried something of the past but proved remarkably suited to the taste of the moment. Miguel Cervantes had entered the years of middle age a failure in almost everything he had undertaken. His misfortunes on returning from his ordeals in Algiers had left him disheartened, a state foreign to his trusting and sanguine temperament, and the defeat of the armada increased his depression. For the first time in his life he wrote with unrestrained bitterness. Following the second attack on Cádiz he joined the cruel hounding of Medina Sidonia, mocking the duke's concern and fearlessness *after* the English had departed. For some years, the poet's existence in Seville, and elsewhere in Andalusia, was highly precarious. He continued to work for the commissariat, but received an irregular pittance (even to buy a suit of clothes he had to borrow money) and was hopelessly vague in matters of business. Few who knew him then could have been surprised that he was in trouble over the accounts of his department and was committed to at least one short period in jail. Perhaps it was in prison, with time to reflect and collect himself, that he rallied his more positive qualities and prepared a fresh assault on the literary bastions. There is some evidence that in fact jail life brought him his greatest inspiration. In any case, it was at this lowly and unenviable point of his career, in his early fifties, that Cervantes first became interested in the idea that would put obscurity behind him forever.

His plan, neither pretentious nor altogether original, was quite simply to write a short story about an amusing eccentric so steeped in the romances of chivalry that he imagined himself a knight-errant. It was conceived as a parody of the popular chivalresque hero, and certainly nailed the coffin of that character. But it turned out to be very much more. As Cervantes explored the possibilities, he found himself on such intimate terms with the theme, and its ironic potential, that he dropped the short-story treatment and embarked chapter by chapter on a text of full length. Thus

Don Quixote, the deluded hidalgo who was to become the greatest character in Spanish literature, struck the trail of noble intent toward the first of his endless absurdities and failures. He wore a suit of ancient armor, rode a delightfully decrepit horse named Rozinante, and looked very much like Cervantes himself. Early in the work, Cervantes gave his hero a traveling companion, Sancho, whose down-to-earth peasant attitude to life became the foil to his master's bizarre imagination. The roads they trekked, the inns they stopped at, populated by the people Cervantes knew from his own travels, provided an ever-varying pageant of sixteenth-century society. These were not the pseudoclassic images of the author's earlier novel, the *Galatea*, but recognizable people—brash wenches, grasping landlords, rough convicts, courtly gentlemen, scheming damsels, self-interested tradesmen, farmers, and barbers—sketched with warmth and delightful gusto. To add to the attraction, Cervantes spiced his work with the sly Andalusian wit, full of oblique reference and double meaning, known as *gracia*, and threw in an occasional jibe at the expense of some well-known personality.

Among others so mentioned was Lope de Vega, whom Cervantes liked no better for his voyage with the armada. "No poet is as bad as Cervantes," responded the playwright in disgust, "nor so foolish as to praise Don Quixote." The literati of the day were inclined to agree, but the reading public and commercial publishers thought otherwise. The first part of *The Adventures of the Ingenious Knight Don Quixote de la Mancha*, published in 1605 as a bulky book with the motto *post tenebras spero lucem* (after darkness I hope for light) on the title page, was an immediate sellout. Within a few weeks, reprints were being rushed in Madrid; rights had been sold for Portugal, Aragon, Valencia, and Catalonia; pirate editions were already on the market. Ten years later, Cervantes brought out a second part, widely claimed to be better than the first. By now, *Don Quixote* had been published in Italy, the Netherlands, France, and England. Its success was almost unknown among Spanish books of the period. In Madrid and Seville, strangers hugged its author delightedly. Though Cervantes lacked the business instinct to exploit his popularity financially, and never grew rich, there was no doubt that he had caught something of the mood of the moment. Quixote himself, the mad knight, the uncompromising optimist who set out to reform the world at lance point and was defeated by the very futility of the project, was essentially Spanish in character: tolerant, kindly, wise, until the mad dream of destiny beckoned, then as morally impassioned as the great peninsula crusaders, as romantic and violent as the Muslims who preceded them. Ever since Berber zeal had provoked responding ardor in Spain's embattled Christians, a tendency to fanaticism had stalked Spanish life. Sancho, worldly-wise, saw the folly of it, but Quixote was not to be restrained by a peasant.

Profoundly human by any standards, the universal qualities of the work were less immediately important. Humoristically, Cervantes had explored the root of all pathos, the difference between aspiration and achievement. Philosophically, he had examined romance and reality as interacting agents on human nature. Psychologically, he had profiled what would later be termed the superego. Allegorically, he had sown the seeds of endless speculation. Yet these were not conscious intentions so much as the result of direct and honest observation. The simpler theme Cervantes sealed with the ultimate return to sanity of his hero was disillusion. On that note, Spain entered the seventeenth century.

Chapter 8

MAKE WAY FOR THE FOREIGNERS

"God, who has given me so many kingdoms, has denied me a son capable of ruling them," Philip II complained. It would have been surprising had it been otherwise, for men of great authority and personal stature seldom produce their sons in the same mold, and the Emperor Charles had already strained the proof of exception. To have looked for three outstanding Spanish Habsburgs in succession would have been to expect too much. In fact, the two colossi, Charles and Philip, had pretty well exhausted the strength of the line in their efforts. Mental reaction, plus the physical effects of repeated inbreeding among the Habsburg family, was to bring the Spanish branch of the house of Austria to an inauspicious end after three more generations, each of which represented a new level of decline for the nation.

The combined reigns of Philip's son, grandson, and great-grandson almost exactly spanned the seventeenth century, leading Spain from an ostensibly dominating position in Europe to a situation in which she was virtually its powerless victim. To the specter of decaying political influence was added one of unalleviated economic embarrassment which, if not unique in Europe at the time, was heightened by a singular unwillingness to adapt to new conditions. So demeaning had labor come to appear to a nation of conquerors that for many Spaniards poverty seemed preferable to any form of salvation through industry. Though it frequently meant begging, if not actual robbery, the most impoverished of hidalgos sought to emulate the indolence and opulence of courtiers. "Not even a carpenter, saddler or any other artisan was seen but he must be dressed in velvet or satin like a nobleman." The Spanish ethos had lost touch with practicalities. Buttressed by an increasingly fervent Inquisition, religious faith, once the driving power of the people, became more and more an inner retreat, too seldom matched in public by Christian ethics. Corruption and self-interest thrived at all levels of government.

In 1604, the Castilian satirist Francisco de Quevedo wrote to the Flemish humanist Lipsius: "As for my Spain, I cannot speak without grief. If you are a victim of war, we are the victim of sloth and ignorance. In your country, we consume our soldiers and gold; here at home we consume ourselves. There is no one to protest, but any number to tell lies." Yet even Quevedo, who repeatedly warned of the ruin ahead, was a reactionary when it came to answers. As belligerent and superstitious as the most ignorant of his fellows, he disdained foreigners, deplored commerce and industry, and believed vehemently in the very Inquisition that was stifling the truthfulness and protest he called for. Quevedo, perhaps the sharpest voice raised against the standards of his time, was still bound to the dream of a now irretrievable past. Already, in the later years of Philip II's reign, the conflict between tradition and changing circumstance, between the assumed and reality, had begun to create confusion in the Spanish psyche. The accession of his son Philip III, a young man of such aseptic tastes that the old king had been reluctant to call him to his deathbed, did nothing to diminish the process.

The new king, a product of his father's last marriage (to Anne, daughter of the Emperor Maximilian II), inherited all the old man's piety and none of his diligence. His life was a strange concoction of frivolity and devotion, allegedly blameless of venial sin but lavish in the vanity and exhibitionism, the love of theatrical display and elaborate festivity that sometimes marks the inhibition of sensuality. Already given to opulence, despite the personal habits of the late king, the Spanish court needed little encouragement to indulge its appetite to the full. Under Philip III, the cost of the royal household quickly trebled, while, for the first time in its history of mounting penury, the crown sank to the indignity

of begging door-to-door to help meet its expenses. Plainly, this
idle if amiable spendthrift was incapable of taking over the work
of his father and, between periods of extravagance, the knowledge
filled him with guilt. At such times, Philip incarcerated himself
among the saintly relics to which he looked for comfort, praying
for pardon and the strength of character nature had denied him.
Contemporaries observed that he emerged puff-eyed from fatigue
and weeping. Toward middle age, the incidence of depression
mounted and his limited vitality was submerged in ill health and
remorse.

In the hard struggle for absolutism, from Isabella to Philip II,
Spain's monarchs had varied in method and effectiveness, but none
had turned his back without a fight. The novelty of a king who
lacked even the resolution to begin to govern came as yet one
more crisis upon a system tuned as never before to the notion of
monarch as autocrat. Philip II had been his own minister, personally supervising all departments of the state. Philip III rejected
such duties, appointing instead a chief minister to govern in the
king's name. In this, he initiated the so-called rule of the favorites. The first favorite was a Valencian nobleman, Francisco
Gómez de Sandoval y Rojas, Duke of Lerma, who, swiftly appointing his own favorites to key posts, held power through most of
Philip's reign. The problems he took on would have taxed the finest
and most principled of statesmen. Lerma, though overvilified by
the many former officials his regime had displaced, was neither.
Faced by the gigantic debt inherited by his monarch, he took the
desperate step of debasing the coinage, copper currency assuming
twice its face value, while silver, in consequence, was driven from
the country. If Lerma had not the stature to fight corruption, he had
the guile to exploit it to his own purposes, and titles and appoint-
ments were sold on a grand scale to help finance the court's ostentation. When the people of Madrid protested at the many abuses
inflicted on them in the king's name, the minister moved Philip
overnight to Valladolid, well knowing that a shift of court would
bring ruin to business interests in the capital. Before long, the
king was back in Madrid, better off by 250,000 ducats plus a
percentage of all rents for the next ten years—the bribe paid by
the city to secure his return. From this transaction, Lerma him-

self gained a palace on top of the considerable perquisites he was already amassing.

In foreign affairs he set out on a better tack, anxious to curtail where possible the wars that above all had drained Spain's resources. Here he was helped by two hefty strokes of fate. In 1603, Elizabeth of England died. Her successor, James I, did not possess her rabid anti-Spanish sentiments, and, by delicate diplomacy, Lerma was able to secure a peace in which James promised "not to succour the Hollanders or allow English ships to trade in the Indies." A ceremonial visit to Spain by six hundred Englishmen, the majority Protestants, led by none other than Lord Howard, defeater of the armada, was managed without untoward incident, both sides sworn to discreet silence on topics of controversy. Coupled with some effective generalship by Parma's successor in the Netherlands, the Marquis of Spinola, this development enabled Lerma to negotiate a truce in the crippling Dutch war, Spain admitting the United Provinces as a government de facto in return for what amounted to a twelve-year breathing space. Seven years after the death of Elizabeth came the second stroke of fortune. In 1610 a demented assassin put an end to the life of Henry IV of France and the threat to Spain of that monarch's collision course with the emperor. Once more, Lerma was able to press friendly overtures, this time with the government of the French regent Marie de Médicis.

In home affairs, however, he had no such luck. Not the least of the problems he seized in conjunction with power was the old question of Morisco incompatibility. The frustration of the Alpujarras rising, and the subsequent resettlement of the Moriscos elsewhere in the country, had merely increased the complexity of a situation which had defied solution now for more than a century. The dilemma was a fine one. In a population of some nine millions, well over half a million were Moriscos; moreover, their prolific tendencies were gradually diminishing the ratio. Unlike so many "old Christians," they did not regard farm laboring beneath their dignity and, since they were notably industrious and frugal, their services were valuable both to the landed proprietors and Spain herself. It was more than coincidence that the Moriscos were most numerous where the land was most fertile. In short, they formed a uniquely productive labor force. Such uniqueness did not endear

them to the majority of Spaniards. Nor did their manifest lack of
enthusiasm for the religion they professed less from inclination
than as a form of visa and work permit. Against them, it was
charged with some measure of justice that they practiced Islam
in secret, that they were in treasonable contact with Spain's enemies, and that their numbers constituted a threat to the realm.
Where feeling ran highest, mass extermination was advocated, or
at least deportation to the mines of America. On the other hand,
their employers held them indispensable to agriculture and urged
the Church to greater efforts in religious education.

When a theological commission convoked in the name of Philip
III at Valencia pronounced it impossible to continue administer-
ing the sacraments to those who so clearly regarded them in
mockery, the problem facing Lerma became critical. In a letter to
the deputies of Valencia, Philip wrote with his minister's approval:
"I ordered the commission about which you are informed . . . for
the greater ease of my conscience, to see whether it was possible
to avoid expelling them [the Moriscos] from the kingdom. Yet I
have learned through various, but certain, channels that those of
Valencia and Castile pursue their evil courses. At the moment we
were concerned with their conversion, they sent emissaries to
Constantinople and Morocco to treat with the Turk and King
Mouley-Sidan, asking for forces to be sent to their aid next year
in the assurance that such would find a hundred and fifty thousand
men in arms ready to adventure life and property in this enterprise. The difficulties, they asserted, would not be great, since our
kingdoms were lacking in men, arms and trained soldiers. In addition, I have learned that they are in communication and intrigue
with the heretics and other princes, enemies of our monarchy who
have offered aid in the fulness of their strength."

Fear of the Morisco minority was eloquent of Spain's increasing
weakness, and, during the first decade of the century, their expulsion seemed inevitable. Even so, the pope and a number of
Spanish bishops spoke against it, together with the rural magnates.
Lerma delayed until 1609, then produced the first of the expulsion
orders (for Valencia) which, in the next two years, would clear
the whole country of the offending communities. Troops and ships
were called home from abroad to supervise the exodus to North
Africa, hundreds of thousands suffering incalculable losses and ter-

rors. Spain's own losses were greater. New areas of land joined those already in waste. In 1618 the Council of Castile reported: "The depopulation is such as has never been seen or heard before, and the realm is being utterly ruined and exhausted." Yet while the lowly grew abject and the Cortes protested in a wilderness, the nobility continued to neglect its holdings for an endless whirl of courtly extravagance, and the minister's parasites stuffed their pockets. In October of the same year, Lerma paid the price of a regime based on greed, falling to a conspiracy headed by his own son, the Duke of Uceda. While the deposed favorite consoled himself with a cardinalate and a personal fortune estimated at more than forty million ducats, Uceda proceeded to undo the one constructive aspect of Lerma's policy by plunging Spain back to war.

In 1620, the new Austrian emperor, Ferdinand II, roused the fiery ghost of Luther in Europe by striking at Protestant Bohemia. Heedless of the painful lesson of history, Uceda supported him. Spain's involvement in the series of bitter religious and political conflicts which followed in Germany, the Thirty Years' War, destroyed any hope of extending the truce with Holland and obliterated all prospects of peninsula recovery that century. Meanwhile, having neglected the welfare of Portugal for more than twenty years, allowing not only the violation of her eastern empire by Spain's enemies but also the exploitation of her homeland by Lerma in contravention of all earlier promises, Philip embarked in the last years of his life on a characteristically immoderate state visit to that country, leaving Lisbon to pay his expenses. Portugal seethed with unprecedented resentment toward her neighbor. It was the last helpless fling of a futile monarch. His death in 1621, at the age of forty-three, left the crown with a boy of sixteen whom even Philip III thought unworthy.

Philip IV, child of yet another marriage to Austria, this time represented by Margaret, sister of the Emperor Ferdinand, was born into an oasis of sumptuousness unrivaled anywhere in Europe. A titled Englishwoman visiting the Spanish court during his reign could not believe the country was impoverished. "There is not in the Christian world better wines," she asserted. "They have the best partridges I ever ate, and the best sausages, and salmon, pike and seabream . . . The cream, called nata, is much sweeter and thicker than ever I saw in England. Their eggs much exceed ours; and so all sorts of salads, roots and fruits . . . Besides that, I have ate many sorts of biscuits, cakes, cheese and excellent sweetmeats . . . Their perfumes of amber excel all the world . . . They are very magnificent in their houses, furniture, pictures of the best, jewels, plate and clothes; most noble in presents, entertainments and equipage." No ostentation had been too great to celebrate the birth of the future king. Mounted parades, bullfights, splendid banquets, and balls were attended by nobles from all parts of the realm. Grandees in costumes that were themselves masterpieces of finery knelt in rapt thanksgiving before sacred images encrusted with priceless gems from the empire. Armies of monks and friars chanted praises before gold-plated altars, while the impoverished of Valladolid, the temporary capital, scrambled for twelve thousand silver coins scattered in the plaza by the authorities. By night, palaces and churches glittered with myriad candles. Thirty thousand wax torches were distributed free in the city to enable the poor to join their peers in giving vent to their rapture, a facility employed with such inexpert abandon that the church tower of St. Benedict was gutted by fire, its seventeen bells "melted in shining tears of joy."

Surrounded by the escapist trappings and fatuities of his father's circle, the child grew up a sheltered and aimless youth with a strong fondness, not unreasonably, for horses and dogs. A tall, strapping fellow with fair hair, vague blue eyes and pendulous lower lip, topping a huge chin, there was about him a seedy reflection of the more illustrious of his ancestors. He was more sensuous and virile than his insipid parent, and looked for a tough and masterful hero in his young life. The man he found was Gaspar de Guzmán, Count of Olivares and first Duke of San Lucar, known impressively as the count-duke. Nearly twenty years the boy's senior, forceful, dominant, decisive, and dashing, Olivares was everything Philip missed in his father. He was a man who meant business, and he looked it. His shoulders were massive, his head square with a black fringe and twirling mustaches, his whole appearance heavily, darkly handsome. Like the black bulls of the Marismas, he drove hard at his objectives and was not given to fearing his enemies. Olivares brought tang and action to Philip's life. They galloped horses together, partnered each other in tourneys and adventured in the common places of the capital in a manner which filled the king with dread for his son's soul. By the time the monarch died, the youth was clay in the hands of his worldly companion. An anecdote retailed by one who was present at the new king's chambers on the morning of the accession told how the count-duke, sweeping aside those waiting to pay homage, entered Philip's bedroom, threw back the curtains and peremptorily told the lad to get dressed and prepared for some hard work. Philip meekly complied. By the time Uceda arrived to present himself as chief minister, his fate had been decided. Indeed, the mourning services were scarcely over before the ax had fallen among the late king's favorites: Uceda was persecuted, Lerma hounded for his plunder, their lieutenants in jail or executed. The clansmen of a new royal favorite were in office.

Though lacking Lerma's diplomatic and conciliatory talents, Olivares was the more inspiring statesman, his sentiments strictly those of the traditional Spanish imperialist. He loved power and was intolerant of opposition, but his motives were less personal and opportunist than those of his predecessors. His boundless energy, coupled to a sincere if vain faith in Spain's ability to sustain the counterreformation and refurbish her tarnished greatness, was reflected in the burst of new hope that marked the early years of his regime. A well-intentioned endeavor was made to curtail luxury and extravagance in which Philip played a part by reducing court expenses. A new fleet was amassed, and a sea victory over an impudent Dutch force off Gibraltar did something to restore Spanish naval prestige after the hammerings of Cádiz and the armada. In the Netherlands, Spinola captured the Dutch stronghold of Breda after a siege of ten months; in America, incursions by the same enemy were repulsed; in the Mediterranean, a wide sweep against Moorish pirates was successful. Optimistically, Spain looked ahead to fresh victories. Writers and painters renewed the old theme of armed glory. In Madrid, Philip, now hailed "the Great," strutted out like a cockerel while the capital preened its somewhat tawdry feathers.

If Olivares kept a tight hold on the king, it could not be said that he isolated him from reality or denied the young man worldly pleasures. No Spanish monarch since the reconquest had been so intimately acquainted with society or so absorbed in its expression in the form of music, the theater, art, and letters. The reaction that had driven him from the artificial climate of his father's circle to the earthier values of the stables and sporting life led on to a wider field of sentience. He was fascinated by the picturesque aspect of the seventeenth-century city: by the penniless slickers in gaudy doublets and frayed shirts who promenaded like lords in the capital, by the gamblers and cutpurses, the reckless bloods with ready rapiers, the rouged actresses, the sham soldiers, the endless beggars, the hired satirists, and the hungry artists. From the so-called Mentidero, or Liars' Walk, at the end of Madrid's Calle Mayor, the high street, came the latest society scandal concerning such familiar names as Lope de Vega, or his successor Calderón, whose private passions were as much discussed as their plays. Philip was especially intrigued by the theatrical fraternity and often attended public shows incognito. He also explored the city with Olivares at night, when few people of honest intent were abroad. Foreigners were fond of proclaiming the shamelessness of the women on the streets of the capital, and the boldness with which total strangers accosted them. The impression doubtless owed something to the lingering oriental tradition of feminine seclusion which, together with the prevalence in public places of ruffians and vagabonds, kept the bulk of respectable females at home. Certainly, after-dark Madrid, no less than any conurbation of the period, earned its reputation for "wickedness," and the king's nocturnal jaunts became the talk of a scandal-loving society.

"People," wrote the king's tutor, the Archbishop of Toledo, "are gossiping all over Madrid, and things are being said which add little to the Sovereign's dignity." Such adventures, he told Olivares, were a bad example to the nation. The count-duke was furious. The archbishop, he said, should have something better to do than collect vulgar gossip. Philip was sixteen, he pointed out, and ought not to be ignorant of the world. "It is right that the King should see all sides of life, the bad as well as the good." It would be well for the prelate's safety, he hinted, if he had the sense to mind his own business in the future. There have always been opposing views about the count-duke's influence on Philip. The chief minister's detractors claim he subverted royal morals for his own ends; his supporters, that he tried to make a manly king of a doubtful prince. At all events, there can be no question about one aspect of Philip's virility. It is only curious to ponder that of the thirty and more illegitimate children he produced, not to mention those by his two wives, none could have been less fitted to rule than his legal successor. Philip was greatly attached to his first wife, Isabel de Bourbon, the daughter of Marie de Médicis. Contracted to him in their childhood as part of Lerma's diplomacy with France, Isabel grew into a pretty and vivacious woman, and he squired her with jealous attention. For her part, her sportive French instincts found no shortage of compensations for her husband's misalliances, and she brought a gay, if not always ladylike, spirit to court.

Like Philip, Isabel delighted in the drama of intrigue then flourishing and financed from her own pocket plays with such titles as *The Scorned Sweetheart, The Woman's Avenger,* and *The Power of Opportunity,* on one occasion herself representing the goddess of beauty. Like Philip, too, she was a frequenter of public theaters, where she watched secretly through the grille of an enclosed box. At times, her appetite for entertainment went further, and she would have snakes let loose in the auditorium, or gleefully play Peeping Tom on specially provoked fights between country wenches. The royal couple were seen regularly together at bullfights, while elaborately staged autos-da-fé, with their huge crowds, lurid parades, and powerful sermons, provided an equally deadly climax for their presence.

Yet, for all the count-duke's efforts to draw out the young Habsburg, Philip's interests remained largely personal. Among his most enduring acquaintances was that with the artist Velázquez, who was appointed court painter when he was twenty-four and the king eighteen. Velázquez, who shared Philip's interest in horses and adored the dogs which littered the palace, got on with the king from the start. Few days passed without their meeting, and the association went on to outlive that of the king and Olivares. There is a strange equity in the fact that the boldest and most independent of painters, the first and greatest truly Spanish giant in the world of art, should so consistently have found inspiration in a subject as visually undistinguished as Philip. From youth to age, Velázquez studied those ignoble features, that limp flesh, the weak eyes, the oddly fish-like mouth, bringing to each picture new insight and sympathy. His gradual transformation of Philip's portrait, through rigid formality of feature to a more yielding, impressional awareness, catalogued the artist's development and has been likened to "that tireless climb of the Greek sculptors, through so many stiffly-studied athletes, to the breadth of Phidias's gods, or the suppleness of the serene Hermes of Praxiteles." Philip, whose feeling outweighed his resolution, deserved the credit he received as a patron of the arts. When Velázquez died in 1660, he was Marshal of the Palace, having risen from social obscurity to an eminence second to few in the land.

Meanwhile, the forceful hand of Olivares was provoking ominous reactions both at home and abroad. Imperialist successes in the Thirty Years' War, notably at Nordlingen in 1634, when the renowned Spanish infantry was crucial to the destruction of an army of Swedish and German Protestants, were drawing France to the point of full-scale intervention. Already, fearing the old menace of encirclement by a strong Austro-Spanish Habsburg alliance, she had struck at the Valtellina, the valley connecting Lombardy with the Tyrol, and had subsidized Swedish opposition to the Habsburgs. Still, French Catholic sentiments complicated her predicament, a factor Olivares held to his advantage. Unfortunately for the Spanish favorite, however, there had come to power in the France of Louis XIII a chief minister whose ambition and iron will matched his own, and whose political adroitness surpassed the count-duke's. Cardinal Armand Richelieu, ailing author of A Defence of the Main Principles of the Catholic Faith, virtual ruler of France since his appointment as premier in 1624, had no doubts about the relative dangers of Protestantism and a Germany reconciled to the Habsburgs. In 1635, he declared war on both Spain and the emperor, calling on the Dutch to take the offensive.

The full implications of Spain's new involvement were beginning to emerge. Victories, as well as defeats, cost money, yet nothing spendable could come of this striving for glory. Despite his curbs on idleness and luxury, Olivares had been beset by a diminishing income and rising prices from the first. In some cases, the cost of tax-collecting itself had actually exceeded the revenue proceeding from it. Moreover, the burden was unevenly spread. Too often, Castile, the heart of the Spanish system, bore the brunt of demands, both in men and money, while the more independent states used their long-guarded rights to dodge the issue. Olivares determined to put an end to such evasions. "You should not be content," he told Philip, "to be king of Portugal, of Aragon, of Valencia and count of Barcelona"; it was necessary "to reduce these realms to the same order and legal system as Castile." This indeed was the logical conclusion to Isabella's policy of unity. It was also true, as Olivares realized, that much of Richelieu's strength lay in his grasp of a centralized authority. But if the count-duke's intentions were reasonable, time and his own impatience were against him. Exhausted Castile, bedeviled by her own anti-quated administration, was a poor advert for centralization, while the favorite's crude persuasive tactics did nothing to help. Convening the three cortes of Aragon, Catalonia, and Valencia, Olivares and the king bluntly asked for troops and money. When the members caviled at demands which, they insisted, undermined their liberties, the count-duke lost his temper. The members of the Valencian Cortes were upbraided as traitors, and one threatened with garroting; the Catalans were provoked to demand the repayment of former loans to the king before they would vote a ducat.

While the eastern states seethed with resentment, Olivares turned to an already indignant Portugal and proceeded to attack the last traces of her autonomy. In 1636, he introduced a Castilian property tax to that country. When the Portuguese offered to resist, he countered with an additional imposition and a proposal to abolish the Portuguese Cortes and reduce the kingdom to a Spanish province. By 1639, tensions throughout the peninsula were at breaking point. That year, the Dutch reversed their defeat off Gibraltar by smashing a Spanish fleet of seventy ships in the English Channel. Gone were Spain's hopes of regaining her old naval power, or of commanding the sea lane to Flanders. At the same time, Richelieu pushed troops into Roussillon, drawing Castilian soldiers into Catalan territory where their abuses inflamed existing grievances so thoroughly that the people were ready to go over to the French. The year 1640 saw the cataclysm unleashed. In a single year of crisis which threatened the whole process of peninsula unification, Catalonia declared herself a republic under Richelieu's protection, the Castilians there were massacred, and

Olivares, calling on Portugal for reinforcements, was answered with a lightning rebellion which toppled Spanish authority in Lisbon overnight. It took less than four hundred armed conspirators a mere three hours to obtain the regent's surrender and assure the throne for its strongest Portuguese claimant, the Duke of Braganza, thereafter King John IV. With every enemy of Spain in Europe behind them, the Portuguese were to thwart all efforts at reconquest by her larger neighbor.

The debacle finished Olivares politically, and forced Philip to take personal action. With French armies pouring south through the Pyrenees, he raised the best army he could and, a brace of pistols at the saddle of his favorite charger, set out from Madrid to meet them. Reaching Saragossa in 1642, he found not only Cerdagne, Roussillon, and Catalonia thick with French troops, but a good deal of Aragon, too. In Madrid, Isabel wrote him stirring letters of encouragement, and roused the capital to her admiring support. Despite her nationality, Spain had always found the queen's liveliness and bold charm good value for money. But Philip's resolution was wavering. He had never commanded an army before, and the need for experienced leadership at so critical a moment was obvious. When his army marched to face the enemy near Lérida that autumn, the king was not with it. He was still at Saragossa when he learned of its defeat. Sick at heart, he returned to Madrid and put pen to the dismissal of his chief minister, whose last throw had been a vain plot to murder Richelieu. Not even the blandishments of the count-duke's wife, deployed in a final bid by her husband to exploit Philip's best-known weakness, could save the fallen favorite. He died, insane, on his estate some thirty months later.

Now the blows were falling with a vengeance. In northern France, a Spanish force from the Netherlands had advanced into the Ardennes and laid siege to Rocroi, a small town near the present Belgian frontier. The invading army, twenty-seven thousand strong, included a formidable array of the famous *tercios viejos*, the incomparable Spanish infantry. Against it sallied the young French Duke of Enghien, later known as Prince de Conde, with an army smaller by several thousand and nothing to compare with the invader's reputation. With a combination of great dash and good luck, Enghien succeeded where many a better-equipped commander had failed. In the first place, he attacked against experienced advice. Then, when he did attack, his orders were several times misunderstood or miscarried, with the result that the French plan broke down into something at once more unorthodox and opportunist than expected. To the Spanish commander, Francisco de Mello, the battle was puzzling. The French advanced and retreated on all sides with disconcerting irregularity, while his infantry in their formal ranks stood bewildered. At last, when the enemy on his flanks were retiring in disarray, his own cavalry pursuing them, Enghien appeared in his rear with eight mounted squadrons and swept stunningly down the center. The verve of the young duke, who had disdained a helmet in favor of a soft white-plumed hat, routed all but the first line of Spanish infantry, which formed a square with some eighteen heavy guns on a ridge. Three times, Enghien led his men against the formation, each time hurled back with heavy losses from point-blank fire. The *tercios* stood firm, but luck had deserted them. Their ammunition was low, and their officers signaled for quarter.

As Enghien moved forward to negotiate, however, the Spanish musketeers misread the situation and reopened the engagement. Enraged by what they took for an act of treachery, the French fell on the Spaniards regardless of danger or mercy, and the battle ended in massacre. Eight thousand Spaniards were killed; seven thousand captured, mostly wounded. The French dead numbered two thousand, with a further two thousand injured. The result was of more than strategic significance. Rocroi, with its grim proof that Spanish infantry after all was so much less than invincible, heralded a new era of French military prestige, and the final collapse of the legend that had started with the Great Captain, Gonzalo de Córdoba. Hailed among Spain's enemies as a revelation comparable with the defeat of the armada, Rocroi destroyed the last illusion of Spanish might in Europe. From Flanders to Italy, the erstwhile conquerors were on the retreat, while dissent was so rife in the peninsula that at one moment even Andalusia was on the verge of becoming a breakaway kingdom. Had the deaths in quick succession of Richelieu and Louis XIII not distracted France, and had the Catalans not reacted as violently in the end to French occupation as they had to the Castilians, Philip might never have gained the Peace of the Pyrenees, a pact settling Spain's border with France on that mountain range. By the time it came, in 1659, Europe could finally take stock.

The imperial dream of the Habsburgs, like that of religious domination, had evaporated a decade earlier with the end of the Thirty Years' War. The German states had obtained independence. Holland had established her sovereignty, as had Switzerland, and gained trading rights in the Indies. France had extended her boundaries to stretch from the Pyrenees in the south up to and including most of Artois, plus various footholds in the Netherlands. Cromwell's England had relieved Spain of Dunkirk and exploited her preoccupation in Europe to seize Jamaica (1655). Portugal had shed sixty years of dependence, and even Catalonia, returned to the Spanish fold, had gained confirmation of her much-prized *fueros*, or privileges. Spain had gained nothing. Indeed, her losses were beyond estimation. Not for two centuries had the country touched such depths of penury and decadence. Of the cheating and robbery abounding on all sides, even among priests, one well-placed ecclesiastic wrote: "I do not wonder, for the pinch of poverty is so general that everyone is forced to do it." The same authority, Jerónimo de Barrionuevo, told how the king was reduced to dining on eggs while the queen went without her favorite sweetmeats, so bad was royal credit. "For two and a half months the usual rations have not been distributed in the palace, since the King has not got a real. On the day of St. Francis, they served the princess [María Teresa: betrothed to Louis XIV of France under the Peace of the Pyrenees] with a capon which stank like a dead dog. When she ordered it away, they brought chicken on slivers of toast, but it was so infested with flies that she almost overturned the lot. This is how things go on in the palace . . ."

While the royal family pulled in its belts, the staff in the royal kitchens became a law unto itself. On one occasion, six were killed, twenty wounded, and others dragged to prison as the result of a dispute between guards and the scullions. Idleness and contempt for authority were so advanced in Madrid that few except foreigners were willing to work. Thousands of Frenchmen took advantage of vacancies, dressing like Spaniards to avoid a special tax on aliens. They did not diminish the violence and profligacy in the capital. Wastrels with swords and daggers under their capes fought over plunder and the ubiquitous prostitutes. Philip made unavailing attempts to clean up the streets. "They are arresting all the women they find loitering unaccompanied," wrote Barrioneuvo ironically, "and hauling them in tens and twenties to prison with their hands tied. The jail is so crammed they have barely room to stand. If this goes on, either the building will have to be greatly extended, or vast supplies of wood will have to be laid in to burn them." Instead, most bought themselves out in cash or kind, and the germ of corruption spread ever wider.

To add to Philip's personal depression, Isabel had died a year after Rocroi, soon followed in death by their popular teen-aged son Baltasar Carlos. To his increasing misery, the king renewed the old Habsburg habit of close intermarriage by taking as wife his niece, the Archduchess Mariana of Austria. Mariana, a sour-faced young woman whose discontent was as remarkable as Isabel's ebullience, produced yet one more blow to Spain and the dynasty, a tragic infant, mentally and physically deficient, upon whose puzzled brow was to fall the crown of chaos. In the declining years of his life, Philip, who had always found comfort in women, fell under the influence of a female counselor named María Coronel, abbess of a convent at Agreda, in the Sierra de Moncayo, bordering Aragon. While the king unburdened his soul to María, a nephew of Olivares, Luis de Haro, took on the duties vacated by his uncle, accomplishing little save the enrichment of himself and his kinsmen. The year 1665 saw the humiliation of Rocroi repeated at Montesclaros, in Portugal, when the last effort of Philip's life, an attempt to regain that country by force, was overwhelmed by a combined army of Portuguese and Englishmen. Three months later, Philip joined the four thousand Spaniards who had died in the battle. Before its consignment to a tomb in the Escorial beside his forebears, the king's body, painted and clad in a suit of silk and gold, lay in a hall of his palace often used as a theater, surrounded by many of his pictures. If it was a fitting farewell to an amiable dilettante who had proved as unequal as his father to the sterner tasks thrust upon him, it drew few tears in the capital. Mariana was immediately absorbed with the power that would be hers as regent to the pathetic child, Charles; the Marquis of Malpica, captain of the guard, promptly ordered his men away from the death chamber to keep watch on the new king, while a succession of nobles refused to accompany the coffin from Madrid to the Escorial for fear of losing some advantage in their absence. Those eventually pressed into service turned the body over to the friar of that establishment with almost indecent urgency and raced back to the capital as fast as their horses could carry them.

Charles II, last of the Spanish Habsburgs, was the ultimate and tragic result of a consistently interbreeding family, a mere parody of its features and tendencies. Physically, he possessed the ancestral chin to such grotesque proportions that he could neither eat nor speak normally. Mentally, he inherited the melancholia of his progenitors to the extent not simply of religious fatalism but of the most puerile superstition. Faced with reconciling the divine right of the monarch with his patent incapacity, his guardians pronounced him bewitched by evil spirits, a diagnosis the sad creature believed all his life and which filled his mind with unspeakable horrors. The implications of his frailty were clear to all Europe. Senile at an age when most men are approaching their prime, the King of Spain would die without children. While his court became a battleground for all with hopes of succession, the country's rivals gathered like wolves on a blood scent. Only their fears of each other, particularly of France, unequaled in power under Louis XIV, kept Charles's inheritance anything like intact through his lifetime. As it was there was no peace and, despite the balancing efforts of England, Holland, and Sweden, the restlessly ambitious Louis bludgeoned the French Comté, Luxembourg, and further strongholds in the Netherlands from a groggy Spain. That a nation with scarcely visible means of support, her armies decimated, her commerce paralyzed, her communications severed, her leadership incompetent, should have continued to resist at all was a remarkable tribute to the tenacity and spirit of the Spanish race.

But Louis could afford to wait. On any grounds, he was strongly placed in the scramble. His formal claim to a stake in the peninsula rested chiefly on the rights of his wife, María Teresa, Charles's half-sister, betrothed to Louis at the Peace of the Pyrenees. Though María had then renounced her rights to the Spanish throne, the renunciation had been agreed with France on the condition of a hefty dowry which her father, Philip, predictably had been unable to honor. In practice, Louis relied heavily on the French faction at the Spanish court. This was led by a member of Philip's large company of illegitimate children, a young man, known like one before him as Don John, who had inherited something of the glamour of his mother, a Madrid actress. Their candidate, and Louis's, was Philip of Anjou, the grandson of the French monarch. Implacably opposed to the French, however, and consummate in her loathing of Don John was Charles's mother, Mariana, who led an Austrian faction backing the claim of her own great-grandson, the young prince Joseph of Bavaria. For a while, these opposing factions tugged the simple Charles one way and another.

Since he was only four years old on his father's death, Mariana was able at first to grasp power as regent. She did little for her cause by elevating her Jesuit confessor, a German named Johann Nithard, to the offices of Inquisitor General and chief minister, or, following his abject failure, by promoting an equally useless adventurer from Naples, Fernando de Valenzuela. On the wave of indignation caused by these meddlesome foreigners, Don John swept impressively into authority, compelling Mariana to retire to a convent. But the swaggering Don John was disappointing in power, at once vain and ineffectual, and his death in 1679 returned Mariana to her son's side. The one major success John had scored for his faction had been to persuade Charles to marry into French royalty in the person of Louis XIV's niece, Marie Louise of Orleans. If the marriage meant nothing to Charles, it was an embarrassment to the Austrian party for ten years, at the end of which Marie's death enabled the scheming queen-mother to find her son a wife of her own choosing. The result was that the bewildered Charles found himself married to Anna of Neuburg, sister-in-law to the Emperor Leopold, who had proposed the match with a keen eye to his own interests. At this point, the intrigue became doubly involved, for, to Mariana's frustration, Anna turned out to be an imperious and strong-willed person who soon threatened to take complete command of her husband. In this, she was backed by her redoubtable governess, the Baroness Berlipsch, and other members of her entourage.

The Austrian faction was thus divided. While Mariana supported the claim of Joseph of Bavaria, Anna promoted a new clique behind the candidacy of Leopold's second son, the Archduke Charles. The emperor's hand was now revealed more clearly. At the same time, the pathetic king, growing weaker and increasingly demented, was harried, bullied, and wheedled from all sides. He signed a will in favor of Joseph, but Anna forced him to destroy it and he wrote a letter recognizing the archduke as his heir. He was ready to sign almost anything put before him. When Mariana died, the Bavarian cause was weakened and Louis of France turned his wiles on Anna, proposing her marriage to the dauphin as soon as her husband should succumb to the effects of his premature senility. France, while gambling to win all, was nevertheless hedging her bets. In 1698 Louis had suggested a scheme to divide the Spanish Empire among the rivals. Spain, Flanders, and the American colonies should go to the Bavarian, he recommended, Naples and Sicily to Anjou, and Milan to the archduke. Shortly afterwards, Joseph of Bavaria died and Louis amended the proposition to offer the archduke the share previously assigned to Joseph, while Anjou took the rest. The astuteness of the partition schemes was that they distracted much of Europe from Louis's true ambitions, proving particularly comforting to England and Holland, whose safety depended on a balance between the larger rivals. Leopold could only draw attention to his own greed by protesting. Anna gave vent to her fury in private. It was said that she smashed the entire contents of her room.

For Spain, the sight of her enemies cutting up and wrangling over the future of her empire was the final indignity. The nation that had once ruled half the world was destitute, a fifth of her ludicrously small annual income spent on maintaining the royal establishments alone, but at least she could still choose the power to whom she must make her subjection. Since the majority of Spaniards gave priority to keeping the empire intact, and since the only candidate with a chance of protecting the entire inheritance was French, feeling veered, paradoxically, in favor of Spain's bitterest enemy. In Madrid, the French faction, now led by the Archbishop of Toledo, Cardinal Portocarrero, had established a hold on the dying king through his confessor, and Charles was carefully tutored to their point of view. On November 1, 1700, Charles and the Habsburg dynasty passed from Spanish history. Less than a month earlier, he had made his last will and testament, naming Philip of Anjou heir to Spain and all her dominions. France was triumphant. At Versailles, Louis called the Spanish ambassador to the royal chambers and presented him to the seventeen-year-old Philip. The duke, listening patiently while the ambassador, on his knees, made a long speech in Spanish, did not understand a word. Eventually, turning to his court with an arm round Philip's shoulder, Louis declared blandly: "Gentlemen, this is the King of Spain. His birth entitled him to a crown, and the late king has recognized this right by his will. All the nation desires his success and has entreated it at my hands. It is the will of heaven, to which I conform with satisfaction." The house of Bourbon had come to the Spanish throne.

Early in 1701, the youthful Anjou, chubby-cheeked and prettily handsome, took leave of his homeland and, as Philip V of Spain, headed south for Madrid with widening eyes. In France he had led a life of easy privilege at the heart of a powerful and thriving nation. Her strong, centralized administration, organized systems of commerce, well-equipped armies, elegant capital, and cultivated countryside had been things for an untraveled boy to take for granted. Now, descending to the desolate plains of the peninsula, he found a very different picture. French travel writings of the period provide a useful clue to his impressions. For much of the day, the land seemed devoid of activity, only the sails of an occasional windmill defying an all-pervading lethargy. Muleteers, munching garlic and tortillas, spread themselves drowsily at the wayside among a tatty assortment of slumbering beggars and vagabonds. In little towns clustered on hilltops, near Roman ruins or along wizened rivers, the same supine shapes could be seen wherever a church porch, or perhaps an orange tree, offered shade. Not until evening did the nature of the populace truly assert itself. Then the hidalgos commenced their promenade, hordes of monks and priests stirred in multitudinous holy establishments while the sound of guitars drifted from taverns and courtyards. From village hovels, old women in black ushered vivacious, raven-haired infants and imperious sucking pigs, children and animals decked alike in a profusion of ribbons. In dwellings of greater pretension, shutters opened on marbled lounges where ladies with painted lashes and rouged shoulder-blades nibbled dried fruit from vessels of a splendor uncommon even in Paris.

Their menfolk, affecting a giraffe-like hauteur, encased their necks in huge starched collars, called *golillos*, and peered through equally outsized spectacles. These, known as Quevedos, after the shortsighted satirist, had little bearing on vision, being merely a fashionable aid to dignity. Now, at the day's end, the city bloods grew restless. As if impelled by the lurid twilight, the Spanish male clapped on a felt hat of ostentatious proportions, hitched his sword belt, and assumed his finest swagger. Even the most impeccably reared of maidens was enchanted, plotting and prevaricating to escape her duenna. Women visitors from other countries exclaimed with horror at the flirtatious precosity of the well-bred Spanish female, despite (maybe, because of) her highly circumscribed environment. One French matron, scandalized by an amorous singer, likened her performance to the "caterwauling of a lascivious puss."

Above all, perhaps, it was the marked contrast between principle and practice that would have intrigued so rational a foreigner as Philip. Many Spaniards, though mortified by the slightest slur on their personal honor, accepted corruption and self-interest as staples of public life. Others, while pious to the point of morbidity, had little to learn from the profligate. Trivial incongruities stamped themselves on the mind of the visitor. Women counting rosaries at the theater gave rise to the malicious quip that they did as much while succumbing to the demands of their lovers. Spain's enemies were quick to charge hypocrisy and bigotry. On the whole, however, the duality of Spanish character was less unappealing and considerably more complex: at least as conducive to compassion and self-criticism as to anything worse. In fact, neither poverty nor piety was capable of diminishing the panache of the Spaniard. Indolence, arrogance, devotion, courage, and passion: such things did not simply *exist* in Spain as elsewhere in Europe. In Spain, they staged a perpetual exhibition. The reign of the first Bourbon monarch of the nation was to add a troupe of astonishing characters to the pageant.

Conspicuous from the start were Philip's child-wife, Maria

Louisa of Savoy, and her aging counselor Marie Anne de la Trémoille, self-styled Princess des Ursins, appointed by Louis to keep a watchful eye on the young pair. Maria Louisa, ten years old when Philip moved to Madrid, was something of a novelty in Spanish history, a boundlessly energetic tomboy of a queen with a passion for games of mock warfare. Organizing the ladies of the court as her army, the effervescent Maria would give the order to advance and as many as fifty otherwise decorous women would charge after her flying petticoats against the king, who held his lines stoutly supported by the palace dwarfs. Philip, boyish enough to enjoy dodging an artillery barrage of flying plates and even an occasional butt in the stomach, was entranced by the playful girl. There was a childish carelessness about their early relationship that must have reminded the ever-attentive Princess des Ursins of her own past. Once celebrated from Paris to Rome for her beauty, the princess had crowned two brilliant marriages with an international reputation as a hostess and diplomat. At sixty, having outlived both husbands, she was not only a woman of rugged will power and ambition, but still possessed of considerable feminine charms. Her fine figure, blue eyes, and distinctive grace were envied by those young enough to be her granddaughters, while the daringly low-cut gowns she affected quickly galvanized Spanish society.

It was not the past, however, that consumed her formidable attention. Soon, the princess knew, the royal playtime must end; the battles become bloodily earnest. Europe could hardly accept the French coup in Spain peacefully, and when war distracted Louis and called Philip to the front, the woman who controlled Maria would be true queen in Madrid. Of one thing the Princess des Ursins was certain: Maria was the key to managing Philip. For, as the mock wars became overshadowed by reality, so the romps between the royal couple would lose their childish innocence, and Ursins was sufficiently familiar with Bourbon masculinity to anticipate the role sex would play in the king's life. Her friend Madame de Maintenon, Louis XIV's second wife, was eloquent on the subject of the Bourbon appetite. Philip, in fact, proved only marginally exceptional, lacking the elasticity of conscience to take a mistress. This, in the words of one student of Spanish history, "meant that he must be married early, and that he must remain married; if one wife died, another would have to be found with as little delay as possible. Such uxoriousness could have only one result, namely that Philip was at the same time the tyrant and slave of woman." Diligently, the aging princess prepared her young charge for the tyranny and the enslaving.

Predictably, war provided a thunderous accompaniment to the process. In Austria, the outwitted emperor proclaimed his son Charles rightful King of Spain and ordered an army into the nearest theater of dispute, Italy. Though militarily no match against France, the Austrians knew very well that neither England nor Holland dared contemplate the prospect of further gains by Louis. Before 1701 was out, the assumption had been justified by a grand alliance between the three powers, who now marched in concert behind the banner of Charles against the Bourbons. In Spain, the allies were quick to exploit the weak points of their enemy, soon winning to their cause Portugal, Catalonia, Aragon and Valencia. Philip, vigorously leading a largely French army, was torn between a mounting threat from east and west. Meanwhile, in the south, Cádiz was menaced by an allied fleet and barely saved by a scratch army of stunned Castilians. When the English overran Gibraltar, they found it defended by a meager sixty Spaniards.

For more than a decade, the War of the Spanish Succession, as posterity would know it, swung to and fro across the peninsula in a frenzied rhythm of marching and countermarching that conveys in summary the giddy pace of an early movie epic. Withdrawing troops from the Portuguese front to oppose an allied landing in Catalonia in 1704, Philip was beaten before Barcelona and learned that his denuded western line had broken to imperil Madrid. Making his way back to the city, he was too late to forestall an allied occupation, and retreated to Burgos. Charles, advancing from Barcelona through Aragon, discovered in turn that he had been beaten to the capital, now retaken by Philip with fresh troops from the north. In 1707, the Bourbon cause gained a boost at Almansa, where an army of French and Castilians heavily defeated one of Germans, Catalans, English, Portuguese, and other allies. Once more, Philip was advancing to the east. Once more, the allies, reinforced now by sea from Italy, turned the tide. Once more, Charles panted through Aragon on the tail of a retiring enemy. In 1710, the allies were back in Madrid. It was a dubious advantage. "We are masters of no more than the ground we camp on," wrote the English general, Stanhope. And that, of course, only until Philip popped back into the picture, when the whole cast shuttled off jerkily, mechanically, across the bleak, familiarly body-strewn terrain.

The country that had once used all Europe as her battleground had now become the battleground of Europe. After two centuries of spectacular self-assertion, Spain had returned in spirit to the days when her plains had been war fields for Moor against Arab, barbarian against Visigoth, Carthaginian versus Roman; her people the battle fodder of rival aliens and their ideologies. It was a role that would be repeated grimly in the future as the weakening pendulum of the peninsula swung hopelessly between the great new powers of Europe. Even the sustaining impetus of faith was obsolete: increasingly irrelevant, as the War of Succession demonstrated, in an age when balance of strength had at last replaced religion as the major theme of international politics.

Still, whatever war's motive, exhaustion remained the ultimate assurance of its termination, and Bourbons and opponents alike were weary indeed by the end of the decade. Louis had already tried to pull out. Apart from his military losses in Spain, savage maulings sustained by French armies at Blenheim, Ramillies, Oudenarde, Malplaquet, and elsewhere had sickened him of the very thought of the Spanish inheritance. England, too, was ready for peace. Thus, when the emperor died in 1711 and the imperial throne beckoned Charles away from the frustrating campaigns of the peninsula, the scene was set for an armistice and the talking of terms between nations. The resulting treaties of Utrecht (1713) and Rastadt (1714) stripped Spain of yet more of her empire. To Austria went Naples, Milan, Sardinia and Flanders; to England, Gibraltar and Minorca, along with the sole right to traffic in slaves with the Indies. To complete the reshuffle, Sicily went to Savoy, leaving Philip with Spain herself, Majorca, the Canaries and the Spanish possessions in the New World and the Far East.

Abandoned by their allies, the Catalans made a desperate last-ditch stand against the king, well aware that submission at this stage meant ruthless Castilianization. For thirteen months, Barcelona held out against hopeless odds, the defenders determined to die with their lingering dream of autonomy. The last of them fought on from street to street and house to house, at last yielding only to prevent the complete ruin of the city. Surrender brought the suppression of their laws, of the official use of their language and all their universities. From now on, with the exception of the Basque territories (allowed to retain their *fueros* as a reward for siding with Philip), the writ of Castile was the writ of all Spain. The traditional "kingdoms" gave way to provinces, each under a captain-general; municipal councils were required to submit accounts annually and deposit surplus moneys with the crown; a new unity of administration was aimed at throughout the country. Though the Cortes remained deprived of initiative in Philip's reign, the crown still governing without consultation, the interests of the nation as a whole were better served than before by these changes. Nor was the pruning of a costly empire in Europe and the Mediterranean a bad thing. What was needed above all was a concentration of energy at home, and a long, long period of peace.

If that now seemed possible, Philip's well-known psychological and physical idiosyncrasies had yet to reveal the measure of their latent disadvantages. Though separation from his wife during hostilities had caused him some mental strain and ill health, he had conducted himself for the most part with courage and energy. Reunions with Maria had not been lacking, two sons resulting. Then, in the very year peace promised the full marital existence his nature craved, tragedy struck at the palace. In 1714, her own health undermined by the war years, the queen died. Philip, despairing, was not alone in his anguish. For the Princess des Ursins, the loss of the attractive young woman she had shaped from childhood as the instrument of her authority came as a grievous setback. Through Maria, the princess had established herself well in Philip's favor, competently holding the fort in his absences, urging forward his administrative changes, and even frustrating the interference of Louis in Spanish government. None better appreciated the urgent need to provide the king with a new wife. For a moment, it actually seemed possible she might be contemplating taking on the duty herself. When Philip retired in mourning to the home of the Duke of Medina Celi, the princess moved into an adjacent monastery, ejecting its inmates and constructing a passage to facilitate her trips between buildings. The ensuing scandal was at least a compliment to a lady in her seventies.

It did not, however, resolve the problem, and diplomatic efforts were extended feverishly wherever the rustle of skirts could be heard in Europe's chancellories. It is eloquent of the anxiety with which Ursins sought a tractable successor to Maria that the tough, sharp old woman was taken in by an altogether questionable adventurer from Italy, a glib opportunist named Giulio Alberoni. Surely one of the most improbable celebrities in Spanish history, Alberoni, son of a gardener from the Po Valley town of Piacenza, had first arrived in Spain during the War of Succession as a sort of jolly padre and clerk to the Duke of Vendôme. Alberoni was egg-shaped, one of those bald, podgy people whose features gleam like lard above multiple chins, and who are customarily rated tiptop company. With great success he had cultivated the image of an earthy raconteur and gourmet, being, as it happened, an excellent cook. But behind the Rabelaisian exterior ranged an astute mind, and, while Madrid lapped up his yarns and *risotti*, the plump priest was quietly calculating the main chance. On the death of Vendôme, he had managed to secure appointment as consular agent to the Duke of Parma at Philip's court. Here, aided by lashings of Lombardian soup and Parmesan cheese, Alberoni ingratiated himself with the king and his entourage. The quest for a royal bride proved his big opportunity. The Duke of Parma had a daughter, Elizabeth Farnese, who was twenty-one and unmarried. If Alberoni could make her Queen of Spain, he might himself usurp the role of the Princess des Ursins. Accordingly, he represented Elizabeth to the redoubtable dowager as a meek and somewhat simple country girl, a serviceable bedmate for the king, and a pliant servant for the older woman. To her shame, the princess fell for it. On September 16, 1714, before either she or Philip had set eyes on Elizabeth, the marriage was sealed by proxy and the bride urged with all speed toward her distraught and impatient groom.

From the beginning, the allegedly docile Elizabeth showed scant aptitude for submission. She had, according to the Prince of Monaco, with whom she stayed in the course of an eminently leisurely journey along the Riviera, a splendid figure, noble head,

glinting eyes and fine, strong teeth in a big mouth. She liked riding
and hunting, and "her will is extremely strong." Indeed, Elizabeth's approach to Spain was less a dutiful response than an imperious progress. In Monaco she amazed her host by her ferocious
appetite. As the guest of the Bishop of Arles, she drank as formi-
dably as a man and was unashamedly sick in the garden. Throughout the trip, she rose late, contemptuously ignored all pleas to
hurry, and drove Alberoni to a torment of anxiety by flirting
outrageously with a handsome Italian chaplain in her suite. The
Princess des Ursins, too, was growing apprehensive. "I tremble,"
she wrote to Madame de Maintenon, "for fear his Catholic majesty will not find this woman pleasing." Reports on Elizabeth,
preceding her arrival, gave the princess some reason to fear she
had been duped. Alberoni, finally able to announce the bride's
imminent appearance, found the old woman furious. "She said to
me that the qualities of this queen were very different from what
I had informed her," he wrote later. Apparently she went on to
elaborate. "You represented her to me as a heroine, but I declare
she is a low creature, from her appetite downwards. I am told she
eats nothing but garlic and hard-boiled eggs."

Philip was waiting at Guadalajara, a short way out of Madrid;
the princess had advanced farther on the road. On the evening of
December 23, the two women met. It was snowing, the going had
been hard and Elizabeth swept up in short temper. Ursins, resplendent in low-cut court dress, refused to descend the stairs to
meet her, gesturing instead to her private room. Outside, a small
group of courtiers and soldiers listened breathlessly. "Madame,"
came a voice, "you have treated the king most impertinently . . .
have you no respect for his impatience to see you . . . turn round
. . . God, madame, you are poorly put together . . . what a
dress!" A pause. Then Elizabeth, violently: "Count Alberoni! Arrest this mad woman who insults me . . ."

It was still snowing as the fuming princess, a few hours back
the most powerful figure in Spain, was hustled toward the
Pyrenees and exile, a prisoner of the same guards who for years
had jumped to her command. For a moment, Philip was of a mind
to countermand the sentence, but that was before Elizabeth arrived at Guadalajara. One night took care of the rest. The new
queen handled her husband with regal assurance. In his thralldom,

Philip actually saw her as nature's ardent innocent. "He tells me her character is quite open and that he gazed to the very depths of it from the first," Alberoni informed Parma sardonically, " . . . I wouldn't dare say as much." In fact, there were few things Philip could do that Elizabeth could not do better. "On Thursday last," stated the court news a few weeks after her arrival, "the Queen, in gentleman's attire, went out shooting and killed two stags and a boar, also shooting from horseback at a running rabbit, leaving it stone dead to the admiration of the King and bystanders who witnessed Her Majesty's extraordinary skill and agility." Had she been content to hunt animals, admiration might have lingered longer.

It was Alberoni who introduced the lusty Elizabeth to politics, for his own purposes. He lived to regret it. The woman did nothing by halves, and her new interest grew until it devoured everything. Her consuming passion, when she began to bear children, was to assure them positions of power, which, since Philip's two sons by Maria were first in line for the Spanish crown, meant gunning for new possessions overseas—or rather, old ones, for the queen resolved to recover Spain's lost dominions in Italy. To this end, she gave most of the remainder of her life, not to mention the lives of countless Spaniards, incurring the wrath of the Utrecht signatories and involving her adopted country in conflict after conflict. That she had the driving genius and dexterity of a second Isabella the Catholic is evident. Before the reign ended she had established two sons against all odds on the thrones of Naples and Parma, propelling a third to a cardinalate. But for Spain, her genius was evil, leading the country once more into wars it could not afford and from which only foreigners were to gain.

For a while, Alberoni rode this tiger of his own creating with dexterity. Nourished by his culinary accomplishments, gratified by the undoubted vigor with which he organized Spanish armies and fleets for her ambitions, the queen encouraged the plump Italian to ever greater endeavor. Whirled on by the greed of his feline mistress, the scheming minister plunged into a jungle of Machiavellian intrigue that involved half the courts of Europe and forced even France to join England and the emperor against Spain. Alberoni was cunning, but he was no Ferdinand. Staking everything on a grandiose plan to persuade Sweden and Russia to invade Scotland and restore the Stuarts, his plans sheered into disaster. Sweden and Russia were antipathetic, a Spanish expedition bound for England to support James, the pretender, was dispersed at sea by storm, and the whole thing fizzled out in the fiasco known to British history as the Nineteen. Alberoni's ride was over. Incensed by his plotting, England sent warships to pound Galicia, the French struck in the Basque provinces, and the emperor hammered Spanish forces in the Mediterranean. In December 1719, he was dropped without qualm by Elizabeth and banished to Italy. Incredibly enough, Alberoni turned up at the election of Pope Innocent XIII, two years later, as a cardinal, and was actually proposed himself, in due course, for the chair of St. Peter, apparently winning ten votes for his peculiarly bland charm. He lived to a great age, and died a very rich man.

Alberoni was replaced in Elizabeth's confidence by a minister of even more blatantly adventurous instincts, this time a Dutchman, the Baron of Ripperda. For Ripperda, power in Spain was merely a prelude to dreams of greater statesmanship, in token of which he soon persuaded the queen that he could further the cause of her children by a personal approach to the emperor. His aim was a rapprochement between Philip's Spain and her bitter enemy of the War of Succession: a coup appropriately matched in size with his vanity. The timing was excellent. Austria's well-known commercial ambitions in the Indies had severely strained her alliance with England. At the same time, the French government, now managed in the name of Louis XIV's successor, the sickly child-king Louis XV, was on most uneasy terms with Philip. A general shuffling of alignments seemed feasible. In 1725, Ripperda pulled it off. As well as signing a treaty of mutual defense at Vienna, the emperor promised his daughters to Elizabeth's two eldest sons, recognized the senior of these in his Italian pretensions, abandoned his claim to the Spanish throne, and agreed to help Spain in recovering Gibraltar and Minorca. In return, he was offered the trading concessions he coveted for his Ostend Company in the Indies. For Spain, it was a poor exchange of substance for avowals; but to the queen it looked fine. Ripperda was made a duke and grandee for his trouble.

In triumph, however, the baron's boastfulness was intolerable. "I know I am hated by the Spaniards," he admitted in public, "but

I despise them, protected as I am by the queen, to whom I have rendered the most important service." The importance of his service was less evident to others. "The King is extremely uneasy," wrote the British ambassador on the subject. When the emperor refused to lift a finger in the face of Spain's consequently abortive siege of Gibraltar, the whole shaky edifice of Ripperda's diplomacy shuddered. Already, the architect was scuttling for cover. In 1726, his house surrounded by an angry mob, Ripperda took refuge in the English embassy, where he promptly disclosed the state secrets of his government. Like Alberoni, he had yet to exhaust his resourcefulness. Finding a frigid welcome in Portugal, England, and Holland, he eventually sailed for Morocco, vowed himself a Muslim, and became grand vizier to the sultan.

Meanwhile, Philip, taxed by his early wars, battered by a domineering wife and her favorites, retained little of his youthful promise save an occasional gleam of wry humor. At one time, when relations with France were at a low ebb, his wife's minions ordered all Frenchmen out of the country. The order was quickly rescinded after Elizabeth found the Bourbon king ostentatiously packing his wardrobe. Even then, there was a note of defeatism in the gesture. In January 1724, he had sought to change his whole life by abdicating in favor of his eldest son, Louis, but the boy's death seven months later allowed Elizabeth to drag her husband back to the throne. Henceforward the king became increasingly subject to depression, retiring for long periods to La Granja, his palace at San Ildefonso, near Segovia, built in a style to remind him of Versailles. With little stomach for Ripperda's vaunted compact with Austria, he drew closer in his later years to the country of his birth. Undeceived by the true beneficiary of the Treaty of Vienna, most Spaniards readily endorsed such a policy, and the interdependence of the neighbors, and their link through the house of Bourbon, was recognized in two Franco-Spanish treaties: the so-called Family Compacts of the Escorial, 1733, and Fontainebleu ten years later, during the War of Austrian Succession.

By the time Philip died of apoplexy in 1746, Elizabeth's hungry soul had largely been satisfied. It was not possible to say the same of the king or the country. Not once since he had crossed the Pyrenees at the turn of the century had Philip revisited France, nor had he ever fully reconciled himself to Spain. For all but six years of his seemingly interminable reign, the country had been at war, and, for most of the time, governed by, and in the interests of, foreigners. Even when Ripperda went, the queen had found a new favorite in the Austrian ambassador. One man alone towered above the greed of such aliens and their disregard for the crying needs of Spain, and he came late in the day and did not live for long. Nevertheless, it was to a great extent the doing of José Patiño, a former financial minister and a genuine Spaniard, that Spain emerged hopefully from the rule of Philip despite the long years of squandered government.

Patiño, coming to an office choked with the stale odor of Parisian scent, Italian soup, and Dutch cheroots, threw the windows wide to fresh air and revived the ideal of integrity. Though he was forced to fight constantly against court hostility, denied to the end the accolade of premier, his sound emphasis on the suppression of financial abuses, the protection of industry, the stimulation of commerce and marine and military reconstruction helped to bring renewed pride and prestige to Spanish life. While the old imperial pretensions persisted, Patiño did his best to exploit them realistically. His psychological master stroke was the recapture of Oran from the Moors in the thirties. At once a campaign truly Spanish in conception, execution, and advantage, and accomplished with the finest fleet raised by Spain in a century, it quickened the national spirit and opened the eyes of all Europe. Spaniards wept with gratitude at the tidings. Self-respect was redeemable; honor was not dead.

Part 3

COMES THE REVOLUTION

"Each nation is a prey to its particular furies . . .
Spain's furies are the anarchical spirit, negative
criticism, extremism and mutual enmity"—
Francisco Franco

Chapter 9

COLONIAL DAYS AND
ENLIGHTENED DESPOTS

Through the wars and crises, the depressions and hopes of the homeland, Spanish America had flourished and developed. In the west, Spaniards had moved on to discover the New Hebrides, New Guinea, and the coast of Australia; in the north, they had pushed through Florida and California; in the south, they had explored Cape Horn and the great rivers of the lower continent, adding vast tracts to the world as perceived by Europeans. The great incentive to expansion was the search for precious metal. When the conquistadors had stripped the temples and tombs of the Indians, they began to seek the source of the treasure. It was this quest for unearthed gold and silver that lured them from the coastlands and fertile valleys into jungles, mountain ranges, and deserts, opening areas they might otherwise have balked at. Where they struck seams, they built camps and roads, hacked out plantations and imported Indians to form a cheap and expendable labor force. Underfed, overworked, and brutally manhandled, the Indians died in thousands, far from their homes and their relatives. According to one description of the Mexican mining camps of the sixteenth century, "It was almost impossible to walk except over dead men or bones, and so numerous were the buzzards which came to feed on the bodies that they cast a huge shadow in the sun."

Many Spaniards protested against such callousness, especially the ecclesiastics who sailed with each new wave of emigrants. "Tell me," asked the Dominican friar Antonio de Montesinos of the Española settlers as early as 1511, "by what right or justice do you keep these Indians in such cruel and horrible servitude? Are they not men like yourselves?" And when the angered colonists complained of his scathing sermons, demanding his ejection from the island, the Dominicans stood firm behind their brother, bidding the mob take heed of his words. To Aztec and Inca, who had always tended to exalt one deity, a creator-god, above their others, Catholic religious organization offered much in common with their own. There was nothing new to them in the idea of an hierarchic priesthood, even in convents, nor in feast days, fast days, and baptism by water. Shrewdly, the Spanish missionaries smoothed the process of conversion by tolerating many pagan customs, adopting sites of worship favored by the natives, and linking local dances and rituals with Christian celebration. The result was a triumph seldom matched in proselytizing endeavor, and the Church was loath to see its efforts upset by the crude and lustful methods of the early adventurers.

Among the type of men Montesinos had staked his welfare to castigate was an educated fortune hunter from Seville named Bartolomé de las Casas. Three years later, Las Casas relinquished his gold, his land, and his native serfs to devote a stormy career to the championship of the Indians. At first, he gained honors. Cardinal Jiménez pronounced him "Protector of the Indians," Charles I supported his aims, time saw him ensconced as Bishop of Chiapa, Mexico. But the very nature of colonial expansion was against him. Appalled by the increasing decimation of the people he had sworn to protect, Las Casas became an advocate of Negro importation, soon perceiving, however, the error of his judgment. Discouraged by failure, he retired for some years to write a history of the Indies. Having returned to the fray with varying success, he finally vented his accumulated fury and bitterness in his much-quoted Brief Recital of the Destruction of the Indies, an indictment of colonial greed and cruelty too appallingly graphic for even his supporters to stomach. Las Casas ended his long life largely discredited in Spain and America. It was left to Spain's enemies to raise him, delightedly, to prominence. For two centuries and more they made full use of his tract for propaganda, thankful their own colonial misdeeds had been spared such a chronicler.

Contemporaneous with but less controversial than Las Casas, was another defender of Indians, Juan de Zumarraga, a Franciscan and the first Bishop of Mexico. Zumarraga's dignified protests to the crown were instrumental in ridding the early Spanish government in Mexico of some of its most heartless men. He campaigned stubbornly against the branding of the natives, and their use as beasts of burden. Asked by fellow-Spaniards how he could possibly associate with people they regarded as so "foul-smelling" as Indians, the bishop replied that to him their smell was heavenly. Typical of the compassion of Zumarraga was his support, in 1531, of the claim of an Indian named Juan Diego to have witnessed the apparition of the Mother of God in the form of a dark-skinned Mexican maiden. His vision was soon famed throughout New Spain as the Virgin of Guadalupe. Many ecclesiastics, among them Zumarraga, worked for the education and social welfare of the Indians. Even the Inquisition, once established in the New World, was far more lenient on the indigenous people of America than on peninsula converts. But the Church, for all its power, could not save the natives from the consequences of European acquisitiveness, and, in the end, grew complacent and comfortable, with its own share of land and riches.

Of riches there were plenty. As the mining program made headway, gold, and increasingly silver, poured in a glittering stream from the earth. Suddenly, camps became towns, towns grew into cities, and traders, manufacturers, and farmers moved into the vicinity to meet the needs of the people. All types of men shared the brash new affluence, not excluding some of the surviving Indians, whose toils were passing to a growing army of Negro slaves from West Africa. It was an age of unfettered greed and unrestrained passions. Among several spectacular silver cities, none better illustrated the peculiar madness of the boom period than fantastic Potosí, thirteen thousand feet high in the Bolivian Andes. Here, in 1543, Spanish prospectors discovered one of the most remarkable mounds of treasure known to the history of mining: a two-thousand-foot hill of silver from which, in their colonial heyday, the Spaniards dug more than sixty million pounds weight of precious metal. Alongside this intoxicating heap of wealth grew the biggest, gaudiest and most riotous city in America. By the middle of the seventeenth century, Potosí, with a population of 160,000 had attracted more inhabitants than even the Mexican capital. In its gilded salons and gaming rooms, fortunes changed hands overnight.

A glimpse at the early annals of the city suggests something of the character of its astounding community. On Corpus Christi day, the entire thoroughfare between the mint and the treasury was lined with silver bars, likewise the altar surrounds of the fabulously baroque churches. Mineowners and wealthy merchants held masked balls and receptions regardless of cost, or staged mounted tournaments for prizes fit to ransom a crown prince. Through the streets rode tough frontiersmen and adventurers bespangled from hat to hip in gold chain, and Indians in shirts of silk and brocade. From the lavishly embroidered curtains of sedan-chairs swung the dainty feet of young ladies of mixed blood, "their slippers tied with silk and gold, and studded with rubies and pearls." Pretty Indian girls sported diamonds and emeralds in their coifs worth thousands of pesos. Women, married or otherwise, whether Indian, mestizo, or white, attracted by dint of their minority a host of impassioned admirers. The privilege was frequently paid for in blood. In 1658, for example, one Luciana Cordero was stabbed thirty-five times by her husband because "he suspected her of having offended his honour." About the same time, jealousy, the endemic scourge of Potosí, reached new limits when a certain Gervasio de la Rea excused himself for killing his wife on the grounds that he had seen "a fantastic man (reputedly the devil) pawing her legs."

Necessarily, many women learned to fend for themselves. When two daughters and their mother were attacked at home by a gang of outlaws known as the twelve apostles and Magdalen, they not only put the intruders to flight but profited to the tune of two thousand pesos left behind in a sack. This particular gang, among many, specialized in house robbery and abduction. "Magdalen," one of their number dressed as a woman, gained the first entry to a chosen premises by pleading refuge from a murderous husband: a subterfuge all too plausible, it seems, in this mecca of lust and cupidity. Two other sisters, Juana and Louisa Morales, daughters of a well-to-do household, defended their honor in a mounted duel against a couple of brothers, Pedro and Graciano Gonzales. The contest, fought in 1641, the year of a notably lecherous governor, the General Acuna, was less obviously one-sided than might have been expected. Pedro and Graciano were "pitifully killed." Not all of Potosí's formidable females confined their vigor to self-defense. Clara, daughter of one Juan Pasquier, ran away from home to join a rebellion, fought a battle, was captured by the victors and narrowly saved from execution by a kinsman. Eustaquia de Sousa and Ana Brinza, apparently bored by the Casanova treatment, stepped out one night dressed as men and shot dead two servants of a local crown officer. For years they roamed Peru toting their pistols until, legendary in their notoriety, they returned to Potosí to die—as they proudly claimed, virgins.

Potosí was not lacking in civilized diversions. There was a theater, and *comedias* were staged and attended with great elegance. Few citizens, however, were content for long with passive entertainment. They did not, as their historian put it, "disport in gardens and pleasant fields, but rather in eight fencing academies where they learned how to kill one another." Participation was the essence of their pleasure. At carnival time they indulged themselves heartily. In highest spirits, the gallants and ladies of the town assembled in brilliant battalions "with costly costumes and hats, with plumes and jewels, with their flags." The object was to wrench these flags from their carriers, to which end they applied themselves so excitedly that "they knifed each other and killed each other," leaving the streets littered with anything up to a hundred bodies, "men as well as women." Such a life could not endure forever, and the pitch was maintained for only a few decades. Gradually, the passion, like the mound of silver that had lit it, subsided. By the end of the seventeenth century, the height of the fever was over; by the end of the next, Potosí was again little more than a village.

Inevitably, the wealth of America had attracted many Europeans other than Spaniards. Drake of England was only one of the privateers of the sixteenth century who had ranged as far as the Caribbean to prey on Spanish treasure ships, and by the beginning of the seventeenth century many Englishmen, French, and Dutch, as well as others, had extended their activities to defy Spain's holy dispensation in the New World. In large areas unoccupied by the Spaniards, particularly in the north, the old claim of exclusive ownership was now clearly beyond hope of enforcement, and tacit recognition of foreign colonies was followed by explicit agreements. Yet understanding over the rich killings Spain had made in her established possessions was less readily forthcoming. Repeatedly, she refused demands from England and France for a share in her trade. Jealously, those powers refused in turn to acknowledge her rights to a monopoly. As a consequence, the Indies for long reposed beyond the bounds of normal European relationships, a zone of contention, of troubled waters, in which some very rough customers ventured to fish.

They came from an assortment of European countries, their departure often precipitated by urgent necessity—fugitives, paroled convicts, and ne'er-do-well adventurers—encamping in coves and on beaches either ignored or deserted by the Spaniards. The golden reaches of Española were especially popular, for here, by the early seventeenth century, a number of original Spanish settlements had been abandoned, and quantities of imported pigs and cattle had since bred profusely in the wild. Depopulated of Indians and alive with good hunting, the island coast became well known for its rough and ready tramp communities and the provisioning facilities they offered such illicit operations as smuggling and piracy. From the remaining natives, these bands of foreign outcasts learned to preserve the meat from their hunting expeditions by a combination of sun curing and smoking known as buccaning. This skill gave rise to the name buccaneer, a term synonymous to Spain with piracy and trespass, to rival powers with a form of retributive justice. Hounded by Spanish warships, desperate, resourceful, and savage, the buccaneer developed a bond of sorts with his polyglot fellows, a common detestation of the regular enemy.

As France and England established colonies on other islands and the mainland, the buccaneers gained allies and became better organized. In 1630, they seized the small isle of Tortuga, off northwest Española, building a substantial stronghold and stores depot there for smuggled goods, pirate loot, and foodstuffs. Tortuga became famous in buccaneer history. The same year, a London company occupied Providence Island, off the coast of Nicaragua, with the declared intention of fattening on Spanish trade. The Providence company had plenty of work for tough, unscrupulous seamen, and for some time it employed and directed the men of Tortuga. For a decade, the settlement survived repeated Spanish attacks and the constant squabbles of its rowdy members, a growling ulcer in the system of Hispano-American commerce. In 1641, the Spaniards determined to cut it out. Destroying the English colony on Providence, they fell on Tortuga with grim efficiency, massacring all who failed to escape. Those who returned when the warships departed found themselves back in business under the auspices of the French West Indian authorities. Others took to sea, leading a roving life as best they could until, in 1655, they helped an English fleet to capture Jamaica. At last, with good harbors to work from, and the Spanish navy decimated by the English and the Dutch, fortune swung in their favor. Desperadoes and fortune seekers from every European trading nation flocked to their ranks. The buccaneers were set for a thirty-year reign of terror on the Spanish Main that was to end by horrifying even the governments which had formerly encouraged them.

The first taste of things to come was provided by an overland attack on Segovia, Nicaragua, which was barbarously sacked, as were Maracaibo and Gibraltar on the Gulf of Venezuela. The wholesale murder of prisoners, including the entire crews of captured vessels, plus the abuse of women and children by the degenerates who swarmed with the buccaneers, quickly disenchanted the civilized world of the time. In the late sixties, command of the buccaneers passed to a Welshman named Henry Morgan, who had reached the Indies from Bristol in a lowly capacity, then schemed and bullied his way to the top. Grasping, pitiless, and intrepid, Morgan swept the Caribbean unchecked, adding to a mounting list of depredations. "Between the years 1655 and 1671 alone, the corsairs had sacked eighteen cities, four towns and more than thirty-five villages—Cumana once, Cumanagote twice, Maracaibo and Gibraltar twice, Rio de la Hacha five times, Santa Marta three times, Tolu eight times, Porto Bello once, Chagre twice, Panama once, Santa Catalina twice, Granada in Nicaragua twice, Campeche three times, St Jago de Cuba once, and other towns and villages in Cuba and Espanola for thirty leagues inland innumerable times."

In 1671, Morgan climaxed a lawless career with his notorious raid on Panama, leading two thousand buccaneers across the isthmus to capture the bullion city. Panama was taken and burned, but the Spaniards had removed their stores and treasure. Exhausted and hungry, many of the marauders starved to death on the return journey to Jamaica. Meanwhile, an increasingly apprehensive English government had signed a treaty with Spain (1670) agreeing to help restrain the buccaneers in return for formal recognition of its West Indian colonies. Morgan was arrested, metaphorically declawed, then sent back to Jamaica as deputy governor with a knighthood. There he died, without further distinction.

After Panama, the most effective buccaneering activity switched to the Pacific, where the coast of Peru was ravaged repeatedly and Spanish trade menaced from California to Chile. By the mid-eighties, the power and prosperity of the Pacific marauders was at its peak. But dispersal in such a wide theater meant a gradual diminution of strength, while the increasing rivalry of France and England in the New World was reflected in fresh animosities in the pirate ranks. In the Caribbean, the buccaneers of Tortuga and western Española found their old stomping grounds overrun by a growing band of French settlers. Eventually, by the simple expedient of importing several shiploads of women from France, the French governor, Bertrand d'Ogéron, turned the very birthplace of buccaneering into a hard-working agricultural colony. The days of terror were over. Groups of pirates still operated in the Indies, but by the opening of the eighteenth century all governments were against them, as was the populace of the New World in general. Many former buccaneers used their ill-gotten profits to buy land and slaves on the islands or the mainland, waxing rich and establishment-minded as planters.

Experience, and with it sobriety, induced many Spanish colonists to seek an alternative livelihood to the mines. Men who had started by sifting the earth in search of gold and silver began to wonder if they might not be looking at treasure in the simple earth itself. Time was to prove the conjecture an apt one. Before the eighteenth century was out, the income from the Mexican mines was less by almost a fourth than the value of the agricultural produce. The process of farming development was based on a combination of crops and methods from both the Old and the New Worlds. Through the Indians, the Spaniards discovered such commercial items as tobacco, maize, tapioca, chocolate, quinine, and turkeys, all hitherto unknown in Europe, and learned the benefits of fertilizing with guano, a residue from bird-droppings found in great abundance on the islands off the coast of Peru. "Some say," wrote an early Spanish visitor to this country, "that it is soil placed there by God for the purpose." In return, the settlers gave America the wheel, such draft animals as the horse, the mule, and the oxen, and a whole range of meat-producing animals, cereals, and fruits, together with a crop particularly well suited to Central and South American conditions, sugar. In Mexico and Peru, farming followed in the wake of mining; but in Chile it came first, wheat and grapes being harvested about the halfway mark of the sixteenth century. The lands of the Río de la Plata, poor in minerals but rich in grass, became the home of the stockmen. Juan de Garay, the founder of Buenos Aires, introduced some fifteen hundred cattle and horses in 1580, many of which escaped on the Pampa to lay the seed of an industry that would be shipping nearly a million and a half hides a year from that city before 1800, already salting meat for overseas consignment.

Industrialization in Spanish America was boosted by the eventual relaxation of the trade monopoly system, which had first seemed so admirable, later much less so. The formula had been simple and obvious. Spain would import gold, silver, and other raw products from the Indies; the Indies would import manufactured goods from the homeland. By a strict veto on all foreign trade, either way, the last ounce of profit would be squeezed from the enterprise to the exclusive benefit of Spain and Spaniards. For a time it seemed to work. Then the flow of treasure began to wreak its curse. At home, inflation sent prices spiraling. Easy money lured workers from the land and kings into grandiose imperial projects. The faster the silver poured in, the deeper the nation plunged to debt. Loss of Spanish naval supremacy laid the Atlantic trade lanes open to attack, necessitating a convoy system protected by warships. The cost of such protection meant an import and export tax. Diminishing productivity in the peninsula led to the purchase of more and more manufactured goods from Northern

Europe, both for home consumption and shipment through to America. Before the seventeenth century was very old, 90 per cent of all goods shipped from Spain to the Indies were of foreign manufacture; an increasing quantity of colonial bullion earmarked for its payment. As far as America was concerned, Spain was no longer the manufacturer but a middleman. The monopoly system was forcing her to pay through the nose for goods she might have obtained on keener terms elsewhere, or manufactured for herself.

Faced with such conditions, and the potent argument of contraband activities that threatened to undermine the whole basis of legal trading, the monopolists were forced to give ground. Though trade was still confined within the limits of the empire, the old single-port rule was rejected after 1750 and traders from any port in Spain allowed to buy or sell anywhere in Spanish America. By the same token, factories and mills sprang up in the colonies. These produced a large variety of requirements, from cannons to stockings and church bells to porcelain. As in Europe, this early industrialization grew on the weary shoulders of the peasant orders. The eighteenth-century traveler Baron von Humboldt told how Indians in the textile mills of Peru often died of exhaustion at work, or were beaten and tortured to maintain productivity. But the general economy prospered, and the growth of trade helped to tame new frontiers, establishing carrier trails, river services, and a system of coastal shipping. One famous land trail spanned three thousand miles from Buenos Aires to Lima. There was also a trade link with China through the Philippines, Spanish ships making annual trips from Acapulco, Mexico, to Manila during most of the colonial period to exchange American silver pieces, hardware, and other stuffs for oriental silks and spices.

Humboldt's German taste for efficiency was gratified by the colonial postal services. "The courier system has been so well organised," he wrote, "that an inhabitant of Paraguay or the province of Jaen de Bracamoros (on the banks of the Amazones) can correspond quite regularly with one of New Mexico or the coast of New California, across a distance equal to that between Paris and Siam, or Vienna and the Cape of Good Hope. Similarly, a letter posted in a little town of Aragon will reach an Indian village in Chile or the missions on the Orinoco . . ." If the visitor had thought to find an outdated backwoods society, he was surprised.

Cultural progress, he declared, was "most notable in Mexico, Havana, Lima, Santa Fe, Quito, Popayan and Caracas," the study of mathematics, chemistry, minerology and botany especially marked in Mexico, Santa Fe, and Lima. "Everywhere," Humboldt wrote, "one observes a great intellectual movement . . . a rare facility for understanding and the principles of the sciences." Nor was beauty neglected. The Academy of Noble Arts in Mexico possessed a collection of plaster modelings "more complete and beautiful than any in Germany." In Mexico, too, Humboldt found "the most perfect flowering of the architecture we have traced from the Kingdom of Naples through the individualistic environment of Spain." There were buildings, even in provincial towns, which "might form a part of the most beautiful streets of Paris, Berlin or Petersburg."

Humboldt was struck by the high quality of the metal crafts in New Spain. "The smallest towns have their goldsmiths whose shops employ craftsmen of all castes, whites, mestizos and Indians," he reported; colonial silverware "can vie with the loveliest of its kind in the most civilized parts of Europe." Turning to other fields, the German noted that the Spanish government "had made the most important sacrifices, with extraordinary liberality, towards fostering nautical astronomy and the accurate charting of the coasts . . . few charts of Europe are better drawn than those of Western America from Cape Mendocino to Queen Charlotte Straits . . ." while "the study of natural sciences has made great progress in all the Spanish colonies." Not least to his own advantage, Humboldt could keep in touch with events in Europe as well as the New World through any one of several sophisticated newspapers published in Spanish America. Lima, with a record of printing dating back to 1584, produced an excellent example in *El Mercurio Peruano*, a credit to its founder, the Viceroy Gil de Taboada.

Above all, the traveler was struck by affluence: unequally shared, but nonetheless evident. By the turn of the century, Spanish America, with Portuguese Brazil, was supplying nine tenths of the precious metals produced in the world. Humboldt reckoned that the mines of the two empires had so far yielded a total of nearly six thousand million pesos (pesos roughly equivalent to modern dollars), of which less than a sixth was accounted to Brazil. At all events, mining profits were fabulous. On top of which, the manufacturing industry was lining some very large pockets, with farming set to outearn either. The cities of this New World, with their straight avenues and spacious plazas, reflected the affluence. Yet there was restlessness. Its focus was the city center, with its complex of government buildings, churches, and the low, colonial-style palaces of the rich. Here dwelt the *peninsulares*, the men of the peninsula—governors, generals, judges, bishops, and others, with all their retinues—sent from Spain to fill the top offices. Mexico reviled them as *gachupines*, the spurred ones. In the south, they were ridiculed as *chapetones*, tenderfeet. Yet the barriers of their privilege were complete, and neither wealth nor prowess could breach them. "The most wretched European . . . thinks himself superior to the whites born in the new continent," wrote Humboldt. "He can reach positions to which access is almost forbidden to the natives, even those distinguished by their talents, their learning and their moral qualities."

None resented the *peninsulares* more bitterly than their immediate neighbors, the Creoles, American-born of full Spanish stock. Men of business, property, and the professions, the Creoles regarded themselves as the true inheritors of the conquistadores, their rightful place on the pride of the plaza, not in the streets, however salubrious, just beyond. Third in order of social status came the mestizos and mulattoes, progeny of Spanish and Indian or Spanish and Negro unions. Well endowed with physical and mental blessings, yet set apart from either clan of their parents, these children of two worlds had grown up to fend for themselves, to rely very much on their wits. That they thrived as well as they did was due partly to the peculiar conceit that afflicted Spanish society in the mid-colonial period. The developing disdain of even poor Spaniards for any form of laboring activity gradually opened the way for the mestizo to assert himself as artisan, skilled worker, and foreman. With his brothers, he came to form the colonial middle class, a stratum of rising influence, often better off than a great many whites, whose ranks included thousands of shiftless and indolent paupers. Finally, on the hutted outskirts of the city lived the Indian who had succumbed to the white man's scheme of life, and the Negro, most deprived of all classes. Beyond the city altogether, an increasing source of trouble to the government, dwelled the nonurbanized Indian of the frontier, clinging grimly to his old way of living, raising up his own leaders, nursing a deep hatred of the rulers who had murdered his ancestors and stolen his country.

As the colonial era moved toward its climax, the antagonisms of these groupings, and their complex variations, mounted in explosiveness. Life in the cities, with their violent histories of earthquake, epidemic, and plunder, was fraught with an undercurrent of profound dissatisfaction. The administration itself was an imposition upon an imposition. The settlers, having suppressed the Indians, were in turn suppressed in their own rise to power by the forces of the crown. Hernando Cortes had symbolized the independent spirit of the conquest by giving his first settlement, Veracruz, a city council even before the town had been constructed, thus snubbing the authority of the King of Spain's representative in Cuba. Other settlements had likewise established councils, or *cabildos*, which elected magistrates with powers of law enforcement and justice. Moreover, insisted the colonists, the sittings of their *cabildos* should be free of outside interference; privileged, if the occasion warranted, to maintain the privacy of their discussions. This evolution of a spontaneous political force from the bottom, from the people, was quickly and heavily smothered from the top. In 1524, the Emperor Charles had created the Council of the Indies to supervise the whole government of the colonies in the name of the crown, its jurisdiction "supreme over land and sea and in all affairs of peace and war, political, military, civil and criminal." The council had maintained its prestige throughout the years. In the New World itself, the monarch was represented by his viceroys, who demanded by right the same respect, privileges, ceremonial, and obedience due to their royal master. Not only could a viceroy appoint his own nominees to most vacant posts, he was often president of the *audiencias*, the courts of the frontier territories, and asserted his influence in other spheres through governors, corregidors, and *alcades mayores*, the crown watchdogs in local areas.

Basking in the warmth of viceregal magnificence, the *peninsulares* had deftly plucked the plum jobs of the Indies while the Creole frontiersman nourished his resentment. Neither, any more than the Indian or the mestizo, had the settler happily witnessed the milking of America to support the futile imperial pretensions of Madrid. Yet isolation, and the powerful forces of religious and loyalist convention, had kept him in his place for well over two centuries. Only when the relaxation of trade and travel restrictions began to take the wealthier Creoles abroad, and to induce a brisk importation of radical ideas from Europe, did conservatism begin to loosen its iron grip. Works by Rousseau and the French encyclopedists appeared in the cities. They were banned, and the bans provoked wider interest. The prosecution of printers and distributors stimulated passions. Two momentous foreign events brought tensions to breaking point. In North America, the people took up arms against the English government. Madrid, eager to further England's embarrassment, unwisely supported the rebels, whose dramatic successes were watched keenly by the Creoles of Central and South America. Then, from France, came news of the proletarian rising, and mestizo, Indian, and Negro leaders took fresh heart. The days of colonial rule, of the *peninsulares*, were numbered. The only question was how much of Spanish America would fall with the hated government.

In Europe, the second half of the eighteenth century brought that short, ill-fated relationship between juggernaut kings and the new enlightenment that gave rise to the so-called benevolent despots. Absolute monarchy, based on the philosophy of the king as God's deputy on earth, had reached the peak of its political development. "*L'état, c'est moi*," (I am the state) Louis XIV of France is said to have pronounced. At the same time, a growing taste for knowledge, for reappraisal, was beginning to undermine the old creed. Montesquieu satirized kings and prelates; Voltaire harangued the great; Rousseau affirmed that government should be based on the consent of the governed. More directly illustrative of the curiosity which tempered the period was the famous encyclopedia compiled by Diderot. Though the work was repeatedly attacked and suppressed, in the end not even kings could deny their interest.

In 1774, Voltaire told how the French monarch became involved with Madame Pompadour and the Duke de la Vallière in a debate on the constituents of gunpowder. The discussion prompted Madame Pompadour to remark that she did not know how her rouge or her stockings were made, whereupon the duke observed that they could find the answers in the encyclopedia had not the king ordered its confiscation. The king replied that he understood that the books were dangerous. Wishing to resolve their problems, however, he sent for a copy. It took three servants to carry in the twenty-one volumes, and the party was soon thumbing through the pages. To the delight of the king, each of their queries was answered, and he ordered the confiscated works to be returned to their owners. As a parable, the tale had validity. For kings, no less than commoners, knowledge was irresistible. Indeed, though absolute monarchy, raised as it was on dogmatic assertions unquestioned for centuries, was doomed ultimately by the new intellectual freedoms, in several instances the monarchs forced the pace of reform from on top. The spirit of their government has been described as "All for the people, but nothing by the people." In Spain, the system brought startling results.

After the distressing chronicle of misdirection and self-interest handed down by past governments, Spain's "benevolent despots," Ferdinand VI and Charles III, sons of Philip by Maria and Elizabeth respectively, opened a novel and refreshing chapter. Ferdinand, succeeding his father in 1746, gave the nation at last the foreign policy of neutrality it so desperately needed. Middle-aged on accession, wise and moderate, the new king was possessed of that form of sound, constructive mentality whose processes are perhaps the more effective for being unspectacular. His professed philosophy, *"Paz con todos y guerra con nadie"* (Peace with everyone and war with nobody) was by no means a doctrine of weakness. Ferdinand accepted a proposition which had long been evident: that for Spain to try and match the powers of the French army and the English navy was economic folly. Instead, he strove to raise his sea and land forces, within a reformed financial framework, to a state of efficiency that would deter potential aggressors and make neutrality and independence effective concepts. Accordingly, many points on the coast and the Portuguese frontier were strengthened with new fortifications, including Barcelona, Cádiz and La Coruña; an annual construction quota was imposed on certain peninsula and American shipyards, and new regiments were formed and put into training.

Ferdinand's program of reorganization, reflecting in part the earlier efforts of Patiño, was well engineered by his outstanding ministers, Cenón de Somodevilla, Marqués de la Ensenada, and José de Carvajal, Duke of Huescar. Though Ensenada inclined to French sympathies, and Carvajal to English, both were Spaniards before everything, and Ferdinand held them true to the cause of Spain's recovery. In this he was ably supported by his Portuguese wife, Barbara of Braganza, a determinedly peace-loving woman, who did Spain the useful favor of replacing Elizabeth Farnese as first lady of the capital. Ferdinand treated his stepmother most generously, allowing her at first to remain in Madrid, a privilege not customarily granted the nation's queen dowagers. But the proximity of the two women caused some embarrassment, and when Elizabeth was discovered intriguing against official policies she was banished from the city, retiring to her late husband's palace at San Ildefonso. Ferdinand was to tolerate only one Italian favorite at court for the rest of his reign: Carlo Broschi, better known as Farinelli, the singer, who became honored and much loved by the royal couple as their director of opera.

For more than a decade, Ferdinand stubbornly resisted the rival blandishments of France and England, determined to ally himself with neither against the other. As Spain's forces, especially her navy, developed in response to his prudent measures, the diplomatic pressures upon him intensified. Minorca and Gibraltar were dangled as bribes. But even when 1756 brought the start of the Seven Years' War—that momentous clash between the trans-Channel giants whose repercussions would be felt from North America to India—Ferdinand kept Spain aloof from the conflict. It was phenomenal: a Spanish king who refused to get embroiled in a European war. Diplomats chafed and soldiers fidgeted. Ferdinand held to his counsel of peace. As a result of his policy, the domestic revenue increased by five million ducats annually while that from America was almost doubled. After his father's death, he had arrived at an agreement with the nation's creditors on the basis that the resources to pay off the huge burden of past debts simply did not exist. Of a population between seven and eight million, Ferdinand had found more than a quarter on the verge of starvation; upwards of fifty thousand square miles of farming country entirely neglected. Philip had abolished internal tolls and customs; Ferdinand put an end to the wasteful and oppressive system of tax-farming, removing, too, a ban on the export of minerals so that many once-abandoned mines in the peninsula began working again. He also set up factories for the processing of Spanish wool, formerly sent abroad to be treated.

In keeping with his role as benevolent despot, Ferdinand lent the safeguard of his authority to the controversial Galician essayist Benito Jeronimo Feijoo, sometimes called the Spanish Voltaire. Feijoo, a Benedictine monk and scholar of great mental breadth, was the most important of the school of didactic and reformist writers which arose in the absence of any major creative literature in Spain since the death of Calderón in 1681. His aim was to bring the light of reason and humanity to bear on the depths of superstitious ignorance to which his countrymen, in their long intellectual isolation from the rest of Europe, had descended; to spread the spirit of independent inquiry which motivated the best of the encyclopedists. In a land still cowed by the Inquisition, his clear and sober arguments in favor of intellectual freedom, in defense of women against the inferior role assigned them by men, in opposition to the practice of torture, and even in admiration of what he considered the judicious attributes of the heretic English put him in dire need of influential protection. In 1750, Ferdinand placed a prohibition on the tirade of abuse encountered by Feijoo. Soon afterward the king founded an academy of fine arts and set up an observatory of astronomy. He also supported the subsidization of intellectual activities of many sorts, encouraged Spanish scholars to study abroad, and helped to attract foreign scientists and craftsmen to Spain.

Within a dozen fruitful years of his accession, Ferdinand and his ministers had transformed a weak and groping nation into one refreshed in substance and confidence. New philosophies and ideals were stirring, new factories in production, new ships and armies standing in readiness. Most remarkable of all changes: there was actually a credit balance in the treasury. A tremendous amount remained to be done, but Spain was better placed to get on with it than she had been in two hundred years. Sadly, Ferdinand was already an ailing man. Fortune, having finally granted the land the king it needed, had set a jealous time limit on his valuable services. In August 1758, Queen Barbara died and, though her husband lived a further year, the shock of bereavement virtually ended his active life. A month after the queen's death, the English ambassador wrote of Ferdinand: "He has kept his bed for seven days, he was blooded twice within a few hours, and has been physicked, but his reluctance to see anyone, except the two physicians, increases daily . . . no direction can be given, nor any order issued. It is impossible to see what will be the result of this unsettled scene." But, added the ambassador, for all his torment the king "had not uttered a weak, extravagant or injudicious sentiment." He died childless in the autumn of fifty-nine, leaving his eldest half-brother, Charles, to succeed him, thus crowning all Elizabeth's dreams for her sons.

But if the old queen thought that her son's accession would bring a return of her own power, she misread the nature of the man. "Her Majesty, one may infer from many little artifices, has not yet discovered what every person is convinced of, that she neither has nor will obtain any influence in affairs," wrote the English ambassador again. Unlike his father, Charles was free of female influence for most of his long reign. Widowed within a few months of accepting the throne, he never remarried, nor did he give his mother a chance of meddling in politics. At forty-three, he was very much his own master. He had served a substantial apprenticeship to kingship in Naples (a realm he now turned over to one of his sons), had lived also in Parma, and was familiar with French as well as Italian civilization. Experienced, cosmopolitan, and progressive, he came to Spain with a happy record and a sincere concern for the land and its people. He was to prove one of the most energetic and successful of Europe's enlightened despots.

Charles was considerably more colorful than Ferdinand. Though blessed with his predecessor's capacity for patience and reason, as well as with his reforming aptitude, the new king was far less of an introvert, more forthright, doctrinaire, and robust. Of average height, slightly built, and sinewy, he was something of an open-air addict, taking regular and vigorous exercise for his excellent health. Exposure to the elements had given his naturally fair complexion a ruddy, weather-beaten appearance. He had bushy eyebrows, a big nose and affected the sporty attire popular with many later-day liberals and republicans. "His dress," reported an English visitor, "seldom varies from a large hat, grey Segovia frock, a buff waistcoat, a small dagger, black breeches and worsted stockings; his pockets are always stuffed with knives, gloves and shooting tackle. On gala days, a fine suit is hung upon his shoulders, but as he has an eye for his afternoon sport, and is a great economist of his time, the black breeches are worn to all coats. I believe there are but three days in the whole year that he spends without going out a-shooting, and those are noted with the blackest mark in the calendar . . . No storm, heat or cold can keep him at home; and when he hears of a wolf, distance is counted for nothing; he would drive over half the kingdom rather than miss an opportunity of firing upon that favorite game."

Such activities did not conflict, as he saw it, with his social principles. "You see," Charles told a foreign diplomat in his old age, boasting a personal record of 539 wolves and 5323 foxes killed, "my diversion is not without benefit to the country." The country did not grudge him his diversions, which provided a lot of scroungers and layabouts with casual employment as beaters. It is an interesting commentary on the conservatism of the people, however, that they responded swiftly and resentfully to the reforms he soon initiated for their own betterment. Charles was shocked by the conditions he found in Madrid. The city lagged far behind other European capitals in commonplace amenities. Its streets were unpaved, litter and liquid of the vilest kinds accumulated in the thoroughfares, undrained and unswept. There was no lighting at night. The more nefarious elements of the community often did as they liked. In parts, the squalor made even Hogarth's London seem desirable, let alone Paris and the elegant cities of Italy. To the hale king, with his wholesome private regime and his modern outlook, it was all especially repugnant. That the heart of Spain, the seat of his government, should be a place unfit for ordinary, decent people to live in, scarcely matched his ideas of the bright new world, and he lost no time ordering radical changes. Sweepers were organized, pipes and gutters brought in, pavings laid and a city police force established to maintain the public safety. Surprisingly enough, at least to Charles, many Madrileños were less than delighted by the sudden clean-up. In particular, a decree against the carrying of arms, a custom favored by almost all classes of Spaniards, was taken unkindly.

Nevertheless, the essential aims of the operation probably could have been achieved without trouble had its supervisors used a little tact. Charles had been absent from Spain too long to remember the subtleties of prejudice and conceit among the people. The man he charged to execute the reforms, his Italian finance minister, the Marquis de Squillace, was even more of a stranger in the country. Though efficient in his own field, he was a gruff man and no diplomat. Squillace was strongly opposed to the broad-brimmed slouch hats fashionable among Spaniards, and to their long, voluminous cloaks. They made citizens look like conspirators, he protested, rather than subjects of an enlightened king. More to the point, they made the concealment of weapons very easy, the identification of criminals difficult. Undoubtedly, some form of modification was in the interests of all law-abiding people, but as Squillace was to discover, dress habits conceal sensitive nerves of personality. When he attempted to alter the fashion by decree, posting officers in the streets to cut lengths from offending garments, the howl from the mob was formidable. As in the story of the magic broomstick, each divided remnant of material seemed to grow into a replica of the original. The more the officers cut, the more the sinister garments multiplied until, on Palm Sunday of 1766, black cloaks and slouch hats converged on the center of Madrid in an openly defiant mass, and shots from an apprehensive royal guard turned the demonstration into a riot. A contingent of Walloon troops employed for the king's protection bore the brunt of the fury, many being killed and mutilated, and an angry crowd called for the death of Squillace.

Charles, not immediately endangered by the dissidents, arranged for his minister's escape from the country, then removed himself discreetly to Aranjuez. Here he remained for several months, impatiently striding the banks of the Tajo, while disturbances rumbled in Madrid, Barcelona, and elsewhere. The last thing Charles had expected was to see the people rebelling against measures instituted in their favor—crying, as he put it, "when they had their faces washed"—and it taught him to tread more stealthily on the road to reform. His first change was to bring a strong Spanish hand to his ministry in the person of the Count of Aranda, a man who combined progressive ideas from France with a good deal of influence in his own country. He also reduced the cost of certain commodities whose high price had been blamed on Squillace's economic measures. The matter of the offensive costume was dealt with most conveniently by making it the uniform of the official executioner. After that, it was seldom encountered on the streets.

The spring storm of his reign behind him, Charles resumed his reforming activities. Aranda, a confirmed anticleric, believed that the clergy, particularly the Jesuits, had been behind the city risings, and Charles determined to reduce the Church as a reactionary power in Spanish government. As a beginning, an investigation was ordered into the cause of the 1766 troubles. This was conducted by an eminent economist, the Count of Campomanes. In June 1767, Campomanes reported that the true responsibility for the outbreaks lay with the Jesuits. The verdict suited almost everyone except the society. It whitewashed the uncompromising attitudes of both the people and the government, and it exonerated other members of the clergy involved, men who were only too pleased to see blame laid on an isolated section of the Church regarded by most ecclesiastics as arrogant and unduly privileged. For some time, the Society of Jesus had attracted increasing hostility, not merely in Spain but throughout the rest of Christendom. For one thing, its avowed loyalty to Rome above all other authorities cast suspicion on the loyalty of its members as nationals. For another, its programs were uncomfortably efficient and successful. Jesuit educational institutions diverted students from the universities, and, in the New World, provided a strong hold on local populations. In Spain, the insidious grip of its members on religious and civil affairs through inquisitional offices and a long succession of confessors to royalty had made the Jesuits widely feared and detested. In France, where their ideas had clashed with the new liberal doctrines, they had already been expelled. Portugal had banished them several years earlier.

Charles acted swiftly on Campomanes' report. His eviction order caught the society by surprise, and Aranda pursued it to a prompt and unsparing conclusion. Some ten thousand Jesuits were shipped without ceremony from the peninsula and Spanish America, and every one of their houses closed. Six years later, the combined pressure of Spain and France compelled the pope to issue a bull suppressing the society altogether. Charles and his ministers turned briskly to the former Jesuit colleges, secularizing curricula, modernizing textbooks, introducing new philosophies and methods of science. Old theological chairs were discontinued; fresh ones were filled on the basis of academic merit. At the languishing universities, too, Charles burst open creaky doors and let in the intellectual breezes from the north. Having established his own directors of education and a regular system of inspection, the king could stride out on his daily exercise with mounting satisfaction.

But the dismissal of the Jesuits did not end the power of the Church. From the earliest days of the reconquest, it had grown in partnership with the Spanish monarchs, a great ally while aims remained undivided, a formidable obstacle to a king whose ambitions were inimical to its interests. Clerics were everywhere, their fingers in all aspects of life. A year after the eviction, there were something like 150,000 ecclesiastics in Spain, perhaps one to every twenty or so adult Spaniards. In Olmedo, for instance, there were seven churches and as many convents serving a total population of two thousand. More than three thousand communities were under ecclesiastical jurisdiction during that half of the century, Church property holdings were tremendous, while its revenues from these and such sources as stipends, fees, and tithes amounted to an annual income of little less than a billion reales. Not surprisingly, enlightened opinion found such wealth and influence excessive, especially since the vast majority of clerics were credulous, ill-informed folk with little to commend them to the beneficiaries of modern education. Above all, the notorious Inquisition attracted reformist attention. Accepted at first as an agent of public protection, the Inquisition had soon become a public menace. Its early activities, directed mainly at Jewish and Moorish converts, had fallen among the most talented and industrious sections of the populace, undermining enterprise with fear and suspicion. Culture and commerce languished in its odious climate, while the institution itself had grown rich.

Time and again it had been put to the Emperor Charles V and the later Habsburgs, often by the Cortes, that the Inquisition should be subject to closer scrutiny by the state, which at least should be responsible for the revenues of the system. But, to the kings in their constant fiscal embarrassment, one of the conveniences of the Inquisition was that it lived on its victims and seldom troubled the crown with financial complications. The iniquity of the process was not only that it gave the Holy Office a vested interest in heresy; it encouraged, too, a degree of independence that amounted to a virtual carte blanche on operations. The Inquisition had become a state within a state, paying no taxes, accounting to no one for its confiscations, maintaining armed guards and a network of secret agents, seizing and condemning all who challenged it. Its operatives had infiltrated armies, fleets, and universities until no one was safe without the direct protection of the crown, and even the will of kings was occasionally challenged. The Emperor Charles had had to invoke the aid of the pope to obtain freedom for his own chaplain, the friar Alonso de Virues, imprisoned on a fatuous charge. The inquisitors also had the right of prohibiting any books they disliked, and were assiduous in hunting down works condemned by the Church. Any bookseller or private individual found in possession of a banned book was liable to death, accompanied by the confiscation of his property.

With the expulsion of the Jews and Moriscos, the Holy Office had been deprived of a regular market of victims. Lutheranism raised a new source of heresy, but its appeal was not considerable in Spain, and the burning of a few foreign Protestants had brought international repercussions which outweighed the satisfaction. Mysticism, on the other hand, was more in keeping with Spanish character, and a diverse assortment of mystics, from zealots to simple eccentrics, next attracted the Spanish inquisitors, as those of France and Germany in earlier centuries. Among their more notable targets were Ignatius de Loyola, who was twice put in prison, and Teresa de Cepeda, later St. Teresa. Teresa, the sixteenth-century founder and reformer of many Spanish convents, and author of a number of works of a mystical nature, was charged with misconduct and some of her writing prohibited. Quietists and Jansenists were persecuted, often mercilessly, as were the freemasons in their turn, and a whole range of progressive scholars and politicians. The new ideas which came in with the Bourbon dynasty were poison to the system, and the inquisitors countered them with more anger than caution. By the death of Philip V, they had already crossed swords with the government, and, though Ferdinand was not personally antagonistic, the liberalism and humanity implicit in his policies created a mood unfavorable to the Holy Office. Among the powerful politicians of the new school unwisely attacked by the Inquisition was the Count of Aranda. In Aranda and Charles, the forces of vengeance, regalism, and intellectual enlightenment would finally combine to suppress the worst of the inquisitional terrors.

It is indicative of the mounting tolerance and thoughtfulness of the period that the burning of heretics ceased in Charles's reign. The last victim of the holy fires, a pathetic old woman charged with sorcery, was burned at Seville in 1780. By a series of timely decrees, the once unassailable Inquisition was swept from the field of normal judicial matters, forbidden to execute any order from Rome without permission of the Council of Castile, and instructed to refrain from interfering with writers unless it was willing to hear their defense. It was also invalidated from passing judgment on any noble, minister, or other servant of the king. Far removed from his introspective predecessors and their claustrophobic cells, the brisk and logical Charles had no intention of suffocating amid a welter of religious trappings. Of priests, the country had plenty. What it needed was more crops, greater industrialization, better social services. Here Charles took up zestfully where his prudent half-brother had left off.

Among the popular innovations of the reign was the now familiar state lottery, a revenue-raising device unique in being welcomed by its subscribers. Coupled with a new rent tax on land and property, it helped the treasury to stand a drastic reduction in the traditional and less discriminating taxes on sales and foodstuffs known as the *alcabala* and *millones*. At the same time, vigorous efforts were made to put an end to the cult of honorable idleness that had bedeviled the land for so long. Charles took pains to proclaim quite emphatically that no loss of prestige attached to the hidalgo who engaged in a craft or technical work. Enlightened noblemen and other people of influence banded together in the Sociedades Económicas de Amigos del País, the Economic Societies of Friends of the Country, which established teaching centers for applied science and industrial skills in many parts of the land. Experimental work in land reclamation and industrial processes pushed ahead, and agricultural workers, including some six thousand Bavarian immigrants, were settled in new villages to revitalize underpopulated areas.

Stimulated by Charles and his practical ministers, the government built new factories for a variety of products, including glass, porcelain, and furniture at Madrid, glass also at San Ildefonso, hats at San Fernando, cotton and wool fabrics at Avila, Guadalajara, and Segovia, and brass at Alcaraz. Aranda, and another prominent statesman of the reign, the Count of Floridablanca, embarked on public works programs which gave Spain hundreds of miles of new roads and canals, and enabled stagecoach services, officially run and protected, to ply safely between the urban centers. Overseas, fresh markets and ports were sought not only in the New World but to the east, where the commercial importance of the Black Sea was appreciated, especially by Floridablanca, an energetic advocate of free trade. Hand in hand with this surge of activity went a sense of social responsibility that no longer regarded the saving of souls as justification for ignoring their minds and their bodies. Hospitals, asylums, and poorhouses were established throughout Spain, many run by members of the Church in the tradition of compassionate service that had contrasted so radiantly in peninsula history with the reverse side of the religious coin. Savings banks and philanthropic societies flourished, the population began to increase, revenues soared despite the easing of taxation.

In foreign affairs, Charles was less successful. The pressures exerted against Ferdinand's policy of neutrality had become more and more uncomfortable, and, though the second of the brothers cherished the same ideal of peace, events forced him to compromise in practice. Primarily, the problem was one of England's expanding pretensions, and the failure of France to hold them in check. It was Charles's misfortune to see the frontiers of French empire overwhelmed by the British both in Canada and India, and to watch the acquisitive aspirations of what was to become the greatest imperial nation of the modern world grow increasingly flagrant. He needed no one to tell him that every new advance of that power in the west inevitably meant a loss to the Spanish government. Even his Saxon wife, Amalia, by inclination pro-British and anti-French, had seen the danger before her premature death. "London," the queen had declared, "needs to feel a powerful blow, or she will be insufferable, deeming herself mistress of the globe."

The king's peaceful disposition had been tested sorely from the start. Regardless of Spanish neutrality, England had seized ships from Spain, discriminated against her merchants, and threatened her territories in an arrogantly provocative manner. In the New World, the British refused to share the Newfoundland fishing banks, established log-cutting settlements in Honduras without Spanish permission, and encouraged contraband trade and piracy. When Charles proposed mediation, he was rebuffed. When he protested, he was asked for an explanation of Spain's own program of naval redevelopment. In 1761 Charles responded by signing the third Family Compact with France. His ambassador in that country at the time, the Italian Marquis of Grimaldi, had argued the advantages of an alliance obligating France to defend Spanish interests in the Americas, but, in fact, the French gained more than the Spaniards by the treaty. For the latter, it meant belated involvement in the Seven Years' War, an abortive march into Portugal, whose government refused to join the compact, overt English aggression in the Caribbean and the Philippines, and, within two years, a hasty scramble to the peace table on the losing side. Far from sustaining Spain's interests in the west, the Family Pact cost her government Florida, which went to Britain as a condition of peace, and forced Charles to acknowledge the British claims regarding Newfoundland fishing and Honduras logwood. By way of placating her ally, France transferred to Spain the large but undeveloped territory of Louisiana, which brought more trouble in the shape of its disapproving inhabitants.

A decade later, it seemed that Spain and France had a chance to get their own back. In 1773, Boston harbor was blackened with tea and the brew of revolution wafted through Britain's North American colonies. Next year came the First Continental Congress, and, in 1776, the Declaration of Independence. France moved swiftly in support of the rebel English colonists, but Charles was apprehensive. For one thing, he was not convinced of the outcome, and well remembered the earlier Franco-Spanish fiasco. For another, as an imperialist himself, he was not unaware of the dangers of condoning colonial revolt. Consequently, he moved cautiously, supplying the rebels with money and arms under terms of close secrecy, but reluctant to force a new break with England. In this policy of wait-and-see, he was supported by Floridablanca, who had replaced Grimaldi as secretary of state, but opposed by Aranda, now in Paris, who favored joining France in the open. Aranda, anxious to forestall the possibility of a reconciliation between London and the rebels, need not have feared. The poor showing of British arms in America considerably encouraged her enemies. Combined with Spain's own state of heightened military preparedness, it made the advocates of war in Madrid sound all too plausible. When Floridablanca himself joined their number, Charles was almost convinced. Still, he played for time by offering to mediate in the hostilities, a gesture suavely rejected by London. Finally, in April 1779 he concluded a secret treaty with France, formally declaring war on England in June.

Spain was more than ready to fight. Her people were eager for revenge against England, and even beggars contributed their alms to the cause. In Europe, the Franco-Spanish plan was an invasion of England and the expulsion of the British from Gibraltar and Minorca. The first of these moves proved a failure. The combined fleets of Spain and France, under the French Admiral d'Orvilliers, were plagued with bad weather, bad health, and bad management, while d'Orvilliers was inferior in ability to the English admiral, Hardy. Not a man was landed, and the armada returned dejectedly to the coast of France after several miserable months at sea. Nevertheless, England had been alarmed, and the operation prevented her sending much-needed reinforcements to America. Gibraltar was first blockaded, then attacked with fierce determination by the allies. In their efforts to reduce the stronghold, they used huge floating batteries, the joint invention of a Spanish sailor named Barcelo and a Frenchman, d'Arcon. The defenders replied by bombarding them with red hot shot. At two crucial points of the siege, which lasted more than three years, British ships ran the blockade to avert the imminent starvation of the garrison and to replenish its arms. In the eventual peace talks, London offered to exchange Gibraltar for Puerto Rico, but nothing came of it. Minorca, on the other hand, fell relatively easily to a surprise attack. Meanwhile, in the New World, the Spaniards had reversed their earlier misfortunes, freeing Honduras from the British and advancing in Florida, where Mobile and Pensacola were soon in their grasp. By 1783 the inevitability of American independence, and the desire of France and England to make peace, was urging Spain toward settlement despite her unsatisfied claim on Gibraltar. For a change, she came out of a war in credit. She had regained Minorca and east and west Florida, and seen her great colonial rival humbled in America. It was a gratifying experience—provided too much thought was not given to the future of her own western colonies.

Charles was now sixty-seven. The wolves and foxes lived less in fear of his gunshot, and the increasingly bitter rivalries between his ministers suggested a relaxing of the master's hand. Nevertheless, the last years of his reign were not without achievement, particularly in an area somewhat obscured by the pressing affairs of the west. Reign after reign, the Muslim powers of North Africa had made trouble for Spanish garrisons at Ceuta and elsewhere on that continent, continuing to terrorize the Mediterranean sea lanes and coastal communities. A major Spanish expedition against the notorious corsair haunt of Algiers, led by an Irish Jacobite, the Count O'Reilly, had failed with ignominy some years earlier. Now Charles returned to the attack, bombarding Algiers and enabling Floridablanca to conclude a series of treaties with the Muslims of Africa and Turkey. The ending of the centuries-old nightmare of Islam brought a sense of tremendous relief. Indeed, it was a triumphant finale to a regime that had done more for the people of Spain than any other since that of Isabella the Catholic. When Charles died in 1788, the population of the country had increased by a million and a half since the death of Ferdinand, and the revenue was three times its quantity a century earlier. His benevolent despotism had severed the bonds of sloth, persecution, and poverty and set free the ideas and energies of a proud race. Ironically, he had also sealed the fate of the monarchy. For, by relegating the Church, as the nobility and Cortes before it, to strict subservience, he left the crown on the topmost peak of isolation. No other king would be able to survive on the summit.

Chapter 10

THE PATRIOTS

Francisco José Goya was born in March 1746, of undistinguished parentage, at Fuendetodos, a village on the Aragonese plain near Saragossa. A rugged son of Aragon, tough and independent, brawny as a blacksmith, he grew up very much his own man, noted by his friends for his lack of fear and prejudice. These characteristics, coupled with a frank and earthy understanding of human passions, provided the country lad with a form of integrity, an obstinate honesty, that was to stamp itself sharply on his chosen career as an artist. Though he served some time in Rome, was influenced by the Italian and French painters then popular in Madrid, and had, at first, to meet the orthodox demands of provincial patrons, his individuality was too strong to be contained in convention and his native genius burst through in a smoldering, spurting blaze of talent; sensual, vivid, volcanically Spanish. Goya, while acknowledging Velásquez, among others, his master, was in temperament quite removed from his illustrious compatriot. Where Velásquez, the stylist, worked systematically toward perfection, Goya was given to experiment. When he wished, he was capable of great technical brilliance, but the key to his work was the urge to make personal statements, and that which fell outside the focus of his interest (for instance, the backgrounds and animals in many of his portraits) he tended to treat somewhat carelessly. Above all, he was the master of animation and feeling, qualities he brought with extraordinary effectiveness to the often stilted art of portraiture.

At the age of forty, Goya was appointed painter to Charles III, and was in demand by the grandest people in the land. He ran his own coach, had shares in the bank of San Carlos, and picked his clientele to suit himself. But, again, he differed in type from Velásquez, the loyal companion and honored servant of royalty. Goya was no more made for the establishment than are bulls for china shops. Though it would be false to pretend he lacked charm and guile when he wished to employ it, his nature was disrespectfully frank. Deafness, brought on by illness in middle age, contributed a tetchiness which recognized neither wealth nor rank. His appeal to society was rather that of the licensed eccentric, and if some found his manner distasteful, many more preferred to be fashionably daring and take his candor to their hearts. Goya captured them on canvas with uncanny intensity, complete in their vanities, vacuities, and lusts. Often his portraits were finished in a day, the basic work done at a single sitting then completed in Goya's studio at night by the light of candles ingeniously attached to his hat. Urgency appears to have been important to achieving the impression. Background details, sometimes even faulty draftsmanship, tended to be ignored. For Goya, success depended on the human statement, not the precision, so to speak, of commas and full stops.

The results were quite startling. The effect of encountering a Goya portrait was to come under the spell of a living personality. It still is, today. Each new sighting of his superbly imperious Duchess of Alba in mourning (now with the Hispanic Society, New York), the wistful little Marchioness de la Solana, or the formidable actress Madrid knew as La Tirana (Real Academia de San Fernando, Madrid), among many others, elicits an uncanny feeling of being observed oneself, as if a spirit had materialized from the past. Perhaps his subjects sensed the immortality Goya would bring them. At all events, they continued to offer themselves to his sharp analysis until his work constituted a remarkably comprehensive gallery of the leading figures in the Spain of his age. Together with the war pictures which interspersed it, it now provides a unique introduction to the impassioned events which follow, one painting in particular compelling attention at the start. On the death of Charles III, Goya became official court painter to the old king's son and successor. Charles IV, already middle-aged, was possessed of a wife as prolific as she was daunting, and in 1800, the artist was commissioned to put the family on canvas.

Goya's *Family of Charles IV* is an outstanding work in any light: to the Spanish patriot, a picture so foreboding of the agony of the next two centuries that, artistic merit apart, it might deservedly hang in black in the Prado. The figures, seeming somewhat self-conscious and apprehensive, are arranged frieze-like against a dark wall, curiously suggesting the identity parade used in detecting modern culprits. Three characters dominate: the king, his queen, Maria Louisa of Parma, whom he had married when she was fourteen and who bore twenty-two children in all, and their son and heir to the throne, Ferdinand, Prince of Asturias. Charles, a bulky figure with an amiable but flaccid face, was then fifty-two. Like his father, he was an inveterate countryman, never happier than with a sporting gun in his hand, but there the similarity ended. He had little appetite for politics, no talent for statesmanship, and displayed scant awareness of the value of time save as a collector of curious clocks. Under Charles, the progressive strides made in the last two reigns promptly stopped. He lost the respect of old campaigners and could not inspire new ones. Had he done so it is unlikely they would have got far, for he was firmly in the hands of his wife, who had strong views on who should run the nation.

Aptly, Goya placed the queen in the center of his picture, portraying her in the strongest, most dominating light. It is not the harshest study he made of her, yet the image is hardly endearing. In a superb gown of silver, overset with black and gold and cut low across splendid breasts, she commands the scene with the effortless dignity of a woman accustomed to having her own way. Even in repose, the head is awesome, at once dainty and tyrannical, somehow crowning a matronly body with the features of a diabolical child. Maria's was a face molded by the most grotesque of middle-aged excesses, from girlish infatuation to the tempestuous fury of the fish market. "It surpasses," wrote one who met her later, "anything you dare imagine."

Set slightly apart from this couple, the artist placed the foremost of their offspring, Ferdinand, then sixteen, a supercilious, frustrated youth with enough of his mother in him to lust for power, and enough of his father to prevent his grasping it full-bloodedly or nobly. Narrow in mind and experience, frightened of one parent, resentful of the other, Ferdinand was already committed by nature to a dodging, flinching, unprincipled retreat to the past. The queen described him picturesquely as "a spiked vine of cowardice." At the side of the prince, Goya painted a female figure, her face obscured in shadow, who is generally assumed to be the heir's future bride, then still blissfully ignorant of her destiny. The marriage two years later, revealing this unenviable creature as Ferdinand's cousin, Maria Antonieta of Naples, did nothing to relieve tensions in the royal house. The bride's mother denounced her son-in-law as a fool and numskull "good for nothing and not even her husband as an animal," while Maria Louisa, seldom bettered when it came to invective, called her daughter-in-law "a poisonous viper," "her mother's spittal," and "a half-dead frog." The poor girl survived the ordeal for four years, then precipitately died.

Goya's portrait omitted one person of crucial interest to this point of the story. Manuel Godoy, though not a member of the royal family, by all accounts acted much like one. Godoy had first seen the light of day in 1767 at Badajoz, the old Roman and Moorish stronghold on the western frontier of Estremadura, his people possessing a lengthy pedigree and an equally well-established background of impoverishment. At the age of seventeen, he moved to Madrid to join the royal bodyguard, in which his quick mind, somewhat indolent elegance, and a natural air of authority quickly led him to prominence. The queen, as the court was not slow to realize, was obsessed with admiration for the young man, who, rightly or wrongly, was soon regarded in Madrid as her lover. "Your fame and memory will end only when the world is burnt to ashes," she wrote, and her efforts on her guardsman's behalf were extravagant. At twenty-five, he became the first minister. Whatever the domestic relationship—and it seems reasonable to suppose the aging and monotonously pregnant Maria Louisa was more in need of a sophisticated confidant than an augmentation of the creature services supplied by her husband—Charles was complacent. "Every day, winter and summer," he declared later, "I went shooting till twelve, had dinner, then went shooting again until evening. Manuel told me what had been happening, and I went to bed to repeat the routine on the morrow, unless some imperative formality forbade it."

Charles had barely succeeded to the throne when revolution erupted in France, and the fall of the Bastile and Louis XVI's imprisonment brought a stream of French émigrés to the Spanish frontier. The dilemma for Spain had been acute. Recognition of the new government in Paris, the National Assembly, meant flouting the Family Compact, ignoring the Bourbon heritage, and admitting the most ominous implications for the Spanish monarchy itself. Defiance, on the other hand, implied a possibly ruinous war and the certain murder of the hostage royal family of France. It was a situation that would have taxed the most resolute of leaders, and Charles IV had never begun to look like that. At first the responsibility had fallen on two of his father's chief ministers, Floridablanca and Aranda. The former had adopted a tough line of negotiation with the French assembly, demanding the liberation of Louis, alerting Spanish warships in Cádiz, and imposing rigid security measures in Spain, including the dissolution of the Cortes, the suppression of popular papers, and the screening of all foreigners, especially Frenchmen. For his trouble, he had been the subject of an attempted assassination, while incurring the increasing hostility of France.

When these measures reached the point of increasing, rather than diminishing, the peril to Louis, Charles, who was humane if indecisive, dismissed Floridablanca and called in Aranda. Aranda's sympathies with reform would help, it was hoped, to restore better relations. In fact, things went rapidly from bad to worse. With war flaring between France and Prussia and Austria, the French invaded the Tuileries, abolished their monarchy completely and embarked on a series of political murders which sent a shudder of horror through Europe. In the face of such events, Aranda recoiled and, toward the end of 1792, was seriously considering making war with the new republic to the north when a striking victory for French arms at Valmy shocked him into a more prudent attitude. It was now, with Aranda's stock low and French pressure on her neighbor mounting, that Maria Louisa urged her protégé, Godoy, to the fore. With 1793, and the execution of Louis a mere few weeks ahead, Aranda went the way of Floridablanca and a virtual greenhorn took the helm of the state.

For a while, he ran with the tide of popular feeling. The slaughter of the feeble and hapless Louis by revolutionary heretics aroused the fury of countless Spaniards, and they greeted the predictable declaration of war with enthusiasm. Godoy, already heaped with grand titles, became captain general of the Spanish armies, demanding an unceasing fight to an honorable conclusion. Aranda, who opposed him, was exiled to Jaén and, later, interned in the Alhambra. The campaign opened with some Spanish successes on French soil, but all too quickly kicked back across the Pyrenees. For a while, Godoy held out for the restitution of the French monarchy and the withdrawal of the republicans to America, but successive reverses had damped the spirit of his war camp and, in 1795, French advances in the Basque country brought him to terms on conditions which barely preserved the territorial integrity of Spain. Indeed, he actually gave ground in the Indies, where Spain's share of Santo Domingo was ceded to France. For this achievement, the captain of war was granted the title of Prince of the Peace.

It is easy, with hindsight, to vilify Godoy for his next stroke of statesmanship. While the immensity of the forces unleashed by the revolution still dwelled beyond reasonable prediction, the imperial bogey of Great Britain had never ceased to haunt the Spanish government. In deciding, now, to bind himself closer to revolutionary France, thus courting a mistress whose deepest instincts were anathema to Spanish tradition, he was not, as it has seemed to critics of a later age, flying in the face of all logic. Sooner or later, it was felt, France would restore her royal house. Meanwhile the treaty of San Ildefonso, which he promoted in 1796, provided an offensive and defensive alliance between the two lands against Britain, turning thoughts once more to a united front against English sea power, and the long-awaited recapture of Gibraltar. Unfortunately, neither Godoy nor Charles, who had uncomplainingly joined hands with the slayers of his cousin Louis, had the strength to stand up to their allies. From the first, they were treated as junior partners, dwindling, as the senior gathered her formidable martial potential, into the tragic tools of a new power.

In 1799, a *coup d'état* in France put that country in the hands of a dynamic general named Napoleon Bonaparte, a shrewd Corsican of prodigious and ruthless ambition who, in the service of the

French government, had already overrun Italy and invaded Egypt. When Napoleon created his own government, the Consulate, Spain's alliance with France against Britain had already cost her a naval defeat off Cape St. Vincent and the loss of Trinidad, while Gibraltar seemed as far from reach as ever. France had both ignored and betrayed her ally when it suited her, and Napoleon regarded Madrid with scant respect. Having lavished a few compliments and gifts on Godoy and the royal couple to assure their help against the British in the Mediterranean, he promptly extorted Louisiana from his neighbor. His promise, by way of recompense, to create a new kingdom for the Prince of Parma, son-in-law of the Spanish sovereigns, was the less overwhelming since he had himself displaced the prince from the duchy. His next step in the peninsula was to force Spain to move against Portugal, which country, continuing in alliance with Britain, was providing ports for English ships. In 1801, Godoy, backed by twenty thousand French troops, marched a Spanish army across the Portuguese border and progressed arrogantly, one might almost say Napoleonically, through the Alemtejo. The campaign, known as the War of the Oranges (after an orange-branch sent as a memento by Godoy to the queen), was over in three weeks. Dismayed by sheer weight of numbers, the Portuguese government agreed to ban English shipping from its waters, and to pay the allies certain indemnities.

Godoy, flushed with success, now demanded the withdrawal of the French troops from Spain. Napoleon replied with reinforcements and the laconic comment: "Is the Spanish king tired of reigning?" When it suited him, and only then, did he recall them, in 1802 signing a peace with Britain without bothering to consult his ally on terms. The following year, Spanish feeling was further outraged by the sale of Louisiana by France to the United States in blatant violation of an earlier promise of nonalienation. Napoleon needed money for a renewed war with Britain, and the Spanish government, determined this time to remain neutral, was asked six million reals a month for the privilege. Even the complaisant Charles balked at this. Spain was in a bad way. Military expenses had once more depleted the treasury; an epidemic of yellow fever had claimed eighty thousand lives in the south, and recent harvests had been poor. It was impossible, he reasoned, to make such a large contribution. Napoleon was unimpressed. Unless the money was forthcoming, he intimated to Godoy, he would make it his business to ruin the Spanish minister, a threat quickly substantiated by a letter to Charles accusing the former guardsman of improperly using the queen. Between them, Maria Louisa and her favorite managed to prevent the king from reading it, but Godoy was sufficiently alarmed to agree to the payments.

The so-called neutrality thus gained was a fiasco. Britain, unmoved by formalities, seized a large consignment of bullion from the Indies and pressed further attacks on Spanish shipping to the point when Godoy could no longer shirk the full consequences of Franco-Spanish alignment. In December 1804, Spain declared war on Great Britain and, while Napoleon waited in vain to ferry an army to England, the British navy played a grim game of tag with the French and Spanish fleets in the Atlantic and Mediterranean. In October 1805 the three nations joined battle at sea off the cape of Trafalgar, between Cádiz and the Strait of Gibraltar. The result was an overwhelming victory for the British Admiral, Nelson, against the Admirals Villeneuve and Gravina of France and Spain respectively. More than half the allied fleet was captured and the naval pretensions of both the losing countries were shattered. There, however, the resemblance in their fortunes ended. If Napoleon had missed the boat to England, he had missed little else, and a French triumph at the battle of Austerlitz in December emphasized his supremacy in continental Europe. Spain, by contrast, was frittering her hand disastrously, her awed government accommodating the Corsican's every trick. Godoy's personal ambitions did not help. In 1806 he was deluded into advancing a huge sum from an already inadequate exchequer against Napoleon's feigned backing for a project to set him up with an independent kingdom in southern Portugal. Soon afterward, his culpability in further machinations prompted the French ruler to demand twenty thousand Spanish troops for use in Germany. Acquiescence left Spain itself shockingly vulnerable.

It was at this stage that Ferdinand, the Prince of Asturias, chose to step into the act. His wife's death, linked malevolently by rumor with Godoy, had intensified the bitterness he felt for his mother and her favorite, and there was no shortage of Spaniards looking for a lead against the party which seemed bent on humiliating the country. Had the prince been a man of positive action, he could now, perhaps, have ousted his father from the throne. He was by nature an intriguer, however, and as yet a very green one. Like Charles, he seems to have seen Napoleon as a champion of royalty against the revolution, and his first fumbling move was an attempt to supersede Godoy in the emperor's favor. In the autumn of 1807 he communicated to Paris through his closest confidant, Juan Escoiquiz, a canon of Toledo, a fulsome plea for help against the "malignant conspirators" surrounding the Spanish throne, offering, in token of his good will toward "the hero sent by providence to save Europe from anarchy," his hand in marriage to some lady of Napoleon's choosing. To Ferdinand's discomfort, this attempt at a back-door transaction reached the ears not only of Napoleon but of Godoy, who promptly persuaded Charles to have his son arrested and accused of plotting to overthrow his parents. Shut up alone, and in fear of his life, the prince was soon scribbling an abject confession: "Dear Papa, I have done wrong. I have sinned against Your Majesty as King and as father, but I have repented and proffer the humblest obedience . . . I crave Your Majesty's pardon for having deceived you, and beg, as a grateful son, to kiss your royal feet."

How far Godoy would have pressed the punishment cannot be known, for at this juncture Napoleon informed the palace that any mention of Ferdinand's letter to himself would be displeasing, and Godoy, now more than ever anxious to curry favor, advised Charles to let his son off with a warning. The incident, the so-called Affair of the Escorial, split the court wide open. Godoy, who had thought publicly to discredit Ferdinand, found himself popularly believed to have engineered the whole scandal, while the prince, so recently begging forgiveness, found himself the white hope of the people against the hated minister. Charles, in his willingness to blow one way and the other at Godoy's behest, had sacrificed the last of his scanty personal authority. The queen regarded him as a piece of royal baggage, and her son as an increasingly execrable threat to the favorite. Napoleon, now ready to add Spain to his empire, could hardly have wished for a more helpful situation. As the sordid squabble gained ground in Madrid, the French General Junot crossed the Pyrenees and, ostensibly in accordance with the plan of dismemberment hungrily awaited by Godoy, marched through Spain to occupy Portugal. By the beginning of 1808, that land was in French hands, the Portuguese army disbanded and absorbed in Napoleon's forces through Europe. In Lisbon, whence the royal house of Braganza had fled to Brazil, Junot took office in the name of his master. Except for some unflattering comments in the Paris press, Godoy was not even mentioned.

Once more, as in the earlier War of the Oranges, French forces were stationed in strength in northern Spain. This time, however, no one in Madrid had the nerve to demand their withdrawal. Neither Godoy nor Ferdinand could now hope for success without Napoleon's blessing, and each affected to see the troops as guarantors of his own future. By March, there were 100,000 French soldiers in Spain, one force under General Dupont at Valladolid, others strung across the neck of the peninsula from San Sebastián to Barcelona. Their insinuation in several key points had made the most of the widespread confusion in the country regarding the role of its alleged allies. At Pamplona, a vital citadel on the road south through Navarre, the Spanish garrison was ousted from its fortress by a well-timed ruse involving a snowball fight. While a number of unarmed Frenchmen diverted the Spanish guards with some high-spirited winter sport, a battalion of their fellow countrymen, already quartered in the town, rushed the gates and took command of the stronghold. The local troops were almost too surprised to protest. At Barcelona the garrison was similarly outwitted by French troops supposedly in transit through the city. As they drew level with the citadel, the French officers gave the order to wheel left and calmly marched their men through the gates. Within a matter of hours, the flummoxed Spaniards were turned out on the streets.

While French grenadiers and cavalry poured through the Pyrenees, Napoleon's brother-in-law, Marshal Joachim Murat, now appointed commander-in-chief for the emperor in Spain, lavished assurances and gifts on the court at Madrid. By the time Charles and Godoy awoke to reality, it was too late. With the gates of the peninsula already in French hands, and Murat's armies threatening the capital, Napoleon's attitude became suddenly and grimly explicit. Bluntly, he demanded the Spanish territories north of the Ebro. Godoy, at his wit's end, arranged the removal of the court to Aranjuez as the prelude to a further retreat to Seville, and, ultimately, America. This southerly movement of the royal family, complete with the Madrid garrison which was earmarked as its escort, presented the Spanish people with a clear indication of the fate which had befallen them. In Madrid and elsewhere, crowds began to demonstrate their anger in the streets. Caught between the advancing Murat and the belated fury of his own long-suffering subjects, Charles was persuaded by Godoy to perpetrate the most blatant of deceits. With flight fixed for the eighteenth of March, the king issued the following proclamation to the people:

"The noble feelings you express in the present situation assure me anew of your hearts. Loving you with the gentleness of a father, I hasten to soothe your anxieties. Breathe peacefully; rest assured that the army of my dear friend, the French Emperor, crosses my kingdom in the spirit of peace and amity. Its intention in making ground is to obviate the risk of an enemy landing, while, for my part, the mustering of a houseguard is neither to defend me nor to escort me on a journey, as the malicious would have you believe. Surrounded by such tangible proof of the loyalty of my beloved subjects, what have I to fear? Were this an emergency, how could I doubt your support? But the people of Spain must not believe this an emergency. Be calm. Behave as always towards the allies of your King and, in a few days, you will find tranquility reaffirmed in your hearts while I enjoy the blessings of Heaven in the intimacy of my family and your love."

Even as the message was being drafted, that intimacy, that love, was under fire from the agents of Ferdinand. For the Prince of Asturias, Godoy's anguish was sweet, and, fired by the urge for revenge, he set his own men to stir up the crowds. At Aranjuez, the night before the arranged departure, the scene was uncomfortably reminiscent of the French Revolution. Gangs of malcontents from Madrid mingled with anxious evacuees and court followers at the palace gates, rumors of an escape by Godoy and the royal couple were prevalent and there was no mistaking the tone of the voices and gestures. When, shortly before midnight on the eve of the eighteenth, a carriage with drawn blinds and a mounted escort turned out of Godoy's drive, the word went up that the king and queen were leaving. In fact, it was not so, but the mob was now sufficiently excited to rush the building shouting for the blood of the minister. Abandoned by his guards and unable to escape,

Godoy climbed to the attic, where, concealed by a roll of matting, he escaped notice for thirty-six hours.

Ferdinand made good use of the time. Acclaimed with enthusiasm by the crowd, he quickly announced the dismissal of his enemy and set about restoring law and order. Demands for the abdication of Charles in the prince's favor were already pressing when, on the nineteenth, Godoy was apprehended and forced to throw himself on Ferdinand's mercy. With new demonstrations mounting against the minister, and the queen obsessed with his safety, Ferdinand made his offer: a cessation of disorder and the life of the favorite in return for the crown. Charles, now ready for any way out of his ruin, immediately accepted, pleading ill health in a brief statement of abdication in favor of his son. With Godoy safely in prison and his partisans banished from office, the men of the new king dominated the Council of State. It remained for Ferdinand (VII) to reach an accommodation with Napoleon, who, in the giddy atmosphere of the moment, was expected by many to be favorably impressed by the events. Murat, arriving in Madrid just in time to witness Ferdinand's triumphant return to the capital, was himself perplexed by the changed situation. He reacted cautiously, careful to avoid any gesture which might indicate recognition of the new king. In this, he anticipated the emperor perfectly.

Meanwhile, Maria Louisa, distraught at Godoy's imprisonment, had soulfully implored Murat to help her obtain the release of "the poor Prince of the Peace," so that, together with her ailing husband, they might retire to France and "all live in some healthy place far removed from conspiracy and the affairs of State." Appraised of the marshal's coolness toward her son, however, the queen altered her attitude. Regaining her familiar venom, she now regaled the Frenchman with an all-out attack on the character of Ferdinand, who, she asserted, had engineered the overthrow of the rightful government by forgery, bribery, and treacherous incitement. "Expect from him only outrage and torment. Do not believe a word that he says." This was more to the liking of Murat. On his advice, the queen prodded her weary husband into sending to Paris a formal protest against the legality of his abdication, claiming he had acted under duress in order to save more trouble and bloodshed. Napoleon received news of these happenings at the end of March and in April moved down to the Pyrenees to be handy for the last act. It was, in the tradition of Charles and his calamitous family, a tragic farce.

The setting was Bayonne, on the French side of the Bidassoa, where the emperor now prepared to observe the stars of the Spanish cast in person. The first to take the stage was Ferdinand, lured to the venue in the extravagant hope of being hailed as a brother sovereign by Napoleon. Napoleon kept the young man waiting a while, then invited him to dinner. His view of Ferdinand was not flattering. "He is indifferent to everything and has ideas about nothing," the emperor wrote. "He is a thoroughly uninteresting person." Certainly, he was a very shocked person, for, far from sustaining Ferdinand's authority, Napoleon politely informed his guest that he thought it best to relieve him of the Spanish crown and pass it to a member of the Bonaparte family. Making a brief appearance on a balcony later, Ferdinand waved bleakly to a small group of Spaniards surrounded by French soldiers. "I have been betrayed," he shouted feebly. Since he refused to discuss anything at all from that moment, Napoleon summoned Charles and the queen to Bayonne. They came readily, especially as Godoy had been released to accompany them, and were treated to a royal reception. Charles, crippled with rheumatism, was supported by Napoleon himself as they arrived at a banquet. "I am strong enough for the two of us," jested the emperor, to which Charles replied that he did not doubt it. The meal delighted him as much as the bonhomie of the host. Maria Louisa, bedecked girlishly in red and yellow roses, was equally pleased to be near her favorite. "Eat up," Charles apparently reminded her several times. "You'll like this. This is good."

There was a very different scene later when, having won the parents, Napoleon decided to bring them together with their son for a conference. Even the forceful Corsican, not unaccustomed to family arguments, was startled by the wrangle which ensued over the fate of the Spanish throne. At one stage Charles rose unsteadily from his chair and lunged at his offspring with a stick, while Maria Louisa poured out the full flood of her most virulent abuse. Ferdinand, now plainly terrified, made a frantic bid to flee from Bayonne, failed, and collapsed to Napoleon's demands. A brisk sequence of transactions followed. Ferdinand relinquished the throne to Charles; Charles assigned his rights in it to Napoleon;

Ferdinand agreed to the step taken by his father. For their trouble, Charles received some land in France on which to retire with Maria Louisa and Godoy, while Ferdinand accepted an annuity of a million francs. The act was over. Spain and her empire were sold.

The events unleashed by Aranjuez and Bayonne shocked the nation from the attitudes of centuries, astounded Europe, and set flame to the whole of Spanish America. Almost incidentally, it now seems, they also ruined Napoleon. Napoleon did not expect serious opposition from Spain once the rulers had signed away their titles. He had removed the figureheads, isolated a large part of the army, and established his own troops in vital strongholds. If logic were not enough to convince him that this country still struggling toward the revolutionary era would gladly exchange its preposterous royal masters for the nominee of enlightened Paris, then the peaceful acceptance of a hundred thousand French soldiers on Spanish soil must have sealed the conclusion. "There may be some riots," he forecast, "but the Spaniards will relax once they realise that I stand for the retention of their monarchic boundaries, and the preservation of their religion and customs, as well as offering a liberal constitution." Unfortunately for the emperor, his assumptions were not apparent to the mass of Spanish people. He was right only in anticipating riots, and even there he could be faulted for underestimation. Beneath the impending violence lay a complex of conflicting ideas, old and new, but the primary detonator was simple. On May 2, 1808, by which date they had passively suffered the departure of the best part of the royal family, the citizens of Madrid came to two decisions: That they had been robbed, and that they had been robbed by the French.

The day of destiny, as Spaniards would regard the *dos de mayo*, the second of May, was captured with ferocious vigor in the painting of Goya, whose art, like so much around it, took on a tone of desperation during the deadly struggle ahead. In two violent and agonizing pictures showing the poorly armed Madrilenos rising against the emperor's horsemen in the Puerta del Sol (*The Charge of the Mamelukes*) and the savage reprisals which followed (*Execution, May 3*) his work became as lurid as the passion of the mo-

ment. Against somber, funereal backgrounds, he drenched the
stabbing, hacking, bleeding figures of the drama in a macabre,
electrifying light, well suggesting the frenzy and despair of those
few hours. They began, perversely enough, with a popular demonstration of loyalty to the very family whose senior members were
then wrangling for their own crude advantage in Bayonne. On the
morning of the rising, a palace locksmith ran into the streets of
Madrid shouting, "Kill the French! They have taken the king
from us, and they want to take all the royal family. Kill! Kill! Kill!"
A man took up the incitement from a balcony of the Alcazar, and
others were soon spreading the message through the side streets.
When an officer of Murat's staff was attacked by the crowd that
quickly gathered, the French commander sent a battalion of grenadiers to restore order. Instead, their appearance roused the mob
to greater excitement, and, at the firing of shots, the latent resent-
ments of the city erupted.

While the men and women of Madrid snatched what weapons
they could and hastened to support the original dissidents, Murat
turned his cavalry loose in the capital. The resulting fracas was too
much for the Spanish garrison. Despite the order of their commander to remain in quarters, several thousand soldiers left barracks to join their countrymen against their erstwhile allies. By
the afternoon, with conflict raging in several parts of the city,
Murat realized that the government left behind by Ferdinand had
lost all power to control the people. In consequence, he established
martial order. A military court condemned prisoners to death without trial and, on May 3, French firing squads engaged in mass
executions. At the same time, the death penalty was proclaimed
for all citizens bearing arms. News of these events in Madrid provoked similar risings as far apart as Asturias and Murcia, inspiring
the mass of people everywhere, until the popular front against
the foreign invaders was nationwide.

In Bayonne, Napoleon lost no time completing his own plans.
Finished with Charles and Maria, now political nonentities, he
packed them off with Godoy to the free retirement he had promised them in France. Ferdinand, though pleading loyalty to the
emperor, was sent to Valençay, in Touraine, under house arrest,
where, as the Spanish people gave their blood for independence, he
sought the favor of his captor with felicitations and compliments.

On June 7, Napoleon's elder brother, Joseph, formerly king of Naples, was ceremoniously proclaimed King of Spain in Bayonne. He reached Madrid a fortnight later. Though his manner was affable, and the constitutional project offered with him was by no means disadvantageous to the people, the majority of Spaniards wished no truck with the Bonapartes. Ferdinand's government, on the other hand, had shown no such prejudice, and many of its regional representatives, with some army officers, joined Joseph's adherents. Against them, and the 130,000 French troops now on Spanish soil, the masses declared their resistance to the end.

Spontaneous in nature, and lacking central leadership, the fight for independence gained way on a regional basis, defense juntas forming in provincial centers, guerrillas banding in less populated areas. Farmers, laborers, students, lawyers, priests, and others flocked to the cause, as did many women, to be joined in some districts by regular soldiers. If their arms and tactics were sometimes unorthodox, their spirit was formidable. In two early battles, at Bailén, to the east of the Guadalquivir Valley, and at Bruch in Catalonia, they inflicted defeats on the French, while at Saragossa patriots who had suffered a six-week siege and desperate house-to-house fighting finally put the invaders to flight. By the end of July, Joseph himself had been forced to abandon Madrid and retire with an amazed French command beyond the Ebro. Not since the Iberians stood against the Romans had the people of Spain asserted themselves with such purpose. Wars for other causes they had fought in plenty—wars of religion, imperialism, and succession—and their reward had been little but humiliation and repression. This war was different. At last the ordinary Spaniard was fighting his own cause, for the right to be heard, for a measure of respect.

Early patriot successes, diverting French attention from the west of the peninsula, encouraged the Portuguese to mount their own fight for independence and, before summer was out, Great Britain had landed an army in Portugal which swiftly overwhelmed the French commander, Junot. Ironically, the British general, Sir Arthur Wellesley, who was to win his dukedom of Wellington and numerous other rewards from the Portuguese and Spaniards, had been preparing to attack Spain in the Indies when London decided to throw its power behind the resistance. One of the first

British moves was to transport home from Denmark some nine thousand of the Spanish troops Godoy had sent earlier to Germany. Their fighting defection from the emperor's service in so remote a station had provided an eloquent testimonial of the strength of the patriotic spirit. In September, representatives of the various regional patriot systems met at Madrid and Aranjuez, and formed a central junta. Its first president was the Count of Floridablanca. In November, Napoleon crossed into Spain to supervise the French side of the struggle in person.

The War of Independence, as Spaniards would know it, was to rage another five years, devouring the country as hungrily as had the earlier War of Succession. In those five years, fortunes were to swing from one extreme to the other, almost the whole of Spain falling into the hands of the French before the emperor's armies were eventually rolled back. The year 1809 went dramatically in favor of Napoleon. His own leadership, and the 300,000 men he now had in the country, proved a combination altogether too strong for the defenders, whose armies were nowhere near so efficient and numerous, and whose courage was more commendable than their strategic concepts. Madrid was subdued by bombardment, but Napoleon, judging the feelings of its citizens, wisely lodged his personal headquarters outside the city. The British forces in the west, now joined by a second army under Sir John Moore, advanced with panache but were unable to rely on the unco-ordinated Spanish armies (whose generals mostly ignored the central junta) and withdrew with similar alacrity. Moore marched to Valladolid in a dashing bid to cut Napoleon's line with France, thought better of it, and retreated disastrously to La Coruña, where he was fatally wounded facing his pursuers under the French Marshal Soult. Wellington, foiling Soult's attempt to regain Portugal, advanced to a notable victory at Talavera, only to retire again to the west. The French pressed their advantage. Having secured their communications by a further siege of Saragossa, this time successful, they overwhelmed the Spaniards at Ocaña, south of Aranjuez, and poured into Andalusia. Córdoba, Seville, Granada, and Málaga fell to them rapidly. By April 1810, Cádiz, saved at the last minute by the Duke of Albuquerque and nine thousand men, was the final bastion of patriotic government.

While Cádiz defied the French for month after long month,

groups of resistance fighters kept the war alive in the hills and plains to the north. It was in this irregular type of warfare, waged by small, independent bodies, that the Spaniard excelled, and from him the outside world coined a new phrase, guerrilla (*guerra*, war) tactics. In many parts, guerrilla leaders became popular heroes. A curate named Jeronimo Merino, commanding several hundred horsemen in the Tierra de Campos, made the roads from the north so dangerous that, according to the Spaniards, it took a brigade to deliver a letter from France to Madrid. In Valencia, one José Romeu made a reputation as a mountain fighter, while Juan Martín Diez, a former shoemaker, ranged a wide area of the Cordillera Central with his three brothers and their followers, harassing convoys and raiding outposts. His men, often dressed in captured French uniforms, took their wages in booty, on one occasion snatching a female relative of the French General Moncey complete with her coach, wardrobe, and jewels. Though more than once defeated, and eventually badly wounded, Diez was persistent and of considerable value to the Spanish command, which rewarded him with the rank of general. The three constants of guerrilla strategy were surprise, speedy disengagement, and terrorism, in all of which one man above all excelled. Francisco Espoz, dubbed King of Navarre by the French, operated on a scale that made generals wary. In ambushes on units several thousand strong, he took prisoners by the hundred, captured the royal secretary, and gained enough material to fit out an army. Yet Espoz had started with a mere seven men, founding his rise to fame on an uncanny tactical instinct and a searing hatred of the enemy. Those he killed in battle were not the least fortunate. Some of his atrocities chilled even his followers.

While the *guerrilleros* harassed French communications and generally made life uncomfortable for the Bonaparte government, the Anglo-Portuguese alliance stood firm in the west. The year 1810 saw an all-out French effort to throw the British from Portugal, but Wellington dug in near Lisbon and held on. Napoleon had now departed in person for eastern Europe, where the snows of Russia awaited his legions. His failure to complete the submission of the peninsula left him badly overextended, and Wellington's patience was to be well rewarded. By the spring of 1811, the French were gone from Portugal and Anglo-Spanish forces were besieging Badajoz, on the Spanish side of the border. Soult, marching to aid the French garrison, was defeated at nearby Albuera, after which Wellington took Ciudad Rodrigo, gained Badajoz by storm, and turned north for Salamanca and Valladolid. In August 1812 the French raised the siege of Cádiz and evacuated Andalusia to counter this new threat. Anglo-Spanish forces triumphantly entered Madrid.

For Napoleon, the sun was sinking, the air growing chill. Before the winter was out, he had been forced to shift troops from Spain to the Russian front. On May 22, 1813, Wellington, having retired to spend the winter in Portugal, set out to deal a decisive blow to the French forces withdrawing with Joseph toward their own frontier. Joseph, loaded with all the plunder he could carry, reached Burgos on June 9 but was cut off at Vitoria, routed, and forced to flee empty-handed across the Pyrenees. French control was now limited to Valencia and the northeast. San Sebastián and Pamplona fell to the allies before Christmas, and Wellington, hearing of Napoleon's defeat at Leipzig, struck into France to complete the emperor's embarrassment. On March 28, 1814, came the last French surrender in Spain. A fortnight later, Napoleon abdicated.

The war had been a revelation to both sides. Popular resistance had confounded the invader, who, in turn, had retaught the Spaniard a forgotten political lesson: that the will of the people was stronger than the greatest of emperors, hence that the despotism he had accepted as inevitable for so long was a matter of choice for the future. The notion, for some clear, for others dimly realized, was in any case fraught with complications and confusion. Beneath the oversimple billing of Spain versus Napoleon had occurred a perplexing upheaval, an odd combination of war and revolution, in which, for many Spaniards, the lines had got awkwardly crossed. At bottom, discontent had rested on the evils of absolute monarchy in the hands of such men as Charles IV and Ferdinand. The Spaniard, however, in his patriotic reaction to foreign interference, had largely overlooked the cause for the effect. In this situation, the unworthy Ferdinand had become an object of devotion, known widely as *El Deseado*, the Desired, while the government of

Joseph, a considerable improvement on that of Ferdinand or his father, had been equally widely rejected. Yet by no means entirely. To heighten the paradox, some ardent royalists, especially in the higher ranks of the nation, had taken the view that the abdications at Bayonne, being the acts of kings, were unquestionable, and that Joseph was therefore the only rightful sovereign. A totally different group, the *afrencesados*, or Francophiles, strongly influenced by the doctrines of the French Revolution, had also supported the Bonaparte government.

For the thoughtful patriot, therefore, the war was a profoundly disturbing conflict in which virtue was seldom clearly on the one side. In this respect, the attitude of Goya, as a man of objectivity and intelligence, is once again relevant. He seems to have tried to keep an open if not a detached mind. Though retained as court artist by Joseph, prepared to paint Frenchmen and collect pictures for the Napoleonic Museum, he also portrayed the Duke of Wellington and was invited to Saragossa by its defender, General Palafo, who plainly respected patriotic integrity. Few were better placed than Goya to assess the prewar court and political system, and his belief in the remedies expounded by the French revolutionary writers was a judgment in itself. At the same time, he was disillusioned by Napoleon's methods and appalled by the consequences of introducing doctrines by armed force. The result was a determined concentration in his sixties on the one aspect of the war about which there could be no doubt: its inhumanities and horrors. In a series of eighty etchings, the famous *Desastres de la Guerra*, he turned a steadfast eye on the field of human conflict, immortalizing scenes many would have preferred to forget. The work brought the artist, already depressed, to a state of acute mental crisis. From portraying the corpses and brutalities of real life, he delved inward to echo the nightmare in a series of grotesque, surrealistic fantasies which expressed much of the shock and uncertainty with which Spain would emerge from her torment.

By 1814, the Spanish people stood to choose their own political future. But which future did they want? From the outset the majority, set on independence, had necessarily rejected the constitution put forward by Napoleon, the so-called Constitution of Bayonne, along with the Bonaparte faction that accepted it. It was, nevertheless, a progressive proposition, featuring a common law, an independent judiciary and personal freedoms, among other advantages, and with it came Spain's first taste of constitutional government. On the other side, a constitutional system had early advocates, but, for a while, conservatism prevailed among the patriots, the central junta deferring to a regency council. With the almost total collapse of 1810, however, partisans everywhere demanded a drastic reassessment of the future, and the council, which had clung jealously to its power, was forced to convoke an assembly representing people, cities, and juntas all over Spain, together with deputies from the American colonies. This cortes, the first truly collective and popular national assembly in Spanish history, met at Cádiz in September 1810. As discussions proceeded, the many complexions of its members soon polarized into two main parties: the reformers, or liberals as their opponents called them (thus giving a new term to European politics), who now took the upper hand demanding constitutional guarantees for the future, and the antireformers, or *serviles*, who stood for the return of the monarchy as before.

The liberals, drawn largely from the middle-class intelligentsia, included many intellectual priests, one of whom, Diego Muñoz Torrero, expressed their aspirations in the first parliamentary address of the assembly. When a charter was eventually agreed to some eighteen months later, liberal influence was high and the document, the Constitution of Cádiz, 1812, was indeed radical by Spanish standards. It declared, among 384 articles, that the nation, including Spaniards of both hemispheres, was not the patrimony of any family or person; that sovereignty resided in the nation, which had the exclusive right to establish its basic laws; that the form was a limited, hereditary monarchy of Catholic religion, the king sanctioning the laws of the Cortes with the right of suspension but not of veto: that the Cortes was constituted by a single chamber of elected deputies, one to every 70,000 citizens, to be renewed every two years, and that its responsibilities included taxation, expenditure, the behavior of ministers and civil servants, the size of the forces and the freedom of the press. As in the Constitution of Bayonne, a common law, the inviolability of the individual, and an independent judiciary were cardinal principles. The king was responsible for foreign affairs, matters of war, public order, and the appointment of ministers, magistrates, and bishops.

He would be advised, however, by a council of state nominated by the Cortes, and would not under any circumstances whatsoever suspend or dissolve any meeting of the assembly—a cautious proviso against the tactics that had thwarted the medieval Cortes.

The constitution was proclaimed ceremonially on March 19, and hailed as a charter of popular justice and freedom by the liberals, a huge advance in social and political enlightenment. Indeed, its mere launching as a document was a remarkable achievement, and one that could hardly have succeeded in the face of traditional pressures but for the extraordinary circumstances of the moment. Not only was the liberal majority at Cádiz itself a product of the disintegration of national life under French occupation, but large sections of the electorate it represented neither understood nor cared about the principles of popular sovereignty, a fact very quickly evident. As the French retreat commenced in the peninsula, and new deputies appeared in the Cortes, the liberal majority rapidly dwindled while antagonisms between reformers and their opponents became increasingly bitter. On March 24, 1814, almost six years since he had placed himself in the hands of Napoleon, Ferdinand crossed the frontier into Spain, a free man. As a provision of his freedom and recognition by France, he had signed a treaty at Valençay agreeing to respect the interests of the *afrencesados* and to provide a pension for his parents. This treaty the government of Cádiz had refused to ratify, the liberals demanding Ferdinand's acceptance of the constitution before Spain recognized him as king. He was still reading its articles as his landau drove south from the border.

Ferdinand's return, symbolizing for the masses their final victory over Napoleon, evoked wild enthusiasm in the country. With each triumphant mile, each cheering village and township, his depression over the printed clauses before him lifted more completely, until it dissolved altogether. Many groups and classes who had seen their privileges threatened by juridical equality helped to organize the reception, which was quickly exploited for antiliberal purposes. Among the clergy and the regular military command, in particular, advocates of absolutism were strong, and a royalist conspiracy was well advanced in the capital. Ferdinand's first stroke of unreserved authority fell in Valencia, where the captain general, Francisco Javier Elio, was a rabid reactionary. After declaring himself openly for Ferdinand "in the fulness of all his rights," Elio handed over the baton of military command and invited its bearer to exercise absolute sovereignty in the province. Shortly afterward, the president of the regency, Cardinal Borbón, under government instructions to offer no sign of fealty until Ferdinand had agreed to the constitution, was persuaded to kiss the royal hand. For all the thought that had gone into their program, the liberals were showing strangely little foresight in protecting it. By the middle of May, when Ferdinand resplendently entered the city, Madrid was thick with royalist troops, dozens of prominent liberals had been dragged from their beds to prison, and the walls were already plastered with a royal decree annulling the constitution.

Once more under an absolute monarch, Spain not only failed to progress from the desolation wrought by the war, but, in many ways, distinctly regressed. As a ruler, Ferdinand VII was disastrous. Combining his father's incompetence with a vicious futility seldom, if ever, equaled by a Spanish monarch, he ensured that the rifts in the country would widen and canker until all hope of moderation prevailing was again a mere dream of the future. Surrounded by the most extreme and intellectually barren of *serviles*, Ferdinand embarked on a grim retreat to the past, re-establishing, among other things, the Inquisition, the Society of Jesus, seignorial jurisdiction, prohibition of the press, seizure of foreign books, closure of theaters, and the death penalty for voicing liberal opinions. Within months of his return, a weary nation was harnessed with burdens that had been obsolete a century ago, complete with the financial chaos and foreign contempt that went with them. At the Congress of Vienna, a meeting of European powers provoked by the fall of Napoleon, Ferdinand's second-rate envoy was treated with disdain, a matter which did nothing to appease the king's apparent paranoia. None were spared the rigors of his whim. He ignored the Cortes, sentenced liberal prisoners without trial, abused foreigners in the country, especially the English, and was not above venting spite on his own servile flatterers.

One of his first moves, in flagrant breach of his treaty with the French, was to banish the *afrencesados*. As a result, two separate groups of reformers, formerly divided on the issue of allegiance, now found themselves on the same side of the fence. Some liberal refugees fled to the Indies, where rebellion was already overt, but most sought shelter in France and England. Here, contact with more sophisticated social systems confirmed both their convictions and their bitterness, quickening the will to fight for the reform of their government. Ferdinand and the *serviles* persecuted such tendencies ruthlessly, determined to hold the traditional barriers at all costs. Behind them, they had the ideological apathy and the innate conservatism of the working classes, plus powerful reactionary forces in the Church. Against them, broadly speaking, were the intellectual classes, the bourgeoisie, and the aristocracy. As time passed, the precise nature of this duality would vary, but the problem itself remained unchanged through the century: should the radical or the reactionary ideals prevail? Ferdinand's abuses ensured that the argument soon took a violent form. In the first six years of his office, rebellions flared at the rate of one every twelve months, while conspiracies and secret societies flourished, among them freemasonry, which provided a useful framework for conspiratorial activity. Many of the malcontents were veterans of the War of Independence whose services Ferdinand had failed to recognize. Juan Díaz Porlier, a former guerrilla leader, and General Luis Lacy, by-passed in promotions despite a distinguished war record, were among rebel leaders who paid for failure with their lives, and it is significant that the man who eventually succeeded was also a military commander. In 1820 a new feature appeared on the scene, the military *pronunciamiento*. With it, the army stepped squarely to the front of Spanish politics.

Colonel Rafael del Riego, commander of an Asturian battalion awaiting shipment to America in the far south, had been a prisoner in France and was deeply involved in Masonic activities. These had a pronounced revolutionary leaning in the liberal cities of Andalusia, where an executive was established to organize the co-operation of regimental societies. Plans for a rising centered on Cádiz, not only for its aptness as the cradle of constitutionalism, but because the expeditionary force assembled in the area for use against its blood brothers in the New World was notoriously averse to such a prospect, nor had its temper been soothed by mismanagement. Without reference to the navy, Ferdinand had purchased through a court favorite eight dilapidated Russian warships for use in the venture, at a price which had occasioned a public scandal. He had also parted with Florida to sweeten the United States.

The first day of 1820 was fixed for the insurrection, and a Colonel Antonio Quiroga was chosen as its leader. When the time came, however, Quiroga was detained, and Riego took his place. For a moment it looked as if the rising might go the way of its ill-fated predecessors. Having assembled his soldiers and proclaimed to them the constitution of 1812, Riego quickly found himself faced with a government force under Manuel Friere, the general commissioned to suppress the movement, whose troops opened fire on the people of Cádiz. In the main, however, the army was for the revolution, and another force deployed by the government joined the insurrection. Encouraged by their garrisons, cities all over Spain were soon clamoring for the constitution. Toward the end of February, La Coruña declared for the rebels, swiftly followed by Oviedo, Saragossa, Barcelona, and Pamplona.

Within a week or two, a terrified Ferdinand was protesting undying liberality. On March 7, a special issue of the official gazette announced that the king "in accordance with the general will of the people" had resolved to swear to the constitution. Two days later he took the oath. "Let us advance openly, myself leading along the constitutional path," he croaked painfully. With the tables reversed, the exiles of 1814 poured back while members of the Cortes who refused to submit to the constitution of 1812 were banished. It was now the reactionaries who went underground to plot restoration, the liberals who imposed the inevitable security measures. The American expedition had, meanwhile, been canceled, thus aborting the last possible chance of enforcing Spain's hold on the colonies. The new regime lasted only three years. Apart from the constant threat of its royalist enemies, its own ranks were divided between moderates and extremists, the latter eventually ensuring disaster. Ferdinand, while paying lip service to the constitution, connived at its downfall from the first. In a country totally unprepared by history for such a government, the task was not difficult. Cynically exploiting the immoderates of both sides, he dispatched a succession of appeals to foreign sovereigns postulating a Spain in the lap of anarchy, and requesting help in the overthrow of his own government.

In 1823, a so-called Holy Alliance of France, Russia, Austria, and Prussia, expressing a reactionary temper then prevalent in Europe, responded by demanding that the Spanish government abolish the charter of 1812. When Madrid indignantly refused, France was entrusted by her allies with the "restoration of order" in Spain, and Louis XVIII assured the French Assembly in a memorable statement that one hundred thousand Frenchmen were ready to march. In April of the same year, the Duke of Angoulême led very nearly that number across the border. This time, there was no resistance. The liberals had neither the money for war nor the confidence of their generals, while the mass of Spaniards was not with the government. Only the royalists took arms—in support of the French. As Angoulême advanced to Madrid, the Cortes sought refuge once more in Cádiz, taking Ferdinand, as a hostage, with them. On October 1, having given his meaningless word to a general amnesty and promised a moderate government, the king was handed over to French protection and re-established as absolute monarch. Despite the advice of Louis to be benign and tolerant, Ferdinand's revenge for what he termed his "ignominious slavery" was so atrocious that Angoulême, sickened by the ceaseless creak of the gallows, refused to accept the king's decoration in recognition of his services.

For Goya, whose radical sympathies had come to be clear in his drawings and etchings, liberal government had meant undisguised satisfaction, and Angoulême's advance was the signal to take precautions. In September, he bequeathed his house to one of his grandchildren and found shelter with some friends. Later, on the excuse of seeking a health cure, he managed to cross the border and set up home in Bordeaux. Here, at almost eighty, Goya settled to spend most of the remaining years of his life, painting superbly until the end, in 1828. Of the principals in his celebrated royal family painting, Charles and Maria had already died, also in France, leaving only the dishonorable and prematurely aged Ferdinand still venting the fears and frustrations of his youth. As it happened, Goya lived just long enough to see another of the figures on that canvas, Ferdinand's younger brother Carlos (painted at the right hand of the Prince of Asturias), rise to political prominence. But first, a more sinister spirit of ultrareaction was to take the elbow of the reinstated monarch. His name was Francisco Tadeo Calomarde, and his declared intention was the utter destruction of every trace of constitutionalism in Spain, every inkling that sovereignty belonged to the people. Calomarde, a protégé of Godoy, became the decisive influence in Ferdinand's new government. As a reactionary, he started where Ferdinand left off, supporting an extremist party, the *apostólicos*, which was more royalist than the king himself. With a ruthlessness that made the 1814 purge seem mild, Calomarde persecuted the liberals, intimidating and suppressing institutions of education, threatening anyone who criticized the government, establishing military tribunals to try those who had "conspired, spoken or written in favour of the constitution of 1812." Ferdinand's Inquisition, squashed by the liberals, was not brought back. It was not needed. In its place appeared extralegal *juntas de fé*, fiery reminders of apostolic ardor, and a Society of the Exterminating Angel, an instrument of clerical bigotry whose title amply indicated its purpose.

In 1827, apostolic sentiments merged with a movement of dissatisfaction in the northeast to produce a so-called Federation of Pure Royalists. To the traditionally separatist Catalans and Aragonese, neither the harassed liberals nor the self-centered Ferdinand had seemed much of a consolation for the loss of their regional *fueros*. When Ferdinand responded to their dissent with customary viciousness, they needed no further urging to back a new candidate for the throne. In this, the *apostólicos*, whose "pure" ideals were also less than satisfied by Ferdinand, concurred. The agreed candidate was the king's brother, Carlos, a man of regional sympathies who was also more devout and forthright than the incumbent. Ailing, and still childless despite three marriages, Ferdinand watched the Carlists gather strength, seemingly assured of their candidate's succession. As the king's health deteriorated, Calomarde's true allegiance became increasingly apparent. "The kingdom is behind Don Carlos," he asserted frankly. "The army and two hundred thousand royalists want him." But Ferdinand was not finished while he had another side to turn to. Thus, in the closing years of his life, came the last astonishing change in his colors, with an amnesty for the oppressed reformers and a new program of moderation. Happily for his purposes, the French liberals had taken charge in their own country, establishing the democratic monarchy of Louis Philippe of Orléans. In Spain, Calomarde was dismissed, the universities and other liberal centers encouraged, and radical buoyancy in general raised to offset the Carlists, whose embarrassed candidate moved to Lisbon.

At last, the king was acting as a stabilizing rather than an agitating influence, performing the role so sorely missing since the liberal emergence. But it was too late. To use his own words, the bottle of Spain was surcharged and fermenting. Ferdinand had neither the time nor the aptitude to settle it. Instead, he bequeathed it to an unsuspecting infant who would live to see its fiery contents spill into the twentieth century. María Luisa Isabella, the first daughter of Ferdinand's hastily taken fourth wife, María Christina of Naples, was born in the last three years of his life. By a law of Philip V, females had been excluded from the Spanish throne, but, to the enragement of the Carlists, the king altered the rule in the course of María's pregnancy, announcing that the child, whatever sex, should succeed him. Fresh turmoil was inevitable. In the summer of 1833, Ferdinand ordered his brother to leave Lisbon, where the political climate was conducive to conspiracy, and retire to the less tendentious haven of the papal state. On receiving a blunt refusal from Carlos, the king collapsed with apoplexy. He was dead within minutes. The bottle was already fit to brim over.

Chapter 11

AN EMPIRE CRUMBLES

The upheaval in America began at the bottom, among the lower orders most sorely oppressed by the colonial system. They rose in great undisciplined, ill-kempt, and poorly armed mobs, touchingly invoking the Christian faith their masters had taught them and calling on the Creoles to join in overthrowing the "bad government" of the *peninsulares*. Their objectives were liberty, equality, fraternity; but they were naïve in appraising their allies and enemies. Many Creoles, too, were intent on liberty, but they wanted no part of equality and fraternity with the miserable people their ancestors had conquered. That the colored masses should expend their energies first suited the white Americans perfectly. Far from joining these early rebellions, they were only too pleased to see them smashed down, often mustering with the Spanish forces for this purpose. When their turn came, they would have few proletarian rivals to contend with.

The leaders of the Indian and Negro rebellions were political innocents. Tupac Amaru, chief of the Indian rebels of Peru, and a descendant of Inca royalty, sincerely believed the Spaniards would meet him on terms of justice for his ill-used people. Instead, they killed his wife and family in front of his eyes, cut his tongue out, and tore his limbs from his body with horses. Miguel Hidalgo, the poor white priest who led the revolt of the Mexican Indians, allowed himself to be captured, and consequently executed, by trickery. So did his successor, a mestizo priest named José Morelos. Even Toussaint L'Ouverture, Negro leader of the slave rebellion against French, British, and Spaniards in Haiti and Santo Domingo —the only lower-class rising to succeed with any permanence, leading to the independence of Haiti in 1803—was lured into the white camp by a sham declaration of friendship and imprisoned in irons.

The desperate and tragic gesture of the Indians, and its relationship to the rising of the more resourceful Creoles, was most clearly and dramatically evident in Mexico. Father Miguel Hidalgo y Costilla was a warmhearted fellow. His good works among the humble and needy parishioners of Dolores, a village near the Mexican city of Querétaro, had endeared him to the Indian community. He had helped them to make bricks and pottery, to rear silkworms, to improve their vines, even to organize an orchestra. But the plight of the people perpetually tortured his conscience. Ragged and barefoot, exploited by landowners and industrialists, or scratching a pathetic existence from their meager plots, they seemed in every forlorn expression and movement to Hidalgo a condemnation of Spanish government. Watching the hapless lives of his flock, he could understand the currents of the French Revolution. Indeed, he could sympathize. He had read the modern philosophers and, on his visits to nearby Querétaro, met radically minded Creoles, steeped in the contempt of their kind for *gachupine* authority. Stimulated by their sentiments, he joined the plottings of a young and hotheaded action group, in whose company his compassion found a new and heady outlet. No longer the frustrated local agent of charity and justice, Hidalgo felt born, instead, to lead a great crusade against oppression, a fiery mission of social redemption.

On the morning of Sunday, September 16, 1810, the parish priest climbed to his pulpit and preached a sermon that galvanized Dolores. As the message spread through the neighborhood, excited Indians streamed from their hovels, many carrying knives and machetes. Prisoners, sprung from the local jail by Hidalgo's followers, blinked in the sunshine, surprised to find weapons thrust quickly in their hands. The village church and its environs were jammed with a huge crowd. "Children," cried the voice of the savior, "today brings a new dispensation. Are you ready? Do you want freedom? Will you fight for the lands stolen from your forefathers by the hated Spaniards?" And, when the roar of assent had subsided, the voice came again: "Long live our Lady of Guadalupe! Down with bad government! Death to the *gachupines!*" In those words, Hidalgo coined the battle cry of the Revolution of Mexico. Minted in idealism, traded in terror, it purchased nothing but fresh agony and misery for his people. Before its last echoes faded, the blood of thousands of innocents would have stained the altar of Dolores; the Indians would be doomed to subjection forever. Mexico likes to celebrate the sixteenth as her Day of Independence, but only the Creoles could truly have made it so, and they answered Hidalgo's invitations to join him with chilling silence. The priest and his deluded peasants were on their own. For a while, the deceptive promise of freedom sustained them. They set off on the promised road in high hopes, a horde of tattered and bright-eyed patriots, soon swollen to upward of fifty thousand bodies. Many were women, who cooked and otherwise helped to make camp for their menfolk. Few had firearms. Discipline scarcely existed.

Driven by the accumulated bitterness of three centuries, this motley crowd swarmed on the townships in its path, destroying the inadequate garrisons and murdering and ravaging whole Spanish communities. Only those which offered suitable welcome to Hidalgo, among them the city of Guadalajara to the west, escaped vengeance. Now self-styled "Captain General of America," the unfortunate priest still clung to his delusions, calling on the country to establish a representative congress, to govern "with kindness," to "treat all as brothers." It was a wishful plea amid the maelstrom of hatred and horror he had unleashed. When the authorities responded instead with armies, he found himself in retreat to the north, his followers deserting him as readily as they had once joined him. Six months after the sermon at Dolores, Hidalgo was captured. Four months later, he fell to the firing squad, and his place was taken by his mestizo lieutenant, José María Morelos.

A more efficient and less impetuous rebel than Hidalgo, Morelos switched activities from the north to the south, where he held power in defiance of the Spanish forces for several years before he too was captured and shot. By 1816, the poor man's rebellion had fizzled out, with the exception of a few guerrilla bands in the south. It was time, now, for the Creoles to consider their own play for power. Among them, one Agustín de Iturbide, a shrewd opportunist in his thirties, well born and adventurous, noted the increasing jealousy with which influential white Mexicans viewed the rich Spanish holdings in the country, and decided to bestir himself from a spell of easy living in the capital. What Iturbide lacked in revolutionary ardor was more than compensated for by his infallible eye for the main chance. Hidalgo had sought his help in 1810, but the younger man had wished no part of the crazy priest's campaign. Volunteering instead for the Spanish forces, he had fought with distinction against both Hidalgo and Morelos, a fact he now exploited with cynical brilliance. He needed an army. Unlike the impassioned idealists of the Indian rising, he acquired it without invoking the slightest suspicion. Iturbide calmly arranged his appointment as commander of a strike against the rebel guerrillas in the south. That gave him a nucleus of 2500 first-class soldiers. He needed more. Marching into guerrilla country, he blandly pronounced himself the friend of the rebels he had been commissioned to subjugate, calling on them to join him in the cause of Mexican independence. The last of his requirements was money. Swooping on a silver caravan bound from the capital to the port of Acapulco on the south coast, Iturbide filled his coffers with half a million pesos. With this wealth, and a tough force of regulars, guerrillas, and bandits behind him, the audacious officer put his proposition to Mexico.

This time, it was no crude call to blood and vengeance, but a worldly appeal to the self-interest of each major faction of influence. To the Creoles, Iturbide offered the independence they coveted, with the respectful suggestion that Ferdinand VII should still be recognized as king. To the *peninsulares*, he promised union on the basis of equality with the Creoles. To the Church, he guaranteed continued allegiance to Rome. The timing was perfect. Coinciding with the liberal revolt of 1820 in Spain, it found the Mexican conservatives drained of sympathy for the peninsula government, and the royalist forces inclined to his side. By October 1821, Iturbide was established in the capital and Mexico, together with the rest of New Spain (that part of Central America governed from Guatemala), passed out of Spanish history. The Mexicans were free: the upper classes to suffer the unbounded conceits of

Iturbide once he held power, and the generations of lawlessness and chaos which followed him; the lower classes to continue in despair and deprivation. For the Indians it meant the end of all dreams of liberation.

Meanwhile, the Spanish people of South America were embroiled in struggles of their own, struggles of such epic proportions that the legend of Pizarro seemed to wilt by comparison. In setting, the story ranged from the snowcaps of the western Andes to the steaming delta of the Orinoco, from jagged mountain trails to the flat, interminable pampas of Argentina. Inland, it swept the malarial plains of the Llanos, crossed the reptile-infested Amazon, bludgeoned through bush and jungle and probed the dank mists of the Venzuelan plateau. Spanning three thousand miles of tropical and near-tropical contrasts, this discouraging arena abounded in hostile life, from mosquitoes, tarantulas and scorpions, to crocodiles, jaguars, and poisonous snakes. Indeed, its rigors were scarcely less alarming than the passions of the human beings who now advanced and retreated across it between their scattered and isolated cities. By European standards, their small armies were derisory, their officers eccentric, their drills unknown to the manuals of military science. That they fought with exceptional resourcefulness and savagery owed something to the fact that the protagonists were racial brothers, something to the teaching of the terrain.

In 1783, three years after the ill-fated Tupac Amaru had led the poor descendants of the Incas on their last futile rising, a son was born to one of the wealthiest Creole couples in Venezuela, the Bolívars of Caracas. When, shortly afterward, the father died, the child, Simón Bolívar, became a regular mother's boy, bright-eyed, appealing, pampered, and precocious. Perhaps he might never have been very much more had not a second bereavement soon attended the family. Nine years after his birth, young Bolívar's mother also died, obliging the boy to test his willfulness on a larger world. Through a somewhat unorthodox tutor, one Simón Carreño, alias Rodríguez, Bolívar gained an early introduction to ideas that were to lead to the purpose of his later life. Rodríguez was a gay idealist with a fast and inconstant eye for pretty women and an ardent admiration for the writings of Rousseau, whose *Émile* was the prime source of his educational theories. Twelve years older than his pupil, he was singularly equipped to hold the interest of the other. "You have shaped my heart for liberty and justice," Simón Bolívar wrote him later. "I have followed the path you set me. You were my pilot." At sixteen, Bolívar left Venezuela for Spain to learn the graces of a courtier. He had black, tumbling hair, delicately handsome features, and glowing eyes a girl might have envied. Not unmindful of his inheritance, Madrid society opened its arms to him. He stepped in with style and flamboyance, the products of money and a poetic, self-dramatizing temperament.

After a youthful and tragic sortie into marriage, terminated by the sudden death of his bride, Bolívar embarked on an interlude of idle pleasure in Paris, enjoying the favors of an older woman of some prominence, Fanny du Villiers, the wife of an aging officer in Napoleon's army. Fanny's salon, frequented by many celebrities, introduced the Venezuelan dandy to the top echelons of post-revolutionary society, among whom he held his own with a natural assertiveness. He had read much of the eighteenth-century school of French writers, together with the earlier Hobbes and Spinoza, and sought to make himself felt with loud republican opinions. On one occasion, he was confronted by Humboldt, now back from the Americas. "I believe," said the German, "your country is ripe for independence, but I cannot see the man who will achieve it." If the irony of the statement were still far from evident, a seductive concept of fame was stirring in Bolívar. At twenty-one, he witnessed an event which greatly stimulated his emotional propensities. His words on the subject are revealing. "In the last month of 1804, I saw the coronation of Napoleon in Paris. The spectacle thrilled me, not so much by its magnificence as by the expression of love shown by this great public for its hero. The universal acclamation, the spontaneous demonstration of more than a million people seemed to me the pinnacle of man's desires, the realisation of man's highest ambition. For me, the crown, which Napoleon placed on his own head, was a feeble symbol of obsolete custom. What I found splendid was the homage and enthusiasm his person invoked. This, I admit, caused me to reflect on the enslavement of my own country, and the fame which would come to him who liberated it." Again, later: "All my attention was focussed on Napoleon. I had eyes only for him among the crowd of people. My fascination was boundless."

In 1805, with his old tutor Rodríguez once more at his side, Bolívar left Paris and its many diversions and set out on a trek through Italy to Rome. There, in a characteristically dramatic gesture, he ascended the Aventine Hill, that ancient mound of liberty, fell to his knees clasping Rodríguez by the hand, and pledged his life to the liberation of his country. To his friends, it was the act of a beguiling exhibitionist. The exhibition, however, had only just started. Leaving Rodríguez in Italy, Bolívar bade farewell to a tearful Fanny du Villiers, the accomplished conquest, and set sail for more challenging frontiers. Arriving home at Caracas in 1807, the young millionaire had time to review his properties and other interests before the bombshell of the Bourbon abdication cast its shock waves through South America. In the midsummer of 1808, Venezuela was stunned and appalled to hear that Joseph Bonaparte was King of Spain. Popular demonstrations were organized in favor of Ferdinand, and, when Napoleon's delegates reached Caracas in July, they were lucky to escape unharmed under cover of darkness. The other Spanish American capitals reacted to French approaches in the same way, and soon agents of the resisting patriot assembly of Spain had appeared on the scene to whip up support in the empire. Divided in their loyalties, the colonial authorities wavered and weakened. It was time for the Creoles to take power in their own hands.

By 1809 the threat to the *peninsulares* was explicit. Influential citizens subscribed openly to the movement for American independence. Government officials were publicly snubbed and insulted. At a banquet in Caracas, attended by the governor himself, Bolívar ostentatiously drank to the "freedom" of Venezuela and all America. The governor, a moderate man named Vicente de Emparán, patiently and reasonably explained to Bolívar and other extremists the dangers inherent in the course of revolt, but he made no impression. In April 1810, news of Napoleon's latest victories in Spain brought matters to a head. On the nineteenth of the month, Maundy Thursday, Emparán stepped onto a balcony above the public square in Caracas to appeal to the loyalty of an agitated crowd. He was greeted with a chant of "We don't want him. We don't want him." According to a rebel report of the occasion, he volunteered his resignation from office with a bitter "Well, I don't want it, either." He was banished from the country and a Creole junta proclaimed. By the end of summer, most of the capitals of South America had similarly declared independence, but it was a tenuous revolution, maintained by insecure governments and lacking the support of much of the provincial populace. The whole of Peru remained aloof and loyal to Spain. In Venezuela itself, the people of Maracaibo and Coro, in the west, were unsympathetic to the junta de Caracas, deriding and imprisoning its delegates. If independence were to prevail, the rebels badly needed, they felt, the support of a foreign power. Britain, with her strong navy and her antipathy to Napoleon, was the obvious choice. Accordingly, a mission was sent to London. Its leader was Simón Bolívar.

Bolívar happily paid his own expenses. Colonel of the militia, as he now was, he cut a dashing figure in the English capital, especially attracting the demimonde, and, if he gained little in the way of aid, certainly missed few chances to publicize himself and his cause. The most significant aspect of his visit, as it happened, was his contact with a remarkable Venezuelan exile, Francisco de Miranda, then living as a guest of the British government in London. Historians have disagreed vehemently in interpreting Miranda's bizarre and ambiguous character. Tall and stately, unruffled by the direst setbacks, he cultivated among his eccentricities the gesture and speech of classical Rome, conversing in Latin as well as in Spanish, French, and English, and seldom with less than the most compelling brilliance. He was vain, acutely intelligent, passionate, and seemingly earnest, yet with a godlike detachment which aggravated many associates. If few shared Miranda's sublime conviction of his own infallibility, fewer were so rash as to discount him altogether. Women adored him. Most men were impressed. Born, like Bolívar, in Caracas, Miranda had bought a commission in the Spanish army, being charged in the course of his service with negligence, a matter he dismissed with customary eloquence. Later, he had visited the United States, where, it seems, he was filled with an abiding urge to see Spain's American colonies established in their own independence. Sailing to Europe, he had soon attracted a fascinated audience for an extraordinary scheme to unite a free South America under the presidency of an Inca prince. In England, the government put him on its payroll as a sleeping investment; in France, the revolutionaries made him a general and he twice talked himself out of a Paris prison; in Russia, the Empress Catherine pressed him with favors, including a thousand golden coins and a not ungenerous slice of her affection. As a bonus, Miranda granted himself the title of "count."

Throughout his adventures, the amazing American had never ceased to propound his theme of liberation. In 1806 he had actually landed in Venezuela with a shipload of volunteers in an attempt to provoke a rebellion, but he picked the apathetic western provinces and for once his genius for persuasion was unavailing. Once more, he had turned to London, where Bolívar now found him holding court with some elegance in Grafton Square, an imposing if distinctly pompous veteran of sixty. Prophet, or a king among opportunists? Perhaps Miranda was both. At all events, he seemed to Bolívar the man needed to breathe fire into Venezuela's struggle for freedom. In Caracas, the conservative Creole establishment was less enthusiastic. Arguments against Miranda's brand of radicalism were strong, and events proved them right. But Bolívar held the initiative in London, and, with arrangements made for the exile's return, now proceeded to Venezuela ahead of him to whip up the protagonists of freedom-at-any-price. The result was a public clamor for Miranda, whose arrival in the city at the end of the year, resplendent in the uniform of a general of the French Revolution, was greeted rapturously by the hotheads.

Events began to move quickly. Experienced in the arts of demagogy and revolution, Miranda soon inflamed his supporters not only against Spain and the *peninsulares,* but also against the moderate Creoles and their policies. He waved the red, yellow, and blue flag he had brought to Venezuela, he invoked the power of the press, he urged the self-styled patriots to revile all Spaniards, and he smiled when they burned the king in effigy. Bolívar, learning fast, discovered his own gift of rhetoric, the spate of words that would flow ceaselessly with his career, bewitching crowds and producing an avalanche of letters. At the beginning of July 1811, with the congress still discussing independence, Bolívar addressed the patriots on the need for action. "In the national assembly they deliberate the future," he told them. "And what do they say? That we should start with confederation! As if we were not united against foreign rule! That we should await the outcome of Spanish policy. What do we care whether Spain decides to sell her slaves to Bonaparte or keep them for herself? Are we not determined to be free? These tragic doubts are extensions of the old captivity. They say the great plan should be approached with deliberation . . . are not three hundred years of deliberation enough? Do they want three hundred more. Let us lay the cornerstone of American freedom fearlessly! To hesitate is to perish!"

The pro-Ferdinand moderates could hold out no longer. On July 5, thirty-five years and a day after Jefferson's declaration of independence, the government of Caracas declared Venezuela the first republic of South America. With Miranda quickly its figurehead, dissension in the Creole ranks reached new levels of bitterness. The aging and opinionated general, steeped in a sophisticated European background, was out of sympathy with the frontier attitudes of his homeland. The inexperienced republican government, incompetent and wasteful, dismayed the influential business lobby which had first sponsored self-government in its own interests. On all sides, and by many tokens, the Americans divided, some for the Spaniards, some for the patriots, thus preparing the way, not for a clear-cut dispute between nations, but for the bitter, entangled passions of civil war. In March 1812, after some early successes against the Spaniards grouping in the provinces, the patriots were stunned by an appalling earthquake in the area around Caracas. Thousands were killed, and the very stronghold of republican activity demoralized. It was as if heaven had decided to take sides, and the superstitious rank and file of the country bowed in awe to the argument. Pressing the advantage from their lines to the west, the royalists overwhelmed the patriots at Puerto Cabello, and Miranda, signing papers of capitulation to save a now virtually defenseless capital, fled to the port of La Guaira, where a ship was prepared to carry him to London.

Miranda was a realist. Perhaps he hoped to return again later (he had a large sum of money from the treasury with him); certainly there was nothing more he could do in Venezuela. His patriot lieutenants, however, were less resigned in their attitude. Bolívar, in particular, was disgusted by what he regarded as a sellout. Resentment between the old professional and the young aristocrat had been growing for some time. They were too alike in their theatrical urge for the limelight, while Bolívar's relentless idealism irritated Miranda, who found him "a dangerous youth." Now, at a farewell dinner on the eve of the general's sailing, the earnest patriot officers pressed for an explanation of Miranda's behavior. He responded curtly, with little sympathy for their feelings. When he had retired, Bolívar and the others held a hasty consultation and decided to detain him. Entering his room, they told the general he was under arrest. Miranda dressed carefully and imperturbably in silence, then, taking a lamp, shone it on the faces of Bolívar and his party. "Noise, noise, and more noise!" he pronounced disdainfully. "That is all these people can make!" He was handed over to the Spaniards on their subsequent arrival, and died in captivity. Bolívar, granted an exit permit as a reward for the arrest of his commander, sailed to the Dutch isle of Curaçao, where he planned his next step. The republic of Venezuela had collapsed after twelve months.

Simón Bolívar analyzed the failure carefully. The earthquake and the political errors of the government, aggravated by an antirepublican Church, he listed as major factors. Above all, however, he blamed the junta, in the earliest days of its existence, for abstaining from the use of force against fellow Venezuelans, especially those of royalist Coro. "At that time every sensible man favoured war on so vile and obstinate a city . . . but the junta, vaguely guided by false principles, and contrary to the pursuance of justice, advised moderation and restraint." In the future, he decided, no such principles would hamper the cause. Already, the poison of fanaticism was creeping into his language. Proceeding from Curaçao to Cartagena, in New Granada, the modern Colombia, where Venezuela's neighbors were themselves divided in the fight for independence, the exile from Caracas denounced the royalist forces of his country as "tyrants" and "raging beasts." Embattled Spain, he warned his hosts, had a large number of daring and ambitious officers, long accustomed to danger and privations, ready to descend on South America in search of power to replace that which they had lost in the peninsula.

Bolívar found some six hundred men willing to join him in

invading Venezuela, mostly Colombians. It was a puny force, even by South American standards. Its supplies were inadequate, its weapons second-rate. Its general had never commanded an army in battle. In Venezuela lay a distinguished Spanish officer, Domingo Monteverde, the bold and unscrupulous vanquisher of Miranda, with several thousand well-equipped soldiers. Bolívar's only hope lay in being able to elude the Spaniard in the early stages of invasion, and in rousing the apathetic Venezuelan provincials with his gifts of persuasion. With these thoughts in mind, he crossed the border in March 1813 and climbed into the westerly cordillera of Mérida. Here, the Spanish forces were thin, and he was soon in possession of Mérida itself, where he supplemented his forces with local patriots, pushing on through the hills to Trujillo, farther north. Before descending to contest his native Caracas, Bolívar issued a proclamation which grimly clarified the depths of his commitment. It was to be, he declared, a war to exterminate Spaniards. Alluding to the ruthless severity with which Monteverde had dealt with the former republican provinces, a rule of terror itself not dissociated with earlier patriot atrocities, he announced: "Our revenge shall equal the cruelties of the Spaniards . . . our soil will be cleansed of the monsters that sully it. Our hatred knows no bounds. This is a war to the death." To prove it, Bolívar decreed the murder of prisoners.

There was method in his fervent barbarity. Law for the *peninsulares*, he announced, would not be law for his Creole and colored enemies. To all Spaniards who did not actively support him, he promised "certain death, even if you are indifferent." Americans, on the other hand, he would preserve, "even if you are guilty." It was a terror subtly designed to divide the ranks against him, to induce a traumatic national awakening. The shock on the western forces of the royalists was evinced in the speed with which they fell back, and the recruits which flocked to his banner. Mounting two men to a horse, as the great Gonzalo de Córdoba had once done in Italy, he cut off the enemy retreat in front of Valencia and had won the ensuing battle of Taguanes before Monteverde could reach the scene of action. There was nothing the Spaniard could do but sidetrack to Puerto Cabello while Bolívar advanced triumphantly on Caracas. He entered the city in August amid the pealing of bells, patriotic music, and the applause of large crowds. To shouts of "Long live our liberator" and "Long live Venezuela," a group of girls in white ran up to the young general and wreathed him with flowers. To many, it seemed that he brought an end to their trials and insecurity.

Simón Bolívar was now thirty. His face had lost its youthful prettiness. The fleshiness had gone from the cheeks; the black hair above his high forehead was less curly than before. But his eyes shone as brightly, and women fell before him. He was far from unresponsive. But diversions were momentary. Another passion drove him with obsessive intensity. At the back of his mind was the grandiose concept, once embraced in even wider form by Miranda, of uniting the entire north of the lower continent in a single state. The Liberator asserted that only the creation of such a concentration of power would invite respect. Speeches and manifestoes came from him in seemingly endless succession. Seldom can the El Dorado of human freedom have been invoked so tirelessly by a single politician.

While Bolívar regaled the second republic with the words and emotional gestures of a savior, the city, shorn of Spanish administration, floundered near ruin. The only answer was totalitarianism. In January 1814 the Liberator assumed the role of dictator. The economy was nationalized, all property owners were obliged to subscribe the cost of supporting at least one republican soldier, clergymen were ordered to preach the merits of independence to their congregations every week. Tax evasion and negligence in other duties to the state were punishable with death and confiscation of property. Well aware that opposition, if momentarily silent, smoldered around him, Bolívar organized a network of spies, not only to seek out dissenters, but to infiltrate their activities with a view to conviction on charges of conspiracy. In September, about sixty people were executed as enemies of the state. Many more were thrown into prison. The Liberator was learning the practicalities, the erosive consequences of forcing one's ideals on others. Indeed, he may not have been lacking entirely in sincerity when, in October, protesting once more his defense of liberty, he invited a meeting of his followers to relieve him of his command.

If Bolívar took their refusal complacently, the royalists did not. In by-passing Puerto Cabello with the intention of mopping up the besieged Monteverde later, the Liberator had underestimated the Spaniard. Contemptuous of treating with rebels, Monteverde had looked to his defenses and prepared to hold out. At the end of the summer, he was rewarded by the arrival of twelve hundred soldiers and much equipment from Spain, where Ferdinand was again king in Madrid. Though wounded in battle soon afterwards, and forced to relinquish his command, Monteverde had sustained the royalist cause in its moment of crisis. The Spaniards were back in the fight. Supported by royalist Maracaibo and Coro in the west, they now stood astride the trail Bolívar had blazed to Caracas, isolating republican Venezuela from republican Colombia, and watched Bolívar's war of extinction rebound to his own cost.

The new rumblings of disaster came from the great plain of the Orinoco, unfolding inland of the Caribbean cities and stretching south in the eastern shadow of the Andes. It came from a people beyond the pale of colonial society, less civilized than the humblest Negro or most put-upon Indian: the roaming peasants of the savage hinterlands, the men of the scorching, fever-ridden steppes. The Llanos, or plain of the upper Orinoco, had never appealed much to the Spanish authorities. In the dry season, the shadeless wilderness rendered the sun intolerable; in the wet season, the flooded rivers brought disease and other hardships. In some of the more favored parts, Europeans, attracted by the cattle-grazing, had set up their outposts. On the whole, however, little effort was made to govern, educate, or Christianize this massive area. Across it ranged a crude, nomadic populace, part herdsmen, part hunters, of curious ethnic composition. Originally from the same stock as the warlike Caribs, defying the civilizing influence of both the Andean Indians and the later Europeans, their stock had intermingled in time with that of Negro escapees from the cities and plantations, mestizo outlaws, and even renegade Spaniards. In their wandering, they had rounded up wild European horses and cattle which they drove from plain to plain in search of fresh pastures. They ate the meat, learning to pound it soft between the backs of their ponies and their buttocks. They used the cowhide in their rude, bare huts. Their possessions were minimal, and what they had they fought for against the climate, the rivers, wild animals, and each other. Their pleasures, like their lives, were rough and violent; their passions were ever near the surface. They were called the Llaneros.

Only a handful of whites, contact men for the city cattle markets, were interested in the Llaneros, and the isolated frontier existence of such dealers divorced most of them from urban politics. Tomás Boves, red-haired and bull-necked, as cunning and violent as the animals he dealt with, was a notable exception. Boves was a Spaniard by birth and a smuggler by early calling. Neither the republicans nor the prerevolutionary government of Venezuela had greatly trusted him, and both administrations had at times imprisoned him. For his own part, he had come to hate the former the more intensely and now planned revenge. Boves realized that in the Llaneros he had a perfect weapon. He also realized that idealistic incentives were lost on them. To men as free as the Llaneros, freedom as an abstract meant nothing. What Boves exploited was their lack of possessions. They had almost nothing, scarcely even clothing. His message was simple and potent. Boves preached the gospel of grab-what-you-want. In no time, he had raised a horde of ingenuous cutthroats, any one of whom would fight a battle for a shirt.

At first, Bolívar and his better-disciplined patriots met the galloping plainsmen with fortitude. At La Victoria, in February 1814, an entrenched republican army repulsed the Llaneros in a head-on trial of strength. Two battles at San Mateo in March went in favor of the same side. But Bolívar, relying heavily on infantry and obliged to carry his supplies, was unable to maintain contact with Boves and his horsemen, who lived by indiscriminate pillage off the land. In defeat, the frustrated plainsmen merely turned to some undefended town or village and unleashed their violence with impugnity. Republican citizens who suffered no worse than a severed ear, the standard treatment, could count themselves lucky. Boves was in his element. The Spaniards had made him a colonel, but he treated the commission with derision. His war was a private one in which every man, woman, and child maimed, ravaged, and abused contributed compensation for the indignities society had once paid him. His lieutenant, Francisco Morales, admiring and imitative, was equally sadistic. Encouraged by their example and instructions, the simple Llaneros plundered, murdered, tortured, and despoiled with moronic promiscuity. Neither age nor sex exempted civilians from the sordid orgy of cruelty which accompanied the so-called Legion of Hell and its monstrous leaders.

The contagion of terror was now uncontainable. At Calabozo, a town on the plain south of Caracas, the republicans themselves massacred a quarter of the people for not opposing Boves. At La Guaira, Bolívar ordered the cold-blooded murder of eight hundred prisoners. On both sides, officers dedicated themselves to a crusade of extermination. Fear had passed beyond being a deterrent. It had led to desperation; a desperation which expressed itself in subhuman passions. On these flames was poured the fuel of Negro and Indian frustration. Encouraged by opposing leaders, the underprivileged urban and industrial classes exploited the confusion to rob and murder their masters. Despite his early victories, Bolívar's outlook was bleak. His supplies of arms and munitions were limited and he had no factories in which to replace them. Despite repeated pleas to the United States and Britain, those powers refused him material support. By June, Caracas was jammed with republican refugees from the interior, adding hunger and destitution to the Liberator's problems. Boves and his pack already had their eyes on the capital. On the fifteenth of that month, Bolívar challenged them at La Puerta. For the republicans, everything rested on the issue. There was little finesse or military pomp. The patriots, a miscellany of students, clerks, and other city workers, numbered three thousand, mostly on foot. The royalist infantry, though better equipped, was inferior numerically, relying on the wild Llaneros, with their bizarre assortment of captured uniforms and side arms, to make up the balance. They did so with interest. Galloping in on the flanks of the patriots, already engaged to the front by the footmen, they scattered Bolívar's army in a hundred hectic minutes, slaying most of the republican command and narrowly missing Bolívar himself. The road to Caracas was open before them.

Boves arrived at the city, after a leisurely approach, to find that the bulk of its terrified population had fled before him. Those who remained were subjected to his customary atrocities. The rest struggled east along the coast behind Bolívar in a desperate bid to reach the distant republican stronghold of Barcelona, nearly two hundred miles across barren lowlands and swamps. For twenty days, the pathetic column trudged on. There were few horses or mules, and those which existed were burdened to the utmost. Rich and poor, young and old, sick and wounded, the refugees shared a common lot, humping their foodstuffs and bedding with them, forcing tortured legs to keep moving, scarcely daring to look back for fear of spotting the Llaneros. To their dismay, they found Barcelona as chaotic and despairing as the west. Bolívar had scarcely time to rest there before his pursuers were upon him, now joined by thousands of disillusioned republicans, whose only hope of law and order seemed to lie in a return to Spanish government. Unable to halt them, the Liberator led the weary refugees east once again, this time making for the rebel outpost of Cumana, which offered escape to the offshore island of Margarita.

At last Bolívar was faced with the predicament of his old general, Miranda. The campaign was lost, the people had turned against him, his lieutenants no longer respected him. Perhaps the bravest of all, José Ribas, held out until the end of the year, fighting a series of hopeless actions before his capture and execution, consoled at least that Boves, struck by a spear, had predeceased him. By 1815, Venezuela was back under Spanish control. But it was not the Venezuela of before. Pillage, plunder and corollary famine had wiped out many villages. Churches had been stripped of their treasures and the population decimated. Bolívar had not stopped to see the end. In September he had made good his flight by ship to his earlier place of refuge, Cartagena, leaving behind a last message for the people he had led to ruination. In the flamboyant idiom which had served as a fountainhead of his leadership Bolívar strove once more to rally his disillusioned followers. He absolved his own conscience, denigrated the menacing enemy and exhorted the people to fight on to victory in his absence, invoking the will of God.

The manifesto was received with less than enthusiasm.

It says much for his powers of persuasion that Simón Bolívar was welcomed back in New Granada as a conquering hero. As in

Venezuela, the patriot forces were under heavy pressure from the Spaniards, and Bolívar's appointment as commander-in-chief did little to help. In an ill-timed attack on the Spanish stronghold of Santa Marta, in the north, he was defeated with the loss of a thousand men. Resigning his post, he abandoned New Granada to find refuge on the British island of Jamaica. Here he wrote his so-called Jamaica letter, a sweeping review of the South American situation, past and future. Alone, frustrated in every plan, and down to the last penny of his once-immense fortune, Bolívar still refused to relinquish his vision of independence. Earnestly, he discussed the future government of Spanish America, dismissing the radical democratic system of the north and the monarchic democracy of England as beyond the political talents of the western Latins, and seeking a more appropriate formula. "The American states," he wrote of the south, "need paternal governments to heal the wounds and scars made by tyranny and war." The head of Bolívar's ideal republic, ought, he considered, to be elected for life. Such a head would represent liberty and justice, but, since these had shown little aptitude for flowering on their own, they would have to be imposed through the offices of a powerful social elite. Ironically, Bolívar, in his very abhorrence of all that Spain represented, was proposing the one system Spain above all had made her own in the past—the rule of the benevolent despot.

Jamaica, however, was unimpressed by the exile, who turned next to the Negro republic of Haiti. Here, he found numerous other patriot exiles and a friendly reception from the president, Alexandre Pétion. Pétion agreed to assist in the mounting of an invasion of Venezuela provided Bolívar included the freeing of slaves in his program. After a false start, in which the lack of enthusiasm shown him by the Venezuelan people forced the Liberator to return to the Negro president for more help, Bolívar managed to gain a footing in the east of his country, establishing a temporary headquarters at Angostura, now Ciudad Bolívar, in July 1817. His companions were a strangely assorted crowd, not all of whom took his leadership for granted. Manuel Piar, a wild mulatto whose generalship was instrumental to the winning of the eastern lands of the Orinoco, was seized and executed when he challenged Bolívar's authority. José Antonio Páez, an illiterate

Creole with a brilliant flair for guerrilla warfare, constantly flouted the Liberator's instructions, too strong to be brought to order. Páez, a fugitive at fifteen, wanted for murder, had then fled to the plains to live the life of the Llaneros. A man of huge physical strength and violent temperament—the blood of battle excited him so much that he foamed at the mouth and often fell to the ground in a helpless fit—he was a natural successor to Boves. The rough plainsmen called him Uncle Antonio and would follow him anywhere, rallying to his rescue in his epileptic moments and emulating his berserker fury. It took all Bolívar's tact and charm to win the suspicious and untamed Páez to his side, and the accomplishment proved the turning point of his fortunes. Páez was temperamental and unreliable, but wherever he went the destructive capacity of the Llaneros, the force that had once defeated Bolívar, now brought terror to the royalists.

Another factor was working in the Liberator's favor. His constant calls to Europe for assistance were finally gaining response, not from governments but from the people themselves. In the British Isles, a period of peace accompanied by economic depression had swollen the ranks of unemployed with thousands of demobilized soldiers. Bolívar's agents made the most of the situation. They had no money, but they promised enough of it, plus promotion, when the recruits reached South America. English arms merchants, with stocks left on their hands, were glad to take promissory notes for guns and ammunition. Out-of-work British and German officers assembled entire units to sail with them, proudly dressing them in regimental uniform. Their surprise on reaching Venezuela was swift and unpleasant. Instead of barracks, they found mud huts. The food was terrible, the climate was killing, the sick went untended among people too long accustomed to privation to care, while the promised money was unforthcoming. Instead, the Europeans learned to their astonishment that they were expected to loot. By way of welcome, the Venezuelans offered to buy their uniforms and equipment, Bolívar himself purchasing a fine helmet with plumes, while Páez fitted his delighted bodyguard of tattered plainsmen with brilliant English tunics. Those who could not afford a passage home, or did not die of fever, contrived, in time, to adjust to the environment.

When the problems of assimilation were over, the Liberator

had the most professional army he had ever commanded, a foreign corps of a disciplinary standard he could not have attained for years with home troops. Nevertheless, his attempts to make headway in the more populous coastal areas of the north, held by Spanish forces under an experienced general, Pablo Morillo, were not rewarding, and he decided to monopolize, instead, the plains of the interior, working west toward the Andes. By the beginning of 1819, Bolívar was sufficiently strong in the south and east to contemplate a crossing of the mountains to aid the struggling patriots of New Granada. It was an audacious scheme, not only because it left the unpredictable Páez to contain Morillo in Venezuela, but because the route chosen for the exploit was considered by many to be impassable. South across the tropical swamplands of the Orinoco tributaries, then two miles high into the freezing fastnesses of the sierras sheltering the vital city of Bogotá, it was a prospect to deter the staunchest soldier.

In May, the expedition set out in deepest secrecy. The advance guard, composed of exiled patriots from New Granada, men familiar with the border country, was led by a plump young Colombian aristocrat, Francisco de Paula Santander, the scion of a Creole family with some Indian blood in its history. The hard core of the force was its foreign legion, largely British and Irish, commanded by a robust Anglo-Saxon named Rooke. Irrepressibly hearty and sanguine, Rooke seems to have been molded in the fondest image of the nineteenth-century British adventurer. Each morning, he declared, was better than the last. The malarial plains, he found marvelously healthy. His men, so long as they lived, were incomparable. If necessary, he would take them to Cape Horn and back. To the Venezuelans, Rooke was a madman, but their leader perceived the usefulness of such an optimist to goad on the temperamental South Americans. Together with a column of patriot infantry and a small band of horsemen, the entire force was less than three thousand strong. With it went a herd of cattle for food, and a singularly determined bunch of camp followers, some of whom actually gave birth to babies on the march.

For the first leg of the journey, the small army splashed and waded south through torrential rains, crossing river after flooded river, groping through insect-ridden swamps. At one stage, its members waded through waist-deep water for a whole week. Many of the pack animals drowned and half the cattle were lost. Then, toward the end of June, they reached the rising footlands of the cordillera. Ahead, their pinnacles lost in the clouds, their passes washed out by rain, towered the granite walls of the Andes. As the ragged column struggled upwards, the nights became bitter. Men, reduced to loincloths in the first part of the journey, now shivered in the icy paramo. The rest of the cattle died. Horses' feet were torn to shreds on the rocks. Mules collapsed, blocking the narrow trails with their loads. Looking back on the march across the tropical plains, Bolívar wrote, "I thought the worst was over. But new hazards appear every day, doubling in intensity with every step, and I almost despair of the outcome." Far from their own homes, psychologically vulnerable in the highlands, the Venezuelan plainsmen grew rebellious, but Bolívar had astutely placed the hearty Rooke in their rear, and there was no turning back. To the fore, Santander and his New Granadians gained fresh enthusiasm the nearer they drew to their own lands, tackling isolated Spanish outposts in the passes with relish. On Santander's advice, Bolívar now increased his gamble. To avoid the more formidable of the enemy's defenses, and press the advantage of surprise, he decided to complete his advance across the reputedly impregnable heights of Pisba, aiming to descend to the plains of New Granada via the little hill town of Socha.

The plan succeeded, but only just. Stripped of the last of their animals, threatened by hail, wind, and avalanche, too enfeebled even to carry their rations, Bolívar's units began to disintegrate. Officers disappeared. Companies broke into small groups which lost contact with others. Hundreds died of cold and exhaustion. Sleep was fatal, and men beat each other to keep awake. Finally, in scores and dozens, the patriots limped into Socha, where food and rest awaited them. Rooke's legion was the last to emerge from the mountains. One in four of its members had died on the journey. Rooke was more puzzled than perturbed. The fittest, he consoled himself, had survived. Personally, he had found it "a pleasant hike." There was little time for reflection. With a royalist army of some five thousand moving against him, Bolívar scoured the region for reinforcements, and hastened to make ground. On July 24, at Pantano de Vargas, he emerged well from a preliminary engagement. At Boyaca, on August 7, his men fought like tigers, determined not to go back to the mountains. In the first of these actions, Rooke was wounded leading the British in a bloody hand-to-hand tussle and, afterward, had an arm amputated. "Let me see it," he demanded when the doctor had finished. "Have you ever seen a more excellent arm!" Three days later, he died. But the victory of Boyaca was decisive. The road to the capital was open.

Bogotá gave the Liberator an impressive reception, with a special welcome for its own hero, Francisco Santander, who was made vice-president of a provisional government under Bolívar. Leaving the Colombian to complete the suppression of royalist power in his country, the general quickly returned to Venezuela, picked up the strings of power in Angostura, and turned his attention to the royalist strongholds in Caracas and elsewhere in the north. Helped by the liberal upsurge in Spain, which had resulted in the recall of Morillo and attempts to reach a compromise solution in America, the Liberator finally broke the royalist die-hards at Carabobo, assuring the independence of all Venezuela. He was now free to formalize his grand plan for a union of the northern lands of South America in a single state he entitled Gran Colombia. This he conceived to embrace Venezuela, New Granada, and Ecuador, the last-mentioned yet to be liberated, and, by the end of 1821, he had dictated a constitution naming Bogotá the capital, and was himself the president with Santander as deputy. His next step was to march into Ecuador and notify its people of their new status. The future of the union was, as he saw it, "so sublime that I have no doubt it will be the wonder of Europe. The imagination cannot conceive the magnitude of such a colossus without admiration. Like Homer's Jupiter, it will cause the earth to quake with a glance."

Following the customary verbal overture, Bolívar entrusted the "colossus" temporarily to Santander and, early in 1822, started south for Ecuador with his soldiers. Once more, his small band was engulfed in the hugeness of the Andes. Once more, there was a Spanish challenge to overcome. Once more, Bolívar was the conquering hero. This time, however, there had been fewer doubts, a more triumphant progress. One of the Liberator's most trusted and long-serving officers, Antonio José Sucre, had been sent ahead with an advance force by sea. Landing at Guayaquil, well down the coast of Ecuador, Sucre had rallied many locals to his side, then marched north to meet his chief, defeating the opposition on the slopes of Pichincha, on the ascent to Quito, to enter the ancient Inca city ahead of Bolívar. The Liberator, having dispersed a more northerly Spanish force at Bombona, near Pasto, received the news with some jealousy. In a fit of pique, he wrote Santander: "Sucre has had enough fame . . . he had more troops than I and fewer enemies . . . The victory of Bombona was greater than that of Pichincha . . . General Sucre did not win more glory in battle than I . . ." His petulance dissolved, however, in the reception that awaited him.

Simón Bolívar entered Quito on June 16. Nine thousand feet below lay the plain of Esmeraldas and the Pacific. Sucre, unassuming and efficient, knew his master's foibles well. The entire population of the old Andean citadel was mustered to welcome the conqueror. Bells rang from the churches, flowers garlanded the fine colonial palaces, fireworks soared against a clear sky and the towering, snow-capped volcanoes. As Bolívar rode majestically under triumphal arches, regaled with applause and scented petals, it must have seemed to him the arrival to climax all arrivals. Years ago, he had hear such cheers raised up for his model, Napoleon. Now, across a thousand awe-inspiring miles, through Bogotá and Caracas back to the Orinoco, he had blazed the trail of an empire that was virtually his own. Ecuador intoxicated his senses. "I have no time for anything," he informed Santander. "Not that I lack the leisure for writing, but the thoughts of what can be done with such a great and beautiful country are too numerous." Everything his passionate temperament craved was stretched out before him: respectful warriors, a splendid capital, the adoration of the women for whom he could now spare some moments.

None of the many upon whom he bestowed his passing favors provoked in him, or the scandalmongers of society, such fervent interest as Manuela Saenz, the Quito beauty who became his secretary and mistress. For love of the hero she first saw riding vauntingly into her city, Manuela abandoned the security of a fond and well-to-do English husband, a merchant she described herself as "admirable," and eventually ended her days selling sweets in a small South American port for a livelihood. Like everything Bolívar touched, she paid the price for her moment of privilege. At least, for her it was a generous moment. "The shrine you inhabit will not be desecrated by any other image," wrote Bolívar. "You have made me a worshipper of beauty . . . Believe me, I love you and shall love nobody but you." Her own infatuation was complete. In reply to her husband's repeated pleas that she should return to the hearth of marriage, Manuela declared with passion: "For God's sake! No, no, no! Excellent though you are . . . do you really believe that, having been selected to possess the heart of General Bolivar, I would consent to any alternative, even to being the wife of the Father, the Son or the Holy Ghost?" Torrid and violent, for the lovers were too much alike in temperament to conduct themselves with moderation, the affair was followed rapidly by the first malignant signs of tuberculosis in the general, sickness leaving him thinner and hollow-cheeked. In Manuela's demanding eyes, Bolívar watched his physical image diminish. But his public stature was at its peak. Famed to the farthest cities of Europe, his exploits, title, glory were unmatched by anyone in South America—save, perhaps, one man. And that one was still as unreal to Bolívar as the ghosts of his own bloody battles.

The fortunes of José de San Martín, the Argentinian liberator, in many ways paralleled those of the Venezuelan. Both had suffered early setbacks; both had refused to give up. Each had found his greatest ally in the stern land, making terms with the plains and the mountains; each had known triumph. Neither wished less than a totally independent America. While the Venezuelan's march had taken him south, the Argentinian's advance led north, bringing their spheres of influence closer and closer. What would happen when they met was an interesting point of conjecture. San Martín, brusque, undemonstrative, and averse to the emotional, was in almost all ways antipathetic to Bolívar in temperament.

Buenos Aires, like Caracas, had reacted to the peninsula up-heaval of 1810 by creating a provisional junta. For a while, its dominating personality had been an aggressive young lawyer named Mariano Moreno. Under a strong lead, the rebellion in the far south prospered, but Moreno's death on a mission to England failed to reveal a new leader of the same strength, and indecision and disunity weakened the movement. In 1813, Paraguay broke away to a separate independence, while Buenos Aires struggled over Uruguay with Brazil. To the northwest, in Upper Peru (modern Bolivia), the Spanish regime remained powerful, menacing, and prosperous, its garrisons a stone wall to the revolutionary forces. In 1814, San Martín, appointed to command operations against the Spaniards, decided to establish his base in western Argentina, away from the halfhearted powers of Buenos Aires and closer to the harder-pressed and more committed patriots of Chile. His scheme was to recruit and train his army in the shadow of the Andes, cross the mountains to join the Chilean rebels, then turn his front to Peru.

Born in South America, 1778, the son of a Spanish official, San Martín had received his schooling and military training in Spain. He was a thoroughly professional soldier, commissioned from cadetship, tempered in action against Portugal and Napoleon's armies, and reaching the rank of lieutenant colonel in the Spanish forces. Though a convinced liberal, quick to offer his services to Buenos Aires on learning of the movement for independence, he scorned the mass hysteria of revolution and was contemptuous of mob politics. Speeches and gestures, pageants and processions, titles and acclaim were things which failed to move him. He believed in action rather than words, and when words were indispensable he kept them short. By 1816, when a congress of delegates from all parts of the old viceroyalty finally voted for full independence, the rugged general was itching to go ahead with his plan. At his headquarters at Tucumán he had drilled and disciplined an assortment of Chilean refugees and Argentinian adventurers into a surprisingly businesslike army of several thousand. Impatient of help from the government, he had improvised weapons and munitions in his own workshops, melting church bells and metal ornaments for the purpose, while his wife, a delicate but loyal young aristocrat, canvassed her fashionable city friends for valuables.

At the beginning of 1817, San Martín climbed into the Andes, his army divided into two groups and crossing by different passes. The preliminaries were less arduous than in Bolívar's march on Bogotá, but the mountains were higher, and he had an irresolute government to contend with. He was already on his way when instructions reached him forbidding the venture. San Martín ignored them. His matter-of-fact description of the trek which followed reveals both the thoroughness of his preparations and the extent of the hazards. "The army had 10,600 saddle and pack mules, 1,600 horses and 700 head of cattle. Despite scrupulous attention, only 4,300 mules and 511 horses arrived in Chile, and those in very bad condition. The rest either died or became useless in the crossing of the mountains." Two six-inch howitzers and ten four-inch field pieces were moved on wheeled carriages, "but had to be carried by hand with the help of block and tackle over much of the higher levels . . . Everyone was convinced that the obstacles surmounted obviated all hope of retreat, yet there was great confidence in the ranks, which performed their tasks gallantly and with keen rivalry."

The language, like his leadership, was brisk and professional. At the end of the first week of February, he had thrown back the Spaniards as planned and taken the Chilean city of Santiago. It took just over a year to win the entire country from the royalists and assure its independence, but the general made little fuss of his success. After the decisive fight with the Spanish forces, at Maipú, San Martín observed simply and succinctly: "We have won the battle, completely." He refused all honors and gifts, nor was he interested in acquiring a government title. Having done his job in Chile, as he saw it, he left politics to those better fitted and prepared for his next task, the ousting of the Spaniards from their safest stronghold in the continent, Peru. For three centuries, the prolific mineral resources of that country had made it the richest and most satisfied of Spain's colonies. The wealthy Creoles were complacent; the poorer classes suspicious of change. No army of fiery patriots harassed the Peruvian government, begging San Martín to hasten and help them. Instead, he faced confident, fully attentive defenses, well supported by a firmly entrenched social system.

Had San Martín been less a political innocent, he must at that stage have turned back and made the most of his prestige and victory. Argentina herself was beset by conflicting elements and lacking a strong hand to stabilize her government. The general could have been more effective there than in Peru, especially since his advance had lost the backing of his political sponsors and rested only on the authority of his own officers. But San Martín looked to his front, to things he really knew about, preparing his next step with military thoroughness. It called for a fleet to transport him up the long Pacific coast to his objective, and, painstakingly, he began to assemble one. In this task he placed considerable faith, as had Bolívar at one stage of his own adventures, in the self-assurance and boundless energies of a Briton. San Martín's "Rooke" was a former officer of the British navy, Lord Cochrane, who had turned to free-lancing in American waters after being dismissed with disgrace from his own country's service. Thanks to the miscellany of vessels he managed to purchase or press into service along the coast, San Martín was able to sail for Peru in the autumn of 1820 with a force of between four and five thousand men.

Instead of directly contesting the main city of Lima, the Argentinian hovered for some months on the seaboard, patiently seeking local recruits and hoping for the climate of Peruvian opinion to swing in his favor. "People are asking why I do not march on Lima immediately," he observed. "What good would Lima do me if its inhabitants were hostile politically? What would it benefit the cause of independence if I should take Lima, or even the entire country, by force? My views are quite different. I do not want to step ahead of progressive public opinion. I want the populace to think as I do . . . I shall give it opportunity without danger." If such sentiments scarcely echoed the revolutionary ardor of Bolívar, they by no means reflected a spirit of compromise. When the liberal upsurge in Spain induced the Lima authorities to negotiate, discussions broke down on San Martín's refusal to accept less than complete independence for the country. Time, for the moment, was on the general's side. Belatedly, following a now familiar pattern, the Creole establishment of the city was awakening to the possibilities of a system which could give it control of the government. By the summer of 1821, secessionist pressure had become so strong in Lima that the viceroy, General La Serna, decamped for the interior to establish his headquarters in more congenial surroundings.

San Martín entered Lima unopposed in July, duly declaring Peru's independence. It was an optimistic proclamation. With the exception of the capital, almost the whole of Peru and Upper

Peru remained in the power of the royalists, whose forces, poised threateningly in the sierras, held San Martín in an unseemly defensive posture within Lima and a small neck of the coast. Outside those limits, the Spaniards had a sizable military advantage. Even within, support for independence was not overwhelming, and certainly diffuse in its ideas and methods. Neither the public men of Lima nor San Martín's own officers were happy with the situation, or his ability to handle it, while morale in the ranks of his army was sapped by the climate and inactivity. The first person of consequence to desert was his admiral, Cochrane. Unwilling to wait for the money owing to him and his mariners, Cochrane ransacked the city vaults and made off with the fleet. While conspiracies smoldered among other officers, desertion quickly spread to the troops and confusion gripped the city. Faced either with drastic action or anarchy, San Martín assumed the political mantle from which he had constantly and instinctively recoiled, acting henceforth as dictator. It was to take no more than a single encounter with a born politician and demagogue to convince him that his instincts all along had been right.

A meeting between San Martín and Bolívar had long seemed advisable, especially with regard to the common threat of Spanish arms in Peru. Yet the prospect was fraught with tensions. Neither man could ignore the other's reputation, nor feel entirely happy that his own might not suffer in consequence. To San Martín, the austere professional soldier, Bolívar must have seemed an upstart general and a showoff. To Bolívar, who frequently used protestations of disinterest in conjunction with the acquisition of power, San Martín's disinterest in political reward and station can hardly have seemed convincing, especially when the Argentinian became *supremo* of Lima. Then, personalities apart, there was rivalry for the uncommitted districts between them, notably Guayaquil, which had yet to declare its choice between the two men and which San Martín coveted as a new field of influence to boost his diminishing prestige to the south. It was partly with the annexation of Guayaquil in mind, partly to request material aid against the common foe from a fellow liberator, that the Argentinian now sailed north to meet Bolívar, whom he expected to find in Quito.

It seems hard to believe that San Martín's political naïveté ran to the extent of expecting the northerner to grant assistance in

Peru and concede territory in the same breath. Nevertheless, in anticipating his interview with Bolívar, San Martín apparently visualized the need for no more than a few hours of consultation in the spirit of gentlemen, officers, and patriots. Bolívar's rejoinder was exuberantly fulsome. His letters of greeting spoke of the "goodness," "selflessness," and "glory" of the southerner. He had, he declared, been looking forward to this moment all his life. "With the utmost satisfaction, most respected friend, I give you the title my heart has conferred on you. I call you friend," Bolívar wrote, "because friendship is the only bond for brothers in arms, in enterprise and opinion . . . A few hours, as you say, are enough for a discussion between soldiers, but they will not be enough to satisfy comradeship, to enjoy the pleasure of affection . . ." At the same time, anticipating San Martín with truly brotherly insight, Bolívar moved from Quito to Guayaquil before the other arrived there, pointedly welcoming the traveler to "Colombian soil."

Of the discussion which transpired, very little is known for certain. San Martín's general reaction to finding Bolívar at Guayaquil, and to their confrontation, was that of an aging bull sniffing for the first time an electric fence. He went into reverse very suddenly and seems to have abandoned further interest. At a banquet on the day of their meeting, Bolívar proposed a toast to "the two greatest men in South America: general San Martín and myself." At a ball for the Argentinian the following evening, the guest of honor disappeared. Retiring quietly from the festivities, San Martín had gone to his boat. He sailed the same night. "The Liberator is not the man we imagined," he said later. As far as can be ascertained, Bolívar had made it clear at the intervening conference that he had no intention of providing his rival with sufficient troops to win the ultimate campaign against the Spaniards, not even if San Martín offered, as he seems to have done in final desperation, to act under the Venezuelan's orders. The southerner had revealed his hand, and it was empty. He had cut himself off from Argentina, he had been beaten to Ecuador, he could not handle the Peruvian royalists alone, and his followers had lost most of their faith in him. All too clearly, Bolívar perceived that the stage was his own for the last act. For all his fraternal declarations, he showed no philanthropic urge to share the triumph.

José de San Martín completed his exit without fuss. Convinced that his further involvement could only add dissension to the cause of independence, he resigned his authority in Lima, lingered briefly in the south, then retired to spend his old age in Europe, first in Belgium, then France, where he died in 1850 forgotten by South America. Bolívar took his time in tackling Peru, aware of the strength of the royalist forces there. He reached Lima in autumn, 1823, was invested with the authority of supreme dictator, and set about training some four thousand Peruvians to supplement his Colombian forces. Almost a year later, he scored a bloody victory over the Spaniards in a cavalry action at Junín, inland of the capital, the advantage being consolidated by Sucre soon afterward at Ayacucho, to the south. At last, the liberation of Spanish America was over. The charge of Sucre's patriots at Ayacucho completed the imperial disaster which had first struck Spain in the person of Napoleon. Thirteen years after the start of the Creole rising, the guardians of the western empire were toppled.

Whether anyone had profited from the confusion, the death, the destruction seemed doubtful. The uppermost Creoles had thrown off the restrictions of Spanish government, only to yoke themselves to a succession of frequently more tiresome dictators. Their less well-to-do brothers, and the middle classes in general, had suffered terribly from the struggle and its attendant depression, bearing the bulk of the cost in death and injury while lacking the material reserves to sustain their small businesses. The lower classes could look forward to a life of continued degradation and squalor. A century and more later, the Indians of Peru would still be living on the rubbish of Lima, or in serfdom on the estates of the gentry; few people of the world would seem so pitiful as the poor of Latin America, those lost souls of the west whom Catholic Spain had once dispatched her soldiers and missionaries to save.

Even while Bolívar was in Peru, his grand state of Colombia was breaking up. Having proclaimed the liberation of Upper Peru (renamed República Bolívar) in 1825, he turned north to find separatism rife in Venezuela and New Granada, his commanders defecting, the scene set for further civil wars. First, Páez, of Venezuela, rebelled against the union. Santander of New Granada followed. Bolívar tried desperately to hold the state together, exerting all his powers of verbal persuasion, resigning some of his authority to placate the rebels, marching armies against the dissenters, resigning once more, then marching again. In 1828, an attempt on the Liberator's life, planned in Bogotá, narrowly failed and Santander and others were banished for conspiracy. The following year, Peru turned against Colombia, and Bolívar, heading south, left the northern territories in the throes of fresh trouble. After a critical illness at Guayaquil, the *supremo* set out for his native Venezuela for the last time. He reached Bogotá early in 1830, bestowing the presidency upon the most loyal of his generals, Sucre, but he was not welcome across the border, where Páez was preparing a campaign to "liberate" New Granada from the Liberator. The wheel had turned full cycle. Bolívar was now "the tyrant." In June, Sucre, the last of his trusties, was murdered. In December, disillusioned and too feeble to implement his final plan to follow San Martín to exile in Europe, Simón Bolívar died at Santa Marta, on the north coast.

Among the last of his copious words was a document of despair which indicated that he believed all his struggles to have been in vain and the future of individual freedom in Spanish America sealed with doom.

Chapter 12

FRUSTRATION AND FRATRICIDE

The Cantabrian cordillera of the Basque provinces and Asturias, with its solid front to a thin strip of coastland and the great Bay of Biscay, provides the peninsula map with a northern frieze much akin to that of Granada in the south. In fact, the two poles are quite separate in character. While the Andalusian territory hints on every side of its proximity to Africa, its opposite extremity has more in common with Central Europe. Northerly and northwesterly winds bring an abundance of moisture, checkering the countryside with bright green meadows and luxuriant maize fields, sustaining forests of oak and beech on the hills. From the mountains pour gushing streams and well-stocked salmon rivers; between pastures and farmsteads ply massive oxcarts laden with juicy grass; from the orchards comes a type of cider, *sidra* or *sagardua*, preferred by the people hereabouts to the wine of the south. In the winter, proclaims the northerner with a soulfulness quite distinct from Andalusian exuberance, it is always raining, *"siempre llueve,"* and rather sad. It all makes the parched plains and arid hills on the far side of the range seem remote. Historically, as well as physically, this region lacks the African traces evident in so many other parts of Spain, for it was against the southern slopes of the Cantabrians that the Muslim impetus originally subsided, and from the crags of Covadonga, in these same mountains, that Pelayo and the priests held their ground.

The Carlists, too, bent on reaffirming old traditions, made their bid from the hills of the north. Don Carlos, having waited patiently for the death of his brother, Ferdinand VII, now emerged from exile in Portugal to rally his supporters against the infant Isabella, or rather her mother, Cristina, the regent. The military challenge was centered in the eastern Cantabrian strongholds of the Basques and the Navarrese, Carlos establishing his headquarters in 1835 at Estella. At the same time, other risings in his favor took place in the regions of Aragon, Catalonia, and Valencia. The actual war, fought on the Carlist side largely by mountain *guerrilleros*, was a desultory affair in which the rebels, failing to win either Barcelona or Bilbao, lacked sufficient port facilities for outside supplies and were unable to convince the rest of Europe of their chances. In 1836, an intrepid Carlist general named Gómez led an epic offensive to the west of Madrid as far south as Córdoba, returning north with new recruits and materials, and, the following year, Carlos himself led a sweep to the southeast. But the capital, like other key cities, failed to respond, and, with the Carlist effort spent, the war degenerated into a contest of atrocities in which winning battles became secondary to murdering prisoners. Not the least of the blows struck at Carlos was peaceful. With a subtlety rare among Spaniards in times of emotion, a liberal leader, Juan Mendizabal, persuaded the regent to confiscate the still enormous landholdings of the Church and put them up for sale at attractive prices. As expected, the temptation proved too much for many affluent conservatives hitherto inclined to the Carlists. They invested in the property, hence in the liberals. By 1839, the rebels were ready to talk peace, and, a year later, the war, if not Carlism, had ended everywhere. The pretender and his trusties withdrew to France to await the second chance implicit in the divided nature of their enemies.

Isabella II, declared of age at thirteen, merely completed the contempt felt in Spain for the Bourbons once the roles played by Ferdinand and his parents had been analyzed. A podgy girl, growing to stoutness in time, she had a puffy, petulant face with a sharpness of the eyes that hinted at capabilities which would never develop. Brought up by her mother, a mediocre and self-seeking woman already discredited and remarried, the new queen lacked any philosophy or sense of mission which might have helped constitutionalism to work. Her inclination, like that of her father before her, was to exercise unbridled authority, yet few but the Carlists still accepted such as the royal privilege, and the Carlists were her bitterest personal enemies. At the opposite end of the political spectrum the democrats and republicans challenged the powers of the monarch on principle, leaving only the middle-of-the-road liberals with whom to work. In these circumstances, Isabella followed the pattern of Ferdinand, swallowing the medicine when it was unavoidable and betraying the doctors when it suited her purpose.

The dominating characters of Isabella's time were a succession of army officers, and it was as a consolidation of the process of military involvement in Spanish government that the reign was especially significant. The phenomenon was not without precedent. From the Cid on, and particularly in the days of empire expansion, men of a primarily military stamp had asserted themselves in the politics of Spain and her dominions. The nineteenth century, with its sudden diversification of ideology and the resulting confusion of a people long accustomed to a paternalistic lead, brought striking developments. Rafael del Riego, using the relative stability of military society in an attempt to bring new order to government, had set a fashion that has yet to see its end. Isabella's reign, in which no less than five soldiers vied at varying times for top political office, revealed some interesting aspects of the trend. In some respects, the influence of the soldier politician was benevolent. As a patriot, trained to a code of discipline and honor, he symbolized the nation's desire to be free of disunity, corruption, and foreign intervention. As a creature of positive, unequivocal action on a "common-sense" basis, he appealed at moments of crisis. His values, being uncomplicated and nonintellectual, were understood by the mass of people unconscious of political philosophies and ethics.

Yet this emphasis on externals, on oversimplification, was also a weakness. The road to political goals, as distinct from military objectives, is seldom direct. Social evolution implies doubt, discussion, and argument. These the general regarded as obstacles in his path. As a result, two tendencies emerged with the new vogue in government. One was the gradual retirement of many thoughtful elements from the political arena, leaving more and more ground to the rival extremists. The other was the renewal, albeit in a new guise, of the autocratic system. From the ashes of the absolute monarchy was rising another type of despot, the *supremo*. Not that the process was swift or clear-cut. Civilian premiers would still appear between the ranks of the soldiers, while the latter, working more or less constitutionally with different groups in the Cortes, were by no means conformist in the party sense. Riego had raised a liberal banner. Of the military contenders in the reign of Isabella, the three strongest, Generals Espartero, Narváez, and O'Donnell were of varied persuasions. Baldomero Espartero, the son of a carter who had first joined the army to fight Napoleon, was a "progressive" of the left. Ramón Narváez, who hailed from Granada, pursued a conservative policy. Leopoldo O'Donnell, born in Tenerife of Irish ancestry, had no strong inclination in either direction, and at one time led a coalition. Nevertheless, the military politician was a reactionary at heart, and his development as a species moved predictably to the right in government.

In this sense, Narváez was typical of the type among Isabella's ministers. His self-expressed credo was "the stick, applied heavily," while his attitude to opposition was summed up in an apocryphal deathbed story in which the priest, asking if His Excellency had forgiven his enemies, was told, "I have none. I had them all shot." His government, aided by the queen and the conservative hierarchy of the Church, was resolute and tough, though insufficiently subscribed to hold his liberal rivals at bay all the time. In the foreign field, the soldierly urge to adventure led O'Donnell into costly excursions in Morocco and the Indies. As usual, relations between the Moors and Spain's garrisons on the African coast were strained, and in 1859 the general declared war on the sultan, personally leading an army from Ceuta to occupy Tetuán and threaten Fez. Though hailed as a victory for Spanish arms, the enterprise cost seven thousand men and, followed by withdrawal, gained only a moral advantage. Even that was offset, before long, by the subsequent Atlantic adventure. In 1861, Santo Domingo applied for restitution of Spanish sovereignty to protect herself against neighboring Haiti. Fondly dreaming of the old western empire, now reduced to Cuba and Puerto Rico, Spanish soldiers and administrators descended in swarms on the applicant. As a reminder of forgotten quarrels, their overeager embraces were salutary. Four years later, Spain was rejected by the island for a second time, with the loss of a further ten thousand troops.

By way of venting bitterness, successive governments, now coming and going like shuttlecocks, authorized naval bombardments of the South American coast. This futile activity, arousing more old colonial hatreds, discredited Spain in many foreign capitals. London and Paris refused her loans, and the economy, boosted in recent years by improved communications, especially railways, was again under pressure. Criticism focused, not altogether undeservedly, on the one constant figure in the galleries of power. If Isabella were not, as many felt, the root of all evil, her repeated betrayal of ministers and advisers had never helped matters. By 1868, when her main hope, Narváez, died, the purpose of the next *pronunciamiento* was beyond doubt. It came in September. In a manifesto issued jointly by the army and navy, the point was made bluntly that "the person charged with the defence of the constitution should not be its irreconcilable enemy." Isabella, looking desperately for supporters, was greeted instead by posters announcing "The everlasting downfall of the spurious Bourbons." On the last day of the month, she crossed the Bidassoa to France, declaring her surprise at being rejected by the people she herself had neglected from the start. At thirty-six, there were many years before her. She would live to see the airplane a reality and motorcars in the streets of Madrid. She would still be alive when a twelve-year-old boy named Francisco Franco gazed at the iron cruisers in El Ferrol harbor and dreamed of a career in the navy. But her reign was over. As Spain plunged turbulently toward the end of the century, sometimes rudderless, seldom agreed on her own course, exiled Isabella joined the rest of the world, a spectator.

Once again, as in 1808, the nation had a chance, in theory, of a fresh start. Once again, conflict, confusion, and fear of the untried caused it to cling to the old institutions. Unable to bring the remaining party leaders to agree on a form of government, the military gentlemen, Generals Praxedes Sagasta and Juan Prim, put the question to the Cortes, which voted to retain the monarchy on a limited basis. The constitution, a variation on most liberal manifestos since 1812, was by now too remote from the main lines of conviction to satisfy any side. For many who had helped to oust Isabella, its reforms were hopelessly timid. For others, the same reforms, notably provisions for civil marriage and choice of worship, were anticlerical and offensive. Reaction brought recruits to the republicans and Carlists respectively. Divergence of opinion intensified. Nevertheless, a new king had been called for, and the generals tried to find one. The two most obvious claimants, Isabella's son Alfonso, and Don Carlos, grandson of the original Carlist candidate, were barred by a new law excluding the Bourbons from the throne. The rest of Europe was sufficiently familiar with the situation in Spain to preclude any rush of volunteers. King Luis I of Portugal was offered the crown, but he refused. His father, Ferdinand of Saxe-Coburg, was approached, dithered, then declined. Prince Leopold of Hohenzollern was a candidate long enough to arouse French suspicions and provoke the Franco-Prussian War, but turned out to be another false starter, after which the Duke of Genoa was sounded. He also said "no." Eventually, more than two years after the flight of Isabella, a taker was found in Amadeo of Savoy, brother to the queen of Portugal.

Amadeo, then twenty-six, was earnest, eager to uphold the constitution, and so well-mannered that the Spanish dubbed him the gentleman-king, a title appealing to their sense of paradox. For all that, few in the country really wanted him, with the powerful exception of Prim, whose personal authority had held the nation together in recent months. On December 27, 1870, a few days before Amadeo was due to land at Cartagena, a burst of gunfire ripped into Prim's coach as he rode to his ministry, and the first news to greet the new king on his arrival in Spain was that his sponsor was dead. In the confusion that followed, the real sentiments of the country broke out in alternate Carlist and republican risings. To Amadeo, who could not understand the Spanish tongue, it must have seemed a madhouse. With each gust of wind, the cabinet reshuffled and a new premier was announced. The king had barely grasped one name when it was gone, replaced by another. Prim's death brought the ministry of Serrano, giving way to that of Zorilla, then Malcampo and Sagasta. Sagasta's election was followed immediately by his resignation over a charge of embezzlement, after which it was back to Serrano, and once more to Zorilla. Amadeo stuck it for two years, then announced his own resignation. At last, Spain was about to take the plunge. No sooner had he mentioned it than the Cortes, which had so recently obliged Prim with an overwhelming vote for the monarchy, declared by 258 to 32 for a republic.

The First Republic faced chaos. A large part of the north was Carlist, the south was split by socialists of all complexions, while the government itself, without a strong leader, was hopelessly divided. After a week or two of unitarian policy, its original president, Estanislao Figueras, fled the country without even the formality of resigning, and a federalist group took office. Though fresh elections confirmed support for the system, only a third of the electorate voted. Meanwhile, Spain was reverting instinctively to its regionalist past. Catalonia already posed as an independent state. Seville, Cádiz, Málaga and Granada, among other places, became practically autonomous. At Cartagena, the people took command of ships in the harbor and set up their own navy. It was almost as if the days of the medieval *taifas* had returned, now run by the people and known as cantons. In less than a year, the republic had four presidents, the last of whom, Emilio Castelar, a professor of history and much-respected Spaniard, finally sacrificed his popularity to restore order the painful way. Backed by loyal units of the army, and a reimposition of conscription, he tackled the Carlists and the cantons simultaneously, containing the former, reducing the latter by sheer force. The achievement was considerable, but so were the devastation and suffering, and success brought Castelar's downfall in parliament. "We republicans have many prophets, too few politicians," complained the professor; "plenty of idealism but little experience." His own principles prevented his agreeing to an army coup on his behalf. Instead, troops cleared the bickering assembly and the military was once more in charge.

The republican experiment had proved disastrous. The economy was shattered, credit abroad had dipped to a new low, lives and property had been lost on a huge scale. The people were ready for any sort of peace, and, in December 1874, a brigade of guards proclaimed Isabella's son, Alfonso XII, king at Sagunto. Alfonso differed greatly from his mother. A worldly young man, trained at Sandhurst, England, the new king was most conscious of the need for responsible leadership and stable government. His sincerity evoked a response. In 1876, the second Carlist War, involving 200,-000 government troops in the north, ended in a decisive defeat for Carlos. Two years later, a costly rebellion in Cuba was put down with promises of greater independence for the natives. A blessed calm descended, and Alfonso received the accolade of Pacificador.

Stronger elements than the king, however, were dictating the story. Chief of these was the political disillusionment of the nation, which, sobered by the disasters of partisan rabidity, had become amenable at last to a period of compromise. A considerably restricted version of earlier constitutions was accepted and a conservative government elected to work it, tempered by an unusually subdued opposition. On both sides, the leaders gave their weight to stability at the expense of democratic niceties. For the conservatives, Antonio Canovas del Castillo, a man of erudition, force and personality, proved an expert at manipulating elections in favor of the status quo; Sagasta, for the opposition, more or less went along with the fiction. At least it gave Spain a chance to recuperate.

Even the premature death of Alfonso [1885] was eased for the establishment by the obliging nature of his young wife, Maria Cristina, daughter of the Archduke Ranier of Austria. Not only did she produce their first son a few months afterwards, but, in stark contrast to her namesake of half a century earlier, maintained a most tactful and seemly regency. It was doubtless the most valuable coming-of-age present received by her son, Alfonso XIII. Unfortunately, the regency, if not the regent, produced its own disaster.

In Cuba, where ten years of earlier rebellion had already cost something like a hundred thousand lives, the promised reforms had not materialized. Still a magnet for ambitious officers and aggressive civil servants, not to mention a valuable closed shop for Catalan commerce, the colony remained the subject of strong reaction in the Cortes. The regency was barely underway when the assembly overwhelmingly rejected a proposal sympathetic to reform in Cuba. In 1895, rebellion flared once more in the island and an army was dispatched to suppress it. When this failed, its commander, General Martínez Campos, was replaced by a man of a more ruthless persuasion, General Valeriano Weyler, who instituted a regime of terror and concentration camps.

If the Spanish government was satisfied with such measures, a power much nearer to the trouble was not. Ever sensitive to the complexion of the big island ranged beneath her belly, the United States of America had watched developments there with mounting interest. Apart from Cuba's strategic significance in relation to Panama and Florida, American investments in the colony were more than trifling. With a comfortable excess of might in her favor, it was unlikely the fast-developing western power would take much pushing into open intervention. Weyler's brutal methods strongly influenced American public opinion, providing the war faction with useful ammunition, while the Spanish government, for its part, regarded foreign concern as unwarranted interference. The Spanish people as a whole had no idea of the gravity of the matter until it was too late. On the night of February 15, 1898, the United States battleship *Maine*, in Havana harbor to protect American citizens, was rocked by a violent explosion and sank with a loss of 262 lives. The cause was never agreed upon, but the popular press in America squarely accused Spain. At about the same time, the New York *Journal* published an illegally acquired letter of the Spanish ambassador describing the President of the States, then William McKinley, as a weakling. Though Spain climbed down in the final hour to the extent of ordering a cease-fire against the rebels, the damage was already irreparable. Backed by a wave of popular sentiment, the United States Congress declared Cuba independent and demanded Spain's withdrawal from the island. By the end of April, the two nations were at war.

The outcome was inevitable. America was rich, overwhelmingly strong at sea, and fighting on her own doorstep. Spain was poor, militarily inadequate, and thousands of miles from the scene of engagement. Nevertheless, dynastic pride demanded a heroic gesture, and the Spanish forces gave it. Admiral Cervera, commander of the Atlantic fleet, was ordered to Cuba with four cruisers and half-a-dozen torpedo boats. Though lacking the most elementary conditions for success, he obeyed, putting in at Santiago on the south of the island, already threatened by an American invasion. Blockaded in the harbor by a far superior fleet, and with a disorganized Spanish army in retreat, Cervera was now ordered to go to sea and fight. Once more, he obeyed. Within five hours, every one of his vessels was lost. In the Pacific, another Spanish fleet had already been destroyed in an American attack on the Philippines, and, with Santiago surrendered and Puerto Rico overrun, Spain was soon suing for peace. Under the Treaty of Paris, signed in December, she renounced her sovereignty in Cuba, ceding the Philippines and Puerto Rico to the United States. The last remnants of her colonial splendor had gone.

Strangely enough, the catastrophe did not bring the downfall of the Spanish government. Sagasta, then in office, remained so for the rest of the winter, and, though then replaced, was back in a year's time. The shock to the nation had gone too deep to be assuaged by casting stones at ministers. As the troop ships disgorged their streams of repatriates—broken, fever-ridden ghosts of the great imperial tradition—into a near-bankrupt motherland, Spain knew she had been deceived by more than a handful of mortals, more than a simple state of martial unreadiness. The fault lay wherever a trumpet, a battle color, a rhetorical appeal to the past had blinded men to the facts of the present. And the reaction was the more intense for being quiet, a moral rather than a political matter. Spaniards of intellect and vision had already begun to redirect their efforts from politics to less immediate spheres of influence, and now the cultural renascence became widespread.

History has called the movement, clumsily, the Generation of '98, but it was no organized system and was not defined as a social force at the time. Rather, it was a change of mood, a climate of reappraisal in which the lawyer no less than the writer, the manufacturer as well as the teacher, took a new look at his attitudes and methods in the light of the latest European and western development. Joaquín Costa, the Aragonese scholar and an outstanding spokesman of the "generation," summed it up in two simple slogans: "Let us lock the Cid's sepulchre under triple keys," and "Let us look to the school and the larder."

What Costa and many like him spelled out was that all the *pronunciamientos* and decrees in Spain would not produce political virtue until educational and economic standards were raised. The method they embraced was not political pressure but direct individual effort toward better schools, more efficient industry and agriculture. Since the enlightened despotism of the eighteenth century, Spain's universities, fettered by the fears of Ferdinand and the hostility of Carlists and reactionary clerics, had become little more than factories for government diplomas. No one had better cause to know this than an Andalusian philosopher and jurist named Francisco Giner, twice deprived of the chair of jurisprudence at Madrid for his reforming endeavors. By the time of the war with America, Giner and a group of other outcast professors had established a school of their own, the Institución Libre de Ensenanza, with special emphasis on liberal educational values at elementary and secondary levels. Greatly influenced by the philosophy of Krause, and the need for "all-round" education, Giner constantly sought to widen school activities, introducing games, excursions, art, and manual work to the limited curricula of established schooling in Spain. Very soon, his ideas became fashionable, other establishments appeared to emulate or rival the Institución, influential families sent their children to such academies.

By the first decade of the twentieth century, the government was itself financing an autonomous Committee for the Development of Studies, the *Junta para Ampliación de Estudios*, which founded residential colleges in Madrid, sent students abroad to study, and provided laboratories and centers for further research. Cultural horizons were broadened, and the intellectual reawakening, combined with the inevitable post-Cuba conclusion that the future could lie nowhere other than at home, brought a fresh spasm of economic vitality.

During the reign of Alfonso XIII, who took responsibility in 1902, Spain came of age as an industrial nation and, indeed, turned her capacity to much profit by staying neutral during the great war of 1914–18 in Europe. Alfonso, like his father, was energetic and well-intentioned. A lean, aristocratic face, trim mustache, and a figure to delight any military tailor gave the young king a romantic, debonair aura which was augmented by a hint of imperiousness. If he came to look increasingly like a ruler, rather than a constitutional monarch, the cause lay in circumstances, not perversity. Alfonso was drawn by the repeated failure of others into a nightmare of political problems. They broke like a deluge with the passing of Sagasta and Canovas, both of whom died at the birth of the Generation of '98, the latter by assassination—a grim pointer to the future. For two decades these twin pillars of the reformation had supported an unusually serene political façade. But behind it the old divisions, no longer exhausted, no longer content to play at liberals and conservatives, had drawn fractiously apart. The system now stood revealed in its weakness. No one agreed on anything. Nor was there another Canovas in evidence. By the time Alfonso had reigned four years, there had been eight prime ministers and nearly twice as many major political crises.

Someone had to do something, and the king, constantly sought in support of this or that party, tried to do his best. His best was by no means contemptible. For a young man, he showed an astute grasp of practical politics, maintaining his balance on a shifting and treacherous footing with coolness and patience. When he had a man of authority with whom to deal (and it was rarely), he contrived to work well with him. Such a man was José Canalejas, a radical whose respect for legally constituted power, plus a power- ful gift for oratory, won him a substantial liberal following. But Canalejas proved altogether too statesmanlike for those extremist groups who wished to disorganize parliament, and, in November 1912, he was shot to death at a Madrid bookstore by an anarchist gunman who then committed suicide. Anarchism, a jealous stable- mate of Marxism, had a strong appeal for many Spaniards, espe- cially among the working classes of the south. Based on confidence in the individualistic as opposed to the collective, its professed aim was to abolish all forms of authority, including religion. Official reaction, fortified by memories of the chaotic days of the cantons, was sharp. Persecuted and frustrated, the anarchist turned to violence.

Other new movements had emerged with the industrial era. Bet- ter organized than the anarchists, and sympathetic to Bolshevik successes in Russia, were the revolutionary syndicalists, who formed industrial unions and used strikes and sabotage to further their ends. Communism, however, was not well received by the mainstream of socialism in Spain. This grew rapidly in the early years of the century, stimulated by industrialism and the poor conditions under which the lower classes lived and worked. In 1888 there had been only sixteen socialist groups in the country. By 1912 there were two hundred and sixteen. Meanwhile, the old divisions persisted as stubbornly. Catalan nationalism flared to such proportions that, in 1913, the government went a long way toward conceding autonomy in the region, a policy later reversed. The Carlists, or Jaimists as they had become under the latest claimant in the line, were still strong in Navarre and the Basque lands. Various Catholic and capitalist groups had also appeared by way of protest against socialistic "evils."

Between these old and new elements the mutations were endless, splitting the major parties into fragments. The phenomenon was not, of course, entirely restricted to Spain in this period. It was, however, aggravated in that country by the whole trend of Spanish tradition and the resulting inflexibility and immoderation of its political nature. Thus crisis gathered on crisis; the familiar specter of destruction began to reshape. While the government's capacity to cope with social conflicts decreased, its even smaller capacity to enforce positive programs ensured that such conflicts developed and multiplied. In Madrid and Barcelona, violence became commonplace.

In the late summer of 1921, what remained of Spain's confidence in her parliamentarian leaders received a fatal shock. In agreement with France and Great Britain in 1906, and by a further Franco-Spanish agreement of 1912, France and Spain had undertaken the general supervision of Morocco which, for this purpose, was divided into two protectorates. While France had succeeded in establishing order in the greater part of her own half, Spain, hampered by events at home and by the mountainous terrain of her protectorate, lagged behind in the matter. When famine increased the discontent of the Moorish tribesmen, the Spanish forces on the coast proceeded to deploy in the territory. Two armies were involved. One, based at Tetuán, was directly under the high commissioner, General Damoso Berenguer. The other, based on Melilla, was under a general named Manuel Silvestre. It was Silvestre's misfortune to witness the debacle.

The Melilla command comprised upward of 25,000 men, of whom a proportion was scattered among numerous outposts. Of the rest, a strong expedition was dispatched along the coast to the west, establishing itself by June at the local center of Anual, with a covering force at nearby Igueriben. During June and July, a series of clashes occurred with the warlike Rif tribesmen of the zone whose leader, Abd-el-Krim, a former official in the department of native affairs, had turned against the Spaniards following a personal dispute with Silvestre.

The initial Rif attacks were repulsed but left doubt about the allegiance of some Moroccan troops in the Spanish ranks. On July 19, Berenguer, with no previous intimation of impending crisis, received the first of a series of astonishing communiqués from Silvestre. It said that Igueriben was surrounded by Moorish warriors and that a relief force had been beaten back.

On the twentieth, the high commissioner received a request for naval and air support, which he passed to Madrid. On the twenty-first came a demand for artillery and troops to reinforce eighteen companies already in close reserve. On the morning of the twenty-second, Berenguer learned that the Rifs had stormed Igueriben, ambushing another relief column in the desert, and that Silvestre had decided to withdraw from Anual. "I trust," the commissioner telegraphed in reply, "that the prestige and honour of Spain will be foremost in all minds." His trust was misplaced. Silvestre's army was already in headlong flight. Its general had committed suicide. In the massacre that followed, Abd-el-Krim pursued his enemies almost to the gates of Melilla, overran dozens of outposts and brought the total Spanish losses to nearly 15,000 men. The Moorish terror had risen from the past.

For many Spaniards, Silvestre's incredible march to disaster could be explained only as a blunder of the government or, more directly, of the king. For two years, revolution rumbled in the air and blood stained the gutters. Then came a new *pronunciamiento*. General Primo de Rivera, already in his sixties and with a lifetime of army service behind him, organized his coup in Catalonia, whose return to the national fold he could later claim as his one irrefutable success. It was September 1923. The ministry fell without resistance, and the king acceded to the formation of a military directory.

Rivera had the now familiar faults and assets of the typical army politician. In the material sense, the directory brought many benefits. The most obvious was the restoration of order. In Spain, the gunmen were driven out of sight, and in Morocco the army regained its good name in a long and stern campaign of reclamation. Loud demands for such traditional causes as the restitution of Gibraltar, coupled with an energetic program of public works, helped to gain Rivera widespread popularity. New roads, better railways, and modern irrigation schemes were very welcome. Impressive trade fairs were held at Seville and elsewhere. A new bond of friendship was established with Latin America. Suddenly, Spain's stock in the world was riding high. But it was no more than a seven years' wonder.

As the bills came in for the various projects, especially for maintaining the costly forces in Morocco, public enthusiasm sharply declined. Rising prices and increased taxation were the death of the directory. With the tide against him, Rivera's political ineptitude came to light. In his first flush of confidence, and contempt for the previous government, he had not bothered to have his take-over ratified by the Cortes. Trusting in his early popularity, he had failed to establish a political party to back him. When the time of reckoning arrived, he was alone. At the beginning of 1930, a sick man and no longer sure even of controlling the army, Primo de Rivera resigned, to die in Paris a few weeks later. If there had been little unity left in the old liberal and conservative parties before the directory, its term had completed their disintegration. The only political organizations still intact were extremist. To make matters worse, the king and his provisional premier, General Berenguer, delayed holding the promised elections so long that it began to look as if they were denying the vote. At last, in April 1931, Spain was allowed free expression at the polls for the first time in eight years. Though the country as a whole showed a monarchist majority, the big cities were overwhelmingly republican. Alfonso, accepting the hopelessness of fighting them, followed Primo de Rivera into exile.

The revolutionary committee of a republican-socialist coalition next established itself as a provisional government, placing a former liberal deputy, Niceto Alcalá Zamora, at its head. Alcalá Zamora, who had declared openly in favor of a republic twelve months earlier, proclaimed the event with ardor. The indomitable will of the people, he wrote, had peacefully overthrown a monarchy of fifteen centuries' duration. But, even if he cared to forget that the flight of Isabella II had once been hailed as the end of the Bourbons, it was not as simple as that. Alfonso had retired from Spain, but he had not abdicated, and the elections had demonstrated that despite the diminished stature of Spain's latter-day monarchs, monarchism itself was by no means a spent force. Moreover, it had a powerful ally in the Church. The vociferous reaction of these elements to the new regime quickly inflamed extreme opinion among the radicals, and a wave of incendiarism threatened churches and other buildings in many cities, particularly in the south. Within a month of its formation, the new government had proclaimed martial law in the face of widespread riots and disorders, while a monarchist and a Catholic newspaper had been officially suspended. Once again, an avowedly liberalizing movement was being forced into the suppressive measures it most bitterly opposed in its rivals. It was a poor omen for the Second Republic. Nevertheless, the coalition cabinet pressed forward in earnest determination to create a modern and democratic state from the combustible material around it.

Alcalá Zamora's provisional government was much influenced by the philosophy of Francisco Giner. Fernando de los Ríos, the minister of justice, was a nephew of that great liberal and humanist teacher, while Manuel Azana, the minister of war and the outstanding intellect of the cabinet, was the master's ardent disciple. Los Ríos, together with the minister of labor, Francisco Largo Caballero, and the minister of finance, Indalecio Prieto, was a socialist. Azana was a republican, while the oldest and wiliest of the others, Alejandro Lerroux, the minister of state, was a leading figure in the radical party. By and large, it was a government of thinkers and idealists, and its immediate steps demonstrated its impatience with the old order. Crown property was confiscated, the tricolor was adopted as the national flag and the *Hymn of Riego* replaced the *Royal March*. At the same time, the legislative work of the dictatorial regime was overhauled and a new constitution put under planning. In June, elections for the constituent Cortes produced an overwhelming triumph for the alliance, and the resulting charter passed onto the statute book the same year. Described as a "democratic republic of workers of all classes," the constitution of 1931 instituted a single-chamber Cortes, offered suffrage to both sexes at the age of twenty-three, proclaimed religious freedom and the political equality of all people, and pledged Spain to "the universal rules of international law."

While existing municipal and provincial organizations were retained in the system, groups of provinces might apply to the

Cortes for a statute of autonomy. Federations of autonomous regions, on the other hand, were prohibited. Primary secular education became compulsory, divorce by petition was recognized, freedom of assembly and of the press was guaranteed, and so was freedom from arbitrary arrest and imprisonment. The broad aims of the revolutionary blueprint were clear: to educate the people in the rights and responsibilities of republican democracy, to do away with oppressive privilege of any form, to raise the economic status of the nation and to share the land and its fruits more equitably among the populace, especially to give more to a starving and still semifeudal peasantry. The practicalities of the document were sometimes less apparent. In certain instances, notably in the granting of votes to women, whose inclinations on the whole were predictably conservative, it seemed designed specifically to defeat the republic. In others, such as the banning of the Catholic teaching orders when every available teacher in the country was needed to tackle the problem of education, it seemed self-contradictory. Too often, it was imprudently provocative. Especially was this true of the anticlerical clauses, which profoundly offended wide sections of the public. Not only was the Church disestablished by the new charter, but property belonging to the religious orders was nationalized. Moreover, the Society of Jesus was banned from the country.

Such anticlerical zeal disturbed not only conservative opposition but some members of the government itself. The president and his minister of the interior resigned in protest; Catholic deputies withdrew from parliament. This development propelled a remarkable figure, Manuel Azana, the former minister of war, to the head of the nation. Short and portly with a huge doleful face, heavy lips, and eyes that peered remotely through small, round-rimmed spectacles, Azana was cast less in the romantic image of a Spanish leader than in that of the middle-aged bourgeois of a Thurber cartoon. His public manner was withdrawn and insipid. He seemed made, as one critic had it, of damp clay, and failed to rise to the extravagant passions of his countrymen. Yet his mind was both versatile and brilliant. He held the National Prize for Literature, and had been celebrated, even as a young man, among Madrid's inner circle of liberal thinkers. It was in appreciation of his exceptional mental attributes, and his cool but dedicated attachment to social reform, that he gained elevation—and the savage personal abuse of his enemies, who sought to paint him as a figure of infinite perversion. In all, Azana possessed the classic merits and demerits of the intellectual politician: outstanding powers of diagnosis and prescription coupled with a dangerous tendency to scorn the emotions of the electorate.

None resented him more than the military. As minister of war, he had wielded a sharp scalpel in an attempted republican operation to remove the army from politics. His swift and drastic surgery, aimed not only at service personnel but also at the influence of the ancient military orders, cut across a whole field of time-honored traditions. Concerned in particular with the ludicrously high ratio of commissioned to other ranks, Azana had suspended admission to the military academies, retired thousands of idle officers on pension, rationalized the number of divisional commands to little more than a quarter of their former number and discarded up to 90 per cent of field officers. The resulting bitterness in many circles was to lend backing to two risings against his government. In 1932, retired army officers played a leading part in a monarchist revolt in Madrid. The premier, it was said, stood alone in the window of his chambers quietly smoking a cigarette as police, assisted by loyal troops and civilians, quickly gained the upper hand in the streets. In Seville, a revolt of more dangerous proportions was led by General José Sanjurjo, an officer much admired for his patriotic exploits in Morocco. For a while, Sanjurjo and his rebel troops held sway in the city. Again, Azana disdained to show emotion over the incident. Having dispatched trustworthy reinforcements to the loyal forces on the spot, he took his place in parliament and coolly called up an agricultural bill for amendment. Eventually, Sanjurjo was defeated and sentenced to death. The sentence, however, was commuted and the general later continued his plotting from Lisbon.

More trouble came from the left. While the government grappled with centuries-overdue agrarian reforms and the almost impossible task of stabilizing a falling currency amid world economic depression (and the doubts induced abroad by yet another upheaval in Spanish politics), anarchists, syndicalists, and communists continued in their attempts to disrupt the state. To the methodical Azana, such disturbances were anathema, a blemish on the republican blueprint, and they needed wiping out. The deportation of rebels without trial, the suspension of newspapers, and the severe suppression of demonstrations, among other measures employed by the government, evoked charges of dictatorial methods. Early in 1933, the apparently merciless extinction of a small band of communist rebels trapped in a house in the village of Casas Viejas brought popular indignation to a head. On all sides, Azana's government had lost popularity. The Catalans were upset over the dilution in the Cortes of a statute of autonomy they had presented. The Basques were frustrated because a corresponding statute of their own had not been passed in any form. Meanwhile, a new brand of radicalism inspired by fascist movements in Germany and Italy was beginning to attract Spanish adherents. The elections of November 1933 revealed a sharp lurch to the right. While the left could muster only 99 seats in the Cortes, the conservatives now had 207, with a moderate group, largely of radicals, holding the balance. In these circumstances, the premiership passed to the radical leader Alejandro Lerroux, a wily pragmatist, whose middle-to-right government promptly set about easing the restrictions imposed on the Church by Azana. To the greater fury of the left, a former finance minister of Primo de Rivera's regime, José Calvo Sotelo, returned to parliament to attack the money policies of the republic.

Spain's condition was not up to such stresses of the democratic process, and the temperature rose alarmingly. In the face of conservative pressure to undo everything for which the old coalition had worked, the socialists, led by Largo Caballero and Indalecio Prieto, inclined toward open revolt. Azana deplored the trend but could not stop it. Socialists joined syndicalists and communists in protests and strikes, and Prieto helped to secure arms for the labor unions of the north. In October 1934, a cabinet reshuffle brought three right-wingers into the government and precipitated a general strike. In Barcelona, rebels proclaimed the Catalan state as part of a federal republic and urged the establishment of a provisional anti-fascist government in the city. When the military commander refused to join them, they quickly gave up. In Asturias, on the other hand, some six thousand rebels, mostly miners equipped with Prieto's armaments, converged on Oviedo, where a savage civil war raged for several days. It was put down in the government's favor only after hardened troops had been imported from Morocco for the purpose and well over four thousand people, the majority civilians, had been killed or wounded. The weeks that followed were darkened with martial law, the wholesale arrest of government opponents (including Azana, despite his disapproval of the rebellion), and general political futility and confusion.

By the beginning of 1936, the radical-conservative coalition, like the republican-socialist one before it, had foundered. Moderation had failed. A general election seemed the only hope of sorting things out, but it was hardly a bright one. In February the people went to the polls with an unenviable choice: on one side, a so-called popular front of republicans, socialists, communists and others, and, on the other, the entrenched reaction of the right. The first excluded all real hope of order, the second of progress. Whoever won, Spain herself could scarcely help but lose; and, when the votes showed an almost even balance, the situation relapsed into chaos. In fact, the electoral system gave the left a parliamentary majority, but, though Azana was again raised to authority, its militants were more concerned with destroying than governing. In the first four months of office, the popular front government was asked to answer for more than 250 murders, the burning of nearly as many buildings (including 170 churches and 10 newspaper offices) and more than 300 strikes. Extremists of the right retaliated in kind. The Falange Español, a fascist organization founded by José Antonio Primo de Rivera, son of the late dictator, pledged to overthrow the republic by violence, looking to Europe's other fascist regimes for assistance.

Monarchist opinion sought a different outlet. José Antonio, embittered by Alfonso's failure to support his father toward the end of the directorate, was no monarchist, and a substantial body of conservative sentiment aligned itself with Calvo Sotelo. Sotelo emerged as the prime mover of the opposition in parliament. While the fascists and their counterparts of the left now engaged in uninhibited gang warfare, the leaders of the armed forces hovered on the brink of another *pronunciamiento*, uncertain of the reliance they could place in their regiments. Events did not await their last deliberations. On July 12, 1936, a lieutenant of the republican shock police, the *guardias de asalto*, was murdered. His comrades swore vengeance. At about three o'clock on the morning of the thirteenth, the leader of the parliamentary opposition was roused from his apartment in a fashionable quarter of Madrid by a carload of *asaltos* and asked to accompany them to police headquarters. Apprehensively, Calvo Sotelo accepted the invitation. He would, he told his family, be in touch as soon as he knew what was wanted—"unless these gentlemen are going to blow my brains out!" With Calvo Sotelo in the police vehicle, its driver rammed his foot on the throttle and the party moved off at top speed.

Not long afterward, the vehicle pulled up at Madrid's east cemetery and the attendant was asked to take charge of a body. Two bullets had entered the back of the neck at point blank range. The attendant was only mildly interested. Violent death had become too commonplace to surprise him. It was not until the following afternoon that the victim's identity became known in Madrid and the militants of both sides clamored for weapons.

Four nights after Calvo Sotelo's murder, one of the youngest and most ambitious of Spain's army generals boarded a Canary Islands boat at Tenerife, bound for neighboring Las Palmas. Short and swarthy, with thick eyebrows and large, remarkably bright eyes, Francisco Franco was regarded in many quarters as a model modern soldier. Born at El Ferrol in the extreme northeast of the peninsula, the son of a naval paymaster of modest achievement, he had turned to the army when the navy academy of his first choice had been lacking in vacancies. From that day, he had not swerved from the path of advancement. Solemn and abstemious, Franco had not wasted his time drinking, or with women, or in the fashionable lounges frequented by fellow officers. His career had been everything. In a service riddled with lethargy and incompetence, such dedication could hardly fail to bring notice. Distinguishing himself on campaign in Morocco, Franco had become in turn the youngest captain, major, colonel and general in the army—indeed, for a time the youngest general in Europe. Under Primo de Rivera's government, he had been appointed director of the general military academy where he preached the "sufferings, hardships and sacrifices" of the military life and taught his cadets "never to complain, or tolerate complaints." As adviser to the war minister Diego Hidalgo, of the radical-conservative alliance, he had played an important role in crushing the Asturian revolution of 1934. Unsurprisingly, the popular front government had decided to consign him to the background, restricting him to isolated Tenerife, where Franco had become a cautious conspirator in the mooted *pronunciamiento* centered on the exiled José Sanjurjo.

Events in Spain had forced the plotters to move quickly. While Sanjurjo prepared to leave Portugal and take general command, other officers in barracks throughout the country awaited the signal to rise. Franco had been assigned command of the forces in Morocco, a private aircraft having been chartered in England to fly him from the Canaries to Africa. On receiving word that the plane had arrived at Las Palmas, ostensibly on a pleasure flight, it had remained for him to arrange a plausible cover for his inter-island movement. Oddly enough, the military governor of Las Palmas had at this point accidentally shot himself dead on a target range. Somberly, Franco had phoned the War Department in Madrid and obtained permission to attend the funeral.

He was still at the funeral when a telegraph from Melilla brought news that a leakage in the conspiracy there had forced the plotters to act immediately and seize the city. Again, the revolution had been nudged on by fate. At five o'clock on the morning of July 18, having established martial law on the islands, Franco issued a manifesto from Las Palmas on behalf of the rebels, calling on the army to rise, and promising a better order when the coup was complete. What form that order would assume was unspecified, but one thing was certain: no careerist so dedicated as Franco would have burned his boats in such a fashion without envisaging a radical advance of his position—and Franco was frankly authoritarian with connections in both traditionalist and Falangist camps. Radio Madrid replied by denouncing the rebellion as an "absurd plot" which the government would crush with alacrity. As the day progressed, however, risings made ground on both sides of the Mediterranean. In Seville, General Quiepo de Llano, an avid revolutionary, obtained the surrender of the civil governor by placing artillery in the city center. He had few troops, but an imperious old-guard manner, and his fruity voice was soon heard on the local radio swearing death to "all dogs who resist." By evening, Cádiz, Córdoba, Jerez and Algeciras, among other places, were also largely under the control of the military rebels. So were the remaining centers in Morocco. Franco now flew, as first planned, to Africa.

The second day of the rebellion produced much confusion. Garrisons rising in the north and other areas found themselves sometimes threatened, sometimes encouraged by a militant and impassioned populace. At Pamplona, six thousand men of all ages, wearing the red berets, medals, and crucifixes of the *Requetes*, an organization founded by the Carlists in the nineteenth century, offered their services to the rebel General Emilio Mola, who took over the city to scenes of religious fervor. In Barcelona, by contrast, a rebel division was overwhelmed by armed workers. In Madrid, the main strength of the rebel garrison was trapped and overpowered before it could leave barracks. On both sides, radio stations blared exhortations. The same confusion was reflected in the navy. On a number of vessels, the men responded to admiralty messages by turning on senior ranks suspected of complicity in the rebellion. The officers of the battleship *Jaime Primero* were killed to a man in an astonishing fight with the crew at sea, and an extraordinary fleet, mainly commanded by its lower ranks, appeared off the coast of North Africa. Unsure of the intentions of individual vessels, Franco ordered: "Tell our batteries to fire a shot across the bows of any ship that behaves suspiciously. If she doesn't answer, sink her."

If neither the rebel generals nor the government yet realized that they stood at the beginning of a long and agonizing civil war, it was soon obvious that early expectations of success had been unduly optimistic on both sides. Each had underestimated the wells of passion, the extremes of animosity flooding the country. From the first, the horrors inflicted by Spaniard on Spaniard were appalling. Among the early terrors observed by the United States ambassador, Claude G. Bowers, was the rebel bombing of such places as Irún and San Sebastián. Shortly afterward, he learned that the popular front authorities there had announced their decision to shoot five hostages for every bomb victim. As the war progressed, both sides practiced the arbitrary and wholesale execution of prisoners. Foreign embassies and consulates were besieged by terrified Spaniards in fear for their lives for no better reason than that they held the wrong political opinions. Meanwhile, a rough geographical pattern had emerged from the early phases of the rising. By and large, the government forces, variously described as republicans, loyalists, or (by their enemies) "reds," had retained control of most of that portion of Spain below the central cordillera, including Madrid, plus Catalonia and the coastal and mountain regions of Asturias and the Basque provinces. The rebels, or so-called nationalists, remained unchallenged in Morocco, controlled the western extremity of Andalusia with ports at Cádiz and Algeciras, and were spread widely through Aragon, Navarre, Old Castile, and Galicia in the north. Since the republicans held both the sea between Morocco and Andalusia and the land between their enemies in the north and south of the peninsula, the nationalist forces were dispersed under three separate commanders: Franco, Llano, and Mola.

On July 20, a small aircraft revved-up in a field near Lisbon, and General Sanjurjo prepared to leave Portugal to take his place as generalissimo of the rebellion. The moment had been greeted with much emotion by the friends of his exile. They had welcomed the arrival of the little plane from northern Spain with tears and a rendering of the *Royal March*. Now, as the general perched beside the heavy luggage he had insisted on loading despite the pilot's better judgment, he felt the engine labor and saw the trees at the edge of the field draw close. Suddenly, the propeller was threshing the branches. The machine lurched and burst into flames. The titular head of the rebellion was dead. With Mola preoccupied on the wide and precarious front in the north, and Llano lacking the personal stature of a potential *supremo*, Franco was strongly placed as a candidate for the rebel leadership. He had first, however, to establish himself on the mainland, and his immediate concern was to transport the army of Morocco across the strait. To this end, he had already sent requests to Italy and Germany for transport planes. Within a few days of Sanjurjo's death, these were landing in Africa from both countries, while extra men and material followed by sea from the sympathetic Axis powers.

In the months to come, German air and technical support was to prove especially valuable to the nationalists. The Nazi forces which supported Franco were highly skilled in modern warfare, and their so-called Condor Legion of some six thousand crack troops proved formidable, as did their bomber squadrons. The main supply of foreign arms, however, came to Franco from Italy. Forty thousand Italians were landed in one six-week period, fully equipped and with tanks. Against this rebel aid, the republicans received help, mainly in advisers and material, from Russia, and were obliged to import second-rate arms from various agents in the Middle East. While Soviet citizens never served as combatants in significant numbers, Russia played an active part as time went on in helping to organize the main source of foreign aid to the republic, the international brigades. Altogether, some forty thousand volunteers joined the international brigades, many as communists, others as democrats, liberals or simply antifascists. A large number came from countries, including the western democracies, pledged by their governments to nonintervention. Several thousand were fugitives from the Axis countries themselves. When the rolls were called, Frenchmen topped the lists pretty easily, with Americans and Britons well represented. From Paris, the chief recruiting center, the path led around, or unofficially through, the Pyrenees to Albacete, on the southeasterly plain of La Mancha, where the training took place. The advantage, it now seemed, must go to the first side to organize as a coherent and unified fighting force. The government had started with an army of eager but undisciplined and untrained civilians; the rebels had started with an army of demoralized soldiers. All over the peninsula, troops had found their officers in bitter dispute, their barracks surrounded by angry fellow countrymen. The crucial question was whether or not the nationalist commanders could unite and invigorate the army behind them before the republican leaders could exploit their superior numbers. Franco's transport planes provided the former with a flying start.

Once the army of Morocco was across the strait, the rebels had established a vital lead. Adolf Hitler commented later: "Franco should put up a monument to the Junkers 52. It is to this aircraft that the Spanish revolution owes its victory." (The Junkers 52 was a classic transport plane of the period, and during the world war that followed.) Certainly, from the time Franco could move his headquarters to Seville in early August, the republic was doomed to the defensive. The next aim of the Africa forces was a land link with Mola before turning their front to Madrid. An advance north to Mérida, led by veterans of the foreign legion, was accomplished with little opposition. At each place they occupied, the nationalists reopened churches, held services, and generally contrived to give the movement the appearance of a crusade—an odd twist of history, since many of the troops from Africa were Moors. At the old walled town of Badajoz, near the Portuguese border, they met the first stiff resistance. An assault force of the legion, singing its regimental hymn as it advanced, was decimated by republican machine guns. Fresh attacks carried the fighting to the streets of the city, where the legionaries killed everyone suspected of having borne arms against them. Other republican supporters were slaughtered in the bull ring later. Next, the troops from Morocco pushed on to Trujillo and Cáceres, Franco shifting his heaquarters from Seville to the latter town.

With a sequence of military gains behind him, the general could devote time to exploiting his advantage politically. For several weeks, he scarcely moved from the medieval palace in the San Mateo district of Cáceres which he made his billet. Wireless masts were rigged on the ancient battlements; radio and telephonic equipment piled into rooms lined in red damask. In speeches and interviews, Franco reviled the government as un-Spanish and unpatriotic, lauded nationalism as a pure expression of everything noble and glorious in the national spirit, and appealed again and again to the emotionalism of the Spaniard. In his oddly flat and expressionless voice, the message was doubly monotonous. For years, he insisted, Spain had suffered the influence of "a horde of mistaken intellectuals, despising the true and acknowledged thinkers of our race, peering beyond their own frontiers and absorbing the exotic and destructive in other countries." The result of this "raging rationalism," this savoring of "decadent literature," had been the erosion of patriotism in the minds of the teaching classes. Forgetful of the past, these had lost "the most prominent characteristics of our race" and were shameful of the present. Thanks to the nationalist "liberation," however, Spain was reorganizing "within a broad totalitarian concept . . . the establishment of a strong principle of authority . . . Once the moribund suffrage abused by local bosses and tyrannical syndicates is broken up, the national will can in due course express itself by means of those technical institutions and corporations which, proceeding from the very bowels of the country, truly express its needs and ideals."

Often, he worked in his office from eight in the morning until four in the afternoon without pause for food, returning in the evening to continue into the early hours. When his wife, Doña Carmen Polo—a handsome woman of good family connections in Asturias—arrived at the headquarters, she had to wait over an hour to see him. In September, Franco was ready to assume complete command of the rebel cause. By now, the ill-trained republican militia had been overwhelmed in Estremadura and pushed east along the Tagus Valley to Talavera de la Reina, the last town of importance before the capital. One more drive would have carried Franco's regulars to the gates of Madrid. Instead, he embarked on a dramatic diversion. At Toledo, to the south of the capital, a small nationalist garrison had been holding the Alcázar against heavy odds since the initial days of the rebellion. The defense had attracted widespread notice and admiration, and, by turning now to the relief of the defenders, Franco's concern was not entirely based on military priorities.

Colonel Ituarte Moscardo, military governor of the Toledo area, had barricaded himself in the environs of the Alcázar, a fortress-cum-palace above the Tagus, with some three hundred officers and cadets, about a thousand other nationalist supporters, mainly civil guards, and several hundred women and children. There, hopelessly cut off in republican territory, the bearded, patriarchal figure of the colonel had stood to the flag of rebellion, defying all calls to surrender, even when refusal meant the death of his hostage son. For two months, the garrison had been bombed, mined, and sniped, but its ammunition supplies, unlike its larder, were adequate and the besiegers were unable to press home an attack. Between assaults, Moscardo had taken drill parades and, once, even held a fiesta. But, as September drew on, with half the garrison now killed or wounded, the position grew critical. To eke out food rations, the horses and mules in the stables were killed and eaten —with the exception of a single thoroughbred charger which, becoming a symbol of survival, continued to be groomed and tended. One by one, the towers protecting the Alcázar were mined and demolished by the republicans, forcing the defenders to live increasingly in the foundations. On September 20, the socialist leader Largo Caballero visited Toledo to hasten the fall of the citadel. Fire engines loaded with petrol were brought forward, the buildings drenched and set on fire. The northeast turret, one of the remaining bastions, was mined and blown into the Tagus. Finally, republican reinforcements arrived from Madrid for the overwhelming effort. It never took place. On September 27, the weary defenders saw the spearhead of Franco's army on the hills to the north, and the besieging forces began to vanish. Next day, Moscardo paraded his band of bedraggled survivors in front of the rescuers, saluted, and gave the password that had first signalled the military rising.

"What you have done," Franco told the defenders, "will not be forgotten. You have provided a glorious example to the new Spain which will rise from these ruins." The rescue could hardly have been better timed for Franco's purpose. Within hours of embracing Moscardo before the press cameras, he was in Salamanca presenting a junta of nationalist generals with a decree confirming him as "generalissimo" and "head of the government." The first designation was welcomed, but the second, surprising the meeting, had a cooler reception. It was not until the conference adjourned for lunch that the Franco lobby, backed by organized Falangist and Carlist supporters in the city, was able to persuade the junta individually to accept the decree.

One refinement completed the coup. When the announcement was made public on October 1, the agreed title of "head of government" had been altered to "head of state." Nationalist Spain was in no mood to quibble. The relief of Moscardo had raised emotions to fever pitch, and the influx of Axis arms and personnel added to the general tumult and excitement. Salamanca later became Franco's headquarters, thronging with Italian and German officers. "The exchanging of Nazi and Fascist salutes was incessant throughout the day," wrote a visiting British diplomat. "Every few hours there would be news transmissions terminating with the Franco hymn. These had to be listened to in silence. At the first notes of the hymn, all present would spring to their feet and give the Fascist (or Nazi or Falangista) salute with the right arm aloft. In the hotel, I always managed to slip round the corner, or into the gents, to escape this critical moment . . ."

The year 1937 saw substantial nationalist gains in the north and south. The saddle of republican territory on the Cantabrian coast became the target for a determined push by Mola, whose forces, thanks to Axis support, were now well mechanized. On April 28, the ancient Basque market town and shrine of Guernica was occupied after heavy bombing and strafing by German aircraft. The incident caused an international outcry and inspired the Spanish artist Pablo Picasso to echo Goya's protest against war in a painting named after the stricken town. Adolf Galland, a future air ace of World War II who, like many more of Goering's pilots gained valuable experience at the expense of the Spanish republicans, stated later that Guernica was bombed by mistake. But it was by no means the only town subjected to crippling bombardment. The weight of Franco's support was telling. When, after ten weeks of savage fighting, that great prize of the north coast, Bilbao, surrendered to the nationalists, the republican forces in the northern theater lost fifteen thousand men and much of their will to continue resistance. By the end of October, Franco could announce the sector pacified and turn his attention to Aragon. Meanwhile, his troops in the south, heavily supported by Italians, had completed a sweep of Andalusia culminating in the bloody occupation of Málaga.

Rivalries among the parties of the popular front had constantly bedeviled the republic. Málaga itself received no aid from the communist-controlled forces in Murcia because they were frightened of anarchist power in Valencia, while in Barcelona, a powder keg of extremist emotion, the two groups had engaged in civil war between themselves. Starting with an attack on the communists in an anarchist newspaper, it had spread through assassination to open conflict. Machine gunners of both sides took command of the roof tops, opening up not only on each other and on parties attacking their buildings, but on almost everything moving in the streets. Several hundred participants were killed and at least a thousand wounded before an edgy truce was established. Wrote George Orwell, who fought for the republicans, of wartime Barcelona: "Practically every building of any size had been seized by the workers and was draped with red flags or with the red and black flag of the anarchists. Every wall was scrawled with the hammer and sickle and with the initials of the revolutionary parties [of the left]; almost every church had been gutted and its images burnt . . . No one who was in Barcelona then, or for months later, will forget the horrible atmosphere produced by fear, suspicion, hatred, censored newspapers, crammed jails, enormous food queues and prowling gangs of armed men."

In Madrid, the sound of battle announced the approach of the army from Africa. Azana, resigned to the fate of the capital, retired to a mountain monastery at Montserrat, not too distant from the French border, where his increasing withdrawal from the realities of war exasperated members of the cabinet. Reports of the cruel and chaotic conditions of the country were more than the president's fastidious mind could admit. He dismissed them as gangster stories, informing his ministers: "I am of an analytical spirit, you are not." Constitutional rule was already a fiction.

In July, José Giral Pereira, a druggist, had become prime minister, soon to be followed by Largo Caballero, whose government included anarchists and communists. With the approach of the nationalists, the left-wing parties in Madrid had drawn closer together. The evacuation of the government itself to Valencia, in November, was the signal for extremism to grasp political control of the capital.

On November 7, nationalist shells began falling on the western outskirts. The attacking force, some 20,000 strong, was commanded by the officer who had led the relief at Toledo, José Varela, his line of approach parallel to the sluggish Manzares River. This he sought to cross through the northeasterly Casa de Campo, bringing him into the university quarter of the city. As his Moors and legionaries prepared for the assault, Madrid's loudspeakers called the people to the barricades, masses of workers heading for the front line, some armed, some hoping to arm themselves from the dead. Children helped to put up barriers, women formed a defense battalion and fervent appeals were broadcast for those at home to resist attacks on their dwellings, if necessary by pouring boiling liquid from the windows. Overwhelming numbers were ready to resist: all they lacked, as Madrid's aging military commander, General José Miaja, knew only too well, was the training to make resistance really effective. Many had never fired a weapon. A day passed and the shelling of the university area intensified. Calls for total mobilization came from the radio every few minutes. Neutral observers had already pronounced the capital lost to the nationalists when, through the center of the city on November 8 there proceeded the scarcely credible vision of republican soldiers marching briskly in orderly ranks, steel-helmeted, uniformly equipped, even accompanied by cavalry. The first of the international brigades had arrived.

Its numbers were not great. Commanded by a capable Hungarian known as Kleber, it comprised some two thousand Germans, Poles, Frenchmen and Belgians, with a few squads of British machine gunners. But it provided a sorely needed stiffening for the militia, and more were to follow. The battle which ensued for control of the university area raged more than a fortnight. Several times, Varela's veterans penetrated the outskirts, to be repulsed by Kleber's brigade, which lost more than a third of its men in the effort. The continuing struggle, fought floor by floor, foot by foot through lecture halls and laboratories, devastating libraries and shattering scientific equipment, eerily symbolized the cost in civilized progress of Spain's inveterate disunity. Overhead, Nazi fliers dropped high explosive on Madrid with clinical precision, their leaders fascinated to test the effects of the first systematic bombing of a European city in military history. Public service installations were special targets. A thousand citizens perished, but the determination of the defenders grew stronger. Once there was a wave of panic as a squad of Moors burst through to the Plaza de España, but all its members were killed and the appearance of the once-retired General Miaja at the point of battle helped to reassure the militia. Not until the last week of the month did the protagonists admit their exhaustion. Then trenches were dug and the front consolidated near the Manzares.

During the winter of 1937-38, the focus of conflict switched to the far side of the capital, to Teruel, in the eastern hills of the peninsula, where the nationalists threatened the land link between Madrid and Valencia. Men who had sweated in the summer heat of the central plains now froze in the snows of the cordillera. Terrible punishment was suffered by both armies, but the republicans were the poorer in equipment and fared worse. By March, Franco's northern forces, led by tanks of the Condor Legion, were sweeping through Aragon confident of victory. In Catalonia, the position began to look sufficiently critical that summer for the republican war council at Barcelona to countenance something in the nature of a do-or-die gamble.

In May 1937, the premiership had passed to the former minister of finance, Juan Negrín, a doctor of medicine by profession, with a distinguished scientific career behind him. A moderate socialist, he had worked hard to curb the power of the extremists. Now it seemed likely his efforts had been in vain. His plan, submitted to a supreme committee of officers and ministers, was to launch an all-out offensive across the Ebro River from the north in the hope of restoring contact with the central forces of the republic. It was especially desperate (indeed, fatal as it turned out) since it would stretch the diminishing war supplies in Catalonia to the utmost. Nevertheless, on the dark night of July 25, the loyalist forces crossed the river, some by boat, some on pontoons, some actually swimming in their eagerness to take part in a republican offensive, and the decisive battle of the civil war was engaged.

The ferocious desperation of the attack took nationalist Spain by surprise. Superseding a mood of confidence verging on complacency, it caused serious concern among Franco's supporters, his leadership coming under fire in some quarters. During the next two months there were moments when many nationalists seemed almost despondent. The looming international crisis of Munich, portending a European war that could bring French troops over the Pyrenees, did nothing to offset their worries. But the republicans lacked the power to sustain the offensive and were forced to dig in before achieving their objective. Bogged down in trench warfare, they lost both heart and initiative and could only wait in apprehension for Franco's counterattack. The blow fell at the beginning of October, driving, as had the Cid Campeador's thrust of nine hundred years earlier, clean through to the Mediterranean. By February 1939, Catalonia, cut off from the south, was subdued, a divided Barcelona presenting little trouble to the nationalists. Madrid's position was hopeless. Now racked by the type of secondary civil war that had previously scarred the eastern city, it fell easily to Franco at the end of March, soon followed by Valencia and the remaining republican cities. Negrín, among other popular front leaders, escaped to France, where Azana was to die not many months later. On April 1, the triumphant generalissimo broadcast his last bulletin of the hostilities. "The war," declared the *supremo* laconically, "is over."

Including exiles, Spain had lost a million of her population in three years and spent the equivalent of 3000 million pounds (at the current valuation) on her own destruction. Something like six hundred thousand people had died as a result of the Civil War, of whom perhaps a hundred thousand had been executed without proper trial or otherwise murdered. Yet still, for all the madness, a brotherhood of Spaniards survived. In the course of the savage Ebro battle, the chaplain of a Navarrese regiment had been surprised by the lack of response when he had led an evening prayer "for our dead." Asking what was wrong, he was told: "We want a prayer not only for our own dead but for the dead of our brothers on the other side." Once more, Spain faced the challenge of uniting in a new life.

Epilogue

According to Spanish tradition, the Gallego, or man from Galicia, is austere, inscrutable, and cunning. No one knows what goes on in his head. No one can be sure what he will do next. And when he has done it, the odds are it will still be hard to tell what has happened. By such a reckoning, Francisco Franco, the new chief, or caudillo, was every sixty-three inches of his person a Gallego. Unlike the better known dictators of the thirties, he did not harangue. Franco appeared in public no more than was absolutely necessary, and when he did so his round face was impassive, his rare and fleeting smile an enigma. To the world at large, he gave away nothing. His brief audiences for foreigners, conducted strictly in accordance with protocol, became famed for their brevity and unyielding stiffness. Upon this dour and little-known soldier fell the task of raising Spain from the ruins. His first problem, the sticky one of reconciling the apparently irreconcilable elements of his wartime support, revealed the essentially pragmatic style of his politics. Franco had already, by the end of the Civil War, arrested one leader of the Falange, Manuel Hedilla, for insubordination, and drawn up a policy which, though generally termed Falangist, was in fact a typical Franco compromise.

The state envisaged was totalitarian, anticapitalist, anti-Marxist; a unitary structure in which separatism was a cardinal sin and the gradualness of social evolution in Spain an implicit feature. In place of trades unions appeared the "vertical" syndicate, a Falangist proposal stipulating joint employer-employee representation at all levels. There were, however, sweeteners for the traditionalists. Catholicism was supported as the official religion, while, as time went on, the idea was allowed to spread that an eventual restoration of the monarchy was not out of the question. Few could object to the avowed principles of the state—to defend the dignity, integrity, and liberty of all Spaniards, with special regard to the family as a basic institution—though the accompanying obligation to obey the laws of the regime and uphold the caudillo presented many with a nice contradiction. Above all, the army, the element which alone could ensure Franco's absolute authority, was nurtured and idealized.

Economic recovery, as Ferdinand VI had demonstrated so constructively, meant steering clear of foreign wars, and all the general's stubbornness and guile would be needed to keep Spain from the final disaster of involvement in the second world conflict. The nation was in no condition to take more punishment. As the British ambassador, Sir Samuel Hoare, reported in June 1940: "Famine is the overwhelming fear in Spain and with good reason, for in any other country except Spain I should say that the country is already very near it." At the same time, Spanish defenses were unprepared to reinforce a policy of neutrality with armed strength, and the collapse of France made a German entry of Spain appear imminent. Franco forestalled it with ostentatious signals of good will to Hitler. The caudillo's own brother-in-law, the Falangist leader Serrano Suñer, was appointed foreign minister. A suave man of calculated charm and driving ambition, Serrano Suñer's pro-Nazi sentiments were as familiar as his fascist-saluting minions. After a tour of Germany, where he demonstrated the warmest of feelings toward the regime, he invited Heinrich Himmler to Madrid and entertained the Gestapo chief like a crown prince. Alone among foreign diplomats, the German representatives, Baron and Baroness von Stohrer, were on intimate terms with Franco and his wife. Allied diplomats, who had the greatest difficulty in arranging interviews with the caudillo, were disconcerted to find framed portraits of Hitler and Mussolini adorning his office. At the same time, the Spanish press, which gave little space to communiqués from the Allies, was encouraged to run the wildest attacks on Winston Churchill and the British government.

But, on the question of actually entering the war, Franco kept hedging. In October 1940, Hitler traveled as far as Hendaye, on the Pyrenean frontier, to meet the Spanish leader. It was an unusual gesture from the Fuehrer, and generally regarded as the stage setting for Franco's enlistment as a junior partner of the Axis. If so, Hitler misjudged the man he was up against. After the fulsome pro-Axis propaganda from Madrid, the Nazi leader was surprised to be kept waiting half-an-hour while his Spanish guest allegedly satisfied an abnormal thirst for after-lunch coffee. Having set the interview off on the wrong foot, Franco seems to have parried Hitler's demand for an alliance by stipulating territory in North Africa as part of the bargain price. According to the caudillo, Spanish expansion in Africa, like the recovery of Gibraltar, was "a duty and a mission." But he also knew that Hitler cherished North Africa for himself, and if the shrewd Gallego sought a further delay in developments he had picked the right subject. He had also picked the right moment, for the guns Hitler needed for a move through Spain to Gibraltar had been diverted to the east by British successes in Greece. When the German leader refused to discuss Spanish claims until Franco had committed his country to belligerence, the result was an impasse. Franco returned to Madrid with his hand intact; Hitler fumed over a wasted journey. He would rather have his teeth out, he declared later, than submit to another confrontation with the Spaniard.

In the summer of 1941, Hitler's invasion of Russia was greeted in Spain as an even more comforting diversion of German arms from the Pyrenees. It gave Franco the added satisfaction of posturing in his familiar role as the enemy of communism and anti-Christ, and he actually sent a Spanish division to the Russian front. During the following months, he became as vociferously pro-Axis as ever in his career. In July, he warned the United States to keep out of Europe, repudiated economic aid from America and Britain, denounced "outworn democracy" and declared that the Allies inevitably would be beaten. Speaking to an audience of army officers in Seville, he averred that for twenty years Germany had been the defender of European civilization, and that if

Berlin were ever to be threatened a million Spanish soldiers would be ready to help the German people. Serrano Suñer made the most of the prevailing climate, rebuffing American diplomats, congratulating the Japanese on Pearl Harbor, and inciting a crowd of Falangist supporters to attack the British embassy.

Even in this atmosphere of Axis certainty, however, Franco's native caution was active. Despite Falangist attacks on Portugal for her friendship with Britain, the caudillo had quietly signed a treaty of nonaggression with his neighbor. This had been carefully played down in the Spanish press. He had moved cannily, too, on trade agreements with the United States and Britain, badly needing their oil, rubber, and wheat.

In July 1942, a year after declaring the war lost to the Allies and proclaiming "Europe's new order," he observed in his annual council speech that the form of government suited to one nation was not of necessity suited to another. The promised Axis victory did not seem any closer, and a hint of appeasement toward the Allies was in order. By now, Serrano Suñer had begun to overstep his usefulness, so dominating the political stage that many Spaniards wondered if the persuasive foreign minister were not in fact the master of his remoter brother-in-law. The view was not diminished by the dictator's disinclination to parade in public. Most of the time, Franco lived and worked in the seclusion of the relatively modest palace of El Pardo, an old shooting lodge of the kings' a short distance northwest of the capital. Here, in what remained of the ilex forest once haunted by Charles IV and his shotgun, the caudillo could indulge his own partiality for killing rabbits, deer, and partridge. With armed guards at every corner, and Moorish cavalry covering the gates, at least he was safe.

Those who doubted Franco's grip were disillusioned in the autumn. For some time reports had circulated of a military coup to restore the monarchy, and, in September, a bomb was thrown at the minister of the army, General Varela, well known for his traditionalist sympathies. Varela escaped injury, and the crime was attributed to Falangist youths, a number of whom had associations with Serrano Suñer. Franco exploited the incident with characteristic subtlety. Both Serrano Suñer and Varela were relieved of their ministries, thus killing two birds with a seemingly impartial stone, and their places taken respectively by the Generals Jordana and Asensio. Since Jordana was sympathetic toward America and Britain, while Asensio, though inclined to the Axis, was less emphatically pro-Nazi than his predecessor, the foreign outlook had been modified discreetly in favor of the Allies. As a master touch, Franco assumed leadership of the wayward Falange in person. Two months after this internal crisis, his equivocal foreign policy faced a crucial test with the Allied landing in North Africa, virtually on Spain's back doorstep. He handled the situation coolly, with a minimum of comment. At nine o'clock on the morning of Sunday, November 8, the American ambassador, Carlton Hayes, presented him with a letter from President Roosevelt announcing the offensive, then just commencing. "General Franco, when I saw him, was very calm and cordial," Hayes wrote later. "He showed considerable interest, as a military man, in the landings, and did not conceal his admiration of the strategy involved. He expressed appreciation of the Allied guarantees (of peaceful intent towards Spain and her territories) and said that he accepted them." Not long afterward, diplomatic circles made what they could of a request from the caudillo for a private screening of the Hollywood film *Gone with the Wind* at El Pardo.

Though the Falangist press was still firmly pro-Axis, and Franco continued to flatter Hitler, the caudillo now became increasingly ready to do business with the Allies. By leaving his markets open, he cashed in heavily on the resulting auction in Spanish war goods. Both America and Great Britain engaged in policies of "pre-emptive" buying to keep important commodities from the Axis. By the end of 1942, Spain was much stronger than she had been in 1940, and Franco could possibly contemplate holding the line of the Ebro should the Germans try to break through. Ties with Portugal, strengthened by the forming of a so-called "Iberian Bloc," were no longer muffled but ostentatiously advertised. In March 1943, Franco established a nominal cortes which, though largely appointive, included a considerable number of prominent monarchists. They were not, however, encouraged to step out of line. When twenty-five members signed a petition requesting the restoration of the monarchy, most of them were deprived of office and either jailed or exiled.

As the year progressed, Franco adjusted warily to the changing fortunes of the belligerents. By midsummer he was propounding, for Allied consumption, a policy based on what he maintained were three separate wars. The first war, he explained, was between Germany and Italy on the one hand and the English-speaking countries on the other. In this, he professed neutrality. The second was the Pacific war, in which his sympathies were with the Americans, for he regarded the Japanese as dangerous imperialists and "fundamentally barbarian." The third was the war against communism, and in this he was anti-Russian, for if communist Russia prevailed over the Germans it would eventually dominate all Europe. Nevertheless, by autumn Franco had responded to American and British pressure for the withdrawal of the Spanish division from the Russian front, and was preparing seriously for an Allied victory. On October 1, the "Day of the Caudillo," he announced that the Falange was neither a program nor an ideology, nor should it be connected with any foreign system. The regime was essentially Spanish, he said, and unafraid of meeting the challenge of changing conditions. The Spanish press had already shifted its viewpoint. Allied diplomats called to the inner sanctum of El Pardo observed that the pope's portrait was "in," those of the Axis dictators were "out."

By the time the war in Europe was over, Franco was referring to Spain as an "organic democracy" and the Falangists could not boast a single member in the cabinet. In keeping with the new image, the caudillo pronounced an amnesty for thousands of political prisoners, "offenders" of the Civil War now six years past. All the same, the world looked distastefully upon the Spanish dictator. In 1946, his government was explicitly barred from the United Nations, its members being advised to withdraw their diplomats from Madrid. Franco, it was thought, could not long survive such widespread displeasure. Ostracized on all sides, deprived of the funds badly needed to refloat her economy, nationalist Spain must very soon see the light. The world underestimated the resilience of the taciturn Gallego. It also misread the spirit of many ordinary Spaniards, who might not care to be told what to do from within, but cared a great deal less to be told from without. Gradually, foreign governments began to reconsider their policy. In 1950 the United Nations, prompted by the Latin American republics of Peru and Bolivia, lifted its earlier ban. The same year, the United States of America undertook to loan Franco rather more than half a million dollars, citing his anticommunist attitude. The increasing friction between capitalist and communist ideologies made a big difference to Franco's fortunes. As the cold war intensified, he was not slow to exploit American anxiety to obtain bases in Spain, now driving a hard bargain to gain substantial aid, military as well as economic.

Greatly strengthened, Francisco Franco could afford a few pointed references to foreign attitudes in the past. In 1952, he observed with some relish that Spain was "sought after by those who have hitherto scorned us." To add spice to the sauce, he revived the old claim to Gibraltar, a popular cause with all Spaniards. For home consumption, there was an occasional note of magnanimity. In 1954, he went so far as to agree that a grandson of Alfonso XIII, Juan Carlos of Bourbon, then sixteen, should be educated in Spain. Two years later, Morocco, the earliest scene of Spanish adventure abroad, obtained independence. In the sixties, cultural and trade agreements were concluded with countries in the communist bloc, a sophisticated trend in nationalist attitudes. "You cannot deny that Russian communism succeeded in making Russia one of the world's most powerful nations," said Franco. "There must be some good in it." On the peninsula itself, a new and remarkable invasion had taken place. Western prosperity, creating an unprecedented army of European tourists, was turning the warm Mediterranean coast of Spain into an international playground. Millions of visitors a year vouched for Spain's success in the world tourist market. But in other aspects of the economy achievement was less radical. Agricultural and industrial output, though rising, continued in the main to reflect outdated methods. In agriculture especially, modernization posed the problem of heavy unemployment. Planning, therefore, was based largely on long-term results. The reapportioning of land, its sale to peasant farmers on a twenty-year basis and the establishment of industrial training institutes, among other measures, all looked to the future. The doubt remained that progress would keep ahead of rising prices and a growing population.

Meanwhile, despite a spreading and relatively well-to-do middle-class, the mass of people was still inordinately poor by western standards. Franco, depending on their patience and the horrific memory of civil strife, was alternately sanguine and chastening.

"We have created a Spain on her way to higher achievements," he told the nation in 1966. "It will not be difficult, given our present accomplishments and modern technology, to obtain improved material standards. But do not forget that all things material are superficial, and if we are unable to maintain unity, faith and solidarity, the process will fall victim to inanity and disorder. Let Spaniards remember that each nation is a prey to its particular furies . . . Spain's furies are the anarchical spirit, negative criticism, extremism and mutual enmity. Any political system which fosters these defects in its bosom will sooner or later—and probably sooner—wreak havoc on all improvements in the lives of our citizens . . . Abstract political formulas mean little, and have no value until reflected in the personality of the citizen. Every nation must find the formula most adequate to the needs of its temperament."

For thirty years, Franco had pursued his own formula. His insignia, the yoke-and-arrow symbol of the Catholic Sovereigns, purported to underline its pedigree, and certainly the regime had reflected at least the despotism of the old kings. Only the future could reveal its true significance. To a turbulent and divided Spain, it had brought a remarkably long spell of peace. But how deep was that peace; how real the "unity, faith and solidarity"? How adequate to modern needs was the caudillo's long-term social program and his insistence on the inevitability of gradualness? Most urgent of all questions—that which had bedeviled Spain and her absolutist systems so often—what would happen when the one man above all men was gone? In the seventy-fifth year of the life of Francisco Franco, there was not a lot of time in which to ponder.

Notes

Notes on authorities and works relevant to Chapter One:

Andrés Bernáldez: curate of the Andalusian town of Los Palacios and an intimate of many Christian notabilities during the war in Granada; a vivid writer whose work is most useful, perhaps, as a mirror to the popular sentiments and prejudices of the time (which he shared in full). *Historia de los Reyes Católicos.* 2 vols. Seville: Imprenta que Fué de J. M. Geofrin, 1870.

Luis del Mármol Carvajal: Spanish writer of the immediate postconquest period who interrogated Muslims contemporary with Moorish Granada and may have seen the capital much as it was at the time of the war. *Historia del rebelión y castigo de los Miscos del Reyno de Granada.* Málaga: J. Rene, 1600.

Antonio de Lebrija: versatile and liberal scholar, born Andalusia 1444, studied at Bologna, Italy, and subsequently became a professor of the Spanish university of Alcalá de Henares. His chronicle, though based on the work of Pulgar (see below), contains many facts and observations of his own. Lebrija's *Latin Chronicle.*

Pietro Martire: Italian nobleman and scholar of Milanese extraction who visited Spain in 1487, where he was well regarded by Isabella, and stayed to witness the sieges of Baza and Granada. *Epistolario* in *Documentos inéditos para la historia de España* vol. 39. Madrid: La Viuda de Calero, 1880.

Gonzalo Fernández de Oviedo y Valdés: born 1478, he joined the royal court as a page and was present, though still a boy, during the closing stages of the Moorish war. He later became official historiographer of the Indies. *Las Quincuagenas de la nobleza de España.* Madrid: M. Tello, 1880.

Alonso de Palencia: scholar, politician, and man of the world, Palencia was already a royal chronicler on Isabella's accession and was still writing in 1492. *Crónica de Enrique IV.* Madrid: Hernando, 1904.

Hernando del Pulgar: one of the most important authorities for the war in Granada, much of which he witnessed at first hand, having been confirmed as national historiographer by Isabella in 1482. *Crónica de los Reyes Católicos.* 2 vols. Madrid: Espasa-Calpe, 1943.

Notes on authorities and works relevant to Chapter Two:

Since it would be quite impossible to summarize the documentary evidence for so great a period at suitable length, a brief selection must suffice, both for early and later sources. The reader needing further bibliographical detail is referred to Benita Sánchez Alonso's *Fuentes de la historia española e hispano-americana* Madrid: Consejo Superior de Investigaciones Cinetíficas, 1952 or the *Diccionario de historia de España.* Madrid: Revista de Occidente, 1952.

Primary authorities: The earliest writer to give a detailed and surviving account of the ancient tribal divisions of the peninsula was the Greek geographer Strabo, born about 63 B.C. and still writing some twenty years after the birth of Christ. Though he never went to Spain, Strabo was able to base his thesis on firsthand Roman sources. Among the many classical authors to provide material on early Spain were such familiar names as Caesar, Livy, Lucan, Pliny, Tacitus and Appian, and, in the early Christian period, the historian Crosius and the poet Prudentius. For collections of works see the *Siscriptiones Hispaniae Latinae* in the *Corpus inscriptionum Latinarum,* vol. II and supplements, 1869, 1892, 1896, and the *Inscriptiones Hispaniae Christianae* and supplement, Berlin, 1871, 1900—both works edited by E. Hübner.

The story of the Visigoths in Spain was woven into the literature of a number of rugged scribes who worked in particularly hazardous times. Among them, Gregory of Tours, a courageous cleric of the sixth century who ended his life as governor of that town, maintained a prolific output of historical work though he frequently had to defend his own name and the security of Tours against enemies within the town and without. In Spain itself, Isidore of Seville, a noted encyclopedist who did much to preserve Greek and Roman culture against the barbarians, also produced historical data for the period, as did such others as Idatius, John of Biclaro, and Julian of Toledo. Bibliographies can be found in A. Molinier's *Les Sources de l'histoire de France,* vol. I, pp. 55–63, 91–94, and R. Ballester y Castell's *Las Fuentes narrativas de la historia de España,* pp. 13–28.

Alfonso X, the Learned, dubbed "the father of Castilian prose" after his unstinting efforts to assemble knowledge from many sources into the vernacular, initiated the most influential history of the Spanish Middle Ages, the *Crónica general de España* or *Primera crónica general*. Alfonso carried the work from the beginnings of Spanish history to the year 711, and its extension, after his death, to 1289 provided a Christian slant on the reconquest. Book IV of the *Crónica general* is one of the authorities for the life of the Cid. Another is the epic *Poema de mio Cid*, by an anonymous twelfth-century writer, which, though frequently at variance with recorded history, contains much that is factually convincing. On the Arab side, the Cid was noted in the *Dhakira* of Ibn Bassam and Ibn Alkama's account of the conquest of Valencia, while his marriage settlement, executed in Latin, provided history with a sample of his writing and his signature.

The outstanding historian of events in the fourteenth century, López de Ayala, lived through the reigns of four Castilian kings, Peter I, Henry II, John I, and Henry III, and left personal witness to them all in his chronicles. One of the most cultivated and versatile Spaniards of his time, López distinguished himself as statesman, soldier, and poet, as well as historian, and became the grand chancellor of the realm. His method of writing history as he personally encountered it encouraged a flock of imitators. Another statesman-writer, Francisco de Moncada, though belonging to a much later period (he was not born until the second half of the sixteenth century), was to leave one of the best accounts of the eastern adventures of the Catalans. While his *Espedición de los Catalanes y Aragoneses contra Turcos y Griegos* (Madrid: Biblioteca de Españoles, 1852) is not strictly of basic authority, it is a valuable source. Both scholarly and well traveled, Francisco was at one time ambassador at the imperial court.

Among authorities for the events in fifteenth-century Castile up to the time of Isabella, three chronicles, the *Crónica de Juan II* in *Documentos inéditos para la historia de España* vols. 99–100, Madrid: La Viuda de Calero, 1877; the *Crónica de Alvaro de Luna* Madrid: Imprenta de A. de Sancha, 1784; and the *Crónica de Enrique IV* in the *Colección de escritores castellanos*, Madrid: Hernando, 1904–9, relate directly to the chief characters in Isabella's background.

Notes on authorities and works relevant to Chapter Three:

The most revealing literary authority on Columbus was Columbus, whose writings, so far as they survive, are full of color and character. An account of his first voyage of discovery in his own words exists in the form of a circular letter sent to members of the court (including Luis de Santangel) on his return. His important journal kept on the voyage was badly impaired by its first "editor," Bartolomé de las Casas, whose abridged version, unlike the original, is still available. No details of the second voyage exist by the hand of Columbus (three other participants, Diego Chanca, Michele de Cuneo, and Melchior Maldonada, left accounts), but a report on the third voyage contained in a manuscript in the hand of Las Casas purports to record the words of Columbus. Among the letters of Columbus are several to the Spanish sovereigns and others to Pope Alexander VI, the Genoese ambassador, Diego Columbus, Fonseca, and a number of friends. Columbus also left a will, a book of prophecies, and copious marginal notes in his copies of Marco Polo, d'Ailly's Imago Mundi and Aeneas Silvius, all of which are extant. A classified list of 1395 documents appertaining to the life of Columbus can be found in the *Enumeración de libros y documentos concernientes a Cristóbal Colón y sus viages*, published by the Royal Academy of History, Madrid, 1892.

Among the most useful early sources for the life of Columbus and his explorations are a biography written by his son Fernando and surviving in a sixteenth-century Italian version, *Historie del Signor Don Fernando Colombo . . . e vera relatione della vita . . . dell' Ammiraglio D. Christoforo Colombo*, London edition: Dulan and Company, 1867, and a number of sixteenth-century histories of the Spanish colonies in the Americas: Bartolomé de las Casas, *Historia de las Indias* in *Documentos inéditos para la historia de España* vols. 62–66, Madrid: La Viuda de Calero, 1875; Gonzalo Fernández de Oviedo y Valdés, *La Historia general de las Indias*, Madrid: Imprenta de la Real Academia de la Historia, 1851–55; Francisco López de Gomara, *Historia general de las Indias*, Sargossa: Augustin Millan, 1552–53; Antonio de Herrera Tordesillas, *Historia general de las Indias occidentales*, Madrid: N. R. Franco, 1730. Other early sources include the works of Andrés Bernández and Pietro Martire.

Notes on authorities and works relevant to Chapter Four:

Jerónimo Zurita, "grandfather" of Aragonese historians, devoted a substantial body of his work to the reign of Ferdinand the Catholic. Born of aristocratic stock at Saragossa, 1512, and educated at Alcalá, the brilliant and influential Zurita obtained his appointment by the Cortes General of Aragon as national chronicler at the age of thirty-six. His main commission, a history of the Aragonese monarchy from its emergence following the Arab conquest to the death of Ferdinand, involved extensive research at home and abroad and was completed not long before his death in 1580. Among other things, Zurita provided much information on the North African campaign, and, together with Martire, is a principal authority for Philip of Burgundy's brief spell of power in Castile. *Anales de la corona de Aragon*. Saragossa: Diego Durmer, 1610.

Another Alcalá graduate, Alvaro Gómez de Castro, born near Toledo in 1515, is the main authority for the life of Jiménez. Gómez became professor of humanities at Alcalá and was eventually chosen by the university to write the official biography of the cardinal, its founder. With full access to the archives, and to the reminiscences of a number of the cardinal's personal servants, Gómez produced an exceptionally informed, if inevitably flattering, work. *De Rebus gestis a Francisco Ximenio*. Alcalá de Henares: A. de Angulo, 1569.

The Italian wars brought Spanish affairs and personalities into the orbit of a new and fashionable style of balanced, scientific analysis. Italian writers of the period—among them, Machiavelli, Bembo, Guicciardini—could be relatively impartial in discussing the conflict between Spain and France, while, at the same time, closely in touch with developments. Two are especially worth mentioning here:

Paolo Giovio, born Como, Italy, 1483, studied medicine and philosophy at Pavia and Padua before turning historian under the patronage of successive popes. His principal work, the *Historiarum sui temporis* (libri XLV) published in Florence by Torrentino in 1551, covers the period from the invasion of Charles VIII to 1547. Among a number of biographies, he also produced a stylish and valuable life of Gonzalo de Córdoba. *Vita di Gonsalvo Fernando di Cordova, detto il Gran Capitán*, in *Vitae illustrium vivorum*. Florence: Torrentino, 1550.

Marino Sanuto, Venetian senator and an important annalist of the Italian wars, left his major work in the monumental *Diarii*, spanning from 1496, when he was fifty, to 1533, when he died. It was published in fifty-eight volumes at Venice, 1879–1903. Another of his works, *La Spedizione di Carlo VIII*, Venice: M. Visentini, 1883, covered the earlier events of 1494–95.

Not altogether surprisingly, contemporary French accounts of the Neapolitan campaigns were few and often less than frank. French writers of the time still inclined to the fulsome panegyric of the Middle Ages, a style rendered obsolete by the best of the Italians. One notable exception was Phillipe Comines, statesman and historian, whose position as ambassador to Charles VIII at Venice put him right at the pulse of the diplomatic struggle for power in Italy. Though in the event deceived by the timing of the Holy League, the astuteness and perception of his *Memoires*, written between 1489–98 and published in Paris in 1901–3, placed him among the best historians of his era. Another Frenchman, Jean d'Auton, helped to fill in on later events. *Chroniques de Louis XII*. Paris: Laurens, 1889–95.

Among anonymous works, the so-called *Crónica general del Gran Capitán* provides an early Spanish version, fulsome and given to grandiloquence, of the events in Gonzalo's life. *Sumario de los hechos del Gran Capitán*, in *Nueva biblioteca de autores españoles*. Vol. X. Madrid: Bailly-Baillière e Hijos, 1905–12.

Collections of letters and documents:

Re: Gonzalo and the Italian campaigns: *Correspondencia de los Reyes Católicos con el Gran Capitán*. Revista de Archivos, Bibliotecas, y Museos, 3d ser 1916.

Re: Jiménez and the Oran expedition: *Cartas del Cardenal Francisco Ximénez de Cisneros a Diego López de Ayala*, 2 vols. Madrid: Eusebio Aguado 1867–75.

Re: Navarre: *Calendar of Letters, Dispatches and State Papers relating* to *Negotiations between England and Spain*. London: Longmans, Green, 1862–68.

Authorities and works relevant to Chapter Five:

The richness in contemporary accounts of the conquests of Mexico and Peru, particularly the former, have made these enterprises fascinating fields in which to study the conquistadores in action. Cortés told the story of his Mexican venture in a series of dispatches to the Emperor Charles, *Historia de Nueva-España: escrita por su esclarecido conquistador Hernán Cortés*, Mexico: En la Imprenta del Superior Gobierno, 1770 (English trans. ed. F. A. MacNutt, New York and London: G. P. Putnam, 1908). Several others, including his chaplain, Gomara, wrote accounts of the conquest, but it was not until Bernal Díaz, then an old man living in Guatemala, wrote his memoires that the ordinary soldier's viewpoint went on record: *Historia verdadera de la conquista de la Nueva-España*. Madrid: Imprenta del reyno, 1632 (English trans. A. P. Maudslay, *The Discovery and Conquest of Mexico*. London: George Routledge, 1928).

A key witness to events in Peru was Pizarro's cousin, Pedro Pizarro, a boy of fifteen when he joined his older relative under whom he served throughout the conquest. His narrative, brief and to the point, was first published in 1572. *Relaciónes del Descubrimiento y Conquista de los Reynos del Peru*. A more professional and wide-ranging history was provided by Oviedo, official chronicler of the Indies, who was in Panama at the outset of the enterprise (his son took part in the conquest) and had access both to documents and the dramatis personae. *Historia general y natural de las Indias*. Madrid: Imprenta de la Real Academia de la Historia, 1853.

For a contemporary Spanish account of events in the life of the emperor Charles: López de Gomara, *Annals of the Emperor Charles* V. Translated by R. B. Merriman. Oxford: Oxford University Press, 1912.

Authorities and works relevant to Chapters Six and Seven:

A host of contemporary accounts relates to the armada, in which all shades of reliability (or otherwise) are represented, from the most outlandish propaganda and fantasy to detailed objective reports. Medina Sidonia's own statement of the strength of the armada before sailing—not only in ships and personnel, but down to the smallest items of stores and equipment —was published and on sale across Europe before the action in the Channel had commenced. To this, printers contributed their own errors, both intended and unintentional, Catholics inclining to exaggerate the strength, Protestants adding an horripilating inventory of thumbscrews, whips, and other torture implements. The major naval documents for the campaign can be found in *La Armada Invencible* by Cesareo Fernandez Duro, Madrid: Estampas Tipografico de los Sucesores de Rivadeneyra, 1885; *La Armada Invencible* by E. Herrera y Oria, Valladolid: Academia de Estudios

Historico-Sociales de Valladolid, 1929 (these for Spain); and J. K. Laughton's *The Defeat of the Spanish Armada*, Navy Record Society, 1894, for England. Documents from the family archives of the Dukes of Medina Sidonia are given in *El designio de Felipe II* by Gabriel Maura y Gamazo, Duke of Maura, Madrid: Editorial Cultura Clásica y Moderna, 1957.

Spanish documents relating to Drake's raid on Cádiz are also given by Duro and the Duke of Maura, while English documents appear in J. S. Corbett's *The Spanish War*, Navy Record Society, 1897. Among other items on this subject are a chart by William Boroughs (Public Records Office, London) and a report to Pope Sixtus V (in the Vatican records). For more general documents relating to the reign of Philip II, the reader should consult the *Documentos inéditos para la historia de España*, vols. I, III, VI, XV, XXI, XXIV, XL, XCVIII, CI, CIII, CX, CXI, 1842, etc., also *Actes des états généraux des Pays-Bas*, 1576–85, edited by L. P. Gachard, Brussels: Hayez, 1861–66. For the Escorial: Juan de San Geronimo's *Memorias sobre la fundación del Escorial y su fábrica* (in *Documentos inéditos para la historia de España*, vol. VII) and J. de Herrera's *Sumario y breve declaración de los diseños y estampas de la fabrica de Santo Lorencio el Real del Escorial*, Madrid: Pedro Perret, 1589.

Authorities and works relevant to Chapter Eight:

The marked increase of foreign influence in Spain during this period gave rise to a corresponding interest in the land and its people among a wide European public. Soldiers from England, Holland, France, Austria, and elsewhere wrote accounts of their campaigns in the peninsula, travel writers dwelled in detail on points of social interest, diplomats (and even their wives) wrote their memoirs. It was perhaps to these images of a nation caught in the often picturesque and romantic attitudes of decadence that the immense popular fascination of Spain, and in time her unique tourist trade, owed its birth. For intimate descriptions of life in Madrid and its court in the second half of the seventeenth century, much was handed down, however, by the Spanish writer Jeronimo de Barrioneuvo de Peralta, a gossipy priest of insatiable curiosity whose letters to the Dean of Saragossa and others are collected in *Avisos de Barrioneuvo, Colección de Autores Castellanos*, Madrid: M. Tello, 1892. At the same time, a perceptive visitor from Holland, F. van Aersens, was preparing an informative account of his findings in Madrid and elsewhere: *Voyage en Espagne*, Amsterdam: Elzevier, 1666. In addition, a Frenchman named R. A. de Bonnecase de Saint Maurice published a vividly detailed narrative of the city's life: *Relation de l'état et governement d'Espagne* 3 vols., Cologne: P. Marteau, 1667.

Philip IV's regular exchange of letters with the nun Maria, *Cartas de Sor Maria de Agreda y del rey Felipe IV*, Madrid: 1885–86, contribute to a mass of documentation, including, from a British viewpoint, correspondence by Ambassador Richard Fanshawe, *Original Letters of Sir Richard Fanshawe*, London: A. Roper, 1701, amusingly supplemented by the very feminine memoirs of his wife. With the advent of Bourbon rule, the complexity of foreign observation increased. A whole range of European gazettes, journals, and newspapers was turning its attentions to Spain, while there was no shortage of written comment from such participants and on-lookers as Alberoni, the Princess des Ursins, Earl Stanhope, Voltaire, Mme. de Maintenon, Elizabeth Farnese, Baron Ripperda, and the diarist Duke de Saint-Simon. The tireless abuses of Alberoni indulged by the last-named were later offset by a laudatory life, the *Storia del Cardinale Giulio Alberoni*, published by Stephano Bersani, a priest from the same college, at Piacenza, 1861. For an account of Alberoni published in his lifetime: *Histoire du Cardinal Alberoni*, by Jean Rousset de Missy, The Hague: 1719.

Notes on authorities and works relevant to Chapter Nine:

For an absorbing and commendably unprejudiced account of Spanish America at the climax of the colonial period, much gratitude is due to the German naturalist and traveler Alexander von Humboldt, whose wide-ranging curiosity and illuminating comments were in keeping with the great tradition of travel writing set by his early compatriot Adam of Bremen. Free from the animosities coloring most French and English commentators on the subject, Humboldt was generous in praise of Spain's efforts where he felt it to be due. At the same time, though traveling under Spanish patronage, he was not afraid to criticize, as in his description of the conditions suffered by the workers in the mills. In company with Aimé Bonpland, the botanist, Humboldt sailed from La Coruña in 1799 to Cumana, and then to Caracas. By his return to Europe, in 1804, he had explored the Orinoco, spent several months in Cuba, visited Cartagena, crossed the cordilleras to Quito, explored the Amazon on his way to Lima, and lived a year in Mexico. He also made a short visit to the United States. The story of his experiences is told in *A Personal Narrative of Travels to the Equinoctial Regions of the New Continent during the years 1799–1804* (translated by H. M. Williams), 7 vols., London: AMS Press, 1814–29, and, among other works, his *Political Essay on the Kingdom of New Spain* (translated by J. Black), London: AMS Press, 1811–22, an interesting description of Mexico at the end of the colonial period. Among earlier first-hand accounts of the colonial era, the *Compendium and Description of the West Indies* (translated by Charles Upson Clark), Washington, D.C.: Smithsonian Institution, 1942, provides, for comparison, a commentary on Spanish America circa 1600.

Authorities and works relevant to Chapter Ten:

It is interesting that Godoy, to whom much is owed for knowledge of Spain and its court under Charles IV, far outlived the principal associates of his heyday. He was with María Luisa when she died in 1819, and then received an assurance of continuing friendship from her husband ("come and see me whenever you wish"), who, however, survived his wife by only a few weeks. For many years after the royal deaths Godoy was almost destitute, Spain disallowing the legacies bequeathed him by its former monarchs. Eventually, the liberal government of France, under Louis Philippe, granted him a modest pension, and on this he lived quietly in Paris until his own death in October 1851, eighteen years after that of Ferdinand. His memoirs, published in five volumes under the title *Cuenta dada de mi vida politica*, Madrid: I. Sancha, 1836–42, provide a valuable, if not unquestionable, view of events in his period. Among other useful contemporary material is the *Memorias* of Escóiquiz, Madrid: Hernando, 1915, and a three-volume life of Ferdinand published within a decade of his death: *Historia de la vida y reinado de Ferdinand VII*, by D. E. and K. Vays, Madrid: Repullés, 1842.

The most vital documents for the life of Goya are his letters to a lifelong friend, Martín Zapater, a large number of which were published in 1868. Much romance surrounds the activities of Goya, especially a widely reported legend of his alleged intimacy with the handsome Duchess of Alba, sometimes said to have modeled for the famed *Maja Desnuda*. The evidence, however, does not justify such stories.

Authorities and works relevant to Chapter Eleven:

The almost overwhelming bibliography of Simón Bolívar can be studied fully in *Bibliography of the Liberator Simón Bolívar*, compiled in the Columbus Memorial Library of the Pan American Union, Washington, D.C., 1933. The letters, proclamations, and other writings of Bolívar himself have been published in numerous forms including, in Spanish, Simón Bolívar: *cartas del Libertador corregidas conforme a los originales* (edited by V. Lecuna), 10 vols., Caracas: Editorial Gobierno de Venezuela, 1929–30, and, in English, *Selected Writings of Bolívar* (compiled by Vicente Lecuna, edited by Harold A. Bierck, Jr., translated by Lewis Bertrand), 2 vols., New York: Colonial Press, 1951. The letters and documents of other revolutionary leaders can be found in: *Archivo de general Miranda*, 24 vols., Caracas: L. Hernanos, 1929–50; *Cartas de Santander* (edited by Vicente Lecuna), 3 vols., Caracas: Lit. y t.p. del Comercio, 1942; *Paez, archivo 1818–20*, Bogotá: Editorial "El Gráfico," 1939; San Martín, *Documentos del archivo*, 12 vols., Buenos Aires: Comición Nacional del Centenario del Museo Mirre, 1910–19; *San Martín, su correspondencia 1823–50*, Madrid: Bailly-Baillière, 1911.

Notes on authorities and works relevant to Chapter Twelve:

Memoirs, documents, contemporary commentaries, and eyewitness accounts of the Spanish Civil War are profuse, and the types of book available on the subject sufficiently varied to suit most levels of interest. An excellent bibliography can be found in *The Spanish Civil War*, by Hugh Thomas, New York: Harper, 1961, an excitingly readable and thorough reconstruction of the whole episode. Among works which deal with the modern Spanish scene in detail, *Spain*, by Salvador de Madariaga, New York: Scribner's, 1930, and *The Spanish Labyrinth*, by Gerald Brenan, New York: Macmillan, and London: Cambridge, 1943, are both valuable and absorbing.

Bibliography

Addison, J. *Charles the Third of Spain*. Oxford: B. H. Blackwell, 1900.

Aguado Bleye, P. *Manual de Historia de España*. 3 vols. Madrid: 1954–56.

Altamira, Rafael. *History of Spain*. Translated by Muna Lee. New York: Van Nostrand, 1949.

André, Marius. *El fin del imperio español en America*. Barcelona: Editorial Araluce, 1922.

Arbo, Sebastián Juan. *Cervantes*. Translated by Ilsa Barea. New York: Vanguard, 1955.

Armstrong, Edward. *Elisabeth Farnese*. London: Longmans, Green, 1892.

———. *The Emperor Charles V*. London: Macmillan, 1910.

Astrana Marín, Luis. *Cristóbal Colón*. Madrid: Editorial Voluntad, 1929.

Atkinson, W. C. *History of Spain and Portugal*. London: Penguin, 1960.

Azaña y Diez, Manuel. *Mi revelión en Barcelona*. Madrid: Espasa-Calpe, 1935.

Ballester y Castell, R. *Las fuentes narrativas de la historia de españa durante la Edad Media, 417–1474*. Mallorca: Amengual y Muntaner, 1903.

Ballesteros y Beretta, Antonio. *Historia de España y su influencia en la historia universal*. Barcelona: P. Salvat, 1943–48.

Barbagelata, Hugo D. *Bolívar y San Martín*. Paris: P. Landais, 1911.

Baudrillart, Alfred, Cardinal. *Philippe V et la court de France*. 5 vols. Paris: Firmin-Didot, 1890–1901.

Beazley, C. R. *James the First of Aragon*. Oxford: B. H. Blackwell, 1890.

Benzo, Eduardo. *La Libertad de América*. Madrid: Compañia Ibero-Americano de Publicaciones, 1929.

Bertrand, Louis. *Philippe II à l'Escorial*. Paris: L'Artisan du livre, 1929.

—— and Petrie, Sir Charles. *The History of Spain*. London: Eyre & Spottiswoode, 1934.

Blum, N. *Croisade de Ximenes en Afrique*. Oran: (privately printed) 1898.

Boissonnade, Prosper Marie. *Histoire de la réunion de la Navarre a la Castille*.

Paris: A. Picard et fils, 1893.

Bolívar, Simón. *Selected Writings*. Compiled by Vincente Lecuna, edited by Harold A. Bierck, Jr., translation by Lewis Bertrand. New York: Colonial Press, 1951.

Bolós y Saderra, Joaquín de. *La guerra civil en Cataluña, 1872–1876*. Barcelona: R. Casulleras, 1928.

Bourne, E. G. *Spain in America 1450–1580*. New York: Harper, 1904.

Bowers, Claude Gernade. *My Mission to Spain*. New York: Simon & Schuster, 1954.

Brandi, K. *The Emperor Charles V*. Translated by C. V. Wedgewood. New York: Humanities Press, 1929.

Brandt, J. A. *Toward the New Spain*. Chicago: University of Chicago Press, 1933.

Breuil, Henri and Obermaier, Hugo. *The Cave of Altamira at Santillana de Mar, Spain*. Translated by Mary E. Boyle. New York: The Hispanic Society of America, 1935.

Bridge, J. S. C. *A History of France from the Death of Louis XI*. New York: Oxford University Press, 1921–24.

Brown, Vera Lee. *Studies of the History of Spain in the Second Half of the Eighteenth Century.* Northampton, Massachusetts: Smith College, 1930.

Butterfield, Herbert. *The Statecraft of Machiavelli.* London: George Bell, 1940.

Carande Thobar, Ramón. *Carlos V y sus Banqueros.* Madrid: Revista de Occidente, 1943.

Cardell, Carlos. *La Casa de Borbón en España.* Madrid: Agemundo, 1954.

Carpenter, Rhys. *The Greeks in Spain.* New York and London: Longmans, Green, 1925.

Casado, Segismundo. *The Last Days of Madrid.* Translated by Rupert Croft-Cooke. London: Peter Davies, 1939.

Castillejo y Duarte, José. *Wars of Ideas in Spain.* London: John Murray, 1937.

Castro, Américo. *El Pensamiento de Cervantes.* Madrid: Hernando, 1925.

————. *The Structure of Spanish History.* Translated by E. L. King. Princeton: Princeton University Press, 1954.

Chaytor, Henry John. *A History of Aragon and Catalonia.* London: Methuen, 1933.

Ciges Aparicio, Manuel. *España bajo la dinastía de los Borbóns.* Madrid: M. Aguilar, 1932.

Clarke, H. B. *Modern Spain 1815–98.* New York: Putnam, 1906.

Corbett, Sir Julian. *Drake and the Tudor Navy.* 2 vols. London: Longmans, Green, 1898.

Cotte, S. de. *Madame des Ursins, roi d'Espagne.* Paris: Denoel, 1946.

Crawford, J. P. Wickersham. *Spanish Drama before Lope de Vega.* Philadelphia: University of Pennsylvania Press, 1937.

Dahn, Felix. *Die Könige der Germanen,* vols. V–VI. Würzburg: C. A. Fleischmann, 1870–71.

D'Alessio, G. *Bolívar.* Rome: Studium, 1932.

Danvila y Collado, Manuel. *El reinado de Carlos III*. Madrid: El Progreso Editorial, 1892.

D'Auvergne, Edmund B. *Godoy: the Queen's Favorite*. Boston: Badger, 1913.

——. *Queen at Bay: the Story of María Cristina and Don Carlos*. New York: Lane, 1910.

David, Maurice. *Who Was Columbus?* New York: Research Publishing Co., 1933.

Davies, R. Trevor. *The Golden Century of Spain, 1501–1621*. London: Macmillan, 1954.

Davila, V. *Bolívar intelectual y galante*. Mexico: Rafael Ros e hijo, 1942.

Delaborde, Henri François. *L'expédition de Charles VIII en Italie*. Paris: Firmin-Didot, 1888.

Dietrich, Wolfam. *Simón Bolívar*. Hamburg: P. Hartung, 1934.

Diffie, Bailey W. *Latin American Civilization: Colonial Period*. Harrisburg, Pennsylvania: Stackpole & Heck, 1945.

Dixon, Pierson. *The Iberians in Spain and Their Relations with the Aegean World*. London: Oxford University Press, 1940.

Dozy, R. P. A. *Spanish Islam*. Translated and edited by F. G. Stokes. New York: Duffield, 1913.

Enock, C. Reginald. *Peru: Its Former and Present Civilization*. New York: Scribner, 1908.

Entwistle, William J. *Cervantes*. London: Oxford University Press, 1940.

Espinoza, A. M. *The Second Spanish Republic and the Causes of the Counter Revolution*. San Francisco: Spanish Relief Committee, 1937.

Essen, Léon van der. *Alexandre Farnèse*. 5 vols. Brussels: Librairie Nationale d'Art et d'Histoire, 1933–37.

Ferotin, D. M. *El Liber Ordinum de la edad visigoda*. Paris: Firmin-Didot, 1904.

Fitzmaurice-Kelly, James. *Lope de Vega and Spanish Drama.* Glasgow: Gowans & Gray, 1902.

Fonteriz, Luis de. *The Red Terror in Madrid.* London: Longmans, Green, 1937.

Ford, J. D. M. *Main Currents of Spanish Literature.* New York: Holt, 1919.

Forneron, Henri. *Histoire de Philippe II.* 4 vols. Paris: E. Plon, 1882–87.

Fortoul, J. G. *Historia constitucional de Venezuela.* 2 vols. Caracas: Leon Hermanos, 1942.

Galdames, Luis. *A History of Chile.* Translated and edited by Isaac J. Cox. Chapel Hill: University of North Carolina Press, 1941.

García Rives, A. *Fernando VI y Doña Barbara de Braganza.* Madrid: Julio Cosano, 1917.

Giannone, P. *Istoria civile del regno di Napoli.* 6 vols. Naples: M. Lombardi, 1865.

Gimenez-Soter, A. *Fernando el Católico.* Zaragoza: Editorial labor, S. A. Talleres Gráficos Ibero-Americanos, 1939.

Gómez, Carlos A. *La Guerra de España 1936–39.* Buenos Aires: Círculo Militar, 1939.

Gómez de Arteche y Moro, José. *El Reinado de Carlos IV.* 3 vols. Madrid: El Progreso Editorial, 1892–98.

Graham, R. B. C. *José Antonio Páez.* London: Heinemann, 1929.

Grandmaison, Geoffroy de. *L'Espagne et Napoléon.* Paris: E. Plon, Nourrit et Cie, 1908.

Hamilton, E. J. *War and Prices in Spain 1651–1800.* Cambridge: Harvard University Press, 1947.

Harcourt-Smith, Simon. *Alberoni, or The Spanish Conspiracy.* London: Faber, 1943.

Haring, C. H. *The Spanish Empire in America.* London and New York: Oxford University Press, 1947.

Harrison, M. H. *Capitán de América—San Martín*. Buenos Aires: Editorial Ayacucho, 1943.

Hasbrouck, Alfred. *Foreign Legionaries in the Liberation of Spanish South America*. New York: Columbia University Press, 1928.

Herring, Hubert. A *History of Latin America*. New York: Knopf, 1955.

Hill, Constance. *Story of the Princess des Ursins in Spain*. New York: R. H. Russell, 1899.

Houben, H. H. *Christopher Columbus*. Translated by John Linton. London: Routledge, 1935.

Hume, M. A. S. *The Court of Philip IV*. New York: Putnam, 1907.

——. *History of Modern Spain, 1788–1918*. London: Cambridge University Press, 1923.

——. *Philip II of Spain*. New York: Macmillan, 1903.

——. *Queens of Old Spain*. New York: Doubleday, 1906.

——. *Spain; Its Greatness and Decay*. New York: Putnam, 1913.

——. *Two English Queens and Philip*. New York: Putnam, 1908.

Ibarra y Rodrigues, E. *España bajo los Austrias*. Barcelona: Editorial labor, S. A. Talleres Gráficos Ibero-Americanos, 1935.

Ibn-Abd-El-Hakam. *History of the Conquest of Spain*. Gottingen: Sumptibus Dieterichianis, 1856.

Jane, L. C. *The Administration of the Colons in Española*. La Haye: XXIᵉ Congrès International des Américainistes, 1924.

——(trans. and ed.). *Voyages of Christopher Columbus*. London: Argonaut, 1930.

Jurien de la Gravière, E. *La Guerre de Chypre et la Bataille de Lepanto*. 2 vols. Paris: E. Plon, Nourrit et Compagnie, 1888.

Kirkpatrick, F. A. A *History of the Argentine Republic*. Cambridge: Cambridge University Press, 1931.

——. *The Spanish Conquistadores*. London: A. & C. Black, 1934.

Koebel, W. H. *Uruguay*. London: Unwin, 1911.

Koestler, Arthur. *Spanish Testament*. London: Gollancz, 1937.

Lanning, J. T. *Academic Culture in the Spanish Colonies*. New York: Oxford University Press, 1940.

Largo Caballero, Francisco. *Mis recuerdos; cartas a un amigo*. Mexico: Ediciones "Alianza," 1954.

Lawrence, A. W., and Young, J. (eds.) *Narratives of the Discovery of America*. New York: Peter Smith, 1931.

Lema, Marqués de. *Spain since 1815*. Cambridge: Cambridge University Press, 1921.

Lemonnier, H. *Les Guerres d'Italie*; in Laviose, E., *Histoire de France*. Paris: Librairie Hachette, 1903.

Lévi-Provençal, Evariste. *Histoire de l'Espagne musulmane*, vols. I–II. Paris: G. P. Maisonneuve, 1950.

Llampayas, José. *Fernando el Católico*. Madrid: Biblioteca Nueva, 1941.

Madariaga, Salvador de. *Bolívar*. New York: Pellegrini & Cudahy, 1950.

———. *Christopher Columbus*. London: Hodder, 1939.

———. *Don Quixote*. London: Oxford University Press, 1935.

———. *The Fall of the Spanish American Empire*. London: Hollis & Carter, 1947.

———. *Hernán Cortés*. New York: Macmillan, 1941.

———. *The Rise of the Spanish American Empire*. New York: Macmillan, 1947.

———. *Spain*. New York: Scribners, 1930.

Mahon, Lord. *History of the War of Succession in Spain*. London: John Murray, 1836.

Major, R. H. (trans. and ed.) *Select Letters of Christopher Columbus*. London: Printed for the Hakluyt Society, 1870.

Marañón, Gregorio. *El Conde-Duque de Olivares.* Madrid: Espasa-Calpe, 1936.

Marcu, Valerìu. *Accent on Power: The Life and Times of Machiavelli.* Translated by Richard Winston. London: Oxford University Press, 1939.

Mariéjol, J. H. *L'Espagne sous Ferdinand et Isabelle.* Paris: May & Mottcroz, 1892.

Markham, Sir Clements Robert. *A History of Peru.* Chicago: C. H. Sergel, 1892.

Marsland, William D. and Amy L. *Venezuela Through Its History.* New York: Crowell, 1954.

Masur, Gerhard. *Simón Bolívar.* Albuquerque: University of New Mexico, 1948.

Mattingley, Garrett. *The Defeat of the Spanish Armada.* London: Jonathan Cape, 1959.

Maulde La Clavière, M. A. R. de. *Histoire de Louis XII.* Paris: E. Leroux, 1889–93.

Means, Philip A. *The Fall of the Inca Empire and the Spanish Rule in Peru.* New York: Scribner, 1932.

Mecham, J. Lloyd. *Church and State in Latin America.* Chapel Hill: University of North Carolina Press, 1934.

Menendez Pidal, Ramón. *The Cid and His Spain.* Translated by H. Sunderland. London: John Murray, 1934.

——, ed. *Historia de España,* vol. I; *España prehistórica,* by E. Hernández-Pacheco. Madrid: Espasa-Calpe, 1935.

——, ed. *Historia de España,* vol. II; *España romana,* by P. Bosch Gimpera. Madrid: Espasa-Calpe, 1935–56.

——, ed. *Historia de España,* vol. III; *España visigoda,* by M. Torres. Madrid: Espasa-Calpe, 1935–56.

Mercier, Ernest. *Histoire de l'Afrique septentrionale.* Paris: E. Leroux, 1888.

Merrien, Jean. *Christopher Columbus.* Translated by Maurice Michael. London: Odhams, 1958.

Merriman, Roger Bigelow. *The Rise of the Spanish Empire in the Old World and in the New.* 4 vols. New York and London: Macmillan, 1918–34.

Merton, R. *Cardinal Ximénes and the Making of Spain.* London: Routledge, 1934.

Metraux, Alfred. *The Incas.* Translated by Douglas Garman. London: Studio Vista, 1965.

Miller, Townsend. *The Castles and the Crown.* London: Gollancz, 1963.

Millis, Walter. *The Road to War: America 1914–1917.* New York: Houghton, 1935.

Mola Vidal, E. *Obras completas.* Valladolid: Aldus, 1914.

Montesinos, José F. *Estudios sobre Lope.* Mexico: Colegio de Mexico, 1951.

Morel-Fatio, A. *La Comédie espagnole du XVIIième siècle.* Paris: E. Champion, 1923.

Morison, S. E. *A Life of Christopher Columbus.* 2 vols. New York: Little, Brown, 1942.

Moses, Bernard. *The Intellectual Background of the Revolution in South America 1810–1824.* New York: Russell, 1926.

———. *South America on the Eve of Emancipation.* New York: Putnam, 1908.

Motley, J. L. *The Rise of the Dutch Republic: A History.* 3 vols. London: Bell & Sons, 1855.

Muir, Dorothy Erskine. *Machiavelli and His Times.* London: Heinemann, 1936.

Munro, D. G. *The Latin American Republics.* New York: Appleton-Century, 1942.

Nieto Arteta, L. E. *Económica y cultura en la historia de Colombia.* Bogotà: Libreria Siglo XX, 1942.

Oliveria Martins, J. P. *A History of Iberian Civilization.* Translated by Aubrey F. G. Bell. New York and London: Oxford University Press, 1930.

Oman, C. W. C. A *History of the Peninsular War*. London: Oxford University Press, 1902–14.

——. *Wellington's Army 1809–1814*. London: Longmans, Green, 1912.

Parkes, Henry Bamford. *A History of Mexico*. New York: Houghton, 1938.

Parnell, Arthur. *The War of Succession in Spain*. London: G. Bell and Sons, 1905.

Parry, J. H. *The Spanish Theory of Empire in the 16th Century*. London: Cambridge University Press, 1940.

Peers, E. A. *Catalonia Infelix*. London: Methuen, 1937.

——. *The Spanish Dilemma*. London: Methuen, 1940.

Pereyra, Carlos. *Historia de América Española*, vol. I. Madrid: Saturnine Calleja, 1920.

Pericot, Luis. *La prehistoria de la península ibérica*. Barcelona: Editorial Poliglota, 1923.

Petrie, Sir Charles. *The Spanish Royal House*. London: Geoffrey Bles, 1958.

Pfandl, Ludwig. *Geschichte der Spanischen Nationalliteratur in ihrer Blutezeit*. Freiburg in Breisgau: Herder, 1929.

Plunket, Ierne L. *Isabel of Castile and the Making of the Spanish Nation*. New York: Putnam, 1915.

Prescott, William H. *The Conquest of Mexico*. London: Routledge, 1847.

——. *The Conquest of Peru*. London: Blackie & Son, 1847.

——. *The History of the Reign of Ferdinand and Isabella*. 3 vols. Boston: Dana Estes, 1838.

Prieto, Carlos. *Spanish Front*. London and New York: Thomas Nelson, 1936.

Ramos Oliveira, Antonio. *Politics, Economics and Men of Modern Spain 1808–1846*. Translated by Teener Hall. London: Gollancz, 1946.

Rennert, H. A. *The Life of Lope de Vega*. Philadelphia: Campion, 1904.

Rennert, H. A. *The Spanish Stage in the Time of Lope de Vega*. New York: Kraus, 1909.

Reyes, O. E. *Breve Historia General del Ecuador*. Quito: Talleres Gráficos del Ministerio de Gobierno, 1942–43.

Rivas Vicuña, Francisco. *Las guerras de Bolívar*. Bogotá: Imprenta Nacional, 1934.

Robertson, William Spence. *Iturbide of Mexico*. Durham, North Carolina: Duke University Press, 1952.

———. *The Life of Miranda*. Chapel Hill: University of North Carolina Press, 1930.

———. *The Rise of the Spanish-American Republics*. New York: D. Appleton, 1918.

Rodríguez Vila, Antonio. *Crónicas del Gran Capitán*. Madrid: Bailly-Baillière e Hijos, 1908.

Rojas, Ricardo. *San Martín, Knight of the Andes*. Translated by Herschel Brickell and Carlos Videla. New York: Doubleday, 1945.

Romoli, Kathleen. *Balboa of Darién*. New York: Doubleday, 1953.

Roscher, W. G. F. *The Spanish Colonial System*. Edited by E. G. Bourne. New York: Holt, 1904.

Rose, S. *Ignatius Loyola and the Early Jesuits*. London: Burns and Oates, 1891.

Rousseau, François. *Règne de Charles III d'Espagne*. 2 vols. Paris: Plon-Nourrit, 1907.

Rydjord, John. *Foreign Interest in the Independence of New Spain*. Durham, North Carolina: Duke University Press, 1935.

Salas, X. de. *Goya*. London: Blandford, 1962.

Sánchez-Albornoz y Menduiña, Claudio. *España y el Islam*. Buenos Aires: Editorial Sudamericana, 1943.

Santa Cruz, Alonso de. *Crónica de los Reyes Católicos*. Seville: Escuela de Estudios Hispano-Americanos, 1951.

Schurz, William L. *This New World: The Civilization of Latin America.* New York: Dutton, 1954.

Scott, S. P. *History of the Moorish Empire in Europe.* 3 vols. Philadelphia: Lippincott, 1904.

Sencourt, Robert. *Spain's Uncertain Crown.* London: Ernest Benn, 1932.

Sender, Ramón J. *The War in Spain.* Translated by Sir Peter Chalmers Mitchell. London: Faber, 1937.

Silio Cortés, César. *Isabel la Católica.* Madrid: Espasa-Calpe, 1951.

Sismondi, J. C. L. de. *Histoire des républiques italiennes,* 8 vols. Brussels: Société Typographique Belge, 1838–39.

Smith, R. M. *The Day of the Liberals in Spain.* Philadelphia: University of Pennsylvania, 1938.

Starkie, W. *Grand Inquisitor, an Account of Cardinal Ximénez and His Times.* London: Hodder, 1940.

Stevenson, R. A. M. *Velásquez.* New York: Macmillan, 1899.

Stirling-Maxwell, Sir William. *Don John of Austria.* London: Longmans, Green, 1883.

Sutherland, C. H. V. *The Romans in Spain.* London: Methuen, 1939.

Taxonera, L. de. *El Cardenal Julio Alberoni.* Madrid: Editora Nacional, 1945.

Templewood, S. J. G. Hoare. *Ambassador on Special Mission.* London: Collins, 1946.

Thatcher, John B. *Christopher Columbus.* 3 vols. New York: Kraus, 1903.

Thomas, Hugh. *The Spanish Civil War.* New York: Harper, 1961.

Thompson, G. *Front Line Diplomat.* London: Hutchinson, 1959.

Tirado y Rojas, Mariano. *La Masonería en España.* 2 vols. Madrid: E. Maroto y Hermano, 1892–93.

Trend, John B. *The Civilization of Spain.* London and New York: Oxford, 1944.

Trend, John B. *The Origins of Modern Spain*. New York: Macmillan, 1934.

Ulloa, L. *Xristo-Ferens Colón*. Paris: impression française de L'Edition, 12 Rue de l'Abbé-de-l'Epée; libraire orientale et americaine Maisonneuve Frères 1928.

Valbuena Prat, Angel. *Historia de la literatura Española*. Barcelona: G. Gili, 1950.

Van Nostrand, J. J. *The Reorganization of Spain by Augustus*. Berkeley: University of California, 1916.

Vasconcelos, José. *Breve historia de México*. Mexico: Ediciones Botas, 1937.

Velázquez Bosco, Ricardo. *El Monasterio de Nuestra Señora de la Rábida*. Madrid: Fortanet, 1914.

Vignaud, Henry. *Histoire critique de la grande entreprise de Christophe Colombus*. Paris: H. Welter, 1911.

Villaneuva, Carlos A. *Bolívar y el general San Martín*. Paris: P. Ollendorff, 1913.

———. *Fernando VII y los neuvos estados*. Paris: P. Ollendorff, 1914.

Villari, Pasquale. *The Life and Times of Niccolò Machiavelli*. Translated by Linda Villari. London: T. F. Unwin, 1892.

Vossler, K. *Lope de Vega y su tiempo*. Madrid: Galo Sáez, 1940.

Walsh, W. T. *Isabella of Spain*. New York: McBride, 1930.

———. *Philip II*. New York: Macmillan, 1953.

Warren, Harris G. *Paraguay: An Informal History*. Norman: University of Oklahoma Press, 1949.

Waugh, Elizabeth. *Simón Bolívar; a Story of Courage*. New York: Macmillan, 1941.

Whitehouse, H. R. *The Sacrifice of a Throne: an Account of the Life of Amadeus Duke of Aosta*. New York: Bonnell, 1897.

Williams, M. W. *The People and Politics of Latin America*. Boston: Ginn, 1945.

Woodroofe, Thomas. *The Enterprise of England*. London: Faber, 1958.

Zancada, P. *El Sentido social de la revolución de 1820*. Madrid: 1903.

Zugazagoitia, Julian. *Historia de la guerra de España*. Buenos Aires: Editorial La Vanguardia, 1940.

Index